PIMLICO

418

IRISH VOICES

Peter Somerville-Large is the author of the bestselling *The Irish Country House: A Social History*. His other books include *Cappaghglass*, a record of changing rural life in Ireland which was shortlisted for the Ewart-Biggs Prize, *The Grand Irish Tour* and *Dublin: The Fair City*. He has also written thrillers and travel books about the Middle East, India and Tibet. Born and educated in Dublin, he now lives in Co. Kilkenny.

IRISH VOICES

An Informal History 1916–1966

———

Peter Somerville-Large

PIMLICO

Published by Pimlico 2000

2 4 6 8 10 9 7 5 3 1

Copyright © Peter Somerville-Large 1999

Peter Somerville-Large has asserted his right under the Copyright,
Designs and Patents Act 1988 to be identified as
the author of this work

First published in Great Britain as
Irish Voices: Fifty Years of Irish Life, 1916–1966
by Chatto & Windus 1999
Pimlico edition 2000

Pimlico
Random House, 20 Vauxhall Bridge Road
London SW1V 2SA

Random House Australia (Pty) Limited
20 Alfred Street, Milsons Point, Sydney
New South Wales 2061, Australia

Random House New Zealand Limited
18 Poland Road, Glenfield
Auckland 10, New Zealand

Random House (Pty) Limited
Endulini, 5A Jubilee Road, Parktown 2193, South Africa

The Random House Group Limited Reg. No. 954009
www.randomhouse.co.uk

A CIP catalogue record for this book
is available from the British Library

ISBN 0-7126-6532-3

Papers used by Random House are natural,
recyclable products made from wood grown in sustainable forests;
the manufacturing processes conform to the environmental
regulations of the country of origin

Typeset in Ehrhardt by MATS, Southend-on-Sea, Essex
Printed and bound in Great Britain by
Mackays of Chatham PLC, Chatham, Kent

To Freda and Dominic

Contents

Acknowledgements

I would like to thank in particular, Mark Fiennes, Giles Gordon and Penny Hoare. My editor, Mary Chamberlain, has done a superb job; she has a sharp eye, and an Irish background and was able to make numerous suggestions and comments. Once again I am indebted to the staff at the National Library, the Royal Irish Academy and the Trinity College Library. I also received advice from the Kilkenny County Library and the Irish Writers Association. I am grateful to the Arts Council of Ireland for assistance to enable me to carry out research.

For permission to reprint copyright material from the following books these acknowledgements are made with thanks:

For *Dublin Made Me* by Tod Andrews to David Andrews TD; for *Its a Long Way to Go* by Marigold Armitage to Faber and Faber; for *Guerrilla Days in Ireland* by Tom Barry to Anvil Books; for *The Shelbourne, Bowen's Court* and other material by Elizabeth Bowen to the Estate of Elizabeth Bowen, c/o Curtis Brown Ltd; for *Against the Tide* by Noel Browne to Gill and Macmillan; for extracts from Hubert Butler's essays to Anthony Farrell, the Lilliput Press; for *A Penny in the Clouds* and *Collected Poems* by Austin Clarke to R Dardis Clarke, 21 Pleasants Street, Dublin 8; for *Revolutionary Woman* by Kathleen Clarke to Michael O'Brien, the O'Brien Press; for *Cowslips and Chainies* by Elaine Crowley to Anthony Farrell, the Lilliput Press; for *The Tailor and Ansty* by Eric Cross to John F. Spillane, the Mercier Press; for extracts from Dublin Opinion to Belenos, 50 Fitzwilliam Square; for Lionel Fleming's *Head or Harp* to Caroline Bowder; for *The Boys* by Christopher Fitz-Simon to the author; for *Lady Gregory's Journals* to Colin Smythe; for Dean Victor Griffin's *Mark of Protest* to the author; for *No One Shouted Stop* by John Healy to the estate of John Healy, c/o Evelyn Healy; for extracts from the works of Patrick Kavanagh to Peter Fallon, Loughcrew, Co. Meath; for Molly Keane's *Good Behaviour, Taking Chances* and *Mad Puppetstown* to Sally Phibbs; for Kevin Kearns *Dublin Tenement Life* to Gill and MacMillan; for lines from *Brown Bag Bulging* by

Brendan Kennelly to the author; for *Home Before Dark* by Hugh Leonard to Penguin Books Ltd; for Domnall Mac Amlaigh's *An Irish Navvy* translated by Valentine Iremonger from *Dialann Deorai*, London, 1964; for Frank McCourt's *Angela's Ashes* to the author and to Harper Collins Publishers Ltd; for Bridie Mulloy's *Itchy Feet and Dirty Work* to the author; for John McGahern's *The Barracks* and *High Ground* to A.M. Heath and Co; for Nancy Mitford to Peters Fraser and Dunlop, Writers Agents; for Martin Mulloy's *Book of Irish Courtesy* to John F. Spillane, the Mercier Press; for David Mitchell's *A Peculiar Place* to Geraldine Mitchell; for Geraldine Mitchell's *Deeds not Words* to the author and Treasa Coady, Town House and Country House; for *Wheels within Wheels* by Dervla Murphy to John Murray; for Edward O'Brien's *An Historical and Social Diary of Durrow, Co Laois* to the author; for Frank O'Connor's *An Only Child* to Peters Fraser and Dunlop; for George O'Brien's *The Village of Longing* to Anthony Farrell, the Lilliput Press; for Sean O'Faolain *Midsummer Night Madness* © 1932, 1937, 1947, 1980; *An Irish Journey* © 1940; *Vive Moi* © 1963, 1964, 1993; extracts from *The Bell* passim © Sean O'Faolain to the Estate of Sean O'Faolain, c/o Rogers, Coleridge & White, 20 Powis Mews, London W11 1JN; for *Just Like Yesterday* by Leon Ó Broin to Gill and Macmillan; for extracts from the work of Brian O'Nolan to A.M. Heath and Co Ltd on behalf of the Estate of the Late Evelyn O'Nolan; for Patrick O'Shea's *Voices and the Sound of Drums* to the Blackstaff Press; for *I Heard The Wild Birds Sing* by Patrick O'Sullivan to Anvil Books; for David Thomson's *Woodbrook* to Random House; for Signe Tostvig's *Diaries* to Anthony Farrell, the Lilliput Press; for *Nearly Ninety* by Terry Trench to the author; for Virginia Woolf's *Diaries for 1934* to Random House.

My sincerest apologies to anyone who has been inadvertently missed from this list; any omissions can be rectified in later editions.

Introduction

My uncle used to say, 'You don't see fairy rings any more. All the fairies left Ireland when de Valera came to power.'

In those days belief in fairies was general. Not so long before the Troubles was that terrible day on Slievenamon in 1895 when Michael Cleary burnt his wife to death to rid her of fairy power. The Clearys and their neighbours, in the words of Hubert Butler, still 'lived in that perilous region of half-belief which the sophisticated find charming because they are more acquainted with its tenderness than its cruelty'.

My relations in West Cork treasured a shoe found in a little mountainy field which was just under three inches long and worn down on the sole by its fairy owner. Plenty of people saw fairies, like Patrick O'Sullivan's great-uncle who was never the same again after he saw the little men playing football in a field in West Kerry. A decade ago I talked with an old man who described how Monday was a fairy day when you would have no luck: 'You wouldn't go to a bank on Monday or give your neighbours a pint of milk.' He thought that the Tan War killed the old beliefs. People became less gullible; during the Troubles they were out at all hours, moving in the dark 'and that broke it up'.

As a child listening to my uncle, I used to wonder about the man who had the temerity to banish the little people. Eamon de Valera came to public notice after the Rising of April 1916. The former mathematics teacher with the features of a saint painted by Ribera had taken to warfare; it was noted that he was courageous, considerate to his men and compassionate to his prisoners.

Over the years de Valera has been called many names – the Long Fellow, the Chief, the Undertaker. He was described as the Spanish onion in an Irish stew, or as 'a proud and stately type of leader whom Irishmen in their hearts really respect'. To Sean O'Casey he was 'Bonnie Prince Charlie in sober suiting'. Chips Channon, who met him when he was elected President of the Assembly of the League of Nations in 1938, found the Irish statesman 'grey and dignified and . . . like an unfashionable dentist'.

Oliver St John Gogarty condemned him as 'a chilly blend of machia-vellianism and Puritanism'. In the year the fairies left Ireland he wrote, 'I curse that man as generations of Irishmen will curse him – the man who attempted to destroy our country.'

What puzzled English people like John Gibbons was how this exponent of the Gaelic tradition should be so foreign. 'I have many times watched Mr de Valera, and anybody less like our popular conception of a Celt would be hard to imagine. I myself have wondered how much of his make-up may have come from his Spanish father, for in him there is much of the terrible and uncompromising logic of the Latin.' But there were those who believed that de Valera had not a drop of Spanish blood in him.

No young person who lives in Ireland today can find it easy to imagine what day-to-day life was like in the years following the Rising when Eamon de Valera's conduct, as rebel, outcast, politician and president, dominated the course of Irish history. By the time he died on 29 August 1975 at the age of ninety-two, the changes initiated by Sean Lemass were transforming the country at an increasingly rapid rate. Soon the old simple pious Ireland that he had nurtured would vanish, its grey atmosphere only recalled in memoirs, old newspapers and old newsreels.

In recalling Irish life in the heyday of de Valera, I have to acknowledge a Loyalist background with family allegiances both north and south of the Border that came into being shortly before my birth. My mother's family had a house outside the city she firmly called Londonderry; it was named Willsboro in honour of King William who had granted lands to my ancestor Gideon Scott. Scott was a clergyman who read prayers in front of his monarch before the Battle of the Boyne. My father's family, who came from West Cork and were also Loyalist, became soldiers, clergymen, doctors and engineers. My parents attended the coronation of George VI, and at the outbreak of the Second World War my father, together with many of his relatives, served in the British Army. But by then members of my family at long last accepted the new State – if not with enthusiasm, at least with forbearance. They served it with a dedication I am proud of.

When I was young I noticed how my relations took little notice of the violent events that had changed their status for ever. The IRA were detested, the Black and Tans an embarrassment. Like many other Loyalists, while having no sympathy for those who fought for freedom in the War of Independence, they deplored the brutal mistakes made by the British. My clergyman grandfather wrote to the *Irish Times* condemning the execution of Kevin Barry.

I was familiar with the burnt-out big houses owned by people who had been friends of my parents and who had gone to England. But to a great degree my family ignored the changes in Irish politics. For most of my early life I was ignorant of them and until I reached my teens I was unable to recognise the queer-sounding names of the political parties in Dáil Éireann. At school I was taught the names of English kings, and played cricket and rugby. My knowledge of the Irish language was minimal. When the time came for our class to pass the exam which allowed the school to claim a subsidy from the government, we blithely cheated with the aid of our teachers. The divide followed me from school to university, where Archbishop McQuaid had forbidden Catholics to enter Trinity College Dublin. There were ways around the ban – special permission could be obtained – but in general Catholics in Trinity were rare as hen's teeth.

My experience of Irish life is coloured by the aloofness that characterised the lives of people of my background. Since my memories are inevitably slanted, I have used those of others, taking my pick from the wide assortment of voices which have recorded the path that Ireland took following Easter Week and Independence. Although I have quoted from contemporary newspapers and periodicals, and used diaries and fiction where they illuminate the period, I have mainly relied on the memories of those who lived during the fifty years that are highlighted here. The choice of material is immense and it grows by the minute, as people continue to write about their past with relish, nostalgia or bitterness. The views of Republicans, countrymen, islanders, teachers, clerics, Loyalists, politicians, poets, writers and journalists have their place in this book, as do the impressions of visitors to Ireland. Into these voices I have filtered my own recollections of growing up at this time. I hope the medley has evoked those strange, harsh, hopeful years during which de Valera, in power or out, dominated an Ireland created in turmoil, which was struggling to establish herself as a nation.

CHAPTER I

A Great Ruby from God's Ear

The day before the rising was Easter Sunday and they were
crying joyfully in the churches: 'Christ has risen.' On the
following day they were saying in the streets: 'Ireland has risen.'
James Stephens

The 1916 rebellion was a brave clean fight against an empire. Its
protagonists, who volunteered without pay and jeopardised
their careers as well as their lives, deserve all honour.
Declan Kiberd

Early on Easter Sunday 23 April 1916 in Liberty Hall, the printer Christopher
Brady carried out his commission of printing the document that would
proclaim the Irish Republic. The Proclamation had been composed mainly by
Patrick Pearse and had been approved by the Military Council of the Irish
Republican Brotherhood. Six men, Thomas Clarke, Seán MacDiarmada,
Thomas MacDonagh, Eamonn Ceannt, James Connolly and Pearse himself,
had signed the manuscript earlier in Holy Week, probably at a meeting in Mrs
Jennie Wyse Power's house at 21 Henry Street. Joseph Plunkett, who was in a
nursing home, signed later.

Brady used an old Wharfdale Press. There was a shortage of type; wrong
fonts had to be used and he made an 'E' out of an 'F' with sealing wax. The top
half was printed first; then the type was reset for the lower half. The result is a
different density in the two halves. Brady could always recognise a genuine
proclamation; sixteen are known to have survived the destruction of Easter
Week. He gave the first proof to James Connolly who checked it against a
manuscript: '. . . We place the cause of the Irish Republic under the protection
of the Most High God Whose blessing we invoke upon our arms and we pray

that no one who serves that cause will dishonour it by cowardice, inhumanity, or rapine . . .'

A total of 2,500 copies were run off; the idea was that they would be distributed throughout the country. Sean T. O'Kelly was made responsible for seeing that they were posted up around the city centre.

As the printing was being carried out Brady heard Countess Markiewicz shouting from the next-door room, 'I will shoot Eoin MacNeill.' Connolly told her, 'You will not hurt a hair on his head.' That day MacNeill had cancelled the 'Easter Exercises' by putting advertisements in the papers.

The next morning, Monday, as the Pearse brothers left St Enda's 'to wake up Ireland', their mother called out 'Now, Pat, do nothing rash.' At Liberty Hall, before they set out for the General Post Office, their sister arrived to remonstrate: 'Come home, Pat, and leave all this foolishness.'

With the warm spring weather and blue skies many people planned to spend the bank holiday at seaside places around Dublin Bay. Buses and trams were crowded, and so were the morning trains as the rebels – a few, including Michael Collins, in Volunteer uniforms – went from Liberty Hall to their posts. Many of their arms, shotguns, revolvers and German rifles, which had been landed at Howth nearly two years before, were wheeled over the cobbles beside them in a handcart. The total force was small: 1,558 Volunteers led by Pearse and an estimated 219 of the Irish Citizen Army led by James Connolly.

The men split up and made their way to St Stephen's Green, Jacob's biscuit factory, the Four Courts and other designated places which they intended to defend against the might of the British Empire. A contingent reached Sackville Street and took possession of the General Post Office. Two flags were hoisted over the building, one the tricolour, the other, raised by Lieutenant Eamon Bulfin over Princes Street, a green flag with the words IRISH REPUBLIC on it in white letters.

A crowd gathered almost immediately to listen to Patrick Pearse reading the Proclamation from the steps of the GPO under the portico. Crowds would be a continuing nuisance to the Volunteers in the days to come. James Stephens saw a Volunteer who 'held a lady's umbrella in his hand, and whenever some person became particularly annoying he would leap the barricade and chase his man . . . hitting him over the head with the umbrella'.

Shots were heard from Dublin Castle where the first casualties occurred, with the deaths of a Volunteer named Sean Connolly and a policeman caught by surprise. Tramcars were sent to their depots except for one kept as a barricade at the entrance of North Earl Street. All the public houses in the area closed.

Almost precisely at midday a body of armed men marched up to Westland Row Station and took possession of the platforms, using barrows, sweet machines, seats and milk churns for barriers. The staff were driven out at the point of a bayonet. Intending passengers, many of them women and children with packets of sandwiches and buckets and spades, pushed forward showing their tickets, but they, too, were thrown smartly out of the station.

During the afternoon and evening groups of these disappointed passengers were seen wandering aimlessly around the streets until it occurred to them that something strange was happening. According to the *Irish Times*, 'little children with their packets of holiday sweetmeats were pitifully pattering homewards under the pilotage of their anxious parents and all the while there rang aloud the vicious clatter of rifles on every side'.

There were similar scenes around Harcourt Street; no more holiday-makers would reach Bray. But that morning, before the rebels took up their positions, hundreds of racegoers had set out in special trains from Broadstone for Fairyhouse, not a location for little people, but the racecourse where the Ward Union point-to-point meeting, a popular fixture not only with Dubliners but also with the British Army, was being run that day. Every officer who could, attended the races. Horses running in the Irish Grand National while the bullets were already flying in Dublin included Merri Merri and Civil War; the race was won by All Sorts.

A late racegoer arriving with a bullet hole in his car raised the alarm. One of the first to leave the racecourse was Lord Fingall in his cousin Horace Plunkett's car. They drove with a party of officers to Dunboyne Castle, but hearing no definite news, decided to go on to Dublin. They left just in time; the castle was surrounded by rebels hoping to capture or kill Lord Fingall and his friends. They made their way to Plunkett's house in the south Dublin suburbs, Kilteragh at Foxrock. Plunkett had been playing golf when he learnt the news from Lady Fingall anxiously awaiting her husband's return.

'"Horace," I shouted out of the window, "there is a rebellion in Dublin."

'". . . What nonsense, someone is pulling our leg . . . Ring up the Kildare Street Club."

'I rang up the Club . . . Was there a rebellion in Dublin? "Never heard a word of it," said the porter.

'A few minutes later the telephone rang. "Tell Sir Horace there is a rebellion. They have taken the General Post Office and shot a policeman."'

The Royal Dublin Society's Spring Show opened with some disruption, since cattle from the North of Ireland were unable to cross the city to reach the show grounds. For the cattle already in Ballsbridge there were problems of accommodation since the military authorities quickly took possession of a portion of the grounds. By 4.15 on the Monday a contingent of British soldiers had arrived from the Curragh.

Hospitals were beginning to take in casualties. St Vincent's on Stephen's Green received its first fatalities: two respectable middle-aged men, one a buyer in Clery's. At the Meath there were four deaths that Monday, a British officer, a police constable shot through both lungs, Ella Wainbrook aged seventeen from Fumbally Lane and a man named Kelly who resided in Clanbrassil Street. At Dr Steevens' Hospital two soldiers and one Sinn Féin Volunteer died.

In Merrion Square a temporary hospital was established at number 14, the St John Ambulance headquarters. One of its members, Ella Webb, went round the square from house to house begging and borrowing items of linen and other necessities. The Adelaide Hospital's motor ambulance ferried nine casualties to Merrion Square, returning with food since the Adelaide was entirely cut off from supplies during the fighting. Opposite, Jacob's biscuit factory, separated by a narrow street, was occupied by a strong force of Sinn Féiners. Numerous wounded and dead soldiers, civilians and Volunteers would be brought in during the week. When an officer had his brains blown into the roadway in Camden Street, a girl picked up his cap and scraped the brains into it; covering them with straw, she carried them to the hospital so that they might be buried with their owner.

At Jervis Street on the Monday a young woman, Mrs Sheils, died while her husband was at her bedside; he was home wounded from France. Three dying soldiers were brought in with one already dead. These were Lancers.

A troop of Lancers had been escorting wagons of munitions to the Phoenix Park. On their return they entered Sackville Street from the north end and charged with sabres drawn – the last charge of the British Army, in Sean O'Faolain's words 'in the best G. A. Henty, Light Brigade tradition of gallant lunacy'. The shots that killed them came mostly from the roof of the GPO where Volunteers were firing down into their midst. The watching crowd disapproved and threw bricks, bottles and sticks at the Volunteers to cries of 'Would ye be hurting the poor men?' A woman called out, 'Would ye be hurting the poor horses?' and others caressed the animals that survived after the Lancers had retreated up Sackville Street.

Two days later Ernie O'Malley saw the bodies of the dead horses behind Nelson's Pillar, some with their feet in the air, others lying flat. An old man pointed to the GPO and told him, 'These fellows are not going to be frightened by a troop of Lancers – they mean business.' Like a vignette from the French Revolution, a drunken shawly woman squatted on a carcass singing, 'Boys in khaki, boys in blue/ Here's the best of jolly luck to you.'

There was another dead horse, its throat cut, its blood congealed in a pool, on the west side of St Stephen's Green which also lay in the street during Easter Week, 'stiff and lamentable'. Over the College of Surgeons flew a green flag with white lettering similar to the one on the GPO. Some time during the week in the boardroom the life-sized portrait of Queen Victoria would be cut out of its frame and torn to fragments. Other portraits of prominent surgeons would receive bullet holes.

A car returning from Fairyhouse was caught in crossfire; an officer was killed and Miss Mabel McGlyn was shot in the thigh. Two other women returning from the races were also wounded around this time, promoting the Tuesday headline in the *Irish Times* which reflected what the paper considered important: THREE LADIES SHOT IN STEPHEN'S GREEN.

Inside the Shelbourne Hotel the Easter Week tradition of serving an elaborate tea after the races was taking place in the drawing-room until a rebel shot snipped the flowered corsage from an Easter hat. Only then did guests reluctantly tear themselves away from the plate-glass windows and withdraw to the writing-room.

Before their retreat they might have caught sight of forty-seven-year-old Countess Markiewicz waving her gun, Peter the Great. Earlier, the *Irish Worker*, sneering at her habit of 'drilling street urchins on how to kill British soldiers', had remarked that she was easy to mistake as the representative of an enterprising firm of small-arms manufacturers. For the Rising she emulated an earlier aristocratic rebel by dressing up. In 1798 Lord Edward Fitzgerald had worn a green suit with red braid, rose-coloured cuffs and a silk-tasselled cap of liberty. By comparison the Countess's outfit was conservative; she chose Citizen Army green – a green South African-style shirt with green knee breeches, short green boots and a green slouch hat decorated with green feathers. She had driven to her post in an open-topped car flanked by two Fianna boys, members of the Republican youth movement she had founded in 1909. At Stephen's Green she became second in command to Michael Mallin, Chief of Staff of the Irish Citizen Army. When Jack Love, a night clerk at Guinness's brewery, was captured, searched and, according to his story, robbed of his possessions, he was lectured by the Countess on the coming fight before being released.

Did she shoot dead an unarmed policeman as reported? Did the shot that shattered the window of the University Club, nearly killing an RAMC doctor and a High Court judge, come from her gun? Later she would write how 'this work was very exciting when the fighting began. I continued round and round the Green, reporting back if anything was wanted, or tackling any sniper who was particularly objectionable.'

Inside the Shelbourne there was, in the words of Elizabeth Bowen, 'a sort of ghostly shipboard existence'. Many of the staff were unable to reach the hotel; one, trying to return to his job, avoided gunfire by crouching behind 'one of the ladies', a lusty Nubian figure that still graces the Shelbourne's front. Inside, the guests lent a hand, twenty volunteering as amateur waiters and Lady Torrington acting as a still-room maid. Someone called Fred Barnes organised singsongs.

On Tuesday morning a chorus of 'The Soldiers Song' echoed across the Green from the garrison at the College of Surgeons. Later a machine-gun, hoisted up the staircase of the Shelbourne, raked the insurgents. There were soldiers on the roof, and another party of reinforcements was let in by a side door. Further machine-guns were placed on the roofs of the United Services Club and the Alexandra Club.

From parapets above Fitzwilliam Street and Merrion Square, guns threatened hapless passers-by. Sinn Féin and members of the Citizen Army were accused of firing from behind the safety of chimney-pots, as if they were breaking gentlemanly rules. English soldiers, perched on the top of the Kildare

Street Club, were refreshed with large brown cups of tea and plates of bread and butter carried up to them by page-boys; it proved difficult to drink tea without lowering their rifles.

Outside the club, at the bottom of Kildare Street, Maurice Headlam passed some old women, sitting on chairs waiting for a bit of action to take place. From the first sounds of gunfire Dubliners came out to have a look at the rebellion. The onlookers gathered everywhere. Mr J. R. Clegg of Rathgar, who kept a diary of the week, recorded how already by 2.30 p.m. on Monday groups stood on corners and spectators leant out of windows, 'excited and expectant'. The insurrection was to be enjoyed. 'Almost everyone was smiling and attentive,' wrote James Stephens, 'and a democratic feeling was abroad . . . Every person spoke to every other person, and men and women mixed and talked without restraint.' Rumours abounded: the rebels had taken six carts of ammunition from the military; the arsenal at the Phoenix Park had been blown up; the Germans had landed in three places: the city of Cork was in rebel hands.

It was dangerous to be a spectator. Walking along Fitzwilliam Square past the brass doctors' plates, Stephens was pursued by bullets: 'They lazed into the road beside me, and the sound as they whistled was curious . . . like that made by a very swift saw, and one gets the impression that as well as being very swift, they are very heavy.' He counted fourteen bullet holes in the ground-floor windows of the Shelbourne.

People killed for their curiosity included the serving maid who was brought into the St John Ambulance Hospital, having been shot dead as she looked out of a window. Others were luckier, like the girl who stood in the line of fire in Sackville Street cursing in the foulest of language those who did not support the rebels. Or the woman in a shawl observed on the Tuesday at O'Connell Bridge. Mr Clegg wrote how 'she is shouted to by the group of persons around me gathered at MacBirney's corner, but she pays no attention. After a time she proceeds slowly across O'Connell Bridge, facing the firing . . . She is again yelled at, but comes along as if nothing were the matter, although the noise of the firing is deafening. Someone says, "Faith, mebby she's insured." It turns out she is drunk with two black eyes.'

Licensed premises had been closed under the Defence of the Realm Act. But pubs were broken into and looted, and all week there were plenty of drunken people about.

Among the onlookers gathered on street corners or wandering round their sputtering city were plenty who, knowing they were watching history, sought to record it. Together with the noise of gunfire there was the constant scratching of pencils in notebooks. The Rising was logged with immediacy both by writers like James Stephens, Austin Clarke, Sean O'Casey and Oliver St John Gogarty, and by ordinary citizens like Mr Clegg or Henry Beaton, the company secretary of Arnott's, who wrote to his sister, 'Tuesday: crossed the bridge into Sackville Street and saw a flag over GPO "Irish Republic" – then I began to think the tomfoolery more serious than the idiotic joke which at first I had supposed it to be.'

Austin Clarke cycled everywhere, 'down Grafton Street, past the GPO, up Rutland Square to Phibsborough Church and soon was at the barricades again'. He watched the *Helga*, formerly a fishery protection vessel, now termed by the Admiralty an 'armed steam yacht', coming up the Liffey to shell Liberty Hall, and joined the crowd outside the College of Surgeons.

From the steps of his consulting rooms in nearby Ely Place, Gogarty was another onlooker to the events taking place in Stephen's Green. He told his neighbour George Moore that 'the rebellion could do the Empire nothing but good, as it would redeem their credit in Europe, bringing them their sole victory'.

From his office in the National Gallery, James Stephens set out to reconnoitre the different areas of fighting. A short walk took him to Stephen's Green; he continued towards Jacob's factory where sacks of flour were being used as sandbags. He noted a young rebel 'no more than a boy, not more certainly than twenty years of age, short in stature, with curling red hair and blue eyes – a kindly looking lad. The strap of his sombrero had torn loose on one side, and except while he held it in his teeth, it flapped about his chin. His face was sunburnt and grimy with dust and sweat.' Elsewhere Stephens saw a dead man at the barricades: 'There was a hole in the top of his head and one does not know how ugly blood can be until it has clotted the hair.'

The practical Sir Horace Plunkett, as soon as he was aware of the Rising, began organising a Food Committee. Throughout Easter Week there would be food shortages. Patrick O'Shea's mother, a visitor from Athlone, saw horse-drawn vans of bread set upon by hungry people and emptied in seconds. From six in the morning queues formed outside bakeries. Clergymen, professional and commercial men were seen struggling with bundles of cauliflowers, cabbage, meat, biscuit and bread. A girl told James Stephens that by Friday her family had eaten nothing for three days. Then her father managed to get two loaves of bread; 'the whole fourteen of us ran at him, and in a minute we were all ashamed, for the loaves were gone to the last crumb and we were all as hungry as we had been before he came in'. On the Saturday Stephens reported, 'no bread, no milk, no meat, no newspapers, but the sun is shining'.

The 'shameful looting' had started very soon after the rebellion began. The Dublin Fire Brigade was called out between 10.00 p.m. and midnight on Easter Monday to fires in boot shops that had been looted in Sackville Street. On Tuesday there were two calls to looted premises; two people trapped in an upper room of Lawrence's Fancy Goods Warehouse on the corner of Henry Street turned out to be looters.

The spectacle of deprived and hungry citizens taking over the shops had a ring of vengeful truth. Haberdashers, sweetshops and shoe shops were irresistible targets. Ernie O'Malley noted some women sitting on the curb trying on one pair of silk shoes after another and, if dissatisfied, throwing them into the gutter. Boys wandered about with stolen silk hats perched drunkenly on their heads, drilling with golf clubs, airguns and toy drums.

Enid Starkie and her brother risked gunfire to see Clery's department store opposite the fortress GPO, being sacked; she recalled how 'the people poured out of the surrounding slums like swarming black beetles surging in a never-ending stream in and out of the shops'. Men, women and children crowded into Clery's and emerged with what they could carry. The more practical brought along prams to fill up with sheets, clothes, stocking garters, silks, satins, furniture and whatever caught their fancy.

In the same area a witness remembered, 'The plate-glass windows of a confectioners . . . [is] smashed, and a shower of sweet stuffs, chocolate boxes and huge slabs sprays over among the crazy mass of shawls, caps and struggling children. Old women from the slums hurl themselves towards the windows of a shoe store and almost walk through the plate glass which slivers and breaks among the mob, dealing deep gashes and blood which cannot check the greedy and aimless frenzy.'

Children whose great treat might have been the occasional sweet now had their arms full of them. An old woman pushing a laden pram was robbed of her booty: 'I declare to God . . . I don't know what the world is coming to all and all, wid the dishonesty of people.' Another woman came out of Clery's with a pile of underwear which she proceeded to try on in front of the ever-present crowd. A voice was heard: 'It's a disgrace. Are there no police to stop this at all?'

A few people tried to discourage the looting, like the doctor from St Vincent's, who was seen in Grafton Street battering looters with his blackthorn stick. Sean T. O'Kelly was sent across the road by James Connolly to stop the frenzy in Clery's. When he reported back that instead of shooting looters, his men had fired over their heads, Connolly was unimpressed: 'That'll do no good at all. I'll send someone else to do the job right.'

In Sackville Street on the Tuesday Francis Sheehy-Skeffington, unmistakable with his red beard, long hair and knickerbocker suit, was forming an unarmed guard to protect shops and private property. One of those enrolled was Robert Briscoe, Dublin's future Lord Mayor, who years later told Skeffington's son, 'Your father was a terrible man, God rest him. He had about thirty of us with armbands patrolling the streets near the Pillar. But it got too hot for me. When he went up the street, I went home.'

Later on Tuesday when Sheehy-Skeffington was arrested, he declared he was not a Sinn Féiner; although he was in sympathy with the organisation he was opposed to militarism. On Wednesday, in Portobello Barracks, together with Thomas Dickson and Patrick MacIntyre, he was shot on the orders of Captain Bowen-Colthurst who was impelled by verses from the Bible: 'And these mine enemies which will not have me to rule over them bring them forth and slay them.'

Bowen-Colthurst, regularly referred to as 'the lunatic', was absent from the subsequent inquiry, already locked up in Broadmoor. The horrible details were made worse by revelations of attempts to cover up the crime. The three, who were neither pinioned nor blindfolded, did not have time to say their prayers. Another prisoner in the detention room heard the first volley and said, 'There is some poor fellow gone.' Sheehy-Skeffington's corpse bore a badge which read: VOTES FOR WOMEN.

Other civilians were shot in crossfire or in error; these included two clerks from Guinness's brewery, who together with two British officers were mistaken for rebels by a picket in Robert Street. Some rebels were deliberately killed after surrendering.

During the week the three ambulances of the Dublin Fire Brigade worked continually ferrying the wounded to hospitals, often in danger from stray bullets. One of the ambulance horses was shot in the legs. The final casualty lists from the hospitals reflect the casual nature of the slaughter. They included: 'Jervis Street: soldiers six, women two, children two, rebels and civilians twenty-seven. Mercers: soldiers four, police sergeant one, woman one, rebels and civilians twenty-seven. City of Dublin Hospital [Baggot Street]: soldiers fourteen [these would have been casualties from the fierce fighting around Mount Street Bridge and Northumberland Road, 'the Irish Thermopylae'], Veteran Corps four, children two.' 'Small boys do not believe that people will really kill them,' wrote James Stephens, 'but small boys were killed.' One was a fourteen-year-old, shot on the Monday while giving a glass of water to a wounded soldier. A total of twenty-eight children were killed during the week of the Easter Rising.

Twenty-six bodies of insurgents were found in the office of the *Daily Express* which was retaken after heavy fighting on Tuesday. In the College of Surgeons the chemical lecture theatre was converted into a morgue. A crucifix was nailed to the wall made out of coffin plates. By Thursday, many bodies were being buried coffinless in their clothes, in sheets and in blankets. At Mount Jerome cemetery interments were carried out under crossfire from the soldiers at Portobello Barracks and the volunteers at Rialto Bridge.

Martial law had been declared on the Tuesday: 'WHEREAS in the City of Dublin and the County of Dublin certain evilly disposed persons and associations with the intention of subverting the supremacy of the Crown in Ireland have committed divers acts of violence . . .' Curfew was imposed between 7.30 p.m. and 5.30 a.m. All persons carrying arms were to be fired on.

British reinforcements began to pour in. There were troops from England who had no idea where they were; Lucy Stokes heard how soldiers landing at Kingstown thought they were in France and called out '*Bonjour!*' Enid Starkie encountered a soldier who was surprised to hear people speak English since he thought he was on his way to relieve Kut. Men also arrived from Belfast and Templemore. As lorries carrying soldiers and policemen raced through Athlone people cheered them, and when a lorry stopped for a few minutes the men inside were given refreshments. In Athlone after the Rising pictures of executed leaders would only be stocked in a few shops. But towns like Athlone,

Templemore, Fermoy and Castlebar, whose prosperity depended largely on the presence of the military, tended to act differently; as late as 1997 Athlone was accused of having the smug attitudes of a garrison town.

In Dublin, British soldiers took up positions around Sackville Street and began attacking with machine-guns. That was on Wednesday. On Friday General Maxwell arrived and took charge.

But the fires had started long before, on the first day of the Rising. The report by Captain Thomas P. Purcell, Chief Officer of the Dublin Fire Brigade, described how the first call was received on Monday for engines to go to the ammunition depot in the Phoenix Park; the building survived but the ammunition was destroyed. Fires took hold on Tuesday; by Wednesday the brigade was helpless as the crossfire prevented them getting near the fires. The Linen Hall Barracks continued burning for two days and nights unchecked. At half past twelve on Thursday there was a call to Lower Abbey Street, but since the whole district was being shelled by field guns and mortars, in addition to rifle fire, the brigade could not approach.

This was the start of the fires that did most of the damage. The GPO burst into flames at 6.00 p.m. on Friday and burned during the night, together with the Coliseum Theatre and other buildings. Fires in Sackville Street lit the night sky crimson. Sean O'Casey thought 'the heavens looked like a great ruby from God's ear'. Out at Carrickmines, Samuel Beckett's father took him and his brother up the Glencullen Road to a spot where a crowd had assembled to watch the flames of central Dublin that glowed in the distant darkness. There was laughter and jocularity, but the boy Samuel felt horror.

On Saturday Captain Purcell was told that since the GPO had surrendered and military action had ceased, the brigade could go into the Sackville Street area. But a sniper was still at work; shots hit one engine and a ladder. The firemen were sent back to their stations, abandoning their engines. When they returned, the engines were recovered, and slowly the fires came under control. At 8.00 in the evening, Jervis Street Hospital, in danger from sparks, was saved. For six days afterwards smouldering ruins had to be watered and doused.

The surrenders began to take place. At Jacob's biscuit factory the rebels had used bags of flour as sandbags all week, firing rifle shots at Ship Street Barracks. Now flour bags were removed from a lower window and a member of the Carmelite Order from Whitefriars Street was hauled inside. Soon a party of Volunteers marched out.

On Stephen's Green Commander Malin and Countess Markiewicz surrendered. He would be executed on 8 May. She would be reprieved, to go on being a thorn in the side of many people. Now she kissed her pistol and her Citizen Army bandoleer and refused Captain de Courcy Wheeler's offer of a lift in a car. 'No, I shall march at the head of my men. I am second in command and shall share their fate.'

In Lansdowne Road, close to the savage fighting in Mount Street, the house belonging to Denis Johnston's family had been taken over by insurgents for two nights and a day. 'One could rightly regard these intruders as four rather odd guests who wished us no harm, and were trying to do their best in a social condition of which there was no parallel. On the other hand, it was equally true that we were in considerable peril.' When the Volunteers were taken prisoner, Johnston's mother told the British officers that they were very nice civil boys.

The appalling conditions inside the smouldering GPO had been exacerbated, as the days went on, by the smell of the putrefying Lancer horses outside. Wounded with a compound fracture of his leg, James Connolly had been provided with a bed on wheels; he read detective stories to pass the time. 'It's like a Greek tragedy,' Michael Collins was heard to say. He was sneering at Patrick Pearse's propensity for writing poetic memoranda in the middle of the crisis. Finally Pearse accepted defeat. At 3.30 p.m. on Saturday he handed over his sword to General Lowe and the tricolour was hauled down from the roof of the GPO.

Lord Powerscourt, Assistant Provost Marshal, had been marooned in Dublin Castle and had run out of whiskey. Now resupplied, he encountered Sinn Féin prisoners, 'mostly raw lads, much frightened as to the consequence of their actions'. One asked him, 'If we wish to join the Army, will we be let?'

My grandfather, Edward Phillips, watched prisoners being marched along under escort to Kilmainham, 'an extraordinary collection of old men, young men and women, the majority in plain clothes'.

'Seventy prisoners from Boland's march past,' Lucy Stokes wrote in her diary, 'fine-looking fellows, swinging in good step . . . the leader was a fine-looking man called the Mexican; he was educated and speaks like a gentleman.'

CHAPTER 2

Salt of the Soil of Irish Life

Myself: You can't blame it all on nineteen-sixteen.
My father: I can if I want to. Once you give the gun a
blessing you can't revoke it.

Terence de Vere White

A noble failure is not vain,
But hath a victory its own.

Francis Ledwidge

Events might have turned out better for Ireland if the Rising
had not happened and Home Rule had been allowed to take its
course as a state in the process of a movement to an independent
Irish state that might conceivably, if improbably, in time have
included Northern Ireland.

Garret Fitzgerald

Kathleen Clarke, wife – soon to be widow – of Tom Clarke, was among those arrested in the aftermath of the Rising; after she was released she walked in the dark along Westmoreland Street and Sackville Street. Soldiers lay asleep on the pavement rolled in blankets. 'To go down North Earl Street I had to climb over a mountain of bricks and mortar still hot from the debris of houses which had fallen on a tram that was there.'

Daylight revealed the destruction. Henry Beaton, Arnott's company secretary, compared the appearance of Sackville Street to Ypres: 'House after house destroyed utterly. Clery and Co., DBC, Eason's, GPO, Metropole and Imperial Hotels, Freeman's Journal and literally dozens of other establishments in ruins. Henry Street on both sides from the Pillar to Arnott and Co. nearly every house down.' To his relief Arnott's had been spared.

In Middle Abbey Street the premises of the publishers Maunsel & Co were destroyed, together with Harry Clarke's illustrations of *The Ancient Mariner* which they were about to publish. Nearby, portraits by Clarke's wife, Margaret, were burnt in the Royal Hibernian Academy.

The churches escaped. Although they were not targeted, there was a touch of the miraculous in their preservation. Perhaps it was the prayers of the devout like Matt Talbot who continued to hear Mass during the week, heedless of cordons and bombardment.

Dubliners were seen weeping at the sight of their burnt city. The statues on Sackville Street stood above the desolation. Nelson was 'imperturbable, incongruously remote', according to Sean O'Faolain. 'Even during the street fighting all around him . . . he gazed down undisturbed, detached from it all.' The other adulterers, O'Connell and Parnell, also survived the fighting, although one of the maidens below O'Connell has a bullet hole in her breast which is still easily seen.

Twenty thousand British soldiers had been involved in the fighting. Sixty-two Volunteers and 103 British soldiers were killed, many during the fighting at Mount Street Bridge. Far more civilians had bloodied Dublin's cobble-stones; 256 men, women and children were killed and around 2,000 were wounded.

What was public opinion towards the Rising before the executions? The Church condemned it. The Bishop of Kerry claimed it was fought by 'evil-minded men affected by Socialistic and Revolutionary doctrine'.

Edward Phillips, Managing Director of Guinness, considered that 'the attitude of the lower classes generally was one of aloofness; they did not seem to sympathise decidedly with either party, and for the first time since I have been in Ireland I have seen small children waving Union Jacks in Thomas Street'. (He was an Englishman; Tod Andrews would point out that 'the senior management staff of Guinness was, by definition, non-Irish'.) Phillips's messenger boy went off and joined the Volunteers, only returning to work after the surrender. No doubt many others acted similarly.

From the first there was an underlying sympathy for the underdog, for those who went out, in O'Casey's words, 'with knives and forks' to a contest that George Bernard Shaw described as 'a pram fighting a Pickford van'. The Volunteers were Roman Catholic, not the usual pantheon of Protestant martyrs, such as Tone, Emmet and Lord Edward Fitzgerald. They had taken on a powerful regime which inspired hatred and imposed humiliation.

Professor J. J. Lee, who contends that there was plenty of support for the Rising, quotes two of the copious Easter Week diarists. Gordon Clements, a Protestant clergyman, observed on the Tuesday that men in the street were 'not indignant at the rebels, feeling that "they were hardy boys, even if they are fools"'. R. Kain found that at the news of surrender 'many are murmuring,

"What a pity." ' Another diarist, Mr Clegg, saw a crowd burning a Union Jack to howls of glee. The looters may well have been generally on the side of the rebels; the Rising gave them several wonderful days out. It is to be hoped that the stout shoes and boots they stole lasted them well.

Ernie O'Malley came from a family of Castle Catholics who considered his attitude a betrayal of class. 'My brother would join the British Army, that was respectable, acknowledged as such by clergy and laity. I would associate with people who were looked down upon; once they were called "mere Irish"; now people of Irish birth had got into the eddies of the British caste system. I would disappoint their hopes . . . and be a black sheep.'

There was no doubt where James Stephens's sympathies lay. 'If freedom is to come to Ireland . . . then the Easter Insurrection was the only thing that could have happened. The blood of brave men had to sanctify such a consummation if the national imagination was to be stirred to the dreadful business which is the organisation of freedom . . .'

Moment by moment, hour by hour, Stephens felt the mood of the city change from rejection of the rebels to an espousal of their cause. But he found that 'most of the female opinion . . . was actively and viciously hostile to the Rising'. They included both 'the best dressed class of our population' and 'the female dregs of Dublin life . . . The view expressed was: "I hope every man of them will be shot." '

After the surrenders when Frank Thornton was marched off as a prisoner to Richmond Barracks in Inchicore, he felt that he and his companions would have been torn asunder if they had not been well guarded by British troops. The lines of prisoners taken along the quays to board boats ready to carry them to English jails were jeered mainly by women. These were almost entirely soldiers' wives, 'separation women' who were paid allowances, usually their only income, while their husbands fought in France or in the Dardanelles. Since there was no conscription in Ireland, England treated the dependants of Irish soldiers generously. These women have not been regarded well by Nationalist historians; they are condemned as 'shrill' or 'vituperative', while it is men who take off their hats at the sight of Volunteer prisoners and cry, 'Up the Republic!' There is the implication that the anger of such harridans stemmed from the threat to their allowances rather than from their disgust that Dublin was destroyed while their men were fighting and dying. But they were the same stock as the heroic slum mothers of literature and folklore. They cannot all have been irresponsible like those recalled by Leon Ó Broin: 'I saw a couple of them one afternoon lying in the gutter in Golden Lane tearing each other to pieces . . . While their men risked their lives in the trenches, they drank their heads off in the Dublin pubs.' Wives of Cork soldiers were equally derided in the ballad 'Salonika'. 'My husband's in Salonika, I wonder if he's dead, I wonder if he knows he has a kid with a foxy head . . .'

Returning as a schoolboy to Charterhouse, Hubert Butler passed through the smouldering ruins of Sackville Street just after Easter Week; 'the names of

Pearse and Connolly meant nothing to me, but I felt it was my war in a way that the war in which I was prepared to fight in the Charterhouse OTC was not'.

Most Unionists like his parents had nothing but contempt for the rebels who 'had committed atrocious murders not in the heat of action, but by deliberately killing non-combatants'. They shared the view of the Loyalist quoted by Terence de Vere White: 'There was not more than fifteen hundred persons in Ireland in sympathy with this wretched travesty of a rebellion.' 'Larkin's crowd' was the popular description of 'outlaws who spent the week firing indiscriminately through the town from behind curtains, attics and chimney stacks – they wore no uniforms, they held their arms beneath long coats. They sneaked away and were lost in the population when danger approached.'

'Noble minds planned the Rising as an heroic gesture of sacrifice,' wrote Darrel Figgis in 1927. The philosophy of blood sacrifice was not confined to Ireland; in France or Suvla Bay or the Dardanelles, Irishmen were dying in infinitely greater numbers than those who died in Easter Week and its aftermath. For many of those who had relatives fighting in the Great War, the insurrection was 'a petty rebellion' or 'a small anthill upheaval'.

Soldiers of the Dublin Fusiliers had marched off with the memory of ecstatic Dublin crowds. John Hargreaves remembered how 'they crowded the streets from the dockside – they cheered, they swarmed after us, thrust on us apples, cigarettes, lucky trinkets, rosaries, scapulars, packets of sweets into our hands. You'd think we were Cuchillia – heroes one and all – the high screaming Irish pipes wailing "The Wearing of the Green", the Connaught Rangers crashing out "St Patrick's Day", and the Leinster Fife Band swelling and sobbing sad with "Come Back to Erin".'

While Easter Week was in progress, the Battle of Verdun was raging. The Battle of the Somme was six weeks away. In Gallipoli the Dublin Fusiliers and the Munster Fusiliers had so many men killed that they were forced to amalgamate. In Dublin 'there was scarcely a family around us who had not lost someone', Enid Starkie wrote of her middle-class background. At the same time telegraph boys were making their way into the slums to deliver telegrams with a standard formula: 'The King commands me to assure you of the true sympathy of his Majesty and the Queen in your sorrow.'

'The departed dead in all their glory . . . splendid young men with strong bright fearless faces and typical of all that one hopes for in a rising generation' – so old Henry Robinson recalled them. Those who survived came back to an Ireland where pictures of the executed leaders were displayed in many windows and the new tricolour flew defiantly. The important men had died in Ireland in a 'schoolmaster's rising . . . poet's rising'.

In France, generals like Gough dismissed the efforts of Irish soldiers on the battlefield; after the 16th and 36th Divisions were decimated on the Western Front, the 16th Division was disbanded in 1918. When the veterans returned home, their war service tainted by suspicion and betrayal, they would find no welcome; instead they would be targets for Republicans just as members of the

Royal Irish Constabulary would be. Many ex-soldiers were murdered by the IRA.

'O had they died by Pearse's side . . .' Changed attitudes towards ex-soldiers inflamed by the Troubles were reflected in the memory of an officer's wife who recalled how in 1920: 'Early one morning my husband was the only passenger inside a tram. He was in uniform, and the conductor, looking around to see he was not observed, bent over him and drew a divisional Christmas card of the 5th Division in France and whispered: "This is all I have now, they won't let me wear my medal or ribbons. I spent the twelve happiest years of my life in an Irish regiment . . . had I known what Ireland is like now, I would never have left the Army."'

Irish casualties on the battlefield included Tom Kettle, who spent a brief leave in Dublin just after the Rising; his uniform terrified the traumatised Sheehy-Skeffington children. Francis Ledwidge, who had joined the Inniskilling Fusiliers, would die on the Western Front. In May 1916, recuperating in a Manchester hospital, he wrote to his friend Bob Christie after hearing the news from Ireland, 'Tho' I am not a Sinn Féiner and you are a Carsonite, do your sympathies go to Cathleen Ní Houlihan? MacDonagh and Pearse were two of my best friends, now they are dead, shot by England.'

His haunting poem to MacDonagh, which would henceforth be staple for Irish school children, differed from the angry vigour of balladry:

> In Dublin town they murdered them, like dogs they shot them down,
> God's curses be on you England, God strike you, London town.

In 1916 Kilmainham had been abandoned as a prison for some years. Now they made use of it again. The stone cells were pervaded with a smell of damp and the bombardment of Easter Week had deprived the place of gaslight, so that when Kathleen Clarke said farewell to Tom Clarke it was by the light of a candle in a jam jar held by an English sentry. Grace Gifford would be 'a widow, a maid and a wife'; her marriage to Joseph Plunkett ten minutes before his execution was witnessed by fifteen soldiers with fixed bayonets crowded into his cell. After the surrender James Connolly had been tended by Lucy Stokes's brother, Dr Henry Stokes of the Meath Hospital. He was telephoned by the military authorities who asked him to supply a medical certificate to the effect that Connolly was fit for execution. Stokes refused, but Connolly was tied to a chair and shot anyway.

The owner of the *Irish Independent*, William Martin Murphy, has been accused of calling for the execution of Connolly in particular. In fact he was horrified by the events: 'Every drop of Catholic blood in my veins surged up.'

The executions were no more brutal than those that were being carried out by the hundred for military offences on the Western Front. General Maxwell felt justified in punishing those who had caused the deaths of innocent men, women and children and flattened the heart of Dublin. General Blackadder, who was president of the court martial that condemned Pearse, told Lady

Fingall, 'I have had to condemn to death one of the finest characters I have come across. There must be something very wrong in the state of things that makes a man like that a rebel. I don't wonder that his pupils adored him.' But he did not consider a reprieve, nor did it occur to the generals that if they had hanged the leaders of the rebellion from a public gallows the effect would have been no worse than the staggered executions. The mass conversion to the Republican cause of those who had initially agreed with Redmond's call to fight for England and had already been made uneasy by the scale of casualties of the war to which their people had gone singing, was seen in hindsight as inevitable.

> Salt of the soil of Irish life, bone of her bone were they
> Like carrion flung in quick-lime grave in Dublin town today.

Connolly and Seán MacDiarmada were the last of the leaders of the Rising to die; ninety-seven others were sentenced to death but none of the sentences were carried out, although Maxwell would have liked to shoot a lot more. Eamon de Valera was spared because of his American connections.

On 10 May a letter from George Bernard Shaw appeared in the *Daily News*: '. . . the fact that he [the Irishman] knows his enemies will not respect his rights if they catch him and he must fight with a rope round his neck increases his risks, but adds in the same way to his glory in the eyes of his compatriots. It is absolutely impossible to slaughter a man in this position without making him a martyr and a hero even though the day before the Rising he may have been only a minor poet.' W. B. Yeats later repeated this argument more elegantly in his poem 'Easter 1916'.

In those tough times, while many Unionists approved of the executions, others realised immediately that they not only made martyrs but provided a licence for future bloodshed. The Duke de Stacpoole wrote how 'the Volunteers . . . were . . . saved from the indignation of Ireland at their stupid outbreak and raised to the halo of heroes by the savagery inflicted on them by England'. 'We have been put back a hundred years,' Sarah Purser remarked. Edith Somerville wrote a letter to *The Times* pleading for clemency.

Those who wished to honour the dead could purchase poplin ties in the Irish colours, each with a tie-pin which displayed a photograph of the executed leader of their choice at a cost of two shillings and sixpence. Or a cap badge as used by the Volunteers in gold or silver. Or rosary beads painted in the Irish colours. Postcards of the dead sixteen were soon on sale; Frank O'Connor and his mother used to buy them after attending the Franciscan or Augustinian churches in Cork where Mass was said for the martyrs of Easter Week. Bishop O'Dwyer of Limerick, who wrote a strong letter to General Maxwell after the executions ('your regime has been one of the worst and blackest chapters in the history of the misgovernment of this country'), had his portrait displayed in many shop windows decked with tricolour ribbons.

When the Republican prisoners were released at Christmas that year, they were mobbed and cheered on their return to Ireland; 'again the felon's cap had become the noblest crown an Irish head could wear,' Sean O'Casey wrote. April 1917, the first anniversary of the Rising, was rowdily observed. In Dublin the Sinn Féin flag was erected on the shell of the GPO to the accompaniment of cheers. There were more cheers when another was placed on Nelson's Pillar and a policeman had to climb up to remove it. People in the crowd wore black armbands striped with green, white and orange, while girls wore tricoloured papers in their hair and waved paper flags.

All utterly changed, although Sackville Street looked much the same. 'An Englishman' who wrote *Dublin Explorations and Reflections* viewed the city early in 1917: 'So this was modern warfare. I saw in front of me the shells of houses with ruined walls sticking up jagged into the forlorn sky, a great stone building [the GPO] with a long line of empty staring windows, houses all mottled and spattered with rifle fire, dust everywhere; acres of rubble and collapsed brickwork; bent iron; gaping cellars – at least half a great thoroughfare pounded almost to pieces.' He added, 'It had a strange quality of glamour, the glamour which attaches itself almost immediately to events which are destined to live in history.'

In July 1917 when the Clare by-election was won by de Valera, the bonfires lit in Clare could be seen across Galway Bay at Spiddal.

By August, drilling was forbidden and a proclamation forbade the wearing of military uniforms or the carrying of hurley sticks. Frank O'Connor was among the Volunteers who, shouldering the illegal hurley sticks and occasionally a shotgun, went out to marches and parades on country roads on summer evenings. Those prosecuted for drilling might behave like the men reported on a charge of illegal drilling in Castlebar: 'The prisoners' hats and cigarettes had to be forcibly removed in court.' In Co. Cork when Liam Lynch paraded with a hundred Volunteers in November 1917, they marched into the garrison town of Fermoy, 'loyal Fermoy'; a huge number of men marched at their side before they assembled to drill on open ground.

In vain the authorities banned Irish dancing and Gaelic games; the Irish Volunteers, Sinn Féin, Cumann na mBan and the Gaelic League continued to hold their well-attended meetings. When hurling matches were banned, fifteen hundred were played throughout the country on one day. In vain the green, white and orange was proscribed; it was flaunted everywhere.

Raids were made by the police for band instruments; silver and brass encouraged marching and disaffection. Denis Ireland saw an excursion steamer from Bantry coming in to the pier at Glengarriff. A brass band was playing and an enormous tricolour was floating from the stern. The excursionists lined up at the jetty with the band playing rebellious tunes and the tricolour still fluttering, much to the anger of a group of English officers: 'damned scoundrels, traitors, ought to be shot, etc. etc.'

Ireland was full of restless young men who stayed in the country rather than face conscription in England. Inspired by the wholesale martyrdom following the Rising, they rushed to fight a war of their own and join the new secret army.

Many prepared to fight England from the purest of patriotic motives. The awful events of the past and the halting failures of Home Rule encouraged fervent Nationalism and the call to arms against the old foe.

Education had played its part. There was turbulence in many schools after the Commissioners of National Education forbade pupils to wear tricolour rosettes. A typical response was at the end of August 1917, when boys at St Thomas National School, Rutland Street, Dublin, gathered outside, jeering at those who were non-wearers. They formed a procession, marched about singing rebel songs and stoned school windows and, for good measure, the windows of a public house.

Hundreds of passionate teachers with a belief in independence had stoked up the fires of violence. One hundred and twenty-five of the insurgents who took part in the Rising came from the O'Connell Christian Brothers in North Richmond Street in Dublin; eighty-four others were also educated at Christian Brothers schools. (By contrast, boys taught by the Jesuits at Belvedere went off to fight in France; only five joined the Rising.) In Athlone Patrick O'Shea had a teacher with a vision of a 'free Ireland cleansed from everything that came from England including its language. From him we heard that taxes raised in Ireland kept the English in sinful luxury and that in a free independent Ireland there would be little or no need for taxation.'

Encouragement came not only from primary and secondary teachers. Before the Rising Austin Clarke had attended University College Dublin where he had been lectured by Thomas MacDonagh, 'curly headed, speaking vivaciously with quick gestures', who during a lecture on Young Ireland poets took a large revolver from his pocket and laid it on his desk. 'Ireland can only win freedom by force,' he said.

While patriots thought about fighting Britain, the country was flooded with soldiers in the uniform of the Crown. They were either serving in the great Irish regiments – the Dublin Fusiliers, the Munster Fusiliers or the Connaught Rangers – or were men in British regiments posted temporarily to Ireland. They were not yet here to fight in the forthcoming 'little bitter war' as Molly Keane described the Troubles; the Rising was over and they were on their way to far bloodier battlefields than Dublin.

Garrison towns saw a constant stream of conscript soldiers waiting to be sent to France or Mesopotamia or wherever the real fighting was. Athlone was dominated by band parades, regattas, sports meetings and swimming galas for the troops. Recruits adapted to 'crubeens' instead of fish and chips, and on Saturday night eating houses would be crowded with soldiers sitting around large bowls of steaming pigs' feet.

Every now and then the body of a young soldier would be fished out of the Shannon; drowning was preferable to the uncertainties of the Western Front. Soldiers' funerals were accompanied by the regimental band playing a solemn funeral march on the way to the cemetery and returning to a lively tune which Patrick O'Shea was told was 'We'll Get Another Soldier for a Bob'.

Troops sang 'It's a Long Way to Tipperary' or 'I'm Forever Blowing Bubbles', almost an anthem. During the 1921 war a lorry load of Tommies were singing the song as they were attacked in Rathgar Avenue; 'We'll give you f— ing bubbles!' Ernie O'Malley claimed to have killed a Black and Tan singing the song: 'A frothy blood closed his mouth before he finished the chorus!'

By 1918 it was considered that reinforcements were needed if Germany was to be beaten and the possibility of conscription in Ireland progressed from being a contentious issue to a strong possibility. Loyalists had long been pressing for Irishmen to be compelled to go to war. The *Irish Times* had references to 'The Untouched Recruiting Field in Ireland', while correspondents wrote indignantly about 'The Shame of Ireland'. In the House of Commons Sir George Cave said he was advised that there would be resistance to the Military Service Bill, whose aim was to introduce conscription, but resistance could be overcome.

Protests were immediate, general and raucous. On 16 April 1918 conscription was preached against in hundreds of Catholic churches, outside many of which a Solemn League and Covenant to resist was signed by men of military age. DEATH BEFORE CONSCRIPTION was written on many green, white and orange badges. Seventeen King's Counsel in the Irish bar declared themselves against it; so did the Quakers. A typical anti-conscription meeting in Mullingar in April 1918 was attended by Sinn Féin bodies, the local branch of the Ancient Order of Hibernians (AOH), representatives of trade and labour unions and shop assistants, and between thirty and forty priests.

When de Valera went to Maynooth to get episcopal sanction for resisting conscription, his delegation was received with 'a great ovation'. There was a general strike. In parts of Ireland as distant as Belmullet, Co. Mayo, and West Cork blacksmiths made pikes in preparation for rebellion.

And then it was decided that conscription was not needed after all. The Americans had come to Europe to fight and die instead. But the damage had been done. In early 1918 Sinn Féin, having enjoyed unbroken electoral success, had suffered three by-election defeats, partly because of the disapproval of the Church, as well as conservative attitudes among older people. In Waterford the son of the deceased John Redmond was elected on a sympathy vote. But the Military Service Bill smartly put a stop to Sinn Féin's temporary unpopularity. The German plot increased its support when in May 1918 seventy-three prominent Republicans, including de Valera and Arthur Griffith, were arrested without evidence for 'treasonable communication with the German enemy'. Internment is always a particularly contentious issue.

The weary months of 1918 passed with the casualty lists that continued until minutes before the Armistice. A month before, on 10 October, the RMS *Leinster*, one of four mail-boats to England, was torpedoed after leaving Kingstown harbour. Almost five hundred lives were lost, half the total of Easter Week. Many victims were children returning to English schools.

One of the survivors of the *Leinster* was the butler at my school, an austere and dignified man named Flood, who, we were told, had been picked up and returned in time to get a tram home for his breakfast. Lady Anson, who lost her cousin, remembered the uncertainty of the waiting crowd: 'Then boats came back with a few dead bodies, and it slowly dawned on them that no more would return alive; more and more corpses came in and the authorities converted some big picture gallery or school . . . into a temporary morgue.' There was an under-takers' strike and no means of burying the dead. The search for Lady Anson's cousin was a 'most gruesome nightmare . . . in this vast mass of drowned people – their clothes were just like sodden brown paper . . . their hair was hanging down in a tangled mass – the bodies were so decomposed by sea water that they were hardly human'.

Death awaited in another form; at much the same time the influenza pandemic reached Ireland. In Dublin, convoys of funerals passed through the streets. Undertakers had piles of coffins outside their premises, 'towering barricades of them already sold,' wrote Sean O'Casey, 'yet many more were needed for those who died'. On 5 November there were seventy orders for burial at Glasnevin, three times the ordinary daily number. The head gravedigger became ill and coffins were placed temporarily in resting vaults.

Some people died with dramatic suddenness, often within twenty-four hours of being taken ill. For a period of five months during which sickness raged, the daily number of death notices in the *Irish Times* rose by a third. Only a few mentioned the epidemic: 'of heart failure following influenza'.

Advertisements recommended 'Nostroline, a Defence against Influenza, Nasal Catarrh, Cold in the Head and Sore Throat. A touch of this wonderful preparation inside your nostrils makes (and keeps) you influenza proof.' Or 'Jeyes Fluid – Use it in your bath. Spray the atmosphere of the Office, Factory, Home, Cinema.' 'Fight the flu with Formamint the germ-killing throat wash.' There was a shortage of Bovril with its body-building powers. Sandeman's Port was recommended. If hair fell out during convalescence, a common occurrence, the remedy was Ashmore's Pilocarpine Lotion.

Schools closed, police barracks were empty and post offices shut. The King's Bench dealt with applications to postpone trials owning to the illness of counsel. In crowded slum rooms whole families lay ill.

In the country, attendance at wakes of those who had died of influenza was discouraged, since this was believed to spread the epidemic. Among the victims of flu was Pierce McCann, president of the Tipperary Brigade of the IRA; after the Treaty the repossessed barracks in Tipperary town was renamed the McCann Barracks.

In the midst of the epidemic came the Armistice on 11 November. Over 49,000 Irishmen out of the 150,000 serving in the British forces had been killed in four years of war.

At Templemore there was a parade during which a *feu de joie* was fired; on 'At the command, fire!' the soldier at Bart Street fired, and his comrades, who were arranged in a huge ellipse, followed, firing one after another so that the shots went up one side of the street and down the other and back to the Town Hall. Caps were thrown in the air and three cheers were given. At night the Army held a fireworks display.

In Athlone the big gates of the barracks swung open and the entire garrison came running out together. Peace was celebrated with drinking, music and dancing. Many townspeople wore red, white and blue ribbons.

Red, white and blue was also to be seen in Dublin. In the Shelbourne the menu of the Victory Dinner, topped by victorious allied flags, offered *Huîtres Royales Natives, Filet de Sole à L'Americaine, Pommes Parisiennes, Sauce Italienne, Jambon de Limerick Braisé* and *Didonneau Farci à l'Anglaise*.

Down in the town there was brawling between Volunteers and troops – four British soldiers were killed. Michael Collins was pleased.

CHAPTER 3

Will Ireland Ever be Free?

The prospect of dying for Ireland haunts the dreams of
thousands of youths today.

Special Correspondent for The Times, *December 1918*

There is a minority of exceptionally well-fed persons whose flag
is the Union Jack and whose anthem is God Save the King and
these people heatedly call on Dublin Castle to preserve order.
By preserving order they mean cracking the skull of anyone who
sings 'The Soldier's Song'.

Robert Lynd, 1920

Lloyd George's khaki election of 1918, called to take advantage of the
Armistice, brought triumph to Sinn Féin, which returned seventy-three
members, while the moderate Irish Parliamentary Party went down from sixty-
eight to six. The Unionists held on to twenty-six. Henry Harrison, who had
been Parnell's secretary, was one of those who believed that Sinn Féin should
have gone to Westminster in 1918; it would have got what it wanted and it could
conceivably have prevented Partition. But Sinn Féin abstained and the
Volunteers prepared for war.

Among those with a Unionist background, besides the small number who were
wholly on the side of Republican aims there were many liberal supporters,
Redmondites and Home Rulers. Like Lady Gregory and Yeats, these liberals did
not countenance violence. For sympathisers like Lady Glenavy, Stephen Gwynn,
Lady Fingall and even Robert Barton, a signatory of the first Dáil, the bloody
years could never be justified. Sarah Purser was another who could not support
the killings and burnings; since the time of Parnell she had persistently spoken up
for Home Rule and independence by peaceful and constitutional means.

Lady Gordon, a descendant of the Earls of Milltown, had been a Home Ruler long before the Easter Rising; in her circle the tag meant disloyalty. 'To be suspected of Nationalist sympathies . . . was almost as bad in the eyes of one's Unionist neighbours as being suspected of murder.' Her political stance became increasingly unpopular during the Great War when so many of her friends were losing relatives on the battlefield.

In 1918 Lady Gordon, who had been living in London, returned to Dublin to recuperate after an illness. In order to rent a flat in Fitzwilliam Square she had to pass the denominational qualification that was so common at that time. The advertisement in the *Irish Times* specified, 'Flat to let, lady or gentleman, Protestant, dining out, partial attendance . . .' The accommodation was nothing marvellous – a shared bathroom and a cupboard in the stairs described as a 'kitchenette' fitted with a gas ring and sink. The dirty windows were enshrouded with lace curtains, there was no hot water and only partial electric light. Her landlord was a doctor, and she found that she was expected to share her sitting-room with his patients: 'You wouldn't mind, just for a short time like that . . .'

Lady Gordon gives a vivid account of the atmosphere of bourgeois Dublin after the Rising and before the Anglo-Irish war. She found a run-down city, its centre in ruins, where friendliness made up for poverty, and whose slums teemed behind the smart shop fronts. 'In engaging familiarity the shop people, instead of addressing you indefinitely as "Madam" or "Sir" call you by your name . . . "No grey silk stockings in stock today, Mrs Mahoney," says the shop-walker at Switzer's . . . "If you walk upstairs, Miss Murphy, you'll find our latest models on view."' Such practices were not tolerated in London shops.

The few good restaurants like Jammet's and the Red Bank contrasted with numerous small hotels and eating houses where *Hanche de Mouton* disguised ordinary roast mutton. In this period Dublin boasted one nightclub which served only cocoa and was soon to close down. Naturally Lady Gordon did not write about Monto, the teaming brothel area of the city.

This was the period when at-homes and soirées particularly associated with Dublin were at their most popular. Such gatherings would linger into the new Ireland and did not totally die out until the seventies when Arland Ussher was still receiving visitors once a week. 'The unreal atmosphere in which they live,' observed Lady Gordon, 'gives to the mind of the Dublin literati the fantastic turn which each of them displays in different degrees . . . or it may be the tea and buns on which they exist.'

Seamus O'Sullivan held his at-homes on Sunday afternoons. 'The only trouble about O'Sullivan is that when he is not drunk, he is sober,' said Yeats. Yeats's own at-homes on Monday evenings were all male and often the talk was about sex. George Moore's soirées were on Saturday nights, while Sarah Purser held afternoon gatherings known as 'Miss Purser's Second Tuesdays'. One of Beatrice Glenavy's jobs was to hand round tea and sandwiches while Miss Purser, notoriously parsimonious, boasted 'of how many sandwiches she could make out of a few herrings to put before her visitors'.

Miss Purser fed Sir William Orpen more lavishly when he had afternoon tea in her drawing-room at Mespil House in summertime. 'All the birds know it's "teatime". In they come through the open window; the bread and butter, jam and cakes are all covered to protect them; but if you are not careful you will not get a bite of the piece in your hand at all and if you raise your hand to smack the little devils they just hop back a bit . . . It's a true birds' paradise.'

In 1917 Maud Gonne had bought 73 St Stephen's Green; because of the political turmoil she arranged to exchange houses with Yeats who had married George Hyde-Lees in October 1917. The arrangement was for Maud Gonne to take over Yeats's flat in Woburn Buildings in London while the Yeatses moved into Stephen's Green. It was expecting too much of both parties for such a scheme to work. When Maud Gonne came back to Ireland, she called at her house; Yeats refused to let her in, saying his wife was ill with influenza – the pandemic was raging. The two ex-lovers argued for some minutes at the door. According to Francis Stuart, Yeats was paying a very small rent (justified if Gonne was using Woburn Buildings); 'having just married a rich wife, it wasn't as if he couldn't have paid her properly'. Yeats also let his pet rabbits eat up the grass in the back garden.

In due course Maud Gonne got her house back and even invited the Yeatses to supper. Her friends included Charlotte Despard, known as Madam Desperate, sister of the recently appointed Viceroy, Sir John French. The two women shared what Stuart defined as 'an easy assumption of the absolute rightness of the nationalist cause'.

Mrs Despard was in her late seventies, twenty-two years older than her friend. Maud Gonne was over six feet tall, while Mrs Despard was 'a little woman'. The 'formidable but ludicrous pair' always dressed as widows with billowing black gowns and in addition Mrs Despard wore a mantilla and sandals. A novelist, a suffragette and a socialist, she had come to the cause of Irish freedom late in life.

In her full black mourning for Major John MacBride, not an ideal husband, Maud Gonne was not only still beautiful and head-turning, but had a way of attracting a court around her with willing devotees. Among them was Kathleen Kearney, Brendan Behan's mother, who acted as housekeeper. 'I let the visitors in and answered the telephone – so although I got very little for it I didn't feel degraded ever, and that was worth something.'

Maud Gonne's at-homes were on Tuesdays. She had a French cook and the house in Stephen's Green was always full of animals and birds: canaries, finches, a parrot, a monkey and once a hawk from Donegal. She was seldom without a dog; Austin Clarke remembered her striding through a Wicklow glen like a personification of Hibernia followed by a wolfhound. One visitor to Stephen's Green was seventeen-year-old Francis Stuart who went along to meet his future wife, Iseult, Maud Gonne's daughter, and to glower at Iseult's black-draped mother.

A more jolly weekly occasion would have been *chez* Countess Markiewicz.

Sean O'Faolain remembered how 'crowds used to gather . . . at night. We had tea in the kitchen, a long table with Madam cutting up slices of bread about an inch thick and handing them around – she had lovely furniture and splendid pictures. Then we used to go into the sitting-room and someone would sit at the piano and there would be great singing and cheering and rough amusements. She had lifted her lovely drawing-room carpet . . . and on the bare boards there was the stamping of feet.' Among her guests was Michael Collins who recited Emmet's speech from the dock.

On Sunday evenings at 10.00 exactly guests of Æ, George Russell, collected in Rathgar Avenue; he was visited constantly by Americans, Japanese and Chinese in addition to the adoring old ladies known as the Holy Women. They would be greeted by a smelly old dog and served tea and home-made scones by Æ's wife and two sons. No doubt the refreshment was welcome after listening to monologues about politics or fairies. To the young Monk Gibbon this genial tweedy figure resembled 'a Russian moujik or a Jupiter . . . except one hardly expected to find Jupiter puffing a pipe'.

Russell's untidy little office at the top of a house in Merrion Square with its view of the Dublin mountains was painted with fairies, figures with plumes and aureoles and bright woods and glades. Having climbed the seven flights of stairs, Austin Clarke was surprised to find a small countrywoman with a basket of eggs talking to Æ. He assumed she was a farmer's wife seeking advice about butter and eggs or perhaps a problem of the Co-operative movement. But this was Lady Gregory speaking in her rustic accent, saying 'dis, dat and dose'.

Francis Stuart was unimpressed by the dream paintings – 'false and invented' – and by the spectacle of Æ, a big burly Northern Presbyterian from a background similar to his own, reading with great satisfaction to an admiring audience notices of his recent tour of America. (But Stuart attended readings because Iseult was among those listening.) Cecil Salkeld wrote how 'Æ was to me an entirely practical hard-headed business man who had served twenty to twenty-five years behind the counter at Pim's where, I think, he became manager before working as a back room boy for Sir Horace Plunkett in the Co-operative Movement'.

In other words, Æ's place in society was ambivalent because he had been in trade. In the twilight of their power Protestants continued to be absorbed with snobbery. Writing about her status as 'a lady's child', Enid Starkie recalled, 'To be a Lady's Child did not depend on the size of one's father's income and I believe it was very difficult to qualify for this rank if one's family was implicated in business.'

That so much of Dublin's business was in the hands of Protestants did not help them socially. The Quakers might keep to themselves and be immune from threats of social ostracism – Pim's, for which Æ had worked, was a Quaker drapery – but Elvery's, which was not Quaker owned, was another drapery, and Beatrice Elvery and her family were ostracised by upper-class Foxrock. Other families in Foxrock like the Becketts and Orpens, whose heads of household had adopted professions, escaped the awful stigma. Richard Caulfield Orpen was an architect; his neighbour, William Beckett, Samuel's father, who was in fact a well-to-do surveyor, often referred to himself as an architect which was more socially acceptable. Foxrock was so like Beaconsfield or Gerrard's Cross that the painter William Orpen had felt utterly at home in England when he adopted that country. The stifling bourgeois respectability of the Beckett household drove Samuel from gardens and tennis court to imitate John Synge and go out into the Dublin mountains in search of down-and-outs and tramps.

There was the position of 'Castle Catholics'. Enid Starkie hated going to children's parties at Dublin Castle. Her family was Catholic as the result of mixed marriages, which did not stop her father from sending his children to Protestant schools. An admirable and enlightened Minister of Education, he always maintained that mixed schooling was essential for any growth in ecumenism. But he was an unusual man; during Easter Week he had ignored the gunfire which could be heard out at Blackrock, and sat in his garden reading Pliny's letters.

The playwright Denis Johnston, who lived in a terraced house on Marlborough Road, remembered a middle-class world of servants, coal fires and oil-lamps where silences were broken by the sound of a horse-drawn van or the hum of the electric tram. 'You enter these unpretentious houses by a hall door at the top of a flight of granite steps shared with your neighbour on the right which means that everything in the house begins halfway up, with the front drawing-room looking out on the garden behind. Behind the two rooms are so-called folding doors . . . leaving a long room the full depth of the house – very nice for parties, while at the same time cozy for winter.'

Marlborough Road and even Foxrock offered relatively modest and comfortable lifestyles. Wealthier families might prefer to be housed in one of the numerous mini-estates on the outskirts of Dublin which imitated country houses. The Starkies lived on a farm at Stradbrook beside Blackrock with horses, carriages, meadows, cows, a dairy, chickens and pigs. But such estates needed money to maintain them; the Starkies' living standards, featuring hothouse fruit such as grapes and peaches and plenty of other luxuries, could not be sustained on Mr Starkie's official salary of £15,000 a year, so that bankruptcy constantly loomed.

At Roebuck House, three miles from Nelson's Pillar, Cecil King's family lived with more secure wealth on an estate boasting a large indoor and outdoor staff, four carriages, two walled gardens and a telephone that worked on batteries. The Kings were among the many Unionists who regarded the Easter Rising as a stab in the back.

As teaspoons tinkled and croquet mallets tapped in the genteel suburbs of Dublin, members of Sinn Féin were preparing to fight for independence. By the beginning of 1919 Cumann na mBan, the women's Republican organisation, and Fianna Éireann were flourishing, the Gaelic League had never been stronger, and bodies concerned with the welfare of prisoners and their dependants had been established. When the Dáil Éireann sat for the first time in January 1919 the Volunteers were recognised as the Irish Republican Army.

After the Armistice a few demobilised soldiers joined the IRA – less than a hundred. These veterans were more important than their numbers suggested, bolstering the movement by their experience. For example, after the fighting started, Matt Flood, who had learnt his trade in France at Étaples, was able to use a captured Hotchkiss for the first time, firing on a lorry containing English soldiers and killing the driver. Another trained soldier who brought essential skills to a struggle where the majority of his comrades had little or no knowledge of arms was Tom Barry, who had been in bloody conflict with the Mesopotamian Expeditionary Force. He returned to Ireland in February 1919 and joined the IRA some months later. Like so many of his comrades, his first sign of national consciousness had been the news of the Rising, 'a rude awakening, guns being fired at the people of my own race by soldiers of the same army with which I was serving'.

Another old soldier sympathetic to the Republicans was Sergeant Mike O'Leary, VC. During a round-up by Auxiliaries who shouted, 'You haven't got your hands up!' O'Leary turned out the lapel of his coat and flashed the green ribbon of the Victoria Cross. The Auxiliaries immediately saluted and withdrew.

The recruits who flocked to join with Barry included prosperous farmers' sons, a sprinkling of teachers and idealists burning for objectives for which the men of 1916 had died. Some, like the ploughboy in the song ('I'm off to join the IRA, I'm off tomorrow morn'), were sick and tired of the slavery imposed by farming life and consequently were keener than ever to recover 'the land the Saxon stole'. There were many who had missed the Great War and were spoiling for a fight. 'They not only looked tough but were tough,' Barry considered, 'yet I knew them to be lighthearted youths who would normally have been happy working on their farms or in the towns or back at their schools, had they not volunteered to fight the savage British aggression that stalked the land.'

Recruits would become familiar with the Sinn Féin catechism:

Q. What is your nationality?
A. I am Irish.
Q. What does it mean to be Irish?
A. It means that I am part of the Irish Nation, to which I must give my time and best service and to which I must always be loyal.
Q. Why did England wish to conquer Ireland?
A. Because she wished to rob Ireland of her goods and possessions . . . (Conclusion)
Q. But will Ireland ever be free?
A. If we hold firmly to one another, and help one another, and never in any thought or act admit the right of England in Ireland. Then Ireland will once again take her rightful place among nations.

Most young recruits were deeply religious. This would cause problems, at least during the opening stages of the war. Public opinion could be ignored and so could newspaper criticism like the constant 'dreary editorial whine of despair' of the *Cork Examiner*. But for the devout it would be difficult not to heed ecclesiastical authority which persistently condemned the IRA until the Black and Tans went on the rampage.

If they did not initially have the support of the Church, the Volunteers would, above all, have the people on their side. The Black and Tans would make it easy for them. Volunteers had to depend largely on the support, stoicism and silence of local inhabitants of villages or towns or those living in remote cottages and farmsteads. These people were also essential strands in the network of intelligence that would prove so effective in tracing the movements of British forces.

There would be affection and loyalty towards those tentatively knocking on a back door at midnight. Long memories like those of Father Patrick Twohig would evoke 'leaving your warm bed so that some of those tired young men might take it over for the remainder of the night . . . mother baking late into the night to ensure that nobody was short at breakfast'.

In winter such welcome and shelter would prove essential. IRA veterans would blame their arthritis on their guerrilla experiences of sleeping out in the heather or in wet barns, subsisting on a diet of 'loaf bread', eggs and an occasional slaughtered sheep. One remembered how he 'ate hedgehog in late winter or stewed hare with wine-red tinkers in their camp on the sheltered side of a hedge'.

Volunteers were unpaid:

> The night I met the bold O.C.
> 'Remember this,' he said to me.
> 'You'll get no clothing, food or pay
> But just the honour of the IRA.'

If caught they risked torture and bullets either from the indifferent Tans or Auxiliaries or from a firing squad after a court martial. They would be sent to their deaths by the officers of the army they considered they were at war with who persisted in treating them with contempt, not as enemies, but as 'corner boys collected from every district and rounded up'. They might call themselves soldiers of the Irish Republican Army, but their opponents called them Shinners and cowboys and described them as well-paid murderers.

Preparations for the fight included the reading of old Boer War manuals. The Sunday marches and weekend drillings continued. Uniforms evolved out of a medley of riding breeches, gaiters, trench coats with collars pulled up and soft hats pulled low over the eye. For their enemies this sort of gear would become the hallmark of the gunman.

The IRA was always handicapped by having virtually no arms. The brigades and flying columns in the country received little or no help from headquarters in Dublin and had to manage on their own. Arms could be purchased from abroad, smuggled in by gunrunners or bought from British soldiers who were willing to sell their rifles. Before 1919 Volunteers went around collecting shotguns and bicycles from the general public. Some people made a show of resistance in case they were interrogated by police later on. Loyalists resisted; one lady near Ballyvourney, Co. Cork, threw a pan of bacon and eggs in the face of a man who demanded arms from her. At Tom Henn's home, Paradise Hill in Sligo, the swords hanging on the wall were taken by the IRA.

Raids on soldiers' barracks were a more fruitful method of bringing in weapons. A series of small incidents like the disarming of twelve Cameron Highlanders near Middleton in Co. Cork in June 1919, or the disarming of seven British soldiers at a horse fair near Ennis in Co. Clare, added to the arsenal. The other useful source of arms would be police barracks. In 1919 the order went out in the newly formed brigades to collect information about them and their occupants.

Arms of the period included Vickers machine-guns, Lewis guns, Webley and Scott's Long Webley, the Smith and Wesson New Century revolver, the Lee Enfield, the Mauser automatic like the one Tom Barry used, and Winchester repeaters like the one wielded by Ernie O'Malley. Tommy-guns came over to Ireland during the Truce, too late for the War of Independence, in time for the Civil War.

Even when arms were obtained, except for those who had served in the British forces, the newly recruited men of the IRA were unfamiliar with the use of them. The hurley sticks were discarded for a new sort of training. Volunteers learnt to prepare home-made gunpowder, a mixture of saltpetre and sulphur obtained from friendly chemists, and charcoal made from alder bushes. Land-mines were manufactured from sections of drainpipe filled with black powder. Slugs of buckshot were made from iron obtainable from iron foundries. Molten lead was dropped into cold water, resulting in pellets, each one of which had a tail like a tadpole. A fatigue duty was removing these tails-with-pliers. Home-made bayonets put on shotguns proved a disappointment, while many grenades failed to explode. As a Volunteer Sean O'Faolain made bombs; he wrote of a bomb factory during the height of the Troubles located in a house in the heart of Cork city where weapons were assembled with the aid of pestle and mortar, sifters, jars of acid, bags of chemicals and roaring spirit lamps. Books of instruction gave recipes for weapons like grenade cartridges made with dilute nitric acid, cardboard wads and warm shellac.

Michael Collins was eager to fight; in the countryside fire-eaters like Liam Lynch, Sean Treacy, Dan Breen and Ernie O'Malley raided for arms and prepared to die for Ireland, encouraged by MacDonagh's exhortation: 'The generous high-bred youth of Ireland will never fail to blaze forth in the red rage of war to win their country's freedom. Other and tamer methods they will leave to other and tamer men, but for themselves they must either do or die.' The death of Thomas Ashe on hunger strike exacerbated the sense of unease, and the divisions of Irish life were becoming increasingly apparent. But terror was still in the future; de Valera felt that the public would not yet stomach killing. The Republicans waited for more British brutality. After the blundering over conscription there was no real excuse to start a war except impatience at the slow rate of progress towards any form of Home Rule and a conviction that it would never be achieved by peaceful means. Events were moving too slowly. The shooting of policemen at the beginning of 1919 had similarities with the blowing up of Canary Wharf in 1995.

The British were in no hurry to give up their Hibernian kingdom; they had the northern part of the island to consider and savage things were threatened there as well. There was the residue of the attitude of What I've Got I'll Keep. General Crozier, commander of the Auxiliaries, who was later to resign because of the behaviour of the men under his leadership, commented that 'much of the trouble which exists between Ireland and England today arises from the fact that the English got it into their heads long ago that Ireland "belonged to them"'.

Life went on much as before. Oliver Weldon published *The Valley of the Squinting Windows* in 1918 under the musical pen-name of Brinsley MacNamara, exposing life in the village of Devlin, Co. Westmeath, a world of whispering campaigns, land grabbers and corrupt priests.

The real coming tragedy would be that vicious poverty would continue for more than half a century after Ireland gained her freedom. In Iris Murdoch's words, the poor would simply be exploited by P. Flanagan instead of J. Smith.

CHAPTER 4

Janissaries of England

At Solohead the war began
And next was heard the song
Of the rescue of Sean Hogan
At the station of Knocklong.

Ballad, Anon.

The Black and Tans were in Gort . . . a very bad looking troop,
with little ribbons hanging from their caps and faces that were
not shaved since Christmas, and nothing could be more drunk
than what they were, staggering about the street and letting
their rifles drop out of their hands.

Lady Gregory's informant, 5 March 1921

On 21 January 1919, a day that coincided with the first Dáil Éireann assembly,
two constables named MacDonnell and O'Connell, their carbines on their
shoulders, were walking behind a horse and cart carrying 160 pounds of
gelignite and thirty electric detonators from Tipperary town to the quarry at
Soloheadbeg. As they reached their destination they were ambushed by eight
masked men from behind a hedge. Their attackers seized the guns and
dynamite, leaving the constables' bodies lying in the laneway. Later, three of
the ambushers, Sean Treacy, Dan Breen and Seamus Robinson, defended the
overkill and were adamant that the policemen had been challenged before they
were shot. Dan Breen wrote, 'It was untrue to say that our enemies at
Soloheadbeg did not get a "dog's chance".'

It may have been inexperience or impatience to get on with the killing that
made the Tipperary Republicans plan such a one-sided attack. The action met
with much disapproval, including that of the Catholic Church. The Bishop of

Cork, the most Reverend Dr Cohalan, declared that 'the killing of policemen is morally murder and politically of no consequence'. But many already regarded Dan Breen as a hero, 'the man who had begun the war'. A Republican source proclaimed that 'the men who seized the explosives at Soloheadbeg risked their lives for Ireland – by such deeds are tyrants terrified and bullies held in check'.

The slaughter at the Tipperary quarry was the first recognised action of the War of Independence, a phrase that had been coined by Terence MacSwiney in 1912. In practice this meant the first of many killings of policemen. For two years, a propaganda war had been waged in which members of the Royal Irish Constabulary were portrayed not as keepers of the law, but solely as armed allies of the Crown, who did its dirty work.

The RIC bitterly resented the accusation that its men were military oppressors. Ninety per cent of them were Catholics; they were the sons of farmers and teachers, Home Rulers and men of the people. But their duties included unpopular tasks like baton-charging demonstrations and searching houses for arms. Between 1917 and 1919 they carried out over 12,000 raids on houses in search of arms and were responsible for thousands of arrests and deportations.

Kevin O'Higgins would say of the RIC, 'Let us not forget that it was the height of ambition of most young fellows who happened to be five foot nine or thereabouts.' The men had their grievances; the force was structured so that the majority of its officers were Protestants, 'Sandhurst types' according to Sean O'Faolain, who considered it their task to inspire recruits 'with the officers-and-gentlemen traditions of the crack regiments of the British Army'. During the war recruitment to the RIC was suspended and many of the younger policemen went off to fight. Consequently, by 1919 members of the force tended to be elderly, particularly those sent to rural districts.

A policeman in 'the Force' wore a bottle-green uniform modelled on that of the Rifle Brigade, a black leather belt with brass buckle, a black helmet or peaked cap, a black truncheon case and black boots. Officers had swords, while men carried bayonets which they only used on ceremonial occasions. But they also had guns. The fact that they were armed was the usual reason given to justify their subsequent shooting. The public was also encouraged to revile the Dublin Metropolitan Police whose members over the years had used their truncheons vigorously on assembled citizens. But the DMP was an unarmed force covering Dublin city and Co. Wicklow and its men never became specific targets of the IRA. Sir Joseph Byrne, Inspector General of the RIC, maintained that carrying firearms was only an encumbrance. 'If we had no rifles we should be quite safe.'

Men of 'the Force' had local knowledge vital to the military authorities. After the RIC was terrorised and emasculated, sources of intelligence dried up. Without the familiarity with an area built up at every police station, British troops and later the Black and Tans and Auxiliaries were virtually powerless to identify the enemy and as a result they were encouraged to behave with indiscriminate violence.

After an arms raid in Athlone, the schoolboy Patrick O'Shea and his brother, whose father was in the RIC, were beaten up by fellow pupils to howling cries of 'Traitors' and 'English spies'. Divisions in Irish life were becoming more apparent by the day. The stones, jeers and catcalls directed at policemen softened up public opinion in preparation for their coming deaths.

By contrast, the RIC was considered by Loyalists to be one of the best police forces in the world, its men similar to English bobbies. Brian Inglis remembered their reputation as 'genial fellows who bicycled around keeping an eye out for rough village lads who might be tempted to scrump apples, or strawberries out of gardens'. In the country their role had long been accepted. In Eric Cross's *The Tailor and Ansty*, written in the 1940s, the Tailor, Timothy Buckley, says, 'Yerra, no. The old RIC were a decent enough body of men in their way. They had a job to do, and a difficult job. You'll find good and bad amongst every class of men, and you can't condemn the lot for one.' He goes on with a genial anecdote about the local sergeant called upon to search the house for poteen. 'We'd better drink the evidence first and . . . make the search afterwards.'

But after 1916 policemen, 'Janissaries of England', were becoming unpopular with a public whose Nationalist instincts were heightened. They were doing duties that would normally be performed by soldiers. They were described as agents of the British Government who should be ostracised by the Irish people. In Dublin the DMP had slops poured down on them from backstreet tenements. They would be inveigled into dark halls to fall over dustbins that had been piled up ready for them. They would be showered with stones at demonstrations; on one occasion when they stood with their backs to shop windows, shattered glass fell on them in an ice storm.

After Soloheadbeg, Republicans took to shooting policemen with gusto. Tom Barry's tally of members of the RIC shot in 1920 reads like a game book: '25 April – Sergeant and constable shot dead near Upton . . . Three police killed near Timoleague . . . June 12 – Constable shot dead at Anagashel . . . June 23rd – Bantry: Terrible ruffian of the RIC shot dead . . . July 25 Sunday – Sergeant of the RIC shot going into Mass at Bandon . . . July 27 – Constable shot dead at Clonakilty . . .'

The public approved, even applauded. Any judicial inquiry into the circumstances of these deaths became difficult, then impossible. A typical case was that of Constable Brell, shot dead near Bantry in June 1920 after an affray when between twenty and thirty armed men ambushed five policemen who were serving summonses on bicycles. It proved impossible to assemble a jury for the inquest; police in the area were subject to insults and one had his house burnt down.

Policemen were even ostracised when they were dead. Behind the coffin at the funeral of a dead RIC man would be his comrades in their bottle green, some soldiers in khaki, his relatives in their mourning and no one else.

A bounty of £60 was offered for the murderer of any RIC man, later rising to £100. According to William Blackwood, 'people would be heard discussing this openly and wondering if it would go up or down, in the same way as they might discuss Dunlop's or Guinness's shares'.

Officers of the RIC were also killed. Divisional Inspector Phil Kelleher was shot in the back at the bar of the Greville Arms in Granard, Co. Longford. Michael Collins insisted on the assassination of a divisional commander, Colonel Smyth, who had blithely advocated shooting on sight any suspicious persons – which included anyone with his hands in his pockets. (After the massacre at Kilmichael the latter tactic became common among British forces.) So the one-armed colonel was gunned down in the Cork and County Club in July 1920. He was sitting in the smoking-room when eight or ten men walked in, shot him and walked out again. The operation took a minute. Six months later Smyth's successor, DI Holmes, was killed near Ballydesmond.

When it was possible, reasons were given for the killings. DI Swanzy was implicated in the murder of Thomas MacCurtain, and DI Lea Wilson was condemned for humiliating Tom Clarke after his capture in 1916. When Wilson was shot in Gorey, Co. Wexford, on Collins's order, Collins was exultant: 'We got the bugger!' (Wilson's widow went to Scotland where she bought a holy picture which turned out to be by Caravaggio; it now hangs in the National Gallery of Ireland.)

Most dead policemen, however, were ordinary men doing their duty. Patrick O'Shea was bitter that men like his father were 'shot in the streets, in their houses, going to Mass, doing messages for their wives, having a drink in a pub'. From January 1919 through to June 1922, 442 policemen were killed. In 1920 176 were killed and 257 wounded as contrasted with fifty-four British soldiers killed and 118 wounded. By then British soldiers in Ireland numbered 45,000 while the RIC were down to less than 10,000.

There are plaques to the RIC in London, in the crypt of St Paul's Cathedral and in St Patrick's Chapel in Westminster Cathedral where they are remembered together with the Irish regiments who served in the British Army.

Understandably, resignations from the RIC became frequent by mid-1920. If the policemen were not driven by fear of death or at least ostracism, their parents and relatives were urged by Sinn Féin to persuade them to leave. Terence MacSwiney had a plan that parents of unmarried members of the RIC should be approached by some responsible civilian like a priest with a view to encouraging their sons to leave 'the Force'. In the Dáil Countess Markiewicz ordered Sinn Féin clubs to assist those who resigned.

Police barracks faced attacks with sandbagged windows and loopholed shutters. Ernie O'Malley told of the fire started by himself and his comrades at Hollybrook Barracks when the petrol poured over the dozen policemen inside blew back all over the attackers, setting them alight. 'My eyelashes and eyebrows had gone; there were raised ridges on my face and head and on the back of my neck . . .' But that attempt was exceptional in its failure. After the capture of Carrigtohill Barracks in Co. Cork in January 1920, RIC garrisons retreated to larger towns as smaller police posts were closed down. Then on 3 April 1920, over 250 abandoned stations were burnt. The country was full of their ruins, 'stark and black' as O'Malley saw them, 'loose casements rattling . . . in the wind, sandbags piled in the windows through which the sky was seen and steel loopholed sheeting, often twisted by fire over the friendless deserted doors'.

Non-combatants observed the war going from bad to worse as thousands of English troops failed to make any impression on small well-disciplined groups of guerrillas protected by the general populace. In Timoleague, West Cork, Lionel Fleming and his family glumly watched the unsuccessful efforts of English troops to effect a round-up as the rebels slipped away. Things got worse. Fleming remembered how 'there was a constant succession of events which were both shocking and mysterious. The house of some quite respectable man would be burnt down . . . some apparently harmless person would be kidnapped, another would be found dead on the road with the inscription "spy" pinned to his coat. A neighbour's cattle would be driven off his land, someone else would get a warning to quit the country by the next day. There was never any explanation.'

Few newcomers were tempted to Ireland at this time; the traffic was the other way. One exception was a young man called Kevin Fitzgerald, English bred, whose father had unwisely bought a country property going cheap in the midst of the Troubles. As the War of Independence was getting fiercer, father and son journeyed to Ireland. Once across the Irish Sea 'the train journey from Dublin to Thurles was the dreariest I ever remember, through some of the saddest looking country in the world. It made me miserable then, and it still does.'

Their first sight of their 'dreadful' new estate, Symore, was 'a broken-down lodge gate, a broken-down pair of cottages serving as a lodge, three-quarters of a mile of avenue and then the . . . hideous house, built in 1860'. The estate included seventeen tied cottages and 900 run-down acres gone to seed. Fitzgerald's father wanted quick returns and he set his son to work snagging turnips and 'dunging', cutting up tightly pressed wallops of manure with a hay knife.

A neighbouring landlord offered to teach the young farm-hand the practical side of farming. Mr Willington, whose Georgian house was still happily crammed with servants, was a popular man in the area. With his patronage Fitzgerald encountered the siege mentality among dwindling Loyalist families. He indulged in 'the slow garden-party tennis of those far-off days – fishtailed racquets, yellowing white trousers, and rubber soles on soft brown leather shoes, the grass too long, the net too low, everyone happy'. A Catholic, he was nevertheless accepted as a kindred spirit among 'Protestants enjoying the dangerous patronage of a doomed race'.

In Birr he was entertained in the King's County Club where 'everyone present, English, Irish, Scotch or Welsh, was British to the core. In the smoking room lay the Irish and English *Times*, the latter soon to be banished for disloyal tendencies . . . there, too, lay the essential papers for Irish rural life – the *Field*, the *Sporting Times*, the *Winning Post*, the *Shooting Times*, *Horse and Hound* and *Country Life*. The only books I ever saw in the Club was a complete set of *Buff's Guide to the Turf*.'

For Mr Willington and his colleague, Colonel Head, the King's County provided a refuge in a threatening world. By mid-1919 the war had become local. The barracks in Birr had been gutted and Inspector Hayes of the RIC had been shot dead at Thurles Fair. Mr Willington and Colonel Head were Resident Magistrates, whose duties had changed from trying cases of poaching and drunkenness. At their courts, which had to be guarded by armed troops, no one would give evidence if the case had the slightest political content or dealt with land problems. Sinn Féin arbitration courts had taken over that function. These had started in Ballinrobe, Co. Mayo, in May 1919 when it was decreed that the RIC was unable to carry out normal police duties. They continued until July 1922 when the Civil War was launched in a new roar of gunfire.

Sinn Féin courts assumed extraordinary powers. After an area was cleansed of RIC, a group of Republicans would set themselves up as law enforcers. They would be selected Volunteers whose amateur subjective judgements, supposedly derived from the ancient Irish Brehon Law, were invariably accepted by litigants and defendants without question. They patrolled town and countryside, recording complaints of crime and seeing that licensing laws were upheld. In the days before a new use had been found for baseball bats, punishments often consisted of lashes with whips. Two men who broke into shops are recorded as being sentenced to fifty lashes each; two others, similarly sentenced, were stretched on a wooden wheel while observers kept the score 'as if they were marking a handball match'.

The most important function of these courts involved disputes over land. 'Driving' was an established form of retaliation against unpopular landowners where fences were torn down, cattle were released and land was sometimes ploughed up and taken over. In the old days it was the job of the RIC to stop 'driving', a task they hated. Now those found guilty of cattle driving which had not been authorised by the Dáil Éireann Land Commission had to answer to Sinn Féin courts – they were usually fined.

In Mayo, a typical sitting of the Commission in June 1920 involved the kidnapping of three tenant farmers from Kilmaine who were driven by car to an unknown destination to answer charges of violations of land decrees. A court would be held in some derelict house; if Sinn Féin summoned you, it was wise to turn up.

During another sitting in Claremorris, Co. Mayo, the Commission arbitrated as to whether tenants could 'drive' on to the Protestant-owned racecourse whose trustees had not recognised the court. Much disputed land belonged to Protestants who were not substantial farmers or owners of big houses. They usually found it expedient to go to Sinn Féin for justice. A letter to the *Irish Times* in July 1920 from a solicitor acting for a Protestant widow and Unionist who wished to lay claim to a twenty-two-acre farm outlined her dilemma. Should she go to the official Chancery Court to verify her claim? If she did, she would be unable to work the land or even continue to live in the district where she had lived all her life. On the other hand, after she obtained a decision in her favour from the local Sinn Féin Arbitration Court, she could rest assured that without a single soldier or policeman to guard her, 'complete effect would be given to the decision and she would be left in undisturbed possession of the farm'.

Courts such as Colonel Head's were ignored and, overnight, Resident Magistrates – whose role had been gloriously highlighted by Somerville and Ross in their *Irish RM* stories – were made redundant; all over Ireland they were resigning. But Colonel Head refused to compromise. Like others whose families had lived in Ireland for centuries, noted Kevin Fitzgerald, 'the gods he worshipped were not the gods of Ireland. Patriotism meant love of England. Duty meant duty to England; loyalty to the king of England.'

Naturally the Colonel had every confidence in the new corps of men sent over from England as allies of the overstretched RIC to deal with 'thugs and rapscallions'. He considered the Black and Tans 'the usual type of good natured plucky Englishmen'. He approved of the behaviour of these 'smart, clean-looking young fellows to whom my instincts and sympathies were freely extended . . . nothing seemed to me meaner than the outcry raised against them by superior people in England, perfectly safe themselves'.

Others, too, were sympathetic to these 'saviours'. To Mrs Carlton, a neighbour of Lady Gordon, the Black and Tans were 'the darlings', and to Maud Wynne 'they were wonderful in their bravery and daily risked their lives in defending Loyalist and English interests'. Sir Henry Robinson, who had received a note which read, 'Sir Henry Robinson you are doomed – prepare for death', was also on the side of this 'light hearted reckless set of men'. Nevertheless he lamented that 'some of their humorous stunts really exasperated people almost more than their reprisals'. An example of the humour of the Black and Tans was leaving two men they had shot perched against a wall with buckets over their heads.

In early 1920 advertisements had been inserted in papers like the *News of the World*: 'Are you 17 years of age? Are you at least 5 foot 6 inches in height? [The height qualification was often waived with the result that many Tans seemed to be little men. They also had to pass a very elementary reading test.] If so, join the new police force for service in Ireland. Rates of pay £1 a day, seven-day-week and YOUR CHANCES.'

They first arrived in Ireland on 25 March 1920, the Feast of the Annunciation. Patrick O'Shea saw one of the newcomers in Athlone. He wore khaki trousers and cap and the green jacket of the RIC, the darkest of the forty shades of green. He was wheeling a bicycle and he was very drunk. Over the next couple of years O'Shea would observe many Tans, allies of the RIC whose men had originally welcomed them fervently. 'They had neither religion nor morals, they used foul language, they had the old soldier's talent for dodging and scrounging, they spoke in strange accents, called the Irish "natives", associated with low company, stole from each other, sneered at the customs of the country, drank to excess and put sugar on their porridge.' Lady Gregory was horrified to learn that they also shot the woods of Castle Taylor in May when the pheasants were sitting.

A few months after the Tans, the Auxiliaries appeared dressed in an even more bizarre manner in riding breeches, dark blue jackets, augmented by pieces of old service uniform and huge Glengarry berets; many carried revolvers slung cowboy-style from their hips. These 'fine black-bonneted tight-breeched khaki-coated pipe-smoking six-shooter men', as Sean O'Faolain remembered them and as they appear in old photographs, wore the letters TC on their shoulders for Temporary Cadet. They were considered an élite force, ex-officers and public-school boys. According to Winston Churchill, 'they were selected from a great press of applicants on account of their intelligence, their characters and their records in the war'. The IRA learnt that they would not surrender when attacked, preferring to fight to the last bullet.

Like the Tans, Auxiliaries ('Auxies') were often observed to be drunk. Patrick O'Shea used to see them in Clones, Co. Monaghan, on summer evenings; they would drive into the town and sit in their Crossley Tenders in the Diamond, singing and drinking beer carried out to them by the boots of the Lennard Arms Hotel. According to Tom Barry, they would see a man working in a field or bog and 'laughing and shouting would take aim, not to hit him, but to spatter the earth round him. The man would run wildly . . . Sometimes an Auxiliary bullet was sent through him to stop for ever his movements.'

During the winter of 1920 martial law was introduced and a curfew was imposed; no one could be out after 8.00 p.m. All heads of households were obliged to put a card behind the hall door with names of the house's occupants; these would be checked during raids. In Cork after the killing of some British soldiers, for a time it was as early as 5.00. In the city, according to Sean O'Faolain, people would hasten 'within doors, locking doors, bolting doors, chaining doors at a full quarter to the hour'. After the hour was struck the first lorries would be heard tearing along the quays and through the principal streets, the Tans they carried ready to administer random terror.

Curfew duties in the country, usually undertaken by regular troops, were generally more relaxed, but not always. 'God help your father,' remembered Flor Crowley, 'if he had neglected to nail the full room of the legitimate occupants of his house behind the door . . . God help your father most of all if a Shinner was found hiding in the house. It could be a fusillade of shots outside the back door for the Shinner and it could very well be the same for your father.' In the darkness the cheeks of trembling boys would be felt to check if they were old enough to shave, or they were dragged out of bed to see if they were tall enough to be Volunteers. There were reports of men standing outside their houses during curfew being shot dead.

Tans were known to round up farm animals and bayonet them. They stormed into Mary Clarke's garden and bludgeoned her Kerry Blue puppy. Before that they had cut down the unripened grapes in her garden and decorated the neighbours' hall door knockers with them. In Carrick-on-Shannon the statue of Viscount Clements in front of the courthouse was mistaken by the Tans for that of a rebel Irish chieftain, pulled down from its pedestal and mutilated.

There was general disruption of country life with night raids, prohibition of fairs, burnings of bacon factories and the Co-operative creameries founded by Horace Plunkett. These latter were considered legitimate targets as places where Sinn Féin 'outrages' were planned; the Tans, wrote Hubert Butler, believed that farmers hatched sedition over their milk churns. There were reprisals and indiscriminate shootings. Tans would shoot into bushes and long grass from the backs of lorries. At Mitchelstown two men were killed by shots from a military lorry while at a crossroads dance. In Kiltartan Ellen Quinn, a young married woman, was killed when a Tan took a pot-shot at her from a passing lorry. Elsewhere two priests were shot dead.

By now the intelligence of the British authorities was virtually non-existent, confined to men like the old RIC constable in Sean O'Faolain's story 'The Small Lady', with his doubts and his white moustache leading a group of Auxiliaries through territory familiar to him. An ex-sergeant of the RIC told Halliday Sutherland how he was in an open motor-coach filled with Black and Tans. When they drove through a town he noticed Michael Collins who turned and walked away slowly. If he had run the Tans would have shot him – they always shot people who ran. Later the sergeant went to confession with the sin of not reporting his sighting of Collins. The priest said, 'That's no sin. Your first duty is to your country and not to a foreign power.'

Increasingly indiscriminate violence was condoned. In February 1921 General Crozier, who commanded the Auxiliaries, resigned. After he had been ordered by his superior, General Tudor, not to dismiss Auxiliaries for indiscipline, he discharged a number who had wrecked a shop in Trim, Co. Meath, and had murdered two men in Dublin. When they were subsequently reinstated by Tudor, Crozier declared that he had had enough.

The most notorious reprisals were at Balbriggan following a brawl in a pub where two Tans were shot, and Cork, which was set on fire while Auxiliaries cut the firemen's hoses. Frank O'Connor and his mother 'took turns at standing on a chair in the attic listening to the shooting and watching the whole heart of the city burn'. He watched a tank demolishing a whole block of little houses.

Tom Barry told of lorry loads of Tans roaring into a village: 'The occupants would jump out, firing shots and ordering all inhabitants out of doors. No exceptions were allowed. Men and women, old and young, the sick and decrepit were lined up against the walls with their hands up.' People would give warning of approaching lorries with horns made by cutting the bottoms off pint bottles – a development of ancient trumpets made from cow horns.

Half a century later the approach of the enemy in Belfast would be heralded by dustbin lids.

Lady Gregory learnt how the Tans came into Gort: 'Young Hayes was trying to slip away . . . but they fired and hit him in the thigh. They went singing about the streets "Irishmen Come into the Parlour!" and "Who Fears to Speak of Easter Week!"' She was told of Tan terror elsewhere in east Galway: 'They broke into houses and searched them, and they searched the people in the street, women and girls too that were coming out of the chapel. Then they went into Spelmans to drink and got drunk there . . . Look at McMerneys, they burned all the bedding in the house and every bit of money he had . . . At Ardrahan they kept the boys running up and down the road for nearly an hour and a half and they all but naked . . . and the girls the same way. It is a holy crime – it is worse than Belgium!'

Drunkenness among Tans and Auxiliaries was taken for granted. An example of their antics was the behaviour of Fitz, the tiny Tan observed by Patrick O'Shea standing in the corridor on the train from Dundalk to Clones with a huge service revolver, who spent the journey 'shooting out of the windows at trees and telegraph poles, sending shots into the roofs of stations and after cheerily greeting waiting passengers would fire a fusillade over their heads'. At Sligo station Maud Wynne saw a Tan with 'a pistol in his hand strapped to his wrist, which he constantly kept clicking, and another strapped to his leg; he had a dagger sort of knife in a breast pocket, and bombs in each side pocket; that was his active service equipment'.

Caged lorries roared through the streets with guns firing and then the bully boys would knock down a door. Hugh Leonard's mother encountered a Tan. 'He wore a black jacket and tan trousers and was pointing a Lee Enfield at her. She had barely time to say "Ojesusmaryandjoseph!" when the front door was smashed in and my father was dragged out of bed and slammed against the wall, wearing only the old shirt he slept in.' Floorboards were pulled up, the horsehair sofa was bayoneted and the wardrobe ransacked, until rescue came in the person of a polite regular army officer – just as well, since the family was hiding arms under a mattress. Although he was a regular soldier, Major Bernard Montgomery, later the hero of El Alamein, believed in indiscriminate reprisals. He considered that 'my whole attention was given to defeating the rebels. It never bothered me a bit how many houses were burned.' He asserted that 'any civilian or Republican soldier who interferes with any officer or soldier is shot at once'.

Tommies or Tans? wondered Sean O'Casey shivering in his bed. You could tell at once: Tans shouted, 'soullessly breaking glass panels', while Tommies hammered on a door with a rifle butt and waited for it to open. Tommies were jocular. However, regular troops in the British Army were just as able to riot as the Tans. In September 1920, after a duty sergeant of the 17th Lancers was shot dead as he supervised the shoeing of a horse, drunken troops at Fermoy and Buttevant roamed the streets firing at random and throwing petrol-filled bottles into any house that showed a light. Earlier, when General Lucas was kidnapped by the IRA, troops broke out of Fermoy Barracks and broke every plate-glass window in the town. Above the crash and tinkle drunken voices shouted, 'We want our general back! Give us back our f— general!' As they looted Mr Noble's bicycle shop, throwing his stock into the Blackwater, and plundered Mr Cole's gas-lit jeweller's shop, they neither knew nor cared that their targets were Protestant and Loyalist. But troops like these were considered angels in comparison to the Black and Tans.

Members of Sinn Féin had a reputation for exemplary behaviour if they raided a house, unless they intended to burn it or kill the inhabitants. Stella Webb remembered Republican raiders being told, '"Ah, you needn't come here looking for arms, they're Quakers." My father invited them in and when they were leaving they apologised to my mother who had a headache, and us sitting by the fire.'

The artist Sheila Fitzgerald's house was raided by hooded men in the middle of the night. Her mother went down in her nightgown, carrying a candle, and said, '"Oh please put those guns down. I can't stand guns. I'm terrified of them." So they put them down and she asked what they wanted and they replied they needed a bike. She pointed out my father's bicycle to them and they said, "Thank you, Ma'am."'

'On another occasion the IRA took our second hand Ford . . . My sister . . . went to visit their headquarters . . . The Commandant said he was awfully sorry, he had just brought the car back from an expedition, but it was covered in mud and he would have it cleaned and sent back to us. But my sister said she would rather clean it herself.'

The formidable Miss Tynte of Tynte Park, after a conversation through the upstairs window of her barred house at midnight and an absolute refusal to hand over any of her sporting guns, finally threw down the keys of her car to the awkward crew below. While she supposed she couldn't stop them taking it, she said, she wanted it back first thing in the morning with the same amount of petrol and no bloodstains. And it was.

At the Flemings' rectory in Timoleague one party of raiders who announced themselves as belonging to the IRA turned out to be burglars.

Raids by Crown forces stiffened opposition, as did the burnings of houses, hay barns and whole villages. Then there were the executions. After Kevin Barry was hanged on 1 November 1920, many newborn male infants were given his name. Numerous Republicans were sentenced to death. Among them were twelve executed by firing squad in early 1921 after the engagement at Mourne Abbey. Others were shot while trying to escape or picked out to be killed.

Weary of an official policy of reprisals, shootings and destruction, the population's hatred for anyone in British uniform increased. On one occasion, perhaps after Kilmichael, when a string of gun carriages carrying coffins were making their way down Cork quays past shops ordered to shut, followed by soldiers snatching caps from the heads of men in the crowd, a shawled Cork woman is reputed to have cackled, 'Don' forget to sen' back d'empties! We'll fill 'em again!'

Railwaymen co-operated with the IRA against the British by refusing to take soldiers on their trains; their uncompromising stance over the two years of war greatly assisted the Republican cause. In a typical incident in mid-1920 a sergeant and six men of the King's Own Regiment, who wanted to travel to Bray, were told the train would not go on unless they left it. The soldiers refused to leave, with the result that the driver detached the engine and the train was left standing in the station. Other passengers had to drive to Bray in taxis and outside cars.

A terrible means of influencing public opinion was the hunger strike. The lonely ordeal of Terence MacSwiney did more for the Republican cause than any amount of burnt buildings and uniformed corpses. Martyrdom had been highlighted by the fate of Pearse, who was identified with the figure whose portrait highlighting His exposed heart was in every Catholic home. The symbolism of martyrdom never appealed to Protestants; there is no figure on the cross on the altars of their churches.

Most Protestants, however sympathetic to the Nationalist cause, were baffled by the psychology of the hunger strike. Later, in another part of the British Empire, Mahatma Gandhi refined it as a weapon against the Raj. But now nothing demonstrated Lady Gregory's identification with the Republican cause more than her preoccupation with the fate of Terence MacSwiney. When the Danish writer Signe Toksvig visited Lady Gregory in the autumn of 1920, she was told as she went to bed, 'Now I'm going to say my prayer for the Lord Mayor of Cork. I've said it every evening since he has been on hunger strike. It is the one in the prayer book for a sick person "when there appeareth small hope of recovery".'

Long before 1921 not only Irish but also British and Loyalist opinions were united in regretting the coming of the Black and Tans to Ireland. They began to believe that without the Tans' presence in the country the cause of Irish independence would have been lost; such allies only brought shame and terror. The O'Connor Don was quoted in 1921 as saying 'if they don't turn these Black and Tans out of the country we'll soon all be Republicans'. Another Loyalist with similar opinions about 'these blackguards' added 'they are not gentlemen'. By then the British Government knew that it had lost the propaganda war when the Church turned against it. In a Lenten Pastoral, Bishop MacRory of Down and Connor proclaimed that 'the government told the people they had no quarrel except with a handful of gunmen, but they knew in their hearts, and the whole world knew, that their quarrel was with the whole nation's spirit of liberty which they were doing their best or worst to stifle and kill'.

CHAPTER 5

Siegfried

The rebels of 'The Kingdom' swore
Our dear old land to free,
And shot the tyrant Major on
The Golf Links at Tralee.

Ballad, Anon.

If the Sinn Féiners kill a policeman or ambush our troops, the
Black and Tans burn down the nearest village, but there's no
justice in that because nine times out of ten the men who did it
come from some other part of the country, and in revenge for
the burning of the village the Sinn Féiners go down and burn
one of the big houses where the descendants of the invaders are
still living.

Barbara Fitzgerald, We are Besieged

'Every ambush was a "murder" to us and a "glorious battle" to them,'
remembered Lionel Fleming, whose family were conventionally Loyalist.
David Mitchell has concluded that 'few Irishmen or women can write
objectively about those events. The majority see them through green tinted
glasses which show gallant little bands of meagrely armed men facing the
military might of the British Empire, with the added terror of the Black and
Tans, to win the freedom which in the past had so often been snatched from
their peaceful political grasping. The small minority whose lenses may have
been of a pale British red, or even glaring orange, remember the seemingly
senseless murders and burnings and destruction of houses . . .'

By June 1921, there were between 35,000 and 40,000 British troops in
Ireland, many of whom had come from the battlefields of the First World War.

Their limitless armoury included Vickers machine-guns; their transport, seventy Peerless and thirty-four Rolls-Royce armoured cars, together with the Crossley Tenders favoured by the Black and Tans and Auxiliaries. (During the Civil War the anti-Free Staters greatly resented the fact that Michael Collins and his army had inherited from the British forces these powerful little lorries associated with their bitterest foes.)

The IRA had to rely on bicycles and their assortment of captured or home-made arms. In the middle of 1920 the West Cork Brigade was fighting with thirty-five rifles and twenty automatics or revolvers. The largely untrained men were turned into fighting guerrilla forces by ruthless and able leaders, Dan Breen, Tom Barry, Sean Treacy, Liam Lynch, Ernie O'Malley and others.

In Dublin, ambushes were so frequent in the area around Camden Street that it was known as the Dardanelles. IRA successes in the capital came about under the direction of Michael Collins who was considered to be 'without a shadow of doubt, the effective driving force and the backbone of the GHQ of the armed action of the nation against the enemy'. His opponents thought him exceptional. He struck General Crozier as 'a man I should like to have had as a subaltern in 1914 and he would soon have been a captain and, still more, a colonel had he been spared'.

There was a price of £10,000 on Collins's head. When a rumour went around Dublin just after Bloody Sunday that he had been captured, Paudeen O'Keefe, the secretary of Sinn Féin, said, 'That's the end of the whole bloody business.' The momentum for violence was almost entirely provided by the ruthless energy of this Robin Hood on a bicycle speeding through Dublin, evading capture in moments of breathtaking suspense, taking refuge in Vaughan's Hotel in Parnell Square where Mr Maguire and his general factotum, Christy Harte, kept a large room with four beds for the Big Fellow and his associates. If he was not staying the night he often paused to drink a bottle of stout.

The public adored him and protected him. During the Truce he was to be seen writing autographs like a film star. When he visited Dan Dunne's public house in Donnybrook on one occasion, he leant back and touched a hanging bell-push with his head. The man of the house cut it down and proudly showed it afterwards to customers as his most prized possession.

Collins was plump, a drinker, smoker and swearer, unlike most of his peers, and he had the good looks of the hero. To one of his women admirers, Kathleen Napoli MacKenna, he was 'Siegfried . . . the personification of joyous powerful youth'. Shane Leslie felt it was no wonder he was never caught; 'all the women must have been so glad to hide him; he was a real "playboy" with a tremendous twinkle and sudden quick impulsive gestures'.

The families of the men killed on Bloody Sunday or of Sir Henry Wilson might have had other ideas. Patricia Cockburn was a child when she witnessed the old Field Marshal's assassination on Collins's orders in London in June 1922: 'I was walking down Eaton Square when I saw an old gentleman in a black coat standing on the steps of one of the great pillared doorsteps of the houses there, when another man standing below him pulled out a gun and shot him. The old gentleman half turned round and then slowly collapsed.'

In the countryside much of the action was a series of pinpricks, creating a cumulative success as effective as the bigger engagements deemed glorious. A list of 'outrages' reported for two days in June 1920 conveys the general atmosphere:

Daring outrage in Ennis – seven soldiers disarmed – rifles and bayonets carried away . . .

Audacious theft of motor car in Cork. Officer and his chauffeur had revolvers held to their heads by three men . . .

Co. Wicklow – an unsuccessful attempt to burn down Dunlavin Courthouse . . .

Co. Leitrim – a military officer was fired upon in Carrick-on-Shannon . . .

Co. Fermanagh – an RIC revenue boat stolen in Newtownbutler . . .

Co. Limerick – a police sergeant died of gunshot wounds . . .

Later came the triumphs of the flying columns, like the engagement at Cross Barry when scores of British soldiers were killed to the sound of bagpipes played by the piper Flor Begley. Or Kilmichael, where the doomed Auxiliaries cursed and shouted as they were fired on. In remote places children played a game connected with the infrequency of motor traffic, listening to hear how long engine noises were audible. Children living near Kilmichael remembered seeing the lorry loads race past and listening as the rumble of motors diminished in the distance and went silent before the stuttering gunfire began.

Sixteen Auxiliaries were killed; the seventeenth, Lieutenant Guthrie, fled the ambush, but was caught as he sat dazed by the side of the road. He was shot two days later and buried in Annahala bog.

The names of the dead men are in the registry of deaths in Macroom Church and a tablet remembers the 'Temporary Cadets'. They were all veterans of the First World War – late Bedford Regiment, late Northumberland Fusiliers, late 8th Black Watch etc. For many of these men, after years in the trenches a taste for drink and an indifference to human life might have developed.

Writing in *Guerrilla Days in Ireland* years after the ambush, Tom Barry claimed that the Auxiliaries at Kilmichael were annihilated after falsely calling out 'We surrender' and then resuming their gunfire with revolvers when the Volunteers were in target. But other veterans of Kilmichael did not remember this.

An Auxiliary recalled the shock 'not so much at the loss of . . . friends, but the manner of it'. Afterwards, some of their comrades returned to the area seeking reprisals. They set fire to one house (the scorched remains of the Sacred Heart were lovingly preserved) and shot dead a man called Denny Sullivan. Later they burnt Cork.

The Volunteers fought with every means at their disposal. Random destruction was effective. Telephone poles were hacked down, wires cut, roads trenched, railway bridges blown up and buildings burnt – shops, workhouses, Freemasons' halls, warehouses and nearly every coastguard station in the country. The firing of police barracks had been a start that would reach a climax with the burning of big houses; Republicans used the weapons of gelignite, paraffin and petrol with relish in a red rivalry with the Auxies and the Tans.

To de Valera and Collins, every means of combat was lawful. De Valera approved of the ambushing of British troops: 'The English forces are in our country as invaders, on a war footing as they themselves have declared; in fact they are actually waging upon us not only an unjust, but barbarous war.'

Collins had deplored the tactics of the Rising, which went back to Robert Emmet's rebellion of 1803 – seizing strategic points in the city and holding each one hopelessly positioned in a mini-siege against the might of English guns. He believed passionately in the value of intelligence on both sides. So members of the Detective Division of the Dublin Metropolitan Police were shot, and later personnel of the British Secret Service.

From the first, Collins sanctioned assassination, and well before the War of Independence began he made grim preparations. In September 1919 he formed the Squad, which became known as the 'Twelve Apostles', consisting of a group of men trained in assassination. Those he chose were young, twenty or twenty-one, and they were not allowed to drink. When they went to work, at first they used .38 revolvers, but .45 weapons were found to be more effective. One of the Squad, Vinnie Byrne, subsequently described their methods. From a house in Upper Abbey Street which they called 'the dump', they went out on various 'jobs'. If they saw 'their man' they would follow him until they reached a quiet spot. 'One of us would knock him over the head with the first shot, the other would finish him off with a shot to the head.'

The most spectacular demonstration of the Squad's efficiency was Bloody Sunday, 21 November 1920. With the Tans had come the Secret Service agents, the Cairo Gang whom Collins's Squad destroyed on a November Sabbath morning. The Gang has been presented as a group of callous and efficient spies sent over as allies of the RIC, whose elimination was essential. The danger they threatened and the names they knew or would sniff out imperilled the Republican movement. Given the poor espionage record of the Crown forces, especially after the RIC had been eliminated as a source of intelligence gathering, the potential of the Cairo Gang may have been overestimated. More importantly, their cruel deaths struck terror where it was felt the most. One of the shivering men roused from his bed may well have had the privilege of being shot by a future Taoiseach.

Collins was far more efficient than the Crown forces at organising espionage and he was also personally a good spy, inspecting files in Dublin Castle with the aid of Ned Broy. He was obsessed, claiming that one spy was more dangerous than a regiment of soldiers. In the country the guerrilla leaders shared his preoccupation. At Windgap near Carrick-on-Suir a typically fierce notice was posted on a tree: 'The public are warned not to close trenches, cut up trees, interfere with mines or any way undo the work of the IRA . . . Spies, informers, talkers will be dealt with from this day forward. Women and girls must keep their telephone machines closed when in town and in other public places. Parents will be held responsible for the secrecy of their children when in school, mass etc. Look out shortly for a list of spies, informers and talkers in this district . . .'

Such people have always been figures of terror and shame in Irish history. The RIC could be equated with them and so could the pathetic corpses shot and stretched on roadsides so that passers-by peered down to read what was written on their chests. 'Shot by the IRA – Spies and informers beware.' The sense of horror would remain for years. In 1935, near Mohill in Co. Leitrim, Norah Munnay was shown the place 'where the Tans did bloody murder on the poor lads. Upon the hill you can see the ruins of the informers' house, the man that went to Mohill to give them away. It was burned after he was shot and the people pulled down what was left.'

How many innocent Protestants were 'shot and labelled' in Tom Barry's words? People do not like to debate the issue or suggest that there was a pogrom.

Why was John Good of Bandon killed, a harmless old Protestant? mused Lionel Fleming and his family. Sectarian killing undoubtedly took place in West Cork where there were enough Protestants to be considered a threat. During the Civil War armed bands would go round Cork and Kerry shooting Protestants, particularly prominent Loyalists, in their houses; they accounted for a dozen.

It was easy enough to call a corpse a spy. Tom Barry, a great man for lists, cited sixteen executed 'British agents' including Lieutenant Fielding, buried in a bog near Charleville, and 'old Tom Sullivan, the singing beggar man' aged seventy-five, allegedly a spy for the Black and Tans. Old Tom's body, like others, was used as a decoy for an ambush.

Many ex-members of the British armed forces were killed by the IRA. Often they were designated 'spies'. Spies there undoubtedly were among Loyalists, who told the authorities of suspicious movements in their area. They did so in the face of plenty of warnings that such action was punishable by death. Women were not spared. Signe Toksvig was told by Robert Barton and a man named Robinson how a female gossip and spy had been 'done away with'. 'Man told off to do it simply took her out in a boat on the sea, tied a rock around her neck and threw her in.'

The shooting of Mrs Lindsay caused an uproar. It was unwise of her to order her coachman to drive her in her car to Ballincollig Barracks and warn of a possible ambush at Dripsey. In her terms she was doing her duty and as a result a number of members of the IRA were captured and sentenced to death. Mrs Lindsay and her coachman were kidnapped by Republicans in reprisal.

Some time later Mrs Everard was passing the blackened walls of Mrs

Lindsay's house near Coachford and said to her driver, 'A terrible thing was done there, to think of her and the old coachman and the little dog being dragged up the mountainside and all murdered.' (Typical of her class, Mrs Everard felt just as sorry for the dog.)

'And for why would the old lady be giving the British warning?'

'She did it to save young lives and because she was a brave woman.'

''Tis best to keep your mouth shut these times.'

In late 1921 General Crozier talked to Michael Collins. According to his account, '"I was sorry about that," he replied, pausing as he cast his eyes on the ground as if ashamed, "but she wasn't murdered in cold blood. She was executed. She acted as an informer against the rebels – that was damned silly although patriotic. She warned the police of an ambush and was the cause of military reprisals (legal in your eyes) and the arrest of the ambushers – so she was taken by my men. Strickland tried five men and was going to shoot them and did so. My fellows sent word to him that if he did they'd shoot Mrs Lindsay whom they'd tried and found guilty as a spy and informer. The men were shot and so was Mrs Lindsay."'

Sean O'Faolain, who like Liam O'Flaherty and Frank O'Connor turned the terrible times into fiction, put some of Mrs Lindsay's circumstances into his story 'The Small Lady'. In West Cork market towns, he wrote, a ballad on green paper was distributed about the small lady's treachery and death:

> For she sold our boys to England's Tans
> So they fell without a blow,
> Face to face with a firing squad
> All standing in a row.

Writing recently, Father Patrick Twohig considered 'that particularly lurid incident . . . could have been best left to obscurity and fireside chatting'. The trouble with Mrs Lindsay was that she was seventy years old – and it was hard on her coachman as well.

The ugly business of shooting hostages was considered legitimate in the context of guerrilla warfare. Among them was Divisional Inspector Potter, shot in Waterford as a reprisal for the hanging of Republican prisoners. Ten days after his death Mrs Potter received a parcel containing her husband's diary, will and ring. Among the entries in the diary, which was complete up to the time of his execution, was a note that his jailers were an old man and woman and a young man known to Mrs Potter – implying that they were local people. At 11.00 a.m. on 27th April 1921 he was told that he would be shot at 7.00 that evening; he wrote that his guardians were not at all anxious to kill him, but they had received orders from GHQ IRA which could not be disobeyed.

Ernie O'Malley also had to steel himself for this disagreeable duty. He described two captured English soldiers saying goodbye. 'They shook hands with the QM and myself – their hands were limp and cold. They shook hands with each other.

'"Are you ready?" asked the QM.
'One of the officers nodded. They joined hands. "Goodbye old boy" . . .
'"Squad. Ready. Fire!"'

Frank O'Connor dealt with a similar incident in his story 'Guests of the Nation'. 'Why did any of us want to plug him: weren't we all chums? Didn't we understand him and didn't he understand us?' Later O'Connor was made impatient by the number of times his story was imitated by other writers.

Some people ignored the tensions altogether. In spite of the Troubles, George Bernard Shaw continued to return to 'peelerless' Ireland for a stay at his favourite Parknasilla Hotel in Kerry. 'Ireland is a capital place for a holiday. I do not recommend it to Imperially minded terrorists who have been too audibly urging the Castle to put its foot down – but to the average non-political Englishman I can promise a safe and enjoyable holiday, and the reputation, when he returns, of having dared to be Daniel.' It was easy enough for him to scuttle back and forth from Ayot St Lawrence.

Other travellers making a holiday motoring trip through the Irish countryside at an awkward time were Maud Gonne and her friend, seventy-six-year-old Mrs Despard. These two revolutionary ladies, black clad as ever, were not to be put off by potholes and barricades of felled trees or the military stopping the car. It helped that Mrs Despard was a sister of Lord French – not surprisingly they did not get on. 'It was amusing to see the puzzled faces of the Black and Tans who continually held up our car, when Mrs Despard said she was the Viceroy's sister.'

'They were strange days for the gentry of Ireland, these,' wrote Molly Keane, 'strange silent dangerous days. The morning's paper (and if the post was late it was because a bridge had been blown up the night before or the mail raided on its way from Dublin) might tell of the murder of a friend, or the burning of a house that had been . . . careless in its wide hospitality.'

In theory martial law affected Loyalists, although many ignored the prohibition on guns. In January 1921 Lord Dunsany was fined £25 for keeping unauthorised guns; at dinner after a pheasant shoot at Dromoland Castle, host and male guests carried revolvers in their pockets and took their guns up to their rooms at night. Meanwhile the gentry kept up the tennis parties and *thé dansants* to which the military were invited, ignoring the dangers of shooting and ambushes.

Such entertainment could cause strains. Molly Keane gives the tone: '"If there were no Loyalists in Ireland," the little English Major said with sudden nervous anger, "there'd be a great deal less trouble for us in the country."' To which the reply was: 'Loyalists are never very popular or very fortunate people.'

Lionel Fleming tells of a tea party at which a British officer mentioned the name of a landowner who had supplied him with information. 'When one of the company signalled him to stop talking, the officer was quite indignant. "Why," he said, "we're all loyal here, aren't we?" So they were, except of course for the parlour maid, and within a day or so the landowner was forced out of the country.'

'Don't say a word before the servants,' Terence de Vere White was told by his relatives. 'An ominous silence would fall on all when a maid came into the room.

'What were we afraid of?

'Quite simply that the maids would tell our critical remarks to boyfriends in the IRA who would call to burn our house down.'

That the IRA intelligence network was comprehensively efficient was generally recognised. An apocryphal story tells of two British soldiers on Patrick's Bridge in Cork:

'Where are we going tonight, Bill?

'Shh . . . not a word, mate. See those bloody pigeons. They could be Shinners.'

For the White family and others the divisions of society were seen as a matter of class more than Nationalism. 'The hewers of wood and drawers of water were attacking their masters . . . were the Yahoos to drive out the Houyhnhnms? How could peasant boys and shop boys rule a country?' A maid summed up the prospect in an epigram: 'When it's over, Ma'am, yous will be us and us will be yous.'

Those who were struggling to establish a new Ireland resurrected the ogre figure of the landlord. Although much power had been whittled away by the land acts, the big house and its inhabitants still presented a lifestyle that was unacceptable to many. In Diarmaid Ó Súilleabháin's *Those Days have Gone Away*, he describes local people watching 'well dressed aliens' arriving at Mallow Castle for a party. 'A few serfs actually doff their caps as they pass. The people have sunk to the lowest depth in the mire of slavery. But they are not altogether lost. Among them are a few who sigh deeply and turn away in sorrow and disgust. They belong to the "hidden Ireland".'

Tom Barry hated the big house which he would soon be burning down. 'In it lived the leading Loyalist, secure and affluent in his many acres – around him lived his many grooms, gardeners and household servants, whose mission in life was to serve their lord and master. In the towns many of the rich shopkeepers . . .bowed before the "great" families, sycophants and lick spittles.'

By mid-1920 there were few large houses that had not been raided for arms or money. Sometimes raiders faced by an irate owner or his wife remembered the old servile ways and became diffident or faded away. At Killeen Castle Lord Fingall, a Loyalist Catholic, was asked for a subscription to IRA funds:

'"When the Irish Republic is the government of the country I will subscribe to it, not before."

'"Thank you, my Lord, we know you will," they said politely and vanished into the night.'

Intruders could be put to flight by old social rules. In Kerry Lady Gordon faced them. 'Rising to my full height, armed with a silver candlestick, I stood on the lower stair. They were, I observed, very young. It was not unnatural to conclude that they were also very shy. Young Irishmen always are. My attire was exceedingly scanty, my hair was hanging down my back, my bare feet were in pink satin slippers.

'"Would you like to see our bedrooms?" I enquired.

'The leader suddenly became bashful.

'"No . . . no . . . not at all . . . not at all . . ." he stammered. "Come on, boys . . ." and the party clattered hastily past the stairs, back into the hall and out by the front door, apologising profusely as they went for having "disturbed us".'

'Terrible times,' was how people greeted each other, instead of talking about the weather. Lady Gordon was told about a woman tied up in her house and guarded by another shy young man. 'Terrible times, Ma'am,' he told the bound figure.

Hubert Butler's mother faced two men asking for money for the dependants of the IRA. '"I know who you are," she said to one of them. "You're Jim Connell. Take your cigarette out of your mouth when you are talking to me." He took it out and I began to scold my mother for interrupting what might have been an interesting conversation. It was only the second time I had seen a Republican.' Mrs Butler dreaded her son's sympathies. 'If ever I made some heretical remark about the Easter rebellion she would look at me . . . with loving anxiety as if I had coughed up a spot of blood on to my handkerchief.'

Other sons reacted against their Loyalist backgrounds. Terry Trench kept a picture of his hero, Michael Collins, in his school locker and sang Nationalist songs when walking in crocodile down the North Strand. (The next generation, my own, were not stirred into Republican sympathies; our dreams were with RAF pilots fighting Jerry.)

The musician Brian Boydell was 'violently Republican' at Rugby. His father 'took being Anglo-Irish very seriously . . . I think he believed the King of England had been appointed by God.' Ralph Cusack, whose family lived in Abbeville, the house later owned by a future Taoiseach, Charles Haughey, remembered in fiction his rebellion against his parents. His mother was called away during a party; she returned 'trembling with rage and foaming a little at the corners of her mouth: "I have just been subjected to the most frightful . . . insult imaginable. I was called to my own front door, and there stood three common-looking young men with masks – dirty black masks – over their faces. 'Madam,' they had the effrontery to say, 'we have come to ask you for a subscription if you please – to the Irish Republican Army.' Can you imagine such a thing?"'

A family row erupted between Cusack and his brother and their elders; the boys considered the people their parents called dirty Sinn Féiners and murderous brutes to be friends. They refused to join in when the company sang 'God Save the King' and sang instead:

Up de Valera, the hero of the right,
We'll follow him to battle with the orange, green and white;
We'll beat old England and we'll give her hell's delight
Up de Valera, King of Ireland!

Their father threw them out of the house. 'You are both unfit to mix with decent people.'

The exodus of Loyalists was gaining strength. Lady Gregory noted 'the Goughs leave this week and Lough Cutra is to be shut up till they know how things are . . . Edward Martyn is said to have sold Tulira – the Lobdells (because their motors have been searched and put out of action the night they were going to the Roxboro dance) are going to live in England – Amy has let Castle Taylor and lives in England. I will stay here I hope to my life's end; or rather, I hope Coole Park will be kept open for Margaret and her children.'

A few months after this entry in her diary her daughter-in-law Margaret Gregory found reason to fear living in Ireland. She was travelling in a car that was ambushed; among the victims shot dead was Captain Blake, a District Inspector of the RIC and his wife who refused to leave his side. Margaret was the sole survivor. It was dangerous to be associated with the RIC. The day before the Blake ambush Winifred Barrington, daughter of the owner of Glenstal Abbey, was killed in Co. Limerick together with her companion. He was a District Inspector, like Blake; she was dressed boyishly and may have been mistaken for a man. One of the ambushers said, 'Only for the bitch being in bad company, she would not be shot.'

The summer of 1921 was exceptionally hot, a succession of bright cloudless days. Now the burning of Loyalists' houses as reprisal for those destroyed by 'British fire gangs' became a new tactic of the Republicans. It had started with the Crown forces following an order that for every attack by the IRA, houses of Republicans in the neighbourhood would be dynamited; one hour was given to clear out valuables. They were mostly little thatched cottages; among the more substantial burnt at this time was Michael Collins's home in Clonakilty.

Tit for tat: 'For every Republican house destroyed the homes of two British Loyalists will be burned to the ground,' the IRA announced. In June 1921 guidelines were set down for this new campaign. Formal notice had to be served on any person whose house was to be burnt. In some cases families would be ordered out of the country and their lands confiscated by Sinn Féin courts. 'For the purpose of such reprisal no one shall be regarded as an enemy of Ireland, whether they be described locally as a Unionist, or Orangeman . . . except that they are actively anti-Irish in their actions . . .' Perhaps this rule was adhered to when the policy of burning houses was initiated.

A portion of Ireland's architectural heritage soon went up in smoke. 'Any idiot with petrol and a match can set fire to a house,' commented Monk Gibbon. 'It needs trained architects, masons and carpenters to build a house. The latter class of technical competents is rare, the former are numerous.'

'The British Loyalists were paying dearly, the demesne walls were tumbling,' wrote Tom Barry. 'Our only fear was that, as time went on, there would be no more Loyalists' homes to destroy.'

Lionel Fleming's father began to keep a list that would go on to include the houses destroyed during the Civil War. 'On May 26 [1920] Kilbrittain Castle was burnt ... On December 2nd Timoleague House was burnt ...' The Reverend Fleming's rectory was spared, and still stands today in Timoleague. Rectories were not on the list; the incendiaries generally spared the homes of men of God, even if they did not share the same religion.

But many other houses were vulnerable. Some belonged to noted intransigent Loyalists. Others were in the way or were the next to go. Some like Summerhill in Co. Meath appeared to be set on fire for no apparent reason except that they were big and intrusive. A good many were destroyed to settle old scores, however much their owners clung to the fiction that the fire raisers came from outside the neighbourhood. Tyrone House, whose great ruin stands on the edge of Galway Bay, was said to have been burnt as much as a victim of local land agitation as the suggestion that it was used as a hospital for the Black and Tans.

Even a rumour that a house might be taken over by the Black and Tans was enough to condemn it. This was the fate of Dunboy, a mansion newly built in the château style near Castletownbere in Co. Cork. A witness to its burning was its newly arrived English butler, Albert Thomas, who described the event: 'Everything looked so lovely and green, the water blue as the sky – but still the tension was there. You could feel it, the undercurrent of unrest, with the Black and Tans walking about in couples, their revolvers prominently displayed and bombs bulging from their pockets.'

Mr Thomas took refuge on Bear Island, from where he watched Dunboy burn: 'Tonight I was called up and shown a large glow in the sky overlooking the castle about a mile away. The rebels had burnt the castle down as they said they would. I was very, very sorry for all that lovely old silver, the beautiful glass and splendid linen all being burnt, and all those gorgeous statues and pictures, the wonderful drawing room all burning, for what?' My aunt arrived in Castletownbere the day after the fire; the postcard she sent to the family with the news arrived with the postmark CENSORED BY THE IRA.

A woman I interviewed in 1984 was a young girl when the interior of her house was sprinkled with petrol. By the end of the First World War things were changing in the big house; she remembered that the coachman no longer wore livery. Her father, she recalled, was always thoroughly pro-British until he was forced to go and live in England. Early in the Troubles he was shot by masked men. 'He picked up what we used to call a "curate" – a small poker for the fire – and went to the door and they fired at him and got him through both legs ... a whole crowd of them ... and there was a bullet in the table beside my sister and missed bullets were found in the bookcase ... and then they said, "Come on, boys," and they departed and then we got Father up to bed.'

Later, more masked men – or perhaps the same ones – came at night and burned the house. 'We were in evening dress . . . I don't think it was full evening dress . . . we had passed that stage.' The family was allowed to go into the burning house and snatch some coats and the miniature of a son of the house killed in the war. Everything else was burnt. 'My father had buried the silver in a lead-lined box in the kitchen yard, but the morning before the house was burnt he had brought it in because he thought it might be mouldy or something . . . all the silver melted into the lead so that it couldn't be refined.'

Charlotte Despard's cousins, the Franks, had their house burnt; it did not help that they were also related to Lord French. A pet dog died in the blaze. Molly Keane's family house, Ballyrankin in Co. Carlow, was randomly chosen and burnt with three others in the neighbourhood as a reprisal for Black and Tan atrocities. What impressed her was the tact of the Sinn Féiners. 'My father was a militant sort of man and he came brandishing something and they said ". . . Please come quietly or we're afraid we'll have to shoot you."' Her mother, who was watching the conflagration from a haystack, was presented with a wine cooler by one of the men who thought it might have contained her jewels.

When Colonel Skrine was advised to go back to England, he replied, 'I'd rather be shot in Ireland than live in England.' The young Molly Skrine was attending the smart French School in Bray when her house was destroyed; the school was full of girls in tears because their homes had been burnt. At much the same time Michael Collins's niece, the future mother of a big politicised family, but then 'a frightened sad little girl in a black frock', was attending the Dominican convent in Wicklow after the family home near Clonakilty had been burnt by the Black and Tans.

Colonel Head, the Loyalist acquaintance of Kevin Fitzgerald, living on his estate of Derrylahan Park near Birr, was under threat for his intransigent views. He nearly became the victim of an IRA assassination squad, and reluctantly took refuge in England. His wife refused to go and when the arsonists arrived, did not give in without a struggle.

'I could have shot you for that, Madam,' the leader of the squad sent to burn the house told her when she confronted them with a Mini Max Fire Extinguisher. She was given five minutes to leave, while her children were put on the avenue under an armed guard to watch the splendid bonfire their home made.

The two Miss Dreapers of Finnsborough in Co. Kilkenny were determined not to give in. Like Mrs Lindsay, Miss Florrie Dreaper was an informer. She warned the Castlecomer Barracks of news of an impending ambush; two IRA men were killed and retribution was swift. A meeting was called among Republicans where the sisters were denounced as spies: 'As far as Miss Florence Dreaper is concerned, some of our men are ready to execute her . . . right now . . . either by hanging or shooting.'

But Miss Florrie was luckier than Mrs Lindsay and more humane counsels prevailed. It was decided to chase the sisters out of the country and burn down their house. Because of the failed ambush, the IRA decreed that as an extra punishment the sisters should be forced to be spectators of the burning of their home. But when the Upper Hills Company of the IRA arrived at Finnsborough Miss Florrie refused to come out. Instead she threw grenades down on the arsonists from an upper window and fired Very lights to attract the military.

A decision was made to burn the house even though she remained obstinately inside. Windows were broken, paraffin spilt over wooden floors, and the great stone mansion, a local landmark, went up in flames. Soon the blaze could be seen for miles around and a fireball filled the sky. People in the area heard a thunderous crash as the V-shaped roof of the house collapsed. But where was Miss Florrie? Having refused the order to come down, she retreated up to the roof where throughout the blaze she and her dog squatted in the steel water tank. Miraculously she survived the 'Dante's Inferno' to be rescued the next day by British soldiers from Castlecomer.

Local opinion of the Dreaper sisters encapsulated the dilemma of co-religionists of Swift, Parnell and Tone who had forfeited any claim to Irishness. 'They were identified with the life and hobbies associated with the West Britons of that time living in Ireland.' Their accent and political and philosophical ideas revealed 'that they were definitely English and in no way Irish'. Their sports, tennis, croquet and hunting with the Castlecomer foxhounds, were associated with the alien presence; they were guilty of 'possessing a British cultural background which they had inherited, and moving in an environment friendly to England'.

CHAPTER 6

It is All Terribly Sad

The Shoneen and Stater are lords of the land
The church as placator has taken her stand:
My country partitioned, the Saxon o'erjoyed
As outlawed, undaunted, the moorland I ride.
Paddy Cronin, quoted by Father Twohig

Partition was inevitable; the disadvantageous form it took was
due to the Civil War which was started by foolish and/or
unscrupulous young men and women who did not, or did not
want to, recognise victory when it was handed to them.
Tom Garvin, The Rising and Irish Democracy

In 1921 Lord Desart lamented that 'the complete apathy in England adds to one's despair. Football, cricket in Australia and things of that kind fill the bill for the mass of the reading public, and Ireland and Germany are only headlines to them.'

On a visit to England Desart was summoned to see the King.

'I suppose you must have had a great deal of interest to tell His Majesty?' he was asked later.

'He never gave me the chance . . . "Ah, Lord Desart," was his cordial greeting, "I'm delighted to hear that you still wear nightshirts, just as I do; I can't bear those new fangled pyjamas."' The rest of the conversation ran upon nightwear and Ireland was not mentioned.

In May 1921 the IRA added to Dublin's ruins by burning the Custom House. Several hundred people were involved in the operation; paraffin was brought in by lorry. Five men died, many were wounded and eighty prisoners were taken. The dome collapsed and the fire, which raged for eight days, destroyed plenty of paperwork in the way of civil service records.

The staunchly Unionist Mrs Everard saw and deplored 'a shrieking crowd watching flames lick up to the dome. It was utterly horrible how these savages should enjoy such vandalism.' At Baymount Preparatory School off the North Strand several miles from the city centre, parents were watching a cricket match in front of the castellated building which I would attend in twenty years' time. A schoolboy, Terry Trench, observed the charred scraps of government papers falling from the sky as a parent picked up a piece which he recognised as coming from the office where he worked.

The *Irish Bulletin*, the periodical published by Dáil Éireann throughout the War of Independence, claimed that 'the destruction of the Custom House reduced the most important branches of the British Civil Government in Ireland, already gravely disorganised, to virtual impotence'. Certainly it was one of the factors that persuaded the British to seek a truce in July 1921. The King's conciliatory speech was followed by Lloyd George's letter to de Valera: 'We make this invitation with a fervent desire to end the ruinous conflict . . .'

The fighting continued up to the last moment. Suddenly, 'at a knife stroke', there was peace, as if a referee had walked on to a battlefield and blown a whistle. Men who were about to fire on one another took up their rifles and marched away; engagements which were about to take place did not happen.

Frank O'Connor recalled the moment in Cork: 'A little before noon on Monday July 11th 1921 . . . a slow procession of armoured cars, tanks and patrols began to move back on Cork Barracks . . . Then, as the Angelus rang out from the city churches, the barracks gates were thrown open and tanks, armoured cars, officers and men filed in. Here and there a man would turn and give a derisive hoot at the silent crowd.'

For some the Truce was a craven surrender by Lloyd George, leaving them at the mercy of 'the terrible Frankenstein monster which de Valera and Co. have reared up and armed in Ireland'. A few more months and the monster would have been 'exterminated by British bayonets to make this beautiful island of Ireland once more a clean and wholesome land where men might dwell in peace'. Many Republicans, including Michael Collins, also believed that the Truce had come at a critical time to save 'our heroic little army' which was running out of arms and ammunition.

After the guns were silent, Frank O'Connor remembered how 'all that perfect summer young men who had been for years in hiding drove about the country in commandeered cars, drinking, dancing, brandishing their guns'. The painter Sean Keating persuaded some of them to bring their weapons up to Dublin and pose for his painting *Men of the South*, in which a group of stern-looking men in profile are depicted waiting for an ambush. Members of the North Cork Battalion arrived at his studio at the Metropolitan Museum of Art carrying their guns wrapped in brown paper to the consternation of the porters, who were ex-members of the British Army.

On 11 October Arthur Griffith, Robert Barton, Eamon Duggan, George Gavan Duffy and Michael Collins, carrying a gun in his overcoat pocket, arrived in London with a mandate from de Valera to secure the Treaty. Outside the door of 10 Downing Street, men, women and children knelt in prayer. The routes towards the Prime Minister's residence were lined with Irish exiles, including nuns and priests, reciting the rosary, singing hymns and pouring good wishes on the delegates. Banners, flags, lengths of cloth and cardboard carried slogans in Gaelic and English promoting peace.

The Treaty was signed on 6 December 1921, 'in the depths of winter', sighed Frank O'Connor who fought with the anti-Treaty forces. Griffith said, 'What I have signed I will stand by in the belief that the end of conflict of centuries is at hand.' De Valera immediately signed a repudiation of the Treaty. In England the Government of Ireland Act repealed the 1914 Home Rule Act and copper-fastened Partition.

At Ballykinler Number 1 Internment Camp in Co. Down, while they waited for news, Republican prisoners worked with macramé twine, wood, lead, silver and copper to make souvenirs; they also passed the time playing the violin, mouth-organ and melodeon. There was a choir and a drama society which gave a highly creditable performance of Lady Gregory's *The Workhouse Ward*. In *Ná Bac Leis*, the camp magazine which was typed on yellow paper, a poet mused:

> The sun will shine with splendour rare
> Each songster trill his sweetest air
> And buoyant hopes will banish care
> The day that we get out.

In December, after the Treaty was signed, internees and prisoners were released. In Bray local men were met at the bridge by a torchlight procession; St Kevin's Brass and Reed Band fêted them, and bonfires were lit in the winter darkness. But soon there was little occasion for rejoicing in Bray or elsewhere.

The Civil War began as rhetoric, a war of words in the Dáil. When Griffith said that the difference between the two sides was only a quibble, Cathal Brugha replied that it was the difference between a draught of water and a draught of poison. Countess Markiewicz said, 'Now I say that Ireland's freedom is worth blood, and worth my blood, and I will willingly give it for it, and I appeal to the men of the Dáil to stand true.' De Valera said, 'I am against this Treaty, not because I am a man of war, but a man of peace. We went out to effect reconciliation and we have brought back a thing which will not even reconcile our own people.'

Some have argued that the Civil War was the fault of Great Britain for insisting on the oath to King George; in those days taking such a solemn promise meant a good deal. But when it was far too late, de Valera was able to repudiate the oath without any crisis of conscience.

Ireland Over All, the short-lived anti-Treaty paper, argued that 'the national forces are offered two paths . . . the easy path, which sacrifices the unity and independence of Ireland for temporal gains; the difficult path which keeps the nation pledged to strive and work and fight until the Green, White and Gold floats independently over every hill and valley, town and hamlet, castle and cabin in Eire of the Streams'. But the north-east of the island would continue to be under 'England's wretched rag' instead of the tricolour. Ulster was ugly, in Craig's words, 'a rock of granite'. However, the anti-Treaty debates, 'a spate of words', were not about Northern Ireland. They were about democracy.

During the Christmas season of 1921 the churches were full to overflowing with people praying for peace. When the Treaty was ratified on 7 January 1922, bonfires were lit on the Dublin mountains. Republicans condemned the 'clamour' for peace and coined the 'Free Staters' tag in derision.

The British began to pull out. More than a decade later John Gibbons expressed their feelings in a smug paragraph in *Ireland the New Ally*. 'From our English point of view the business was now finished and fairly satisfactorily. There is no ordinary Englishman with the least desire to oppress Ireland or to treat Ireland unfairly. Heaven knows the country had cost us enough, but now we had given her the freedom that she wanted, and were glad that she was going to be happy at last. We also managed to keep her on some sort of terms with the Empire, so that was all right too.'

After eight centuries of English rule the hand-over was casual. In later years as the breakup of the British Empire proceeded, the ceremony of departure would become a well-practised ritual with bands playing and flags raised and lowered. This first transfer of power was low key. Sir Henry Robinson watched the representatives of the former government and Sinn Féin officials 'glowering at each other' and Lord Fitzalan's hasty departure after meeting the new Ministers who seemed 'scarcely out of their teens'. Collins dominated the proceedings; the hunted terrorist was now 'cordiality itself'. Robinson heard 'people asking each other whether civil servants would be expected to shake hands with men whose hands were stained with outrage and crime. But if the civil servants had any doubt on the subject themselves, they were speedily dispelled by Michael Collins who grasped their hands with his iron grip and shook them warmly with the greatest bonhomie.'

Smart British troops were exchanging places with Irishmen in shabby 'makeshift' uniforms, members of the new Irish Army which was, according to Patrick O'Shea, 'the IRA cleansed of sins against the British Empire by twelve signatures on a document in London'.

In Templemore the regimental colours of the Northampton Regiment were marched on parade without a band before the troops left the barracks for ever. On the Bridge of Athlone departing British soldiers met an Irish guard of honour. The officer in charge of the Irish contingent gave the command 'Eyes right!' but the salute was not returned. Down the Dublin quays trotted the cavalry on its way to England accompanied by bands playing 'Come Back to Erin'. In Loyalist Portmarnock housewives wept as they listened to the massed bands leaving their barracks for the last time.

The RIC began to be disbanded in March 1922. On 17 August 1922, in the midst of the Civil War, they left Dublin Castle almost unnoticed by the public. The same day a detachment of 380 members of the new Civic Guard marched in to take their place; the force was so new that only sixty men wore uniforms. These were navy blue – the bottle green was no more.

Sean O'Casey claimed that the Black and Tans departed in sealed vans. Lady Gregory amended this to 'some motors; there was no booing or applause. Just a sort of delighted murmur, a triumphant purr.'

The Tans left Clones in better heart, crowding on to the train shouting and singing. For Patrick O'Shea, 'seeing them depart in civilian clothes, carrying their shabby baggage . . . one was struck by their very ordinariness . . . I have never seen so many drunk men. They got a boisterous good humoured send off.'

A Tan stepping on to the boat at Kingstown, soon to be renamed Dún Laoghaire, is reputed to have shouted to the crowd, 'So long, I'll be back again to separate you!'

The anti-Treaty minority set a precedent for the modern IRA by displaying contempt of public opinion and the cry for peace. At meetings in every town in Ireland de Valera and his supporters, including Liam Mellowes, Cathal Brugha, Maud Gonne, Countess Markiewicz, Harry Boland and red-bearded Darrel Figgis, blamed their defeat in the election of June 1922 on the press, Home Rulers, vested interests, priests, shopkeepers, shoneens, the middle class, reactionaries, ex-peelers and, of course, Unionists. They claimed that the Treaty, forced on an ignorant people, was a renunciation of Pearse's republic.

'It is all terribly sad,' Lady Gregory wrote in her diary in June 1922. In the same month, following the election, recruitment for six months' service began in five Dublin battalions. The response was overwhelming. The anti-Treatyites, or 'Irregulars', claimed that the enthusiasm expressed by the new recruits into the Army of the Provisional Government was engendered by unemployment and the fact that the anti-Treaty forces refused to have ex-British Army veterans in their ranks. But the eager queues and the overwhelmed recruitment officers demonstrated the strength of feeling for the Treaty. The new army, staffed by officers in new olive-green uniforms with shining buttons and belt buckles, and leggings of red leather, prepared to face their old allies.

The Irregulars had prepared early for renewed war with a couple of bank raids that netted them over fifty thousand pounds. As of old, they went about raiding for arms. Victor Griffin, the future Dean of St Patrick's, remembered Republicans calling on the family in Co. Wicklow. 'My father was at pains to assure them that there were no guns in the house. At this moment my grandfather, who possessed a shotgun which he had prized from his youth, emerged in his nightshirt . . . leant over the banisters shouting, "Bert, for goodness sake don't give them my good shotgun!"' Gilbert Griffin told the invaders his father was imagining things.

In April 1922 a hundred lorry loads of arms had been taken from the British

Navy ordnance ship *Upnor* off Ballycotton Bay. In Dublin the Irregulars resumed the age-old strategy of occupying and defending landmark buildings, the tactic that had failed during the Rising. Now they took over places as diverse as the Kildare Street Club and the Four Courts.

Collins knew that the Treaty had to be accepted; renewed war with the British would bring back a massively reinforced Army which might well make life under the Black and Tans seem a picnic. At the beginning of July, nudged by the British, he turned his borrowed guns on the Four Courts. While the place was being shelled, the fire brigade moved in, working gingerly, since the building had been encrusted with barbed wire and there was the fear of further explosions. As the men of the brigade unwound their hoses, little groups of Irregulars watched them and chatted to them.

Before the Irregulars surrendered they mined the records office in an action which mirrored the burning of the Custom House the year before, sending another flutter of burnt paper into the Dublin sky. The explosion shot up 400 feet into the sky in a column of smoke and dust. According to an eyewitness reporting in the *Irish Independent*, it spread into a mushroom of smoke filled with a snowstorm of papers 'dipping, sidling, curtsying, circling, floating as snowflakes do'. But these snowflakes were rising, not falling, and they spread all over the city. 'A freakish eddy drifted one of the great flakes to my feet . . . It was the last sheet of an order made by a probate judge . . . "And the judge doth order that the cost of all parties shall be costs in the cause."' Another paper picked up in Ringsend and reproduced in the *Irish Times* dealt with the annual rent of £106 paid by freeholder James Lewis in Loughrea in 1806. Documents destroyed included much of Ireland's history: census returns for 1821, 1841 and 1851; registrations of births, marriages and deaths going back to 1636; diocesan registers; half a million old wills; records of High Courts, of the Irish Houses of Parliament and the maps of the Down Survey.

By a dreadful irony, it was only some fifty years since the Government had directed that all registers of births, marriages and deaths should be sent from outlying parishes to the central office at the Four Courts. Fortunately, some parish priests had been less than efficient and their records remained intact. But in general the destruction of so many records has made the efforts of emigrants in seeking the names of their forebears infinitely more difficult.

At the same time O'Connell Street, as Sackville Street was now known, was swept by rifle fire and deserted. The heart of the city was in flames for the second time in six years. Nelson stood out, a silhouette against clouds of rose-tinted smoke.

The new premises of Messrs Clery survived this time. Compensation for its destruction during the Rising had paid for its rebuilding by Ashlin and Coleman, a firm which specialised in 'Catholic work'. Architect Robert Francis Atkinson modelled the new building with its Portland stone pillars on Selfridge's. Clery's reopened on 9 August 1922 amidst O'Connell Street's new layers of rubble. Other premises were not so lucky; a notice at 79 Talbot Street read:

I was burnt out in 1916.
I was 'dittoed' in 1922,
What harm – I'm still at your service in a new building.
S. J. Riordan. At your command for Exhibitions, Signs,
Show Cards, etc.

On 4 July the Irregulars in the Four Courts threw their arms into the flames and surrendered; Cathal Brugha was fatally wounded. During the next few months it became obvious that the anti-Treaty forces would be defeated as they were driven back from town to town. But although the war was lost they refused to accept unconditional surrender. Instead they left a trail of devastation behind them.

Initially the impact of the Civil War had been inconvenience. The Irregulars retreated westwards in stolen motors, singing as they went, destroying communications all over the country. In Tipperary they withdrew at the end of July, blowing up two bridges, setting fire to Cleeve's factory and blowing up the water main to prevent the fire being put out. At Clonmel the barracks were burnt. At Carrick-on-Suir all bridges over the river were blown up and the water supply was destroyed. Limerick and Waterford suffered much damage before they were retaken by the forces of the Provisional Government. On one day, 22 July 1922, a railway and goods train was derailed near Thurles; no trains could move in or out of Nenagh; mines were planted at Ballysadare Bridge in Sligo; no trains could move at Ennis, Claremorris, Woodstock, Killroy in Tipperary and Castle Bernard in Kings County. There would be many incidents like that in February 1923 when a gang of workers in Kerry set out on a breakdown engine to mend a strip of broken line. They were surrounded by armed Irregulars who, after seizing the engine and chalking GO AND BE DAMNED! on it in large letters, sent it at full speed back into Tralee.

Roads were blocked with demolished trees or trenched; the great holes dug in them filled up with water. It became commonplace to see columns of smoke on horizons and hear muffled explosions like thunder. In many places, as the Irregulars passed through, careering wildly, they looted towns and villages for food and clothing, leaving semi-starvation in their wake. Lennox Robinson was told by a Republican that the people did not seem to be ready for freedom and they had been betrayed by priests and shopkeepers. Killing and stealing no longer seemed to be crimes. 'An ounce of fear is better than a ton of love,' another Irregular said.

For days, sometimes weeks, there was no post, first because of the general assault on communications, afterwards because of a postal strike. Telegraph wires were cut and newspapers destroyed by Republicans since the news was seldom in their favour. In Kerry Lady Gordon's post usually consisted of an empty newspaper wrapper from *The Times* with a note 'Found without contents in raided mail'. She discovered that a telegram to London from Kerry had to be sent as a parcel, since the wires were cut to Cork and the cross-

Channel telegraph was suspended. As a parcel it could be sent by sea to Fishguard and on as a wire to London.

In Clare and East Galway during July 1922 police barracks that had survived the old spate of burnings were now destroyed: those at Ardrahan, Kilcolgan and Oranmore, and in Galway the Renmore and Eglington Barracks, were all soaked with petrol and fired before the Irregulars slipped away. In Sean O'Casey's words, 'bridges sank sullenly down into the rivers they spanned'. The bridge across the Shannon at Athlone, over which British soldiers had so recently marched away, was broken. Much of the South-west was cut off by the blowing up of the ten-arched Mallow Viaduct across the Blackwater. When the Free State Army came to Cork to chase Irregulars it had to come by sea. Outside cars, cabs and other horse-drawn vehicles did a good business bringing stranded travellers from place to place. When Lady Gordon enquired in the autumn of 1922 whether she could get to Killarney, she was told, 'If you can leap and you can swim you may perhaps get there.' When V. S. Pritchett's railway journey was halted by a broken bridge, he was taken in a car to join another train across the valley; he eventually arrived in Cork in a racket of machine-gun fire. 'The passengers took it for granted and a bare-footed urchin who took my case said, "'Tis only the boys from the hills."' Pritchett went to a performance of *Hamlet*. The theatre was packed; when Hamlet said everyone was mad in England the whole house cheered.

The anti-Treaty collapse largely came about because of the hostility of the general populace. They had been anti-British; now they were anti the antis. They would help fleeing Republicans, but the old enthusiasm was gone. They knew the Catholic Church was against the Republican forces after they had been condemned in May 1922 by the hierarchy. When it repeated its denunciation in the autumn of 1922 a good many Irregulars went home. Others wrestled with their doubts and the fact that they would be refused the sacraments, and took refuge in the mountains. The decree of excommunication might worry them, but ultimately they would not allow it to corrode their Republican allegiance.

Sean O'Faolain relived his experiences as a Republican in his story 'The Patriot' in which the Irregular soldier Bernard wanders aimlessly among 'grey mountains' in West Cork. 'Only once did he use his rifle in those seven months and that was when sniping from fifteen hundred yards a village supposed to contain enemy troops. He slept in a different bed each night and never ate twice in succession at the same table so that most of his time was spent in going from place to place in search of food and rest. He did so less from a sense of danger than a sense of pity towards the farmers who had to feed and shelter him and his fellows, never thinking that, as all his fellows did as he was doing, it saved nothing to the flour bin or the tea caddy on the high mantelshelf emptied almost daily.'

O'Faolain wrote of the Irregulars in the mountains as being 'weak and scabby and sore, not a penny in their pockets, not a pipeful to smoke, nothing to do from one week to another but run when danger approached, never together, badly led, beaten in all but in name'. Scabies, which is induced by dirt, became known as 'Republican itch'.

On 12 August 1922, Arthur Griffith died. When Michael Collins walked in his funeral procession, murmurs of delight arose from the crowd as he passed. On 22 August their uniformed hero would be dead, shot in ambush at Beal na mBlath, Co. Cork. A few days before, Shaw had met him at Horace Plunkett's house, Kilteragh in Foxrock. 'His nerves were in rags; his hand kept slapping his revolver all the time although he was talking pleasantly enough.'

Shaw's letter to Collins's sister after her brother's death may have comforted her: 'So tear up your mourning and hang out your brightest colours in his honour and let us all praise God that he had not to die in a stuffy bed of a trumpery cough, wreaked by age and saddened by the disappointments that would have attended this work had he lived.'

Less than a year before, the painter John Lavery had met Collins in London and had been impressed by the 'tall young Hercules with a pasty face, sparkling eyes and a fascinating smile'. Now he painted the dead leader lying in state. 'He might have been Napoleon in marble as he lay in his uniform, covered by the Free State flag, with a crucifix on his breast. Four soldiers stood around the bier. The stillness was broken at long intervals by someone entering the chapel on tiptoe, kissing the brow and then slipping to the door where I could hear a burst of grief.'

The solemn silence had been preceded by some undignified moments at St Vincent's Hospital where Albert Power was summoned after midnight to take Collins's death mask. The corpse was laid on a slab in 'a place with bottles and vials around'. Power told Signe Toksvig that 'first the embalmers were doing their job and then he was left alone while he was waiting for the mask to set. But he had put no threads in, he wanted to take it all in one piece. Then he couldn't get it off. No one to hold corpse while he pushed. And it was difficult; he had thought MC had only the little bullet hole behind left ear, but the skull was shattered where it had gone out near the right . . . "Worst minutes ever I spent."'

When V. S. Pritchett arrived at Dún Laoghaire in February 1923, he was frisked for guns by a Free State soldier with a pink face and mackerel-coloured eyes. In Dublin there were sandbags and barbed wire round the Government offices to protect Ministers; O'Connell Street was still in ruins. Slogans were painted on the walls: FIGHT CLEAN, MULCAHY, CALL OFF YOUR MURDEROUS TROOPS. MOVE OVER MICK, MAKE WAY FOR DICK. 'Dick' was General Richard Mulcahy. Throughout the winter spasmodic engagements between Irregulars and Free Staters took place; soldiers' funerals in Dublin were constant, sometimes six a day. You could tell a Republican funeral by the fact that only women followed the hearse. Soldiers went to their graves in glass-sided hearses driven by plumed black horses, just like everyone else. Free Staters were buried in a newly created plot in Glasnevin beside Michael Collins; it was he who got the gun carriage.

In Athlone Lady Gregory observed three coffins on a railway platform and overheard a conversation: '. . . the head and shoulders of one of them were sent over five fields . . .'

Rumour abounded: 8,000 Irregulars were marching on Dublin; de Valera had been taken dressed in priest's clothes; the island of St Helena had been borrowed as an internment camp; soldiers were being flogged and shot.

Liam O'Flaherty, another ex-Republican who exchanged the gun for the pen, put into his novel *The Informer* the horror of the Civil War: '. . . gradually he saw the faces growing colder and more cruel, the lips curling into a snarl and the eyes narrowing. Then one man said, "Let's give it to the bastard."

'They both fired point blank into his head.'

The recruits who had queued up so eagerly to join the new nation's Army were undisciplined. Lady Gregory heard 'a sad account' of young Free State soldiers with 'no recreation grounds, no evening resource but the public house' whose drinking was worse than that of the Tommies. After these Irish soldiers had committed atrocities some felt that they had learnt too much from the Saxon enemy, and they compared the behaviour of Free Staters with that of the Black and Tans. But when Lady Gregory was told 'the Black and Tans did nothing so bad as that' she reminded her informant of the murder of the Loughnane brothers. Her own nationalism became unambiguous as a result of the Black and Tan campaign.

The Republicans were surrendering and the prison ships, the SS *Avonia* and the *Lady Wicklow*, so filthy that many on board went on hunger strike, could not deal with their numbers. By November 1922 over 6,000 prisoners had been salted away in Dublin alone. Many women belonging to Cumann na mBan, the women's arm of the Republican movement, were imprisoned in Kilmainham and fed on bread and butter, over-boiled tea, soup and potatoes which were often bad.

There were rumours of torture in Free State prisons. A man told me his grandfather had been an Irregular prisoner. He had a 'straight leg' as the result of a childhood illness. 'The only time his leg was bent was when he was in Port Laoise.'

The Government had decided to move events along with tough new measures. On 27 September 1922 Kevin O'Higgins and Dick Mulcahy had established military courts with powers to execute men for possession of weapons. On 18 November four men were shot as a warm-up for the execution of Erskine Childers – or so Childers believed. He faced a firing squad ostensibly for having in his possession a .32 Spanish automatic pistol given to him by Michael Collins, 'a tiny delicately made gun such as a middle-aged lady of timid disposition might carry in her handbag', wrote Frank O'Connor who had seen it fixed to Childers's braces by a safety pin.

Childers's death heralded the miserable period of execution and retaliation that would engender bitterness for decades. On 6 December 1922 the Free State came formally into existence with William Cosgrave as President of the

Executive Council. Two days later four imprisoned Republicans, Liam Mellows, Richard Barrett, Rory O'Connor and Joseph McKelvey, were shot as a reprisal for the assassination of Sean Hales, a Dáil Deputy. One of Noel Browne's childhood memories was seeing a line of tricoloured coffins of executed prisoners. Later he read a diary kept by a Free State officer which demonstrated the random way prisoners from different counties were selected for execution. The officer, 'known as a deeply religious man', showed no remorse.

In addition to murder as a response to the seventy-seven executions carried out by the new Free State, Republicans revived the old tested revenge of burning houses. Cosgrave's home, Beechmount in Templeogue, Co. Dublin, went up in flames; when the house of Alex MacCabe, Dáil Representative, was blown up in Ranelagh, Co. Dublin, his children and mother were turned out, the baby taken from its cradle and laid on the pavement close by.

Senators' houses were obvious choices and between January 1922 and February 1923 thirty-seven were destroyed. They included Palmerstown, a Victorian house near Naas, Co. Kildare, belonging to a new Senator, the Earl of Mayo, which was burnt as a reprisal for the execution of six men at the Curragh; all that was saved was an old hunting coat of the Kildares and a coloured reproduction of Millais's *Bubbles*.

Mrs St John Gogarty was seen to be weeping after beautiful Renvyle on the Galway coast was burnt in February 1923; Horace Plunkett was in America when his beloved Kilteragh was blown up by a land-mine planted by the Republicans. The explosion blew out every pane of glass, wrecked the electric light and wind blew through the darkened rooms. All his papers were destroyed; looters appeared the next day and dug around the smouldering ruins for precious plants and bulbs. He lamented, 'I built Kilteragh as a meeting place for all genuinely interested in our country, and if I achieved anything worth while, it was by assembling people there.' It was, in Hubert Butler's words, 'the final insult to Plunkett'; disgusted, he retired to live in England. He was followed by Lord Desart, heartbroken at the destruction of beautiful Desart Court, 'an action as meaningless as it was cruel'. Lord Desart, whose house suffered because he was a brother-in-law of a Senator, spent the rest of his life lamenting: 'I can't bear to think of Desart – it is sadness itself. All gone, all scattered – and we were so happy there.'

Lady Glenavy, wife of the new Senator, Lord Glenavy, was more sanguine about the burning of their new house, Clonard. On confronting masked and armed men in the hall, 'I heard myself say, "Gentlemen, what can we do for you?" The leader came forward very politely and said, "We have orders to burn this house . . . we think real bad of it. We'll do as little damage as we can. We'll use paraffin . . . we won't use petrol."'

After directing that her children's Christmas presents should be saved, Lady Glenavy 'had a most wonderful feeling that everything I owned was being destroyed. No more possessions . . . an extraordinary sense of freedom.'

Another Senator, W. B. Yeats, had guards in his house in Merrion Square.

His tower house, Thoor Ballylee in Co. Galway, was broken into; someone left a smell of tobacco and prised open drawers and cupboards. Yeats was advised not to complain of this 'unfriendly act'. The bridge outside the tower was blown up with some delicacy. The Yeats family were told, '"there will be plenty of time, the explosion won't be for an hour and a half. There will be three explosions. I'll warn you when we are coming." . . . We saw men running away, and one came to the door and called out that it was coming and went away saying "Good night; thanks." The explosions were not very loud.'

Often big houses torched in the new round of burnings were chosen haphazardly. When Rathgobbin House in Co. Laois was burnt in April 1923, and the steward asked why it had been selected for destruction, he was told, 'What were the executions for? Ask no more questions.' In the same county, when Greenhill House was burnt after the execution of the Republican Patrick Geraghty, the eighty-four-year-old owner was ordered from her bed; shots were fired over her head as she hobbled downstairs.

Nothing could save Lismullen in Co. Meath, belonging to Sir John Dillon. The raiders arrived: 'Sir John, we are very sorry, but we have orders to burn your house.'

'But what have I done?' (He felt he had a reputation for being a good landlord.)

'Nothing yourself, Sir John, but there was a man killed on the raid above, and this is a "reprisal".'

When Mary Colum was staying with Lord Dunsany he took her on a tour of the stately homes in Meath which had been burnt down. In West Cork, Drishane in Castletownshend escaped when many other big houses were fired; Edith Somerville ascribed its preservation to the guardianship of departed shades, including her beloved cousin, Violet Martin.

No ghosts interfered to save Macroom Castle, which had hitherto escaped occupation by the Black and Tans. Katherine Everard saw 'a tall spiral of smoke, thin and fading at the top. The castle had always appeared to be solid green from the ivy that clothed it . . . now it was rust coloured. All the village gathered outside the castle where furniture, china and pictures lay on the lawn or leaned against the trees.' It was a scene that had become all too familiar. The tearful housekeeper lamented, 'When I saw them spreading tallow and paraffin everywhere, I knew what was in their black hearts . . . Carry out the furniture first, I told them and that I made them do . . . well, I got her Ladyship's things out and Cromwell's cannon balls, for she had great store by them.'

It was not easy for servants and retainers to determine on their own what to save out of a burning house. Patricia Cockburn tells of a butler who had observed how his master had spent most of his time in the billiard room, so decided to save the billiard table. 'This they proceeded to do, but as it was too large for the door, they started to take it to pieces. One leg was unscrewed when the IRA came back. Time was up, and dozens of priceless pictures and furniture destroyed.'

Tired of incursions by Free Staters and Irregulars, Maud Wynne and her husband decided to leave Ireland, putting their house in the charge of two loyal maids. They were no match for thirty to forty Irregulars who made the usual stipulation, 'We will give you ten minutes to clear out.' They began to pour petrol over the floors and break all the windows to make a draught. 'Alice . . . the housemaid . . . wasted no time, and she and the cook threw everything they could save out of the windows – unfortunately Alice's heart was in the linen cupboard and the cook's in the kitchen.' They did not bother with the paintings by old masters and Maud Wynne's father's gold collar marked SS, the symbol of the Chief Justice of Ireland.

Another victim of the Irregulars was Michelstown Castle whose stones were used later to build much of the fabric of the new church at Mount Melleray Abbey. The castle's owner, Willie Webber, nearly ninety years old, was forced to leave, never to return. The fire in August 1922 was followed by general looting. People stacked furniture and other valuables behind trees for later removal. The only pieces retrieved for the family from one of the most imposing buildings in Ireland were some books from the library and some pieces of silver thrown over the demesne wall.

The temptation to loot was not always resisted. Around Gort the local doctor recognised ornaments and items of furniture from looted houses in the rooms of his patients. At Geashill, Co. Laois, elk horns and a beaten bronze cauldron were taken in a raid.

The Free Staters became more ruthless. The remote reaches of Cork and Kerry had put up stubborn resistance, particularly after Tralee had fallen to their forces when troops were brought around to Fenit in the versatile vessel *Lady Wicklow*. Tralee was in their hands, but in the surrounding countryside the anti-Treaty faction continued to resist. Martial law was declared; a Free State regiment known as the Dublin Guard, some of whose members had gained experience in brutal behaviour in their fight against the British, have been conclusively linked to the atrocity at Ballyseedy near Tralee in March 1923. Republican prisoners, their hands tied behind their back, were blown up by a carefully constructed mine; the only survivor took forty years to tell the true story of what happened.

Sean O'Faolain remembered how 'as the spring of 1923 approached and with it the threat of long days and late light – fatal to guerrilla troops hard pressed – the inevitability of surrender became apparent . . . The Army had become a shambling, wandering scattered band.'

The death of the Irregular Chief of Staff Liam Lynch in April 1923 effectively ended Republican resistance. On 27 April 1923 de Valera announced that 'military victory must be allowed to rest for the moment with those who have destroyed the Republic'. It was his way of saying he was surrendering. But the killing continued, including the murder of the Republican Noel Lemass by unknown men in July 1923. When the violence concluded, between 600 and 700 people had died.

During the Truce Sean Keating had painted the brave men of the South and the West in noble and heroic mould. In 1925 he expressed his disillusion in *Allegory*, in which two gunmen from opposing sides in the war dig a grave for the new republic which lies beside them in a coffin draped in a tricolour like those of so many executed men. A family with mother and child, a citizen and a priest look on helplessly. Significantly, at the back of the picture the old order is represented by a big house in ruins.

The majority of the ladies in black had been anti-Treaty and those in the Dáil lost their seats in the election of May 1922. Republican women, particularly those in Cumann na mBan, gave persistent support to the anti-Treaty forces; afterwards, during the twenties, led by Maud Gonne, they would give their wholehearted support to the IRA.

For decades there was guilty silence about the Civil War, and it is only recently that the questions have begun being asked. To some the unhappy period has seemed like the battle between the Big Enders and Little Enders in Lilliput.

Were the British bluffing? Could they have been less insistent on the Oath? For political reasons Lloyd George was limited in his actions, and there was some fear in England that any concession on the nature of the Oath would have had a domino effect on the rest of the Empire.

Could de Valera not have compromised? His actions gave opposition to the Treaty, particularly among those who had fought for freedom so long and felt a sense of betrayal. How much cynicism was there in the way that the new state's longing for peace was totally ignored? The prayers, the bonfires and the votes meant nothing when the hard men made their decisions. What about the North? The North of Ireland was never a factor during the debates, largely because there was a naïve belief that at some golden moment the fourth green field would be smoothly linked to the newly created Irish Free State.

Twenty-five years after the end of the fighting, in April 1941, Sean O'Faolain wrote an editorial in the *Bell* entitled 'Romantic Ireland'. 'The Rebellion . . . was followed by a Civil War and that was the best thing that ever happened to us. It woke us up from the mesmerism of the romantic dead . . . We know, now, that Romantic Ireland's dead and gone . . . The process of liberation is not ended. It will not end until we get rid of that Old Man of the Sea – our glorious Past and that equally tyrannical Old Man of the Sea – Our Great Future. Some may consider that the future has arrived, but perhaps the stains of the Civil War are indelible.'

CHAPTER 7

Once More People Laugh in the Streets

De Valera lived in those days through his Inferno. Like Dante
he descended into Hell and his face began to show the marks of
his journey. All that he had fought for, all to which he had
devoted his life, was in ruins.

Sean O'Faolain

They are the spit of virtue now
Prating of law and honour,
But we remember how they shot
Rory O'Connor.

AusFtin Clarke, 'Civil War'

How far was de Valera blamed for the carnage of the Civil War? To his
supporters he stood for what was most sacred in the struggle for freedom. To
others he was responsible for choosing bloodshed rather than accepting the
verdict of the polls. 'I wouldn't drink a bottle of stout with de Valera,' said one
of his enemies. 'I wouldn't stand beside him at a crossroads.'

'I curse that man as generations of Irishmen to come will curse him – the
man who destroyed our country,' wrote Æ. The scholar Stephen
McKenna, whose poem 'Memories of the Dead', published in 1916, was a
tribute to the insurgents, now left Ireland because he felt he had been
betrayed. But over the next decades thousands would give different reasons
for leaving Ireland.

In August, when an election was held, Sinn Féin took part. A surprising
number of die-hards voted for its members, a substantial nucleus out of which
de Valera's creation, the Fianna Fáil party, would emerge. Proportional
representation had been brought in as a safeguard to Protestants; in fact it

benefited the anti-Treaty people who would have suffered irrevocably in a first-past-the-post electoral system.

Cumann na nGaedheal, whose name derived from the party originally founded by Arthur Griffith, but now covered those who accepted the Treaty, won comfortably with over 400,000 votes. The party was identified with commercial and propertied classes, in particular with rich farmers. William T. Cosgrave, who had fought in the Post Office in Easter Week and had been sentenced to death, stepped into the shoes of Michael Collins and Arthur Griffith.

Ireland was divided and tired. Kevin O'Higgins lamented, 'We had an opportunity of building up a worthy state . . . we preferred to burn down our houses, blow up our bridges, rob our own banks, saddle ourselves with millions of debt for the maintenance of an army – generally we preferred to practise upon ourselves worse indignities than the British had practised on us since Cromwell.' The destruction wrought during the Civil War brought the new state to the edge of bankruptcy almost before it had been established. The miracle was that inexperienced revolutionaries without economic or political skills could restore the wrecked infrastructure and lay the foundations for a stable government.

After the fighting the weary country presented itself as a place of beauty and hardship whose people struggled to survive on uneconomic farms and holdings, or took the boat. Successive governments grappled fruitlessly with this basic situation which would remain relatively unchanged for over half a century.

Even in the worst of times Ireland had its share of tourists, complaining incessantly that food and accommodation were bad and prices were high. At the height of the Civil War in July 1922, travellers arriving in Cobh were 'keenly disappointed to find after the journey that a barrier of steel separates them from their objective' – a tour of West Cork. George Bernard Shaw, a regular and indefatigable visitor, motoring in July 1923 between Glengarriff and Parknasilla in his chauffeured car with the GBS number-plate, found 'the tourist's heart is in his mouth when he first crosses a repaired bridge . . . for the repairs look extremely unconvincing to the eye. But after crossing two or three in safety he thinks no more of them.'

Emigrants returned for a visit, like Tim Cashman who came back in the summer of 1925 after thirty-three years in America. Cashman's heart sank when he saw the recently renamed Cobh, which he had known as Queenstown. 'You'd imagine the houses were built before Abraham's time, ancient looking, everything without life.' He journeyed in the rain to his old home at Killeagh in East Cork, noted the mud-covered street and found the grass-grown ruins of his old home. 'I can't get my eyes to see things as they were to me before I left.'

A year earlier Harold Speakman, an American not of Irish descent, had the gimmicky notion of touring Ireland in a creaking cart pulled by a donkey. 'I started out on my journey with a donkey . . . not through any eccentricity, or any craving for sensation, but simply as a result of a wish to come as near as I could to the people of the land.' Seven years later Orson Welles, inspired by Pádraic Ó Conaire, who had originated the idea, would repeat the experience.

In 1924 the Civil War was fresh in people's minds. Speakman passed the newly planted wooden cross to Georgie Shea and seven other Irregulars who had died outside Tralee in March 1923. An old couple in Inchigeelagh even had fond memories of the Black and Tans who they had living in their house, with a Lewis gun blazing away at snipers. 'And do you mind . . . you were after going out one day in a brown dress and almost got sniped yourself ? . . . and one of the Black and Tans got mad an' said, "Wot kind of fightin' manners 'ave they got anyway! Tryin' to strike a lydy!"' They assured Speakman that 'the Tan time was nothing to the last trouble – with the bridges and police barracks blowing up all around you and the Irish murdering each other like a lot of savages'. But the latest atrocities are always the worst.

Speakman's impressions of the post-war countryside demonstrated how wretched communications still were as a result of the fighting. Dusty or muddy roads were neglected and motorists still travelled at their peril as Shaw had observed. It was as well to take supplies of petrol in any remote rural area since garages were slow to take the place of blacksmiths. An ability to repair a bent axle was useful – a letter to the *Irish Times* described a succession of motorists on the Navan–Clonee road, not far from Francis Ledwidge's white road of Ashbourne, tending their cars which had suffered as a result of steering clear of hazards and potholes. In most parts of the country hens and the collie dogs which appeared from inside cottages and over walls when they heard the car were the chief hazards, as Ann Gregory discovered when she began driving. The dogs would rush at the car and try to herd it; as soon as one had disappeared in a cloud of dust, another would rocket out from somewhere else.

My uncle, who was an engineer, devoted his early career to repairing bridges destroyed during the Civil War. The rural economy depended on trains. They operated as far apart as Ballina and Cahirciveen, carrying cattle to an average of twenty-seven fairs every Monday and twenty-six every Tuesday. They took pilgrims to Westport for Croagh Patrick, Knock and Lough Derg with its penitential threat. They carried enthusiasts up to Dublin for the finals of Gaelic games which offered some unity after the divisions of the war. Immediately after the fighting ceased, repairs of damaged bridges were a priority; after they were completed the wages of railway workers were reduced early in 1926.

There were no long-distance bus services until 1926 when a bus route between Dublin and Cavan was inaugurated. Branch railway lines would continue to network much of Ireland reaching into the remotest places. I can remember travelling on the line from Limerick Junction to Kenmare in an enormous carriage like an Edwardian drawing-room with plush seats and antimacassars, drawn by a small engine crawling through rocky hills and valleys. Many lines had the casual eccentricity of Percy French's West Clare Railway. When Geraldine Cummins visited West Cork in 1926 she found that 'punctuality was a matter of no moment. "Hoult the train for the lady" was the remark made by the Skibbereen station-master to the guard. The former had sighted Edith Somerville who was driving me in her pony and trap.' At Gort station in Co. Galway, there was anxiety lest Lady Gregory and her grand-daughters should miss the train. 'Twas all right in the past . . . but now that the mails travel on it ye can't trust it at all, at all. 'Tis often on time, and wouldn't wait a minyt for ye to catch it.'

For local transport there was the occasional bicycle. Otherwise it was horses, asses and jennets. Ploughing was walking after horses the whole day, exhausting work if the ground was wet. On the western seaboard, Connemara ponies carried turf and potatoes or balanced their hooves on slippery rocks while seaweed was gathered. On market days donkeys and horses were to be seen pulling small flat-backed carts carrying wooden milk churns or high-sided slatted carts with pigs or sods of turf. The first reference to donkeys in Ireland was in the early seventeenth century. Originally from desert lands, Irish donkeys hate the cold and wet. In the twenties they were cheap and plentiful. At fairs tinkers would line the street offering for sale scores of old worn-out donkeys with boat-shaped hoofs. Speakman paid two pounds for his Grania, only to be told he had been swindled: 'You can get donkeys all along the road . . . swap them for ten bob.' (Grania was named by Lady Gregory after another female wanderer; Orson Welles would call his donkey Sheeog (*sídheog*) 'after a certain species of fairy'.)

New signposts in Irish puzzled travellers. Numerous counties and towns had new names, like Queen's County – now Co. Laois – and Bagenalstown – now Muine Bheag. Streets and squares in towns were renamed, usually after heroes and martyrs, to the annoyance of some Unionists who complained that such changes would result in the depreciation of property. Meanwhile temporary writing was to be seen by roadsides, painted slogans referring to the recent past: UP DE VALERA, UP THE REPUBLIC, UP SINN FÉIN, REMEMBER THE DEAD and VOTE FOR CROWLEY, £49,000 FOR TIM HEALY, KING GEORGE'S BATMAN. Speakman was told the sum of money, 'which varied with the quality of imagination of the laddie who wielded the whitewash brush', referred to the supposed annual profits of the Governor General 'in fees, salaries, rentals, atonements, considerations, bonuses, graft, sweepstakes, premiums and loot'.

Decisions were taken as to which ruins were repaired. Compensation courts sat, giving their estimates for the value not only of destroyed big houses, but other property – the Orange Hall with its band instruments in Kingstown (now Dún Laoghaire); the Swan public house in Dublin, occupied by both Irregulars and Free State troops; the shops around the Four Courts damaged by the big explosion; sixty haycocks belonging to Mary Wogan, widow of Garristown, Co. Dublin, maliciously destroyed.

Grandiose nineteenth-century houses like Castleboro and Wilton in Co. Wexford and Dunboy in Co. Cork, or the more ancient Castle Bernard outside Bandon made the most impressive ruins – to this day they retain a romantic magnificence. There were people like Pamela Hinkson who reasoned that total fiery destruction was a good thing. 'To some of those great, grey dignified houses, fallen on evil days, even long before the Troubles, with the new owner perhaps storing his potatoes in the immense drawing-room, under the beautiful decorated ceiling and walls, the Burners must have come as rescuers and a release. Driving through Galway you pass gate after gate of an obviously important place, and nearly always with the tall gate posts looking sadly over your head and the rusty gates sagging between them.'

Casualties of war included coastguard stations, the obelisk to King William on the site of the Battle of the Boyne which lay by the road 'as high as you and me together', the Marconi station at Clifden, and all the police barracks. Speakman, who passed fifty ruined barracks during his journey, was much taken with the Tipperary barracks destroyed in the Civil War, 'gutted, hollow, empty, silent as the ruins of Baalbek, its chimney-pots pointing futilely to the unconcerned sky, a ruin for a few seasons which by its appearance, might have been a ruin of a thousand years'.

The garrison towns went into swift decline – Newbridge, Clonmel, Naas, Castlebar, Carlow and elsewhere. Shopkeepers remembered the good old days when the troops poured into towns to spend their wages. 'Then the pubs were full, the hotels rang,' Sean O'Faolain wrote of Fermoy. '"Yerra, man!" said the inevitable mourner. "For years after they went the shopkeepers weren't even painting the shop fronts."'

The new state would set about rebuilding ex-RIC barracks for the Garda Síochána. There would be few changes in design; some, like those at Bennettsbridge, Co. Kilkenny and Ballyduff, Co. Waterford, would retain the little defensive turrets which gave rise to the rumour that architects had mixed up the plans with those for forts on India's North-west Frontier. Rebuilding of principal buildings in cities like the GPO and Four Courts in Dublin and Cork Town Hall, burnt by the Tans, would take up much of the decade. The Custom House in Dublin was rebuilt at a cost of £326,000, half the original estimate since it was found that some of the existing hall had survived and could be reused. Local monumental masons were putting up statues to the IRA, some of which were already being acknowledged as ugly, like the figure of a Volunteer in Nenagh, which acquired the nickname of 'Jamesy' very soon after it was erected.

Some destruction continued, principally the felling of trees which no one wanted when people were land hungry. Lady Gregory regretted the destruction of trees in 'Lord M's' demesne. 'How sad it is,' she said to Speakman, 'to see all the wood disappearing. When I came through town on Friday I saw a number of carts filled with logs. Formerly it was peat they used.' She would see the woods around her old home of Roxborough annihilated – all the timber cut by 1929 except for some lime trees, 'the wood not being so useful'.

Trees were associated with landlords. One of the most comprehensive tree-felling exercises took place in Co. Laois on the Castle Durrow estate after the departure of Lord Ashford. Over 650 acres of oak, beech and ash were cleared between 1922 and 1928 with great difficulty; long cross-cut saws worked by four men divided up the great trees while the saw-doctor stood by. The Plain of the Oaks became a huge barren space to be divided up among needy farmers by the Land Commission.

Perhaps there was symbolic significance in the death of the last golden eagle in Ireland, caught in a trap for foxes in May 1926. A couple had lingered around Slieve Tookey. The *Irish Times* lamented how 'all Donegal knew these last eagles . . . crossing the high moor land towards Gweedore car-drivers often would halt near the naked slopes of Errigal and bid their passengers search the air for a sight of the kingly birds'.

Speakman found the atmosphere lively in a town like Tipperary, 'attractive, business-like . . . with a spirit of gayety [sic] about it and any number of well-dressed shop windows, and Pola Negri in *Mad Love* and lads in the new uniform of the National Army with laughing Tipperary girls on their arms and an amusement company with merry-go-rounds and fortune tellers and raffle stands in an open lot down the hill beside the railroad'.

By contrast, Liam O'Flaherty's description of a small Kerry town with a population of 2,000 people and fifty-three public houses gave a poor view of provincial urban life – dirty, sordid, the back streets with excrement at every second step. Certainly photographs and postcards of back streets, proudly put on sale by local photographers, tended to show a good deal of what looks like dung and a dog at nearly every door. Most towns and villages, even a village as remote as Belmullet in the far reaches of Mayo, had a smear of tarmacadam. But otherwise they were muddy, ill-lit and without sewage systems. On the outskirts of every town were straw-thatched one-storey cottages weeping with damp.

Paradoxically, in the remotest parts of the West were houses on small-holdings which were superior to any peasants' houses in the British Isles. These had been erected as a result of the Labourers' Cottage Act of 1880. The house of the Tailor, Timothy Buckley, in Gougane Barra, West Cork, has four rooms and some outhouses. Later improvements were undertaken by the Congested Districts' Board, which was established in 1891 by Balfour's administration. The CDB, whose work was ungratefully received by Nationalists as part of the programme of killing Home Rule by kindness, did sterling work all over the West, building harbours, starting industries, erecting houses and supervising the breakup of land after the Land Acts. By 1926 the board was taken over by the Land Commission, which targeted land division; new housing stock had small priority.

In the 1920s clothes still marked a social divide between rich and poor. Men's shabby suits had an odd formality. Best clothes were known as Sunday clothes and worn to Mass; in many areas it was considered unlucky to wear a new garment until it had been worn to Mass. Summer clothes were worn from May to 1 November – often the change from winter to summer kit involved little more than discarding an undergarment or, for boys, throwing off boots and going barefoot.

On rare fine summer days men wore their straw hats. Hubert Butler recalled how in Cavan 'you used to get fine cheap rush hats for haymaking, and potato baskets and clogs made from the local willows and alders'. 'Everyone wore a coat or a hat at that time and I still wear one,' I was told by an old man. 'If you saw Dev holding a meeting they'd all wear caps and that was the way they were brought up. The only person you would see bare-headed would be a clerk behind a counter.' It was fedoras or bowlers for the middle classes, who wore the latter to funerals, and peaked caps for others; Sean O'Casey wore his indoors, whether writing his plays or hanging over the brass rail of the gallery of the Abbey Theatre. It has been said that the decline of the peaked cap, which is still worn by old men, was the beginning of modern Ireland.

Shawls and bare feet were widespread. There were pockets of local elegance – the women of Partry in Co. Mayo, for example, were reputed to dress well. The clothes of island people were gorgeous. Black cloaks with brilliant-coloured linings to the hoods, known as 'Bandon cloaks', would continue to be seen on old women in West Cork until the 1960s. In the 1940s Ansty, wife of the Tailor, wears the West Cork hooded cloak on Sundays and holy days; the material outlasted her lifetime. At much the same period, Sean O'Faolain in *An Irish Journey* muses on the Cork 'shawlies' who 'wear the shawl over the head, and it peaks forward like a nun's cowl, and it falls into a lovely line behind the neck. Or they draw it high up like a collar on the neck on warm days, so that it catches the loose hair in a groove of light.' By then shawls with paisley patterns had been exchanged for black, and many of the younger women had become 'the hatty wans' who wore hats, powdered their noses and painted their lips.

When H. V. Morton visited the Claddagh outside Galway in 1930, he wrote, 'I saw a sight typical of the modern Claddagh . . . From a primitive thatched house came a smart young girl in a fashionable felt hat, blue tailor-made costume and flesh-coloured silk stockings. Her mother . . . wore the wide red skirt of a fisher woman . . . her feet were bare . . . a grey shawl over her shoulders.' Morton was told, 'Some of the smartest girls you see in Galway go home to a Claddagh cabin.'

Since farming was mixed, little isolated farms struggled to be self- sufficient if the market was out of reach. If surplus grain could not be moved, often the only use for it was to turn it into poteen. The persecution of poteen makers by the newly formed Garda Síochána had parallels with the activities sparked by Prohibition in America. Most people, however, continued to drink stout and porter, 'obstacles to the building up for their nation', mused Speakman, '. . . which in many cases among the poorer people seemed to be taken almost as an opiate to relieve the sense of obligation and the sense of strain'.

In areas where holdings were small, the spade was still in use for cultivation, together with the scythe, the mattock, the furze lifter and other tools that required hard work and created custom for the blacksmith. Each region had a different-shaped spade; Munster spades had long narrow blades with fishtail ends, while in Connaught the blade was shorter and broader. In parts of the country it was said that you could tell a man's religion according to the foot he dug with. The blacksmith had the design that was favoured by his local customers. In Beagh, Co. Galway, for example, Brady's forge had the monopoly. 'When you jumped on a Brady spade you'd have potatoes for the hen and cabbage for the cow.' When their manufacture was taken over by spade mills, millwrights copied local types in order to compete for customers; big spade mills would have patterns for dozens of different spades.

The *meitheal*, the co-operative gathering of men to help each other during the seasonal round, eased the hardship of cutting wheat, oats or barley with scythes and the toil of the potato harvest. In mid-October the main potato crop was harvested co-operatively, all neighbours helping with the digging up of Aran Banners, Irish Queens, Kerr's Pinks, Scottish Farmers and the rest. Harvesters would roast raw potatoes at the edge of fields. Sunday work was permissible as an act of charity such as helping a widow get in her harvest. Work had to be completed by 12.00 Mass, when the men laid aside their spades or scythes and marched off to Mass in one group.

People believed in *piseoga*: if you saw a shape like a sail in a candle you'd be getting a letter from America; if an ass brayed very loudly it was a sign that a tinker was dead. Holy wells, pilgrimages and matchmakers, and customs associated with them, were unsullied by new forms of communication. Every area had its own saint to be venerated in patterns or pagan ritual like the strange pattern and veneration of St Gobnait in North Cork that still takes place. (A length of woollen thread or ribbon is measured against a medieval statue of the saint; then it is taken away and used for cures. The priest is usually absent from the ceremony.) Holy water was kept in every house and used like aspirin. For a day every June the most dismal of towns would be made beautiful with flags and flowers for the Corpus Christi procession.

During the year's cycle, candles were lit on window-sills at New Year; the Bridogues or images personifying St Brigid were taken out in procession at the beginning of February; green was placed on front doors on May Day; bonfires were leapt on St John's Eve. Before the towns had asphalt, fires were lit in many streets and boys of each district would gather sticks and kindling for weeks before, as happens today with bonfires in the North on 12 July. In Westport, brass bands played on St John's Eve and old women would be seen going round and round the fire in a blend of Christian and pagan belief, saying their rosaries and throwing a stone into the flames for every decade. Afterwards each would take a red-hot coal into her house. In remote parts of the West of Ireland they still light fires on St John's Eve, often using car tyres which send black smoke into the summer sky.

On St Stephen's Day, Wren Boys thrashed the hedges for little birds to kill. Some time in the late twenties they mostly stopped singing 'Kevin Barry' as part of their repertoire together with 'The Wren, the Wren the King of all

Birds' as they dressed in masks or straw costumes or women's clothes and toured with or without the bird's corpse, according to district. In a few country places the tradition is carried on, without the dead wren.

Ballads were an important means of verbal communication that often referred to deeds of valour. Before popular newspapers they were important. Not only did they refer to the recent Troubles: 'In the churchyard of Shaneglish those two young heroes lie/They gave their blood for Ireland and died for you and I.' Patrick Kavanagh quoted a couple of ballads about football:

> At half-past two the whistle blew
> And the ball it was thrown in,
> Their hero, Murphy sazed it and
> He kicked it with the win.

Or: 'The catchin' and the kickin' was marveel-e-us for to see . . .'

Local events were turned into ballads like this drowning near Belmullet:

> It was a dismal Tuesday all in the month of June
> Young Denny Murphy so sadly met his doom;
> He went out on to an island on the lake of Carrowmore
> And on his return back he sank to rise no more.

So were tragedies like the Cleggan disaster in 1927:

> It caused great sensation along every station
> When brave men were fighting against slash and spray,
> But it left bones sleeping and many weeping
> From Rossadilisk down to Lackan Bay.

Visiting other people's houses, *ag scoraíocht*, still passed the evenings. There were traditional amusements, cards, storytelling or a *céilí*. Donal Foley remembered how 'the dancing was really a kind of endurance test and each couple seemed to dance faster and faster – then there would be singing. Songs that were indigenous, written by men long dead about the deeds of men who revolted against the landlords – they all spoke and sang in Irish.' On Horse Island in Roaring Water Bay, dances were held every night during the winter with fiddlers and 'lads playing the mouth-organ' and cards, while tea, poteen and porter were served.

Storytelling included tales of Cúchulainn, Fionn MacCumhaill, saints and animals, together with folk-tales, jokes and stories from the lives of saints. Ghost stories were exchanged and believed; in Wexford the Danish writer Signe Toksvig grew tired of the lurid supernatural stories, the white woman, the dead woman, the devil as big as a calf with eyes the like of two big balls of fire, the dead priest and the gentleman with a cloven hoof, told by her maid who was convinced they were true. A few years later she was wearied by learning of children lighting a May bush with candles and a bonfire. '*Bealtaine* fires, O *Catholicissimo*!' she wrote in her diary.

In his account of life in Belmullet, Father Noone quotes two examples of entertainment in the home:

A Variety Dance in August 1928 in the house of Miss Ellen Neilis 'began at 9.a.m. and continued till the grey hours of Monday morning . . . Singing began in the small hours. Among the turns Miss McDonnell sang "The Snowy Breasted Pearl", Ellen Neilis recited "Owen Roe O'Neill", Michael Judge sang "I'll tell Tilly on the Telephone", Martin Moran from Bangor sang "The Wearing of the Green" and finally all sang "Auld Lang Syne".'

In 1930, at the wedding of Michael Deane and Annie Kate Cuffe, 'strawboys' appeared 'dressed in their cone-shaped straw hats over their lily-white garb of silk and linens, and decorated with all the colours of the rainbow – captain and mate danced first to the bride and bridesmaid, and the company afterward to their choice of partners in the house'.

Such amusements were changing in the face of new inventions. Already in 1924 Speakman was entertained in Inchigeelagh by a gramophone brought back from America playing 'Silver Thread among the Gold' and 'My Dark Rosaleen'. By the thirties gramophones had become more common; in Charlestown, Co. Mayo, John Healy's mother had one, also brought back from the States, which played jazz music, much disapproved of by the clergy. Apart from jazz, the tenor John McCormack was always a particular favourite. Athlone's favourite son benefited from the widespread distribution of records; the country rang with his voice.

The Irish broadcasting service began on New Year's night, 1926; it was known as Radio 2 RN, the call sign designated by London to reproduce phonetically the last words of the line 'Come Back to Erin'. (The name would be changed to Radio Eireann in 1932.) One of the earliest programmes consisted of folk-songs sung by the first Director, Seamus Clandillon, and his wife. Five thousand radio licences were issued in 1926, although it was estimated that there were five times as many receivers and many listeners for each one. Victor Griffin recalled the first wireless set in Carnew: 'I remember the excitement of the first time I put the earphones on me and I twiddled the knob on top of the little brown box. The locals were invited to sample the novelty – one or two were scared out of their wits.'

Soon they were everywhere, including the islands. On Horse Island in Roaring Water Bay the first little battery set arrived, 'and it was fantastic to the young people that it could be put up on a table and that it could make a sound and there was nothing feeding it'. Sheila Fitzgerald was told that a bus driver had a wireless near her village in Donegal. 'For six pence he would allow people to sit in his bus and listen . . . You climbed in and sat in rows facing the other people – everyone had earphones clamped over their heads.' At the Leeson-Marshalls' big house, Callinafercy in West Kerry, the wireless was kept in the dining-room, but a connecting cable carried the sound to a loudspeaker in the servants' hall.

For those who aspired to listen with something more elaborate than a cat's whisker touching crystal, a wireless was expensive; a four-valve set complete with batteries, coils and loudspeaker cost £12 second-hand – equivalent to £200 today. Licence fees at a pound apiece, later reduced to ten shillings, brought in revenue to pay for programmes, but the service was run on a shoestring and there would be continued complaints about its quality, particularly the quality of news bulletins. Soon BBC programmes were relayed from the Dublin station.

An evening's entertainment on Radio Eireann would be similar to that offered on 6 May 1926: 7.25 p.m. Stock Exchange Report. 7.30 p.m. Talk – The Story of Galway Harbour. 7.45 p.m. French Lessons, Mlle Guidicelli. 8 p.m. Violin Recital. 8.20 p.m. Songs – 'Le Coq de Notre Vieux Clocher' (Fourdran. Gypsy Song), 'Le Petit Chat Blanc' and other songs. 8.35 p.m. Station Orchestra. Clarke Barry's Light Symphony Orchestra. 10.30 p.m. Weather forecast and close down.

Throughout the twenties the cinema was taking hold. In Dublin Lady Gregory, worried about low audiences at the Abbey, wistfully noted a long queue to see Charlie Chaplin. (Dublin was full of queues. There were the Saturday and Monday queues at the pawnshops and every afternoon outside betting shops 'long queues of lowly citizens'.) Elsewhere, casual picture shows took place in town halls or barns. Licences were only required if there were more than six performances a year, but the regulations for audience attendance were so lax that insurance firms would not insure shows. Cinemas were only regularised after the tragedy in Drumcolliher, Co. Limerick, in September 1926 when a fire started by a lamp falling on discarded reels of film in a hall over a flour store during a performance of *The Ten Commandments* resulted in the deaths of fifty people.

Gaelic games offered opportunities to put aside the venom of the Civil War. (The handball courts served the really poor who could not afford hurley sticks.) Hurling and Gaelic football, which had made a vital contribution to national self-determination, were unifying factors in a divided country. The Gaelic Athletic Association, originally formed as part of a campaign of resistance against English domination, now provided neutral territory in hundreds of parishes throughout the country where old resentments could be forgotten in the spirit of competition.

The new Free State Government was gaining in confidence, achieving stability and the rule of law in the face of armed resistance and the threat of assassination. It was fortunate that its remit did not include the North of Ireland and its turbulence. Unification with the North would remain only an aspiration; the Cosgrave Government, with plenty of its own problems, acquiesced at the injustice of the Boundary Commission. In the South there were the makings of unity in a population that was ninety per cent Catholic; the minority was tolerated and its interests safeguarded up to a point.

The British Government had introduced plenty of Catholic middle-class employees into the civil service which made for continuity. Education, health and the welfare system were largely in the hands of the Catholic Church. Fifty per cent of the population was engaged in agriculture. After 1926 Ireland no longer had to contribute to the British National Debt, but it did have to continue two other obligations – to pay RIC pensions and land annuities that amounted to over £3 million a year. Small farmers suffered and had their cattle confiscated; after a decade of stagnant economy they would give their support to de Valera. Most farmers owned their land either through the Wyndham Land Acts and the administration of the Congested Districts Board or, after 1923, by acquiring their holdings through the smooth workings of the Land Commission.

First things first. Cosgrave's Government allowed the Church an increasing role in the management of the country and set about dismantling a reasonably efficient education system by introducing its policy of compulsory Irish. Letter-boxes were painted green and 'The Soldier's Song' replaced 'God Save the King'; at the Horse Show, Unionists refused to stand up while it was played. In 1923 film censorship was brought in. Among many unpopular actions, Kevin O'Higgins, the Minister for Home Affairs, introduced the Holy Hour, during which pubs had to close down for a period each afternoon; he considered that when he was a student he had been given too much opportunity to drink.

By the spring of 1924 the prison and internment gates had been unlocked, and for thousands of Republicans who came flooding out, the new Ireland seemed little better than the old. 'One saw them,' wrote Sean O'Faolain, 'marching through the streets from the railway stations ragged as tramps, their little bundles under their arms – but still singing.' Harold Speakman met Irregulars in Dingle, some newly released from prison. 'They blew my cap off with a bullet and pinked me all the way to jail with a bayonet,' one told him. A woman who had been on the run had lost one brother to the Republican cause and another was crippled. Irishmen were harder against Irishmen than the English had been, they said. Speakman encountered two former prisoners on the slope of Croagh Patrick who told him that at least seventy-five per cent of pilgrims were Republicans. Excommunication was no longer a problem for them.

De Valera had not gone away. In January 1925 at a speech in Cavan he exhorted his listeners that 'no man who stood for the independence of the country or who had any sense of personal or national self-respect would take an oath to a foreign king'.

For the victorious, all roads led to Dublin where the good jobs were. *Dublin Opinion*, which consistently supported de Valera, brought out a famous cartoon complete with signposts, illustrating this fact. There were no jobs for ex-Irregulars like Sean O'Faolain or ex-gaol birds like Frank O'Connor. The best jobs were for those who had supported the Free State forces. 'This was no longer the romantic Ireland of little cottages and the hunted men, but an Ireland where everyone was searching frantically for a pension or a job.'

Another ex-Irregular, Tod Andrews, also had little time for the new

Government. Of his home life he wrote, 'No family with a Free State background ever visited this house or vice versa until well after the Second World War.' Edward MacLysaght went further in remembering 'the terrible events which the healing effects of time can never repair'. Interviewed late in life, Sean Lemass, whose brother had been murdered, burst into tears. He said that 'firing squads have no reunions'.

In this atmosphere Andrews and his fellow Republicans condemned the new Government for slavishly copying the English model. They disliked the newly established Senate, created as a talking shop for Unionists including Yeats and a handful of Unionist peers. Tod Andrews recalled how 'we looked with contempt on our Free State opponents, who, with the pretentiousness of the nouveau riche, had adopted a life style of which dinner parties, card parties, garden parties, dances, and of course, horse racing became the favourite ingredients. Many of them, to our satisfaction, succumbed to debt, drink and fornication.'

Sean O'Faolain, another unreconstructed Republican, also felt 'a strong sense of moral decay'. The Anglo-Irish had given way to a corrupt middle-class Catholic bourgeoisie, 'a new native acquisitive class intent on only cashing in on the changes of Government'. He believed 'in the years after the Troubles that this combination of an acquisitive and uncultivated middle class and a rigorous and uncultivated Church meant that the fight for the Republic as I now understand it had ended in total disaster'.

'The liveried servants of the enemy' who aped the English were despised by the envious defeated, who took on the garment of austerity. Tod Andrews remembered how 'we disapproved of any kind of ostentation – we disapproved of the wearing of formal clothes, tuxedos, evening or morning dress, and above all else the silk hats . . . We disapproved of gambling. We disapproved of golf and tennis and the plus fours and white flannels that went with them. We disapproved of anyone who took an interest in food.' All such habits could be associated with the old enemy and the belief that the Free State Government had become a British puppet. Sean Lemass considered that 'Ireland today is ruled by a British garrison, organised by the Masonic lodges speaking through the Free State Parliament and playing the cards of England all the time'.

During the twenties Armistice Day was still important, not only for Unionists, but for all those veterans who had fought in Flanders and Gallipoli. There might be scuffles, fist fights and poppy snatching by Republicans, but the thousands who continued to remember the dead of the Great War were impressive. As late as 1928, the Pro-Cathedral on 11 November was full to capacity of ex-servicemen attending a Mass commemorating the war. Afterwards, 18,000 marched in procession to the Phoenix Park. Most were gaunt and thinly clad, since, like ex-Irregulars, they found life hard in the new Ireland. In the rain, bands played 'Tipperary', 'Wrap Up Your Troubles' and other wartime songs, and the watching crowds sang along 'heartily'. A guard said, 'I have never seen so many people wearing the poppy.'

Remembrance Day continued to be celebrated on a low-key note up to the Second World War. But veterans of the First World War continued to be ostracised. They found jobs hard to get and in some villages children threw stones at them. The Memorial Gardens at Islandbridge, designed by Lutyens, were completed in the 1930s after long delays, but de Valera refused to have them opened. They became a place of weeds.

Returning to Dublin, which Gogarty had described as being 'stupefied by Celtic chloroform', V. S. Pritchett sensed approaching change. After spending long hours in Dublin pubs 'where the same stories – getting better and better, of course, go round', he 'could smell the coming reaction and the dullness of growing obduracy. I became aware of Irish self-destructiveness.'

However, for those on the winning side and for many others the first years of the Free State or *Saorstát* brought a new sense of optimism. Brian Cooper, a newly elected TD and former Loyalist, expressed his 'passionate desire . . . that Ireland should forget old quarrels and look to the future rather than the past'. For Arland Ussher the new Government comprised 'the most capable and disinterested group of young statesmen who ever . . . midwived the birth of an Irish nation'. They balanced the budget and introduced the Shannon Scheme for hydro-electric plant. The new Civic Guard was created and the Army, although reduced in number and troubled with mutiny, had an important role to play in the new State. The Custom House and the Four Courts were being rebuilt. But the time of disillusion was fast approaching.

In 1923 Yeats received the Nobel Prize for Literature. Was there a special Protestant realism in his reputed response to learning the news: 'How much?' His hero, Parnell, had acted in similar fashion upon receiving a lavish cheque from his supporters: 'Is it crossed?' Yeats's triumph was felt by certain die-hards to be dubious. Many like Monk Gibbon could rejoice that he had 'made the name of his country shine in the imagination of the rest of the world a hundred times more than any of the political nonentities whose names are on everyone's lips here'. But in the emerging puritan Ireland others had their doubts about an international figure whose ideas were too liberal. The *Catholic Bulletin* deplored that 'a reputation for paganism in thought and word is a very considerable advantage in the sordid annual race for the substantial sum provided by a deceased anti-Christian manufacturer of dynamite'.

The house and grounds of the new Royal Dublin Society at Ballsbridge were almost completed. The Horse Show would be graced by the new Governor-General Tim Healy, who was presented as 'an invisible mender, a mender of old antagonisms social and personal'. Healy was said to unite the charms of 'devilled almonds, *crème de menthe* and *pêche* Melba, perfectly blended'. He might be attended by Oliver St John Gogarty, or be seen with Lady Lavery or Lady Fingall who admired the way he collected old Waterford glass, always wore Irish-made clothes and declared that he wished to get away from the pomp and circumstance of his predecessors. But many thought him a shameful figure to be titular head of the State. Sarah Purser refused to shake hands with him.

On one occasion, after emerging from a performance at the Abbey accompanied by Lennox Robinson, old women in shawls shouted at him, 'Who betrayed Parnell?' Robinson told Leon Ó Broin that he would never forget Healy 'who was old and stooped becoming more and more stooped still, and getting into the car as soon as possible'.

Kevin O'Higgins, held responsible for the executions of the Civil War, was another figure who attracted hatred. Ó Broin recalled an occasion in Parnell Square when O'Higgins encountered a mob of screaming women. 'Good night, ladies,' he said, doffing his hat. *Dublin Opinion* had a grim joke: 'Mr O'Higgins said he hoped to visit every prison in the *saorstát*. Wait until there's a change of government, Kevin.' But before that could happen he was assassinated.

At the outset of the founding of the State the new Government planned a festival which would bring into prominence features of the Celtic past and at the same time be an augury of good intentions and an opportunity to forget the years of bloodshed and division, when Irishmen could join hands in celebration. The Tailteann Games were concocted, a re-enactment of the ancient Celtic festival held in the ninth century. They were supposed to take place in 1923, but the Civil War intervened and they were postponed to 1924.

Gogarty was called in to plan the occasion. The guests he chose were 'the people who amuse me and I like, who have spoken out for Ireland at the time of the Troubles'. They included G. K. Chesterton, Compton Mackenzie, Augustus John and the Maharaja Sahib of Nawanagar, otherwise known as the cricketer Ranjit Sinjhi who was so impressed with Ireland that he would buy an estate in Connemara.

The Abbey performed three typical plays, including Yeats's *Cathleen Ní Houlihan*. Francis Stuart received one of the literary awards for his poetry. Already Stuart, who had been interned during the Civil War, felt loftily above it all. His character H 'had seen enough . . . to grasp the fact that it hadn't much to do with him after all. Under either de Valera or Griffith, art, religion and politics would still be run by those who at best used them to give them power, prestige and a good living, and at worst . . . as a means towards a sterile, high-toned conformism.' And yet Stuart knelt in front of Yeats who crowned him with a laurel wreath.

The streets were decorated with flowers and tricolours and the occasional Union Jack. Excursion trains brought in spectators. At Croke Park under the colours of the Tailte, blue and gold, the programme of games and events emulating the ancient Celtic festival included gymnastics, archery, handball, hurling, football and chess. Tiny tots in Irish costume competed in dancing. Aeroplanes performed acrobatics, while a choir of 600 voices sang the specially commissioned Ode which ended with the word '*Fáilte*'. John McCormack, an essential ingredient of Irish celebration, gave a concert.

But senior Republicans refused to attend, and in spite of lights, brass bands, sunshine and tubs of trees and flowers, the festival was not an unqualified success. Harold Speakman found the south and west of the country indifferent to the impending celebrations. A municipal strike involving 30,000 workers did not help. Unemployed men marched beside the Liffey holding placards: WE WANT WORK, NOT PAINT AND DECORATIONS. WE WANT FLOUR, NOT FLOWERS. V. S. Pritchett had noted that 'there were always ragged processions of protesters, on the general Irish ground that one must keep on screaming against life itself'.

Gogarty devised a tease, billeting Augustus John in Dunsany Castle; he told Lord Dunsany that John was an alcoholic and John that Dunsany was a strict teetotaller. John escaped by night and walked all the way to Dublin where he attended the banquet in Dublin Castle. Because of the strike all the lights went out; there was apprehension about the loyal toast, but when Tim Healy proposed it, everybody stood up, including Count McCormack, who, it was feared, might go on sitting.

Were the Tailteann Games a favourable omen for the new age of Irish freedom, or merely, as John described them, 'fatuous self-glorification'? Compton Mackenzie felt that the proceedings had been carried off with dash and imagination. They took place when the gloom was lifting, and the *Irish Times* had no doubt that they mirrored the national mood: 'During the last week the country seems to have shaken off a nightmare . . . once more people laugh in the streets, the furtive expression has disappeared from the faces of Irish crowds . . . Irish women have blossomed again like flowers . . . Irish men have discovered the dignity of the top hat.' De Valera's people abhorred this treacherous symbol. When Fianna Fáil came into power in 1932 great emphasis would be placed on the change to a simple lifestyle, symbolised by the absence of top hats.

But meanwhile Yeats's 'terrific' top hat was worn with panache and even Sean O'Casey was persuaded to don one: 'The terrible beauty of a tall-hat is born to Ireland.'

Like an Irish version of the Olympics the Games were revived at four-year intervals in 1928 and 1932 during the glorious summer when the Eucharistic Congress took place. The spectacle of Queen Maeve and her courtiers, together with some wolfhounds, parading in Croke Park made a striking contrast to the religious ceremonial that had preceeded it.

CHAPTER 8

A Small Eater was Admired

> Six of us slept in one bed. And we had no bedclothes, we mostly
> slept with me daddy's overcoat over you – sure the bed was
> loaded with boys and hoppers – you'd be scratching yourself.
> *Interview in* Dublin Tenement Life, *edited by Kevin Kearns*

In 1922 V. S. Pritchett visited Sean O'Casey in his tenement on the north side of Dublin. The fanlight over the door was broken and so were some windows. In O'Casey's ground-floor room where he did his writing were an unmade iron bed, a couple of tables on which he rested his books, some battered chairs and an oil-lamp for illumination. The Abbey faithfully reproduced this room in *The Shadow of a Gunman*. An old, damaged chimney-piece surrounded the smouldering coal-dust fire in the grate. Georgian houses were being stripped, as O'Casey's stage directions reveal. Hackers, developers and dealers were ripping out chimney-pieces, brass grates and carved staircases. Around this time the new Governor-General, Tim Healy, had replaced two ugly black mantelpieces in the official residence in the Phoenix Park with white Georgian chimney-pieces bought from a house in Mountjoy Square. When he ceased to be Governor-General he had to leave them behind and they are still in Áras an Uachtaráin.

On O'Casey's shabby wall hung a notice: GET ON WITH THE BLOODY PLAY. The play was *The Plough and the Stars*.

His family had shared the hardship of slum life in 'the piggeries' with the multitude. He knew the tenements well. He recalled the roughly cobbled streets deep in dust, strewn with empty matchboxes, scattered straw and paper, and covered with horse dung. Gas lamps were 'deformed from the play of children'. He was familiar with slum houses, 'a long lurching row of discontented incurables, smirched with the age-long marks of ague, fever, cancer and consumption, the soured tears of little children and the sighs of disappointed newly married girls'. He remembered how 'the doors were scarred with time's spit and anger's hasty knocking; the pillars by their sides were shaky, their stuccoed bloom long since peeled away; they looked like crutches keeping the trembling doors standing on their palsied feet.'

There was no plumbing in these buildings where the outside lavatory was shared by scores and slop buckets were hidden by curtains in the corners of rooms. The stench of urine and excrement was overwhelming.

Women went to great lengths to maintain some sort of order. The labours of Monday wash days with water hauled up from the yard and boiled, and sheets and garments hung out of windows, were necessary in the battle for cleanliness. Lily Foy, interviewed by Kevin Kearns, remembered her granny washing clothes, 'but the big vat of water was never thrown out. That water would be taken by a neighbour next door and they'd wash their clothes in it. And then they'd take that water and start at the top of the tenement house and scrub down the stairs. One woman would do her flight and another hers.'

When there was a large family, and usually there was, eighteen to twenty feet, most of them bare, brought mud and dust into a tenement room. The task of keeping it remotely clean required endless physical strength and dogged perseverance on the part of the woman of the house who was likely to be pregnant. For most of the time she washed herself and her family with the aid of jug and basin. The public baths at Tara Street or the Iveagh Baths were luxuries.

During the First World War, rents for slum premises had been frozen. Soldiers going off to fight were reassured that there would be no hardship imposed on families left behind or on themselves when they returned. This situation continued unchanged. Since rents continued to be kept low by law, landlords were generally impecunious, without the means to improve their rotting premises. However, the public perception of them was different; in 1926, *Dublin Opinion* portrayed a 'tenement king' in top hat and tails saying, 'Those three families I let the last room to are a rough lot.'

The Shadow of a Gunman appeared in 1923, marking O'Casey as a new and powerful voice in Irish theatre. In 1924 *Juno and the Paycock* restored the shaky fortunes of the Abbey Theatre. A fracas took place during the first run of *The Plough and the Stars* in February 1926 when a group of women and a man scrambled on to the stage; the man struck Maureen Delaney in the face and aimed a blow at May Craig. Barry Fitzgerald, who was Fluther, sent him sprawling into the wings.

The second run in May 1926 had the house booked out with applauding audiences for every performance. This was in spite of the presence of the usual Greek chorus of black-clad women carrying placards led by Mrs Sheehy-Skeffington. Apart from some stink bombs dropped from the balcony to the ground floor during the second act, everything went well.

Did the plays have their settings in the worst slums in Europe? Worse than the Gorbals or Granada? Thanks to O'Casey, the Dublin slums were the most famous.

Writing in the early thirties in the *Capuchin Annual*, the Reverend T. F. Ryan described how every year tourists in their hundreds sought to view Dublin's slums as one of the sights of the city: 'People give their instructions to the driver of the "jaunting car" telling him to be sure to bring them through some of the poorest streets . . . The routes vary, but practically all include the Coombe. Rarely are the very poorest streets actually included in the itinerary; but the visitors see enough to give them the thrill of horror they anticipated.'

For a time after O'Casey had brought the slums to the world's attention, the eyes of middle-class Dubliners were opened to the shocking conditions in their city. But they continued to ignore them. Father Ryan noted how so many citizens 'made it a point to avoid the poorer districts altogether . . . they talk of "fine old Georgian mansions" falling into decay; but they have never climbed the rickety stairs or penetrated into the rooms and cellars and the garrets that whole families call "Home".'

The new Government was either helpless or obdurate in the face of poverty. In 1924 old age pensions, given to those over seventy, and pensions for the blind were actually reduced. Unemployment rose steadily, while only 14,000 new houses were built from public subsidy between 1922 and 1929. Widows had no allowances; if they could not support them, their children were sent away to grim and squalid institutions which were workhouses under another name, where brothers and sisters would instantly be separated.

The slums of Dublin and those of other cities would exist for decades. In the forties Sean O'Faolain became nostalgic at encountering once again the slums of Cork with their 'hot verminous smell, indescribable and unique'. Recently, Frank McCourt has cast a lurid light on poverty in Limerick in the 1940s which had changed little from the city Robert Graves saw in 1919. Graves remembered, 'the door of a magnificent Georgian house flew open and out came, first a shower of slops, then a dog which lifted up its leg against a lamp-post, then a nearly naked girl-child who sat down in the gutter and rummaged in a heap of refuse for filthy pieces of bread; finally a donkey which began to bray'.

In the country the death rate was lower than in the cities, but the living was dire. The most baneful link with the past continued to be poverty. There were people alive who had been children during the Great Famine; many others had suffered hardship in the later years of the nineteenth century.

Patrick Kavanagh remembered bitterly the Monaghan of his boyhood where 'conditions on the small farm with families of ten and upwards were really dreadful . . . A small eater was admired.' In 1928 a member of Cork County Council described cabins in mountainous districts of the county 'with but a single small window not much larger than the porthole of an armoured car. An up-to-date farmer would not house his pigs in such a house while no man calling himself a sportsman would kennel his cur dog, not to say his game in similar conditions.'

Harold Speakman came across a cabin in Co. Galway with eleven people in one filthy room – an old woman, a young couple and their eight children, the oldest eight years old. The furniture consisted of three chairs. 'Little boys of assorted sizes, resting themselves first on one leg and then on the other, stood against the walls. They seemed to be waiting for something . . . there came to my mind the bizarre notion that they were waiting to grow up and go to America.'

Patricia Cockburn remembered Youghal in Co. Cork in the 1920s as being in 'a position of oriental and African poverty. Ragged, shoeless children ran about the streets, sallow hopeless men leaned against the houses all day. TB was rampant – though food was cheap . . . Most of the people out of work lived on potatoes with salted pig's cheek or crubeens on Sundays.' In the West, where crowds of visitors spent their holidays in order to imbibe Gaelic culture, Nicolette Devas was horrified by Lettermore and Carraroe, 'a poor land with poor crops . . . barefoot children in home-spun shifts'.

Since O'Casey's plays have become overfamiliar, we have forgotten the impact they made on audiences who had endured the events that formed the background to his tragedies. The poignancy of their plots hinged on deaths by violence. But death by other means would have been more familiar to tenement dwellers. Father Ryan observed that however large a family of children he encountered in the slums, 'how often, after the enumeration of the living is there . . . an addendum: "And I buried a little girl when she was two – she'd be thirteen now; and another little girl when she was eleven months – she'd be going on twelve; and a lovely baby boy of three months – he'd be nine and a half . . ."'

Children were more pragmatic; Mary Hanaphy, born in 1908, interviewed by Kevin Kearns, remembered how 'there were a lot of deaths . . . We just knew: "Oh, so and so is dead, and she's twelve."'

During the First World War, Æ had stated that it was decidedly more dangerous to be a baby in a Dublin slum than a soldier in France. Infant deaths in rural Ireland in 1926 were at a rate of 74.41 per thousand births. There was an exceptionally high rate in Dublin of 115 per thousand. One of the biggest killers of small children was gastroenteritis, a disease prevalent particularly in cities. Bottle-fed babies were prone to it (they still are in the Third World), and housing and poverty contributed, as did open lavatories and horse dung, playgrounds for flies. 'Summer diarrhoea' was fatal to young babies who were considered 'intractable to treatment' in spite of the efforts of doctors and medical students, teams of whom were on call during the summer months to rehydrate withered infants with drips.

Scarlet fever and diphtheria were huge problems; in Mary Hanaphy's family four out of nine died of diphtheria. Maternal mortality persisted, mostly from puerperal sepsis in those days before antibiotics. Typhoid lurked in infected water and milk; there were occasional cases of typhus caused by lice.

Writing of circumstances in the thirties and forties, Elaine Crowley described the regular fine combing and inspection of hair that was part of the louse hunt. 'I knelt . . . over a piece of white sheet . . . on to which fell generations of lice; the mother of them all, big, sated and dark grey, younger ones paler in colour and the infants so pale and minute as to be almost invisible. One after the other my mother cracked them between her thumb nails . . .'

Heads were shaved to deprive lice of habitat. According to Crowley, 'it wasn't unusual to see lice crawling on people in a bus, in Mass, on the face of a corpse. Fleas were gone before you saw them, leaving behind their small red bites. And bugs, if not already nesting behind the layer upon layer of wallpaper, came into one's home in second-hand furniture.' Another tenement problem was mice; cereals like porridge had to be constantly examined in case mouse droppings had spoilt them.

Half the population had no teeth. Shaw jeered that 'you teach your children to speak Gaelic, but you don't teach them how to keep their teeth to speak it with'. Frank McCourt remembered the teeth of the 1940s, 'brown and black . . . holes . . . big enough for a sparrow to raise a family'. Then the terrible false teeth: 'Dad claims these teeth were made for rich people in Dublin and didn't fit, so they were passed on to the poor in Limerick.' Mary Doolan, a Dubliner interviewed by Kevin Kearns, had a tooth pulled for one shilling. The dentist 'put his knee on me and pulled'. She rinsed out her mouth with Jeyes Fluid.

Scabies and impetigo, stimulated by dirt, made children ugly. Rickets, the result of a lack of vitamin D, left spindly, twisted legs. Harold Speakman came across three pretty girls in a mountainy district of Cork, all of whom had goitres because they lacked iodine. Trachoma was common.

Of the killers, tuberculosis, which thrived because of malnutrition and overcrowding, was the most feared. A diet of bread and tea and a single room occupied by eight or ten people provided ideal conditions for its spread. A man or woman dying of the disease, coughing all night, trembling from feverish sweats, would often be sharing the bed with other members of the family. Some houses where tuberculosis spread from one to another were known as 'coffin boxes'.

Everyone knew about the correlation between milk and disease which was a running joke in *Dublin Opinion*. (Milkman's Wife: 'Quick, quick, get a doctor! The baby's drunk some of the customers' milk!')

Alice Caulfield, interviewed by Kevin Kearns, had four sisters who were sent to die in the dreaded Pigeon House sanatorium in Ringsend, notorious for its processions of coffins. Not only at Ringsend, but all over the country, the sanatoria gave up their dead in droves. 'Coughin' in and coffin out,' they said.

At St Teresa's Sanatorium near Ballinrobe, converted from a big house from which a landlord family had departed, March and October were considered the worst months. At any one time up to twelve bodies would be lying in the morgue, once the Colonel's coach-house. Milk, eggs and fruit were served to the sick in gracious drawing-rooms. When St Teresa's went on fire, such was the dread of disease that it was difficult to find volunteers to deal with the flames. Such prejudice was universal; when the first pavilion for the sick at Peamount Hospital was built, a group of local men came and pulled it down.

Peamount at Newcastle Lyons, Co. Kildare, which had also been developed from a big house, was a model sanatorium where outdoor pavilions and a farm producing TB-free milk, fresh vegetables, fruit, honey and eggs combated the advance of the white plague. But lungs went on rotting until there was nothing left to breathe with.

Exasperated doctors tended to blame the sick for dying. Fearful of diagnosis, the stricken, often men with families, went on coughing up blood and failed to go to the doctor 'till forced to by weakness . . . too late for active treatment'. The County Medical officer in Co. Mayo complained how 'often patients present themselves at the tuberculosis dispensaries with double lung disease so advanced that death takes place in some instances six to eight weeks after the patient is first seen . . . The disease has been carefully concealed until the patient becomes moribund.'

So there were more black diamonds to be stitched on sleeves, and wakes to be held where the whiskey, clay pipes, snuff and shredded tobacco were laid out for all comers, each of whom took a symbolic sniff of snuff. There was more work for black-plumed horses pulling hearses carrying coffins, often oak, lined with white satin. They had been paid for with 'Society Money', carefully paid each week. Deep purple curtains around the glass were tied with black ribbons, and often a line of iron ivy leaves edged the roof. The horses' harness would be covered with black material. The hearse driver would wear a livery of a double-breasted black coat and a velour top hat; sometimes, if the corpse was a woman, a white band would be tied around it.

Funeral customs differed all over the country. In the Midlands the clocks were stopped in a house where someone died. At Kerry wakes, thirteen candles represented Our Lord and the twelve Apostles; one candle, the Judas candle, was left unlit. Graves were not opened on Good Friday or on any Monday except when a sod had been dug the previous day. Relatives were not allowed to place the last sod on the grave of a dead person. After the funeral the clothes of the dead were given away; the receiver of a dead man's suit was expected to wear it at least three times to Mass, and one of the Masses should be for the soul of the deceased

In spite of the dying and all the hardship, one of the enduring images in Dublin's tenements is of simple happiness. 'When I think of Clanbrassil Street and how it was when I was a child it seems it was always summer, the sun was always shining,' said one old lady. There was so much goodness sustained by a deeply held faith. Countless observers were amazed at the community spirit that kept these savagely poor people afloat. Elaine Crowley has movingly described how 'people were always slipping money to someone less well-off. Slipping shillings into hands, little parcels of food into shopping bags . . . "I made a mistake and bought too many eggs. I hope you won't be offended with a few." Or, if the gift was clothes: "My young wan has had a stretch. This won't go near her . . . It's a sin to throw it out." The gracious giving went on all over the city, all over the country. Money and food, clothes and time. Advice and consolation. People to sit with the dying, to sit all night with the bereaved, to go with you to see the doctor . . . to lend a pledge for the pawn. A woman on the estate kept "the dead bundle" – bed linen, candlesticks and a crucifix to lend to those who hadn't the means to wake their dead with dignity, asking only that the linen should be laundered.'

It was said that Dublin's poor, nearly all devout Catholics, were the Church's brightest ornament. The Ireland of the time was described as the Free State at Prayer. Arland Ussher, a Protestant, considered that 'the Irish people deserve high commendation for holding to the ancient faith in a world that has grown shoddy minded; for the Irish alone among the nations today, religion is still the central reality of life'.

The Irish were constantly praised for their adherence to the traditional values of the Church, which had been a cornerstone of their lives for generations. The authority of priests and bishops was unchallenged. Liam O'Flaherty wrote in 1930 how 'the power of the priests in Ireland has always been very great, and it is still as great as ever. Those foolish people who say that the priests are losing their power, make, in my opinion, a great mistake.' Remembering her youth, Mary Healy observed that 'we do not think the priests are infallible, but I think in those days the Catholic Church did think they were'.

In 1927 when Lawrence Cowen's play *Biddy*, which portrayed a money-grabbing priest, was performed in Limerick, there was a riot; the audience left the theatre except for a few who remained behind to sing 'Faith of our Fathers'. Commending these godly people in a sermon, a Limerick priest, Father Moriarty, declared that 'the priesthood is the sublimest office on earth. In it God has raised a mortal man to the height of His divinity . . . in the priesthood God has raised mortal man above kings and emperors, above angels and archangels.'

Writing in the *Capuchin Annual* about Castlegregory in West Kerry in 1930, the Very Reverend Canon Breen observed how 'in this parish women and girls and bareheaded boys reserve for the priest a salute . . . strangely and strongly reminiscent of the Fascist salute of which we saw so much in Rome'.

Canon Breen revelled in the link between himself and the 'fervent worshippers' of his parish, particularly at the Station Mass and Communion when the priest used a parishioner's swept, garnished, painted and beflowered house as a fitting place to say Mass: 'For priests and people the Stations are a boon bringing both into more intimate contact, establishing new ties of mutual knowledge and respect, affording opportunities to the aged and infirm to receive the Sacrament and to the priest to acquire the knowledge of his flock which Christ Himself teaches to be absolutely essential.'

Liam O'Flaherty's opinion of the motive and opinions of the priest was less lofty: 'He has an idea that Ireland is the only moral country in the world. And yet his personal view of the Irish people as individuals is a poor one. He is firmly convinced that the English people are immoral, principally on the score of lechery. The French are even worse. The Americans are very doubtful people on account of the facility for divorce in that country.'

The parish priest might be 'a stupid, good-natured sort of village tyrant' in O'Flaherty's opinion, but he was guardian and protector of his flock. From the pulpit he told them who to vote for and he denounced the party he did not favour. Usually he was conservative and authoritarian, interfering in the lives of his congregation, unafraid to use the threat of hell as a means of bringing them to heel. Certain topics in particular preoccupied his Church, in the knowledge that her people were in constant peril of damnation. The dangers arose from 'touching pitch'; reading a libidinous poem, joining in an indecorous game, meeting with Protestants, looking on at an immodest dance or laughing at an obscene song were the first steps on the road to hell. Rural dancehalls where 'dark rites' were enacted became an obsession among clerics who denounced them as 'synagogues of Satan'. Lenten pastorals attacked the dangers of bad books, the desecration of the Sabbath, motion pictures, habits of impurity and immodest dress.

In 1928 *Dublin Opinion* offered a joke in the form of a conversation between a modern young girl and her clerical uncle concerning strictures on female dress that bordered on the Muslim:

'Young girl, "Look here, Uncle, these dress regulations of the Bishops are intolerable."

'Uncle: "How so, my dear?"

'Young girl: quoting, "'Sleeves below the wrist, high collar to the ears and frock four inches below the knee.' Why we'd roast in summer!"

'Uncle: "Better roast for a few weeks than roast in eternity."'

When Lady Gregory saw *Tartuffe* in London she knew it would not do for Dublin. Tartuffe's objection to low-cut dresses 'would seem taken verbatim' from the bishops' pastorals.

The *Irish Ecclesiastical Record*, which conscientiously recorded the views of the Catholic Church, discussed subjects like capital punishment (fine – St Thomas Aquinas approved of it), cremation of an amputated limb, and the confessions of children (a priest must not lose patience, however tedious and repetitive they might be). Medical ethics were spelt out clearly. Even 'indirect' abortion was unlawful if the baptism of the child was put in doubt. Doctors had obligations to baptise a child, using a flow of water on the head, or failing that some part of the body. It was always preferable that a man should perform this function. Such baptism, which meant the salvation of the baby's soul, was always more important than the life of the mother. 'A woman, in undertaking the obligation of motherhood, has bound herself to undergo not merely the pains and dangers of confinement, but also whatever additional trials God might be pleased to send.'

By 1926 agitation for divorce had died down. Yeats had urged that 'it must depend upon a small minority which is content to remain a minority for a generation to insist on these questions being discussed'. But the Church insisted that in this matter there would be no talk of liberty of conscience. In 1926 the Reverend P. J. Gannon, SJ, put the position clearly in the *Irish Ecclesiastical Record*: 'Divorce in the Irish Free State today . . . is not only improbable, but unthinkable. Catholic legislators . . . could not pass any bill of divorce without violating a clear dictate of conscience . . . Catholics feel they can as little authorise divorce by law as they could perjury or robbery or murder.'

Education, health and welfare were under the control of the Catholic Church. Already, before the Free State came into existence, there was censorship of films and a Vigilance Committee to keep an eye on morals. In 1911 the *Catholic Bulletin* had been founded 'to warn Catholic faithful of immoral literature', but by the late twenties its chief role was to attack Protestant institutions like Trinity College Dublin, the Royal Dublin Society and W. B. Yeats. James Joyce and *Ulysses* also met with regular disapproval: 'this filthy writer', 'that muck heap'.

The Order of the Knights of Columbanus had been created in Belfast in 1915 to encourage 'fraternal charity and to develop practical Christianity among its members'. The order had a Masonic structure, and its activities, which attracted businessmen and men from the professions, were just as secretive as those of the Masons.

Dissidents fought back, often shrilly. Ireland, they claimed, was 'largely ruled by a priesthood and an atmosphere based on economic conditions of the medieval and Renaissance period'. A liberal periodical endorsed by Yeats, optimistically entitled *Tomorrow*, closed after two issues. Gogarty pointed out that 'almost all Irish priests are sons of well-to-do publicans, shopkeepers or gombeen men'. Francis Stuart sneered at the priest of the time 'with his stomachful of indigestible dogmatics and a half-starved mind, self-poisoned by the complementary toxins of love and authority and fear of its loss'.

Another critic was Sean O'Faolain. 'Catholic youths in my time did not normally talk to priests about their problems – their priests talked to them. This relationship was based on the postulate that while the Catholic religion is intellectually impregnable, the gift of faith is too tender a plant to be submitted to the cold winds of speculation.'

O'Faolain concluded that the caretaker of sacred mysteries enveloped in Latin to whom everyone bowed and touched their cap, 'black, tall, thin and straight as a lamppost', was himself a sacrificial victim. The power of the priest threatened loneliness to many an august figure who had voluntarily taken on a sacred social burden. Frank O'Connor's friend Father Traynor suffered from living in a 'priest-ridden country'. 'I can't ever get on a tram without some old man or woman getting up to offer me his seat. I can't go into a living room without knowing that all ordinary conversation stops, and when it starts again it is going to be intended for my ears.'

When O'Connor called Father Traynor a bloody fool, the priest said no one had called him that since he was sixteen.

The only jobs that O'Connor, whose real name was Michael O'Donovan, could find after his release from internment were among Protestants. For a while he taught in a small Protestant school in Cork whose headmaster told him, 'All the clergymen are the same, Mr O'Donovan . . . Catholic, Church of Ireland or Presbyterian . . . you can never trust any of them.'

With the help of Lennox Robinson who was (temporarily) Secretary to the Irish Carnegie United Kingdom Trust, O'Connor entered the library service. He worked in Sligo and later in Wicklow under the poet Geoffrey Phibbs, the son of a Sligo landowner; he and O'Connor became good friends in spite of Phibbs's 'natural contempt of the educated man for the self-educated'. They united in their efforts to stop the local priest closing down the Carnegie library. O'Connor had already encountered one young man complaining about an indecent book with a dirty word in it. The word was 'navel'.

Throughout the new State, libraries endowed by Andrew Carnegie were frowned on as being full of cheap nasty books. Librarians could not be too careful. The canny Scottish philanthropist had made it a condition of building his libraries that there should be some local contribution. This gave local committees considerable power to reject them. They disapproved of 'light magazines, novels . . . modern English fiction of the sensational kind . . . which have deadened and vulgarised the minds of the people'. Even Lady Gregory deplored 'the mass of rubbishy fiction they fill their shelves with'. At a meeting of one Carnegie Library Committee she objected to readers being supplied with books by Ethel M. Dell. She, herself, had not been allowed to read a novel until she was eighteen, and then only after the lamps were lit.

Carnegie libraries encouraged English work at the expense of Irish. Unfortunately, that was what readers wanted and continued to want. Examining a library catalogue of 1936, Hubert Butler found that ninety- four per cent of the books issued were fiction. 'Among the novels I found no book, banned or unbanned, by Mr O'Faolain or Mr O'Connor, whereas there were nineteen by Edgar Wallace and fifty-one by two ladies called Charlotte M. Brame and Effie A. Rowlands. They write about the sins of English peeresses . . . *Lady Brazil's Ordeal, Lady Darner's Secret, Lady Ethel's Whim, Lady Evelyn's Folly . . .*'

Outside libraries a certain amount of book burning took place. According to Benedict Kiely, when a butcher in Delvin burnt a copy of *The Valley of the Squinting Windows* an old lady said, 'Thank God, the trouble's over now. The book's burnt.' *The Oxford Book of Ballads* was publicly burnt by the Christian Brothers because it contained 'The Cherry Tree Carol', which concerned Joseph's irritability with the Incarnation. In Galway, books by Arnold Bennett, Victor Hugo and Shaw were destroyed by a priest, 'a nice young man with a fearful sense of his own importance, having had an uncle a Bishop'.

Newspapers were another danger to the soul. In 1925 *Irish Truth* wrote that there should be a Tariff Against Filth. 'Every Saturday night the decks of the cross-Channel steamers are piled high with "Sunday" papers compiled largely from pickings in the week's record of murder and lust abroad and at home . . . The lewd newspaper is a far greater danger than the public house. The poisoned minds are many times more numerous than the congested livers.'

Patrick Kavanagh wrote in *The Great Hunger* of Maguire and his people:

> Their intellectual life consisted in reading
> Reynolds News or the Sunday Dispatch.
> With sometimes an old almanac brought down from the ceiling
> Or a school reader brown with the droppings of thatch.

In 1929 the Censorship Board was established on the recommendation of the Evil Literature Committee to prohibit anything 'in general tendency indecent or obscene'. The first publication to be banned was a magazine called *Health and Strength* which had an article on nudity. Henceforth, newspapers would have regular weary headlines: BANNED BOOKS – A BATCH OF TEN. The first Irish novelist to be banned was Liam O'Flaherty who was extremely annoyed. 'The soutaned bullies of the Lord, fortressed in their dung-encrusted towns, hurl the accusation of sexual indecency at any book that might plant the desire for civilisation and freedom in the breasts of their wretched victims.'

Some of the excessive new puritanism arose from disgust with the past. In particular, for decades one of the shameful symbols of the Imperial presence in Ireland was the presence of the huge brothel area on the north side of Dublin, known after a number of name changes as 'Monto' after Montgomery Street situated in its core. The area had been tolerated, if not encouraged, as a place of rest and recreation for the huge numbers of British troops garrisoned in the city.

Monto might provide material for *Ulysses* and evoke wistful memories of the Hay Hotel in old bucks like Gogarty, but it would not be missed in the new Ireland. Most middle-class Dubliners had ignored it in the same way they ignored the slums. If they were to venture into the area insultingly situated right beside St Mary's Pro-Cathedral in Marlborough Street, they would be startled. 'In no other capital of Europe have I seen its equal,' wrote Halliday Sutherland. 'It was a street of Georgian houses and each one was a brothel. On the steps of every house women and girls, dressed in everything from evening dress to night dresses stood or sat.' Their clothes were kept clean by the madams who employed an average of seven or eight prostitutes, most of them women in their twenties. An old lady interviewed by Kevin Kearns felt no shame in coming from Monto, 'but the reputation was there, 'cause of the girls. In them years they were called "unfortunate girls". We never heard the word "whores", never heard "prostitutes". Very rarely you'd hear of a brothel, it was a "kip"; and the madams were called "kip-keepers". But the girls were very good, they were generous.'

According to Frank Duff, 'they ranged from beautiful, trim, elegantly dressed girls to the most awful specimens of the human race'. After the British sailed away came the man who was directly responsible for the reform of

Monto's prostitutes. Like the dogged penitent Matt Talbot, Frank Duff was a Dubliner with a working-class background. Both men aspired to sainthood, following different religious paths, Talbot wrapping himself in four chains, including one 'about the size of a horse's trace', Duff founding the Legion of Mary.

Within a year of its inception in 1921 the Legion had taken on the task of erasing Monto from the map of Dublin, an enterprise which the newly recruited Legionnaires, many of them devout young women, would relish. They were aware that persuading prostitutes to give up their old ways was not going to be easy. Understandably there was reluctance; some whores felt that the new Free State intended to lock them up for life.

In the 1940s Duff wrote a boisterous account of the early exploits of the Legion in its task of rescue, which met with the disapproval of the Archbishop of Dublin, John Charles McQuaid. Duff called Monto Bentley and his book *Bentley Place and Miracles on Tap* makes lively reading.

During the Legion's first mission a charabanc took a number of rescued girls from Myra House in the centre of Dublin out to a retreat at Baldoyle. As the girls boarded, a crowd gathered, singing 'Faith of our Fathers', while old women recited the rosary on their knees. 'Get in ladies, we are a bit late. We must be moving. Out of thirty-one we have twenty-three – our net . . . truly filled with big fishes. Who could have imagined it? Such a wondrous draught!'

The vividly coloured open charabanc with its fair penitents and Frank Duff sitting in the front by the driver stopped briefly at the Franciscan church of Adam and Eve on Merchants Quay, attracting the attention of some soldiers across the river who were pulling down the ruined walls of the Four Courts. Soon they were safely on their way over the Liffey, driving northwards to the Convent of the nervous Sacred Sisters of Charity at Baldoyle. 'Mother Angelo showed signs of double distress – her face was drawn and white. "Will we be murdered in our beds?"'

But the retreat was a resounding success. There was a day full of confessions. 'Surely no confessors ever before heard so extraordinary a story?' What gave particular pleasure was the conversion of two Protestants, one of whom retired to a Magdalen community 'where she has been distinguished for her holiness'.

The Legion investigated the whole area of Monto, finding dreadful things – a woman dying in bed, clutching a bottle; swarms of children used as messengers for buying cigarettes; five women encamped in the same bed – 'heads and legs protruded . . . at every angle! . . . We picked a head and gave a pull or two at the savage mop-like tangle at which the feline glory had been debased – Oh! when had it last been attacked by a comb?' There were encounters with whores, nearly always drunk; Tilly Smith, Katty Edwards, Marcella Dean, and the worst by far, Jess McGuinness, twenty-two years on the streets, saturated with methylated spirits, known as the Queen of the Spunkers.

The final closure of the infamous district was planned with the care of a military operation. On 23 February 1923, reformers and police moved in swiftly, arresting forty-five girls and many gentleman callers who were bundled into waiting lorries and brought to the Bridewell.

A procession passed through Monto with acolytes bearing candles, and every house was blessed. For the most notorious kip-houses a special ceremony took place in which a picture of the Sacred Heart was nailed to every door. One was reserved for a particularly fitting *coup de grâce* conducted by Duff himself. In his actions there was a suggestion of the book about the undead by another Dubliner, Bram Stoker. 'A table was placed against the wall and on the table a chair. It fell to my lot to climb on this chair, to drive a spike into the wall as high as I could stretch, and on that spike to hang a huge crucifix.'

CHAPTER 9

The White Blackbird

You see, your Irish Protestant is always in danger of feeling
himself the white blackbird. He realises that a native character is
as much associated with Catholicism as his own religion with
Ascendancy.

Monk Gibbon

Proddy Woddy on the wall
A half penny loaf will do ye all.

Traditional

The two Protestants most prominent in the Rising, Roger Casement and
Countess Markiewicz, converted to Catholicism after they were captured. In
both cases it was a symbolic gesture, following the new dictum expressed by an
earlier convert, Maud Gonne: 'My nation looks at God or truth through one
prism, the Catholic Religion.' To be Irish was to be Catholic. Later, Lady
Lavery and Mícheál Mac Liammóir, neither of whom were Irish born, would
follow their examples together with other foreigners who combined their new
Irishness with a place within the Roman Catholic Church.

In May 1918, Mrs Kathleen Clarke, Tom Clarke's widow, was taken to
England to Holloway Prison where she found herself locked up with Countess
Markiewicz and Maud Gonne, both of whom had dignified themselves with the
title 'Madam'. While walking around the prison yard they argued about their
status: 'Madam M claimed she was far above Madam MacBride; she belonged
to the inner circle of the Vice Regal set, while Madam MacBride was only on
the fringe of it.' The ladies' Catholicism did not impress Mrs Clarke. Catholics,
if they were Republicans, as Conor Cruise O'Brien has pointed out, 'took such
conversions simply as further establishing what very decent friendly
Protestants these people were'.

Mrs Clarke was pressed to feel her inferiority. 'When Madam Markiewicz did talk to me in those early days, I sensed a certain amount of patronage in her tone and manner . . . It appeared to worry her that such an insignificant little person as myself was put in prison with her . . . Her attitude was that the British were a blundering race of fools to arrest someone like me.'

When she was about to be released, Mrs Clarke was questioned about the difference between herself and the two other ladies. According to her own account, she told the matron of Holloway, 'I am Irish, and as such, knowing my country's history, how can I be other than hostile to my country's only enemy, England? The other two ladies . . . are of English descent . . . and they belong to what they call the Ascendancy or English element . . . They have identified with our struggle for freedom – but they naturally cannot feel the same hostility to England as I do.'

After the Civil War, Maud Gonne, together with Mrs Despard, set out to give trouble to the Free State. In 1923 they filled every room of their newly acquired Roebuck House, once the residence of the King family, with mattresses on which slept newly released prisoners. An ex-prisoner coming up the short drive seeking help would meet a number of untrustworthy dogs; having faced so many Cerberuses, he could walk in and ask for a meal or stay for as long as he liked. Later, Roebuck House was turned into a business centre to make money for deserving Republicans. Like the dogs, the favoured projects, which included floral shell decorations and potted preserves, betrayed Maud Gonne's Ascendancy origins. They made pure jam – one hundred per cent Irish, according to an advertisement in *An Poblacht*. Unsurprisingly, their attempts at industry ended in failure.

The two ladies showed constant antagonism towards the new Government. 'The Unionists and Free Staters have everything their own way,' said Mrs Despard. Roebuck House was constantly raided. When Maud Gonne was imprisoned once again, Mrs Despard kept up a lonely vigil outside Mountjoy Gaol, sitting on a chair. When Gonne addressed a crowd near Parnell's monument in 1927, eighteen-year-old Francis MacManus heard 'a voice that no man forgets. Never had I heard a voice like it, not from any other woman, unless perhaps from one of the renowned Abbey actresses.' He felt 'Dublin was the battlement on which she, Helen, walked triumphant.'

There were more raids, and in 1931 a force of armed CID men turned Roebuck House inside out. Nothing quenched the ladies' spirits. When Mrs Despard retired to the North of Ireland to instigate civil disobedience up there, she wrote, 'People think that because of my age I should take things easy. Why should I? I find life interesting, even at ninety-two, and beautiful.'

Constance Markiewicz had died in 1928 in the public ward of St Vincent's Hospital at the age of fifty-two. The Government, which had imprisoned her as it imprisoned Maud Gonne, refused to give her a state funeral. But more than 100,000 people turned out to see her coffin, together with seven bands and eighty lorry loads of flowers, pass on its way to Glasnevin. Who could forget the enduring image of the Countess in her protective role of helping the poor? As

Brian MacMahon described her, 'she could be found dressed in a smeared apron, whitewashing a latrine in the slums, pausing only to take out a gold cigarette case and from it extract her final Woodbine'. Even a critic like Lady Ardilaun admitted that 'there was something gallant about her. We were each working for what we believed would help Ireland.'

Others felt a desire to be associated with the new Ireland. Edith Somerville declared of her ancestry, 'I don't mind if you say British, if you like, but the only trickle of English blood comes from one marriage. My family has eaten Irish food and shared Irish life for nearly three hundred years, and if that doesn't make me Irish I might as well say I was Scotch or Norman or Pre-Diluvian.' But she was not prepared to go as far as becoming Catholic.

For all the brave posturing of Gonne and Markiewicz, Lady Gregory did as much for the cause of Nationalism, although she did not flaunt her Republican beliefs. Perhaps because she remained a staunch Protestant, driving to Sunday Matins whenever the weather permitted, she came to symbolise the fading Ascendancy. She is remembered as Sean O'Casey saw her, 'mistress of a grand house, dying reluctantly, filled a little too full with things brought from all quarters of the known world'.

O'Casey paid his first visit to Coole in 1923. He himself came from the opposite end of the Protestant spectrum. When he was a boy he had questioned his mother:

– But we're not really Irish, Ma, not really . . . ?

– Not Irish . . . of course we're Irish. What on earth put it into your head that we weren't Irish?

– One day, an' us playin', Kelly told me that us Catholics were really Irish; an' as we were Protestants, we couldn't anyway near be Irish.

– Th'ignorant cheeky little Roman Catholic scut . . . if your poor father was alive, he'd show you in books solid arguments . . . that St Patrick was really as Protestant as a Protestant can be.

After the founding of the new State the question of identity caused uncertainty among Protestants of every sort. The shrinking Loyalist world felt it had little to celebrate. Hubert Butler has written of 'the bitter cynicism and despair which devastated the greater part of the Irish Ascendancy class in the twenties', adding that many treated 'as a personal grievance disasters whose origins were in Irish history'. (In Paris Vladimir Nabokov felt contempt for the attitudes of the dispossessed, the emigré who 'hated the Reds' because they 'stole' his money and land.) But whatever their mental miseries and their disdain for the new order, for the comfortably rich bourgeoisie and the remaining owners of country houses life relapsed into pleasant old ways.

For other Protestants less comfortably situated it was not so easy. On 12 July 1924 the Deputy Grand-Master of the Co. Monaghan Lodge addressed a local Orange rally: 'We are now citizens of the Irish Free State . . . the Government has been forced upon us against our will – we did not ask for it; we did not want it. Now that we are living under it, we are all determined to do the best we can and support it.'

Small farmers and shopkeepers strove to find a place in the new order. The future Dean of St Patrick's Cathedral belonged to this sizeable and often forgotten group. Victor Griffin's father was a grocer in Carnew, Co. Wicklow. The family was on good terms with the Catholics among whom it lived, visiting freely and sharing their lives. Other matters were avoided. 'Keep your head down, look after your family and business, avoid religion and politics in conversation with your RC neighbours – this was the Protestant manifesto.' While they still belonged to the Unionist tradition, this did not mean they felt cut off from being equally Irish in the widest sense of the term.

Griffin concluded that 'whatever crisis of identity the Ascendancy may have had, the ordinary Irish Protestant, farmer or businessman, had no doubts that he was thoroughly Irish, though he may have secretly regretted the ending of the British connection and his political separation from the United Kingdom under the Crown'.

At the same time, given the anguish of the Troubles, there was need for caution. 'I remember my mother warning me, "Victor, steer clear of religion and politics – you'll get us all burnt out if you go on saying things like that."'

It was a question of acceptance – either clear out or shut up. Between 1911 and 1926 the Protestant population of the Twenty-six Counties fell from 327,000 to 221,000. But plenty chose to stay. Some of the reluctance of many Loyalists to leave Ireland for the mother country may have been due to feelings similar to those expressed by Arland Ussher: 'I have always been depressed in England . . . There are probably at least as many intelligent people to the square mile there as anywhere else. I think it's the pressure of the national will weighing you down, as tight as a clenched fist . . . an instinctive "norm" which mustn't be departed from. It's in the air, like a "Thou Shalt", here there's only a "Thou shalt not", which is simpler.'

Some of those who had already departed even returned from England. When Norah Robertson's family reversed the trend and took a house in Raglan Road, 'windows flew up and colonels' and old ladies' heads popped out to see the strange sight . . . it almost affected the property market that anyone for no reason should come and live in Dublin'. A considerable number of Protestants were still to be found in Dublin suburbs like Rathgar and Rathmines, while the seaside town of Greystones had a freak majority – fifty-seven per cent, including a vigorous group of Plymouth Brethren.

There was inevitably a sense of disillusionment and regret for the past. Mourning her burnt house and the loss of society, Lady Ardilaun lamented, 'Those nice young officers . . . our class has gone and who is there to replace it?' Her sentiments were echoed by Maud Wynne: 'Where could one live in Ireland now, but in the tragic past of horrors, for the present is also one of gloom. All the fun and laughter of old times is gone.'

With the departure of the British Army from garrison towns, there was a chronic shortage of suitable partners at hunt balls. Patricia Cockburn remembered attending one at Dromana, in the great circular ballroom that hung over the Blackwater. Even with 300 guests it was considered a flop, because, as the host put it, 'They looked like flies in Waterloo Station.'

When the old warhorse Sir Henry Robinson returned to Ireland in the mid-twenties, he noticed a general air of shabbiness and lack of prosperity: 'The people with money have been destroyed, their place taken by a new class, careful about their money and niggardly about tips.' He encountered a former captain in the Free State Army now employed as a lift boy: '"I'm not a snob. But I declare to goodness ye couldn't but pity me if ye see the class of people I have to bring up in the lift these days."'

After 1918, Unionists came to be known as Loyalists. A popular image of the time was of a group of elderly Loyalists in Ballsbridge or some other prosperous Dublin suburb, sitting down to tea and home-made jam and rubbishing everything the new Government stood for. They sneered at the new Ministers and their education (National University instead of Trinity); they speculated as to whether the interlopers ate peas with a knife or knew how to tackle an oyster. They condemned the brogue. Accent has always been a sore spot in society; in 1998 the *Irish Times* reported how middle-class Dubliners were sending their children to Protestant schools so that they could learn to speak properly.

In the new State there was a reluctance among many Loyalists to accept the new ways. They provoked fearsome disputes about whether or not they should pray for the King in church. Flag trouble would continue for decades. The riots of 11 November almost became a tradition, with poppies being snatched, baton charges and Union Jacks cut down and burnt. When the Kildare Street Club (described by Lady Gregory as 'that exclusive Seat of the Scornful') flew the Union Jack for Armistice Day in 1925, a group of women led by Mrs Sheehy-Skeffington rushed in to remove it; after a tussle, it was wrested from them.

In 1926, to avoid trouble, the club devised a flag of its own which consisted of St Patrick's cross combined with the club badge. Not only was it flown on the King's birthday and Empire Day, but it was also hoisted at the centenary of Catholic Emancipation and during the Eucharistic Congress, a gesture that earned fleeting popularity.

The isolation of Protestants was felt in every class and place and would continue. They were perceived as always being richer than their fellow countrymen, as landlords, prosperous shopkeepers and big farmers. A common answer when someone asked about the health of an acquaintance was, 'I'm as strong as a Protestant but not so rich.' A Dubliner, remembering the fifties, recalled how 'the people were very neighbourly, but they didn't really make friends with us'. Protestants were apart, and there was the idea that they were 'better – more genuine . . . much more truthful, more honest and more upright' than the Catholics.

The old man who repeated this myth to me was a Catholic; he remembered that in the West Cork town where he lived he was not allowed to attend Protestant dances. It was the Protestants who kept him out; the clergyman would take any young Catholic who tried to enter by the shoulder and order him to leave. This worked the other way. Holy men in general were determined to keep the young apart; the fear was that contact afforded opportunities for mixed marriages that began with the intimacies of the dance floor.

Ne Temere, the papal decree on mixed marriages which stated that children of such a union should be brought up as Catholics, was proclaimed in 1910. In 1911, a resolution passed at the Assembly Hall in Belfast at a meeting attended by 6,000 people, stated that it would cause bitterness and sectarian hatred. By the mid-twenties, not only was that Belfast assembly proved right, but the strict application of *Ne Temere* was also having its effect on Protestant numbers.

All sides deplored mixed marriages which brought endless unhappiness. Some Protestant households threw out children (usually sons) who married Catholics and never spoke to them again. In the *Irish Ecclesiastical Record* the Reverend T. J. Hein, SJ, criticised young Catholic men or women attending dances, parties and tennis matches where they frequently met Protestants who were socially 'better off'. 'Add a little carelessness or want of foresight on the Catholic's part in not nipping in the bud the growing intimacy . . .' He believed that Catholics had emerged from the ranks of 'hewers of wood and drawers of water' and lost 'simple virtues'. They tended to be ashamed of their humble parents and dazzled by the social superiority of conniving members of a faith who were all damned.

Outside the Catholic Church there was no salvation. There was the constant danger of the perversion of a Catholic party in a mixed marriage, while the children of this union were also exposed to damnation. Such unions were against the divine law itself.

Father Hein put the hypothetical cases of Jane and Mary. Jane, having been refused a dispensation by her priest, marries in a registry office. 'Her married life becomes a sequence of formal mortal sins. As long as the irregular union continues she cannot make her peace with God . . . She abandons all practice of her faith, thus piling sin on sin.' Meanwhile her pious friend Mary, who has also been refused a dispensation, gives up all idea of marriage. The best solution for both women and for other young Catholics was to aim for 'greater simplicity of life, especially among middle-class Catholics', and avoid Protestants altogether.

'You're a proper little Protestant', would be said by a mother if a baby had to be taken out of Mass for crying. Patrick Campbell spoke of his father's attitude: 'I came from a Protestant home wherein Catholicism and all its works were condemned. "The bottomless squalor of Roman Catholic superstition," my father, half in jest, would say.'

Since in the new State a knowledge of Irish was an essential qualification for a wide range of employment, most Protestants were caught out at a disadvantage. Few of them had taken part in the Gaelic Revival. They had no enthusiasm for Gaelic games. Even Terry Trench, a patriot in every other way, who had learnt Irish and taken up Irish dancing, did not care for hurley: 'It was such a filthy game with players attacking each other with their own *camáin* – I never wanted to see it again.'

In the past little or no Irish had been taught in Church of Ireland schools. Lady Gordon remembered that to belong to the Gaelic League was to be a social outcast; among Unionists 'never did they show any sympathy for those of their countrymen who were struggling to develop the soul of Ireland'. Now Protestant teachers were told suddenly that Irish was compulsory in the educational system. For several years after the campaign for the introduction of Irish into so many aspects of the economic and cultural life of the nation, the Church of Ireland Training College for teachers had the greatest difficulty in obtaining enough candidates to pass examinations in Irish. Even the head of the CITC, the Reverend Kingsmill Moore, confessed that his Irish vocabulary 'could be exhausted by my ten fingers'.

In 1926 the Government introduced seven preparatory colleges in which pupils were offered free secondary education through Irish provided they agreed to become teachers. One of them, Coláiste Mobhi in Glasnevin, was assigned to Protestant teachers, both men and women. Gradually their schools accepted what they described as 'the yoke' of compulsory Irish, though they were seldom ardent. The *Catholic Bulletin* sneered, 'If there are among Protestant schools and teachers enthusiastic workers for the Irish Revival and Restoration movement, these enthusiasts are rather shy.'

The Church of Ireland Archbishop Gregg tried to rally reluctant Gaelic speakers. In 1927 he stated, 'I do not pretend to like compulsory Irish in our national schools. I think it is a bad policy but . . . I would rather see it taught well than ill . . . If the path to [Government] positions is along the thorny track of Irish grammar, Irish cannot be altogether an uneconomic subject of study when it makes the difference between employment and unemployment.'

Dr Gregg was obsessed by the position of his flock in the new Ireland; in 1922 he had led a deputation to Michael Collins which asked whether Protestants 'were permitted to live in Ireland, or if it was desired that they should leave the country'.

Protestants continued to make further trouble for themselves by their own social divisions. The poet Geoffrey Phibbs, who came from a landowning background, despised Yeats because his family had been in trade. The middle classes were particularly conscious of their places in the social hierarchy. Wine merchants, distillery owners and brewers might struggle up the ladder, while those in drapery and grocery might not. Members of the Guinness or Jameson families were members of the élite. Barristers were socially accepted, solicitors not. In Molly Keane's *Good Behaviour*, the girl from the big house receives a proposal from the local solicitor. 'You must be out of your mind,' she replies. In his autobiographical novel, *A Fretful Midge*, Terence de Vere White tells how as a young solicitor he called on a client:

'"My parents would not have allowed a solicitor to sit up with them in the drawing room."

'"I suppose not."

'"When the solicitor called the butler used to show him into a room off the hall. Then to our intense surprise my eldest sister became engaged to him – the solicitor, I mean, not the butler . . . My parents were very good about it – nowadays one cannot be so particular." '

On Sean O'Casey's visit to Coole he was nervous when Lady Gregory met him with her side-car at Athenry: 'Look at her there with all her elegance, well at ease among the chattering crowd of common people; so why shouldn't I be steady in my mind at coming to a big house amongst rare silver and the best of china, sleeping in a bounteous bed and handling divers tools at food never seen before.'

He was not made welcome by the maid who opened the front door. 'Great playwright? I'll give him great playwright. What right at all has a man like that to come into Coole without a tie on his collar, nor a collar on his shirt?'

At table Lady Gregory, 'snapping a finger against a tiny Burmese gong that gave a soft penetrating sound', offered tips on table manners, 'she in simple and most gracious ways showing how things were handled; pointing out that dese things were done, not because of any ceremony, but because dey made one more comfortable, and made things easier to eat'.

At the end of her life, when she felt the house would not long outlast her, Lady Gregory left an obsessive account of Coole, describing it room by room. In the drawing-room with its great windows opening on to the lawn she was accustomed to write sitting at her Empire desk; when an Irregular threatened her life she told him that was where she would be. On the bookshelves were books given by their authors, ranging from Kingslake's *Invasion of the Crimea* in nine volumes to works by Æ, Edward Martyn and Yeats, and James Joyce's *Chamber Music*. In boxes and caskets she kept letters from writers and artists, O'Casey, Henry James, Augustus John, Patrick Pearse and Thomas MacDonagh among them.

Her favourite room was the library with its lines of leather-bound volumes and curtains made from the tent of the Maharaja of Cawnpore. Books and trees were her chief charmers, as O'Casey noted.

A different impression was given four years after his visit by Nicolette Devas, who in 1928 saw only dilapidation and gloom. 'Badly sited' Coole 'squatted dismally on a piece of flat land with trees dripping too close to the house – the famous lake was masked from the house by more trees'.

Devas did not care for the interior that Lady Gregory (whom she considered a 'hooded crow') had so lovingly catalogued. 'I was shown some mildewy and peeling Canaletto paintings hanging crookedly on the wall; a curious trait found in Ireland is . . . a kind of arrogance that prevents people using a tin opener rather than the handle of a Georgian silver spoon. The Canalettos were in such a bad condition that I wondered if they were genuine . . . but then in the moist Irish air everything grows moss, from period furniture to leather shoes.'

She was disgusted by the way her hostess spoilt Yeats. Lady Gregory herself admitted to copying out at Yeats's dictation, 'blackening my fingers as I changed the ribbon of my Remington, or forgetting to reverse the carriage so that the ribbon was in holes through standing still'. Devas was 'deeply shocked by the servile way she waited on him at tea; getting up to place his cup at a certain exact spot'.

In 1927 the Coole estate had been sold to the Forestry Department and Lady Gregory became a tenant; it was her misfortune that her daughter-in-law and grandchildren would not take over their inheritance. She maintained, however, a touching and misguided hope that what she had struggled all her life to maintain would be preserved. In her journal for 20 October 1927 she wrote, 'Today Mr Reed of the Land Commission and Mr Donovan of the Forestry Department came and formally took over Coole . . . It no longer belongs to anyone of our family and name . . . Giving it into the hands of the Forestry people will make the maintenance and improvements of the woods secure and will give employment and be for the good and dignity of the country. As for the house I will stay and keep it as the children's home as long as I keep strength.'

She died four years later. The woods and walled garden of Coole would be preserved, but the house, which Yeats saw as the symbol of doomed aristocratic virtues, would be destroyed, one of hundreds of great casualties.

But there were survivors, among both big houses and their occupants. Those who were wealthy and prepared to accept the changes found that living in the new State was very pleasant. Well-to-do Protestants did not worry about having to learn Irish; their children were either educated in England or in schools in Ireland where the problem could be sidestepped or ignored. They were resigned to the fact that they were unlikely to be seeking positions in the Irish Civil Service. 'There is no chance of any young men of our own class getting employment,' lamented Lady Ardilaun. 'Genteel Proddies – long ceremonial faces' seen by Signe Toksvig were not unduly concerned with the injustices of censorship; many of them would not read those banned books in any case. They did not engage in politics, apart from those who were offered places in the unpopular Senate.

Many Protestant Senators were annoyed with Yeats's speech on the legislation prohibiting divorce. What right had the poet to include them in his pronouncement that 'We are not a petty people'? Rather than being associated with Burke and Tone, they only wished for a quiet life. They wanted to live comfortably in the Free State, keeping a low profile. They murmured in protest when Yeats made such statements as 'The whole system of Irish Catholicism pulls down the able and well-born, if it pulls up the peasant, as I think it does. A long continuity of culture like that at Coole could never have arisen, and never has arisen, in single Catholic families since the Middle Ages.'

When the Censorship Board was set up in 1929, there was little opposition from Protestant ecclesiastics who ignored the sentiment expressed in the *Irish Times*: 'Can we imagine a more precious concern for the Protestant churches than the assertion of their right to think for themselves?' Many Protestants opposed immorality just as fiercely as Catholics; in 1925 a bishop addressed a Mothers' Union to declare 'that the immoral person should be treated, not as at present just as a sinner, but as a criminal, and should receive the punishment meted to other criminals such as robbers or forgers or murderers'.

It was better to ignore controversy. Middle-class Protestants in Dublin lived in comfort, bolstered by servants whose wages were low. In the country there was hunting, shooting and fishing. Huntsmen echoed the prayer quoted at the retirement of the Misses Beresford as joint masters of the Waterford Hunt in 1926: 'Hounds stout and horses healthy, earth well stopped and foxes plenty.'

At many winter hunt balls music was provided by an amateur band run by a master of foxhounds who kept his hounds fed with the fees he earned from his waltzes and jazz. For the young at heart these balls provided frenetic entertainment, and afterwards much scuffling in bedrooms and the butler bringing up champagne late in the morning. During Horse Show Week balls, similar bedroom entertainment took place in the Shelbourne. There was much drinking; one lady used to turn cartwheels on a dining-room table in the hotel. Elsewhere, another used to get so drunk that she was never invited to the receptions at Spike Island given by the British Navy. It all sounds like Happy Valley.

Hunt balls offered 'a phantasmagoria of lights, laughter, mischief and reckless gaiety – lean hunting girls who could speak to Galway without using a telephone, and their bronzed menfolk; an Irish peeress or two with the Irish predominating triumphantly over the peeress; sleek, well-groomed doctors; barristers from Fitzwilliam Street and Merrion Square . . .'

Patricia Cockburn compared her upbringing in the twenties to belonging to a caste system, maintaining that the Anglo-Irish she lived among behaved like 'white settlers in a colonial country'. Nicolette Devas considered women of the landed gentry 'a feudal race of he-women . . . loud voiced, aggressive and brutally outspoken (a spade is called a bloody shovel). The children are treated like gun dogs.'

Problems of the new State could be ignored, as is indicated by a review of 'an Irish Sporting Novel' in May 1926. Molly Keane's *The Knight of the Cheerful Countenance*, published, like all her early books, under the pseudonym of M. J. Farrell (which she had taken from a name over a pub door), was deemed by a reviewer in the *Irish Times* to be 'very entertaining . . . A background of the troubled political conditions prevailing after the establishment of the Free State is vaguely indicated, but does not seem to concern the chief characters in the story very much, unless as a subject of sympathetic small talk to smooth the ways of highly important matters connected with horse dealing.' In the following years M. J. Farrell, or Molly Keane, would continue to write of this inward-looking world.

Aloofness characterised this society, taken to extremes by Mrs Ruth in Co. Kerry: 'When a servant returned from Killorglin with groceries and came to her with change, she would refuse to take any coins in her hand without first donning a glove.' Many still looked for servants of their own persuasion. 'Wanted: experienced single Protestant groom-chauffeur must be a good driver.' . . . 'Can Lady recommend superior young Protestant housemaid for near Dundalk?'

To many Catholics, 'Protestants were very definitely above you, snooty and potatoish in their speech'. Brian Inglis tells how the Protestants of Malahide 'spoke "U" English and only cultivated an Irish accent to tell Paddy and Mick jokes . . . We did not have Irish accents; only an Irish lilt, often a matter of a turn of phrase . . . Some of us have passed for English, except under the scrutiny of Henry Higgins.'

I belonged to this comfortable world. I was born in 1928 in the appropriately named Hatch Street Nursing Home – the street was laid out in the eighteenth century by Sir John Hatch. In the same year, Lady Gregory considered that 'Ireland is, I think, happier than a year ago; the politicians less harsh, though that terrible murder of K. O'Higgins stirred up the old bitterness . . . the Civic Guard have almost done away with those small robberies and personal attacks that had outlasted the Treaty and Civil War.'

From my top-floor nursery window in one of the 'dingy long-faced solemn houses' (Signe Toksvig's opinion) in Fitzwilliam Place, I could look out on the tranquil tree-lined waters of the Grand Canal where canal boats were slowly propelled by barge horses along the mud tow-path. On the street in Fitzwilliam Place an old man played the barrel-organ. The slums were not far away.

Dressed in buttoned gaiters, I attended a nursery school in Clyde Road. Nightingale Hall was mixed – at least, the sexes were. Not long before I went there it had been run on strictly Loyalist lines with a great parade on Empire Day, but since then much had changed. Pupils were no longer required to chant:

> Now first its triple colours mark,
> High meaning in each hue;
> Red flame of love; white blameless life
> Beneath hope's heavenly blue;
> Then bear these colours joyously
> Through threatening clouds of black;
> For you're a little British boy
> And here's your Union Jack.

In preparatory schools like Baymount which I attended later, the Union Jack continued to be raised on suitable occasions. Sometimes a member of the Garda Síochána would cycle up the avenue to request that it be lowered. Small exclusive schools continued to emphasise division, nostalgia for the past and a link with Great Britain – Miss Ahern's Junior School, which one of its pupils, Brian Inglis, described as 'an impeccably English establishment'; Baymount in Dollymount; Castlepark in Dalkey, where one boy was punished for peeing the headmaster's name against a wall; and for girls, Knockrabo in Dundrum and the French School in Bray. The curricula did not usually include Irish history, although we were taught plenty of the English variety. 'The end product of this upbringing and education,' concluded Inglis, 'was not readily distinguishable from an Englishman.'

George White, who attended Baymount, wondered whether the homesickness generated in such schools was not too high a price to pay for the privilege of being well taught in the exclusive company of 'sons of gentlemen'. The aim of such preparatory schools was to coach boys for Common Entrance and further years of misery at English public schools. If parents could not afford English fees, there was always St Columba's College in Rathfarnham which aimed vaguely at inculcating a sense of Irishness in these pseudo-English young gentlemen, or Portora near Enniskillen, renowned chiefly for rowing and for including Samuel Beckett among its past pupils. Until recently, another past pupil, Oscar Wilde, had his name expunged from the list of old boys.

Affluent Catholics had a mirror image of this misguided educational system with prep schools whose aim was to send boys to English Catholic public schools like Downside and Ampleforth. Those who stayed at home might attend Glenstal, run by the Benedictines, or Clongowes Wood where James Joyce had been a pupil, imbibing a system of education 'based on those sound principles which have directed Jesuit Education for Four Centuries'.

St Gerard's, 'a Catholic school for the sons of gentlemen', was unusual in being run by the laity, apart from the resident chaplain who was appointed by the Archbishop of Dublin. Its prospectus, offering such garrison games as rugby, hockey, tennis, cricket, Swedish drill, swimming and badminton, was indistinguishable from that of similar Protestant establishments.

Very few schools crossed the divide and welcomed all denominations and religions. Wesley provided education for Methodists and also attracted members of the Jewish community. The Quakers had inter-denominational schools like Monkstown Quaker Hall and Newtown in Waterford which were also unusual for being coeducational. St Brendan's, founded in 1919 by Frank Stephens, a nephew of J. M. Synge, was also coeducational; it had no corporal punishment, attendance at classes was optional, and boys and girls were encouraged to seek out their own variety of freedom. The school did not last long.

At a time of increasing clerical control and religious division, Sandford Park was remarkable. Begun by Mr Le Peton in the significant year of 1922, it appealed to those few liberally minded people who wanted their children to be educated without being suffocated by conformist principles. Conor Cruise O'Brien went there; so did the fatherless Owen Sheehy-Skeffington, whose family was also divided by religion: 'he thought he would never be so happy again anywhere'.

Naturally the educational split affected teachers. When Patrick Lindsay applied to join the Royal School in Navan as a classics master, his interview included the question 'had I ever ridden with the Galway Blazers? I was told that there were three services the following morning – Church of Ireland, Presbyterian and Methodist. "I am a Papist – what time is the last Mass?" The blood drained from their faces. How could a man with the name of Lindsay be Catholic? The headmaster said nothing, but he was deeply shocked. This was Ireland of the 1930s . . . a small number of people, on learning that I was a Catholic, treated me almost as if I was a leper.' Lindsay subsequently taught at Sandford Park and shared Owen Sheehy-Skeffington's delight in an atmosphere free of religious bigotry.

Trinity College Dublin was disliked by the Catholic Church, by the State and by the majority of Irish people who considered it an alien institution, a corner of a foreign field that was forever England. Its Elizabethan charter, silver plate and entrenched attitudes were condemned. The fact that the Provost was always a Protestant – 'no Papist need apply' – was a perpetual bone of contention. The appointment of the Gaelic scholar Dr E. R. Gwynn in 1927 changed nothing. In the twenties and thirties Trinity adhered to the old ways, continuing to fly the Union Jack on suitable occasions, and drinking loyal toasts. Students went around on Armistice Day wearing poppies and singing 'God Save the King'. In 1929 James MacNeill, who had succeeded Tim Healy as Governor-General, refused to attend Trinity Races because the college authorities insisted on playing 'God Save the King' instead of 'The Soldier's Song'.

The Catholic Church discouraged attendance at Trinity by its flock. A letter by Monsignor Walsh to the *Irish Times* in 1930 made the position quite clear: 'There is, I believe, a considerable number of Catholic students at present attending Trinity College. The College naturally welcomes them; for otherwise her halls would not be full . . . Catholic students who attend Trinity College do so despite the grave warnings of their bishops and in disregard of their opposition and that of the Holy See . . . I may add that the Church, far from moderating her attitude towards Trinity, has become stronger and more stern in her opposition . . . Another University is now available . . . Catholic . . . in tradition and atmosphere.'

The *Catholic Bulletin* was cruder in its condemnation of 'the Catholic "rats" who take the worthless Entrance examinations, the feeble scholarship tests and the ignoble and low-grade degrees put before them in Trinity College'.

The Jesuit schools, Clongowes and Belvedere, refused to be discouraged by such opinions and allowed their pupils to attend Trinity. Not all students were intransigent Loyalists. There was a new Gaelic Society, encouraged by the Provost, and a hurling club, although some verse in the college magazine praising it was found to be in the form of an acrostic which read 'This is all balls'.

'Most of my contemporaries were moderate supporters of the Cosgrave Government,' reported Terence de Vere White, who read law in Trinity. One wonders if in Catholic eyes Dr Noel Browne's opposition to Catholic interference in Irish political affairs could have been blamed on his sojourn there. After attending the university Lionel Fleming changed his views: 'I was aware that there was a stirring in myself and a half-conscious wish for identification with a people who seemed, in spite of every difference, to be my own. It is hard in retrospect to be sure how these things happened . . . it could not be denied that there had been a certain glamour about the Rising; it was rather nice to think that the self-assured English had been pushed out of the country and that it was quite possible to thumb one's noses at them.'

Those Protestants who did not aspire to attend Trinity had fewer intellectual choices. Brought up in a farming community in Wicklow, Victor Griffin was constantly made aware of the religious divide. There was the constant threat imposed by *Ne Temere*, and the occasions when one of their people succumbed to its rules. 'This was spoken of by Protestants in whispers, a certain embarrassment, a feeling of being let down, of one of our own going over to the enemy.' However much they wished to be equally recognised as Irish men and women and felt themselves part of the Irish nation, the reality was very different. 'We were seen as outsiders, not truly Irish, in the nation but not of it. To be Irish meant being RC, Nationalist, Gaelic and anti-English.'

In the years to come their co-religionists in the North of Ireland observed the decline of their Southern kin. 'As a result, the Protestant community as a whole opted out of the political scene – this passive, almost subservient attitude had an unfortunate effect on the RC community and the Northern Protestants.'

Efforts were made to keep the social structure intact. In Cork, for example, many Protestants would meet their friends from around the county once a week in the city; on Thursdays they would collect the wage packets from the bank, do their shopping and have lunch at the Cork and County Club as a way of keeping in touch.

Those who felt there was nothing for them in the new Ireland departed or died if they were not absorbed into the Catholic majority. In 1911, Protestants in the twenty-six counties amounted to 10 per cent of the population. By 1927 this proportion was just over 7 per cent – a fall of 32.5 per cent. The Catholic population had fallen by 2.2 per cent during the same era. The decline of Protestants would continue remorselessly. By 1981 there were only 115,000 left, forming just under 3.5 per cent of the population.

The old Protestant names above shops disappeared. In Skibbereen in West Cork the 'strong British Loyalist group which lorded it over the supine natives' despised by Tom Barry had been predominately shopkeepers. Some of the names that dominated the trade of Skibbereen in the 1920s were A. G. Power, Gents Outfitters; R. Lester, Chemist; Downes and Dolan, Gents Outfitters; W. G. Wood, Motor Garage; Wolfe Brothers Stationers, Toys etc.; R. Vickery, Hardware; Haddens Medical Hall; J. Trinder, Draper; and C. L. Hosford, News and Shipping Agent. There were many others. They have gone. The same is true of most small towns in Ireland, many of whom have not had a Protestant living in them for decades. Logically we know that mixed marriages absorbed a fair proportion of them, while emigration took the rest. But it is hard not to feel a sense of mystery about the vanishing.

CHAPTER 10

Let There be Light

Waves of fresh, youthful and forward-looking energy came up
against stagnant lakes of insularity and entrenched, often
ignorant prejudice, while the new bourgeoisie, formed in the
wake of revolution, was already stabilising into a new
conservatism.

Brian Fallon

Wagtails were first observed in the plane trees of O'Connell Street in the
autumn of 1929. Thereafter, the shrieking winter flocks outside the Gresham
Hotel would be one of Dublin's sights.

In cobblestoned Smithfield in the heart of the city, town and country met.
On Thursday in the early morning I would be woken in my nursery by the
sound of sheep and cattle in Fitzwilliam Street driven down to the market by
whistling drovers and their dogs. A good dog would take the place of a drover,
or several drovers, men who came from all over Dublin. If it was raining they
would put a sack over their shoulders as they kept an eye on their unpredictable
beasts – a bullock might walk through an open door, or seeing his reflection in
a glass window, walk into it.

The capital was changing a little with the introduction of cocktail hours,
wireless, dancehalls and a newly liberated people. The trams trundled along
from the Pillar on top of which Nelson stood; new housing estates would be
built along their routes on the city's outskirts. There was not much traffic, and
much of it was still horse-drawn. In Smithfield there was a sale of hay every
Tuesday, while a horse fair took place on Wednesday. Harness makers did a
good trade; in Stonybatter there were four, all hard at work. They stitched two
different kinds of harness – city and country. Country harness was usually
lighter, while city harness had double stitching and a good deal of brass;

specially strengthened van harness for brakes and milk vans prevented a horse breaking away into a city crowd.

Dairies had sixty to seventy horses while the national transport company CIE (Córas Iompair Éireann) also used large numbers of huge hairy-footed beasts. Bakers and grocers like Findlater's delivered goods to their customers in horse-drawn vans; horses drew the hops to Guinness's brewery and even the Army used them, having decided they were cheaper than motorised vehicles.

Dublin was still the same intimate small town where friends could meet casually. Austin Clarke could saunter happily 'cityward stopping for a drink at a tavern near Baggot Street Bridge where we strolled through Stephen's Green and at four o'clock met at the Palace Bar. Mrs Padraic Colum, who had returned from the United States, ran into Yeats in Nassau Street. "Why, good morning, Mr Yeats!" He intoned: "I hear a voice. It comes from beyond the seas. I know it now!"'

Beside the squalor of tenements, the respectable working class maintained its standards. In a house with one cold tap and a backyard toilet Paddy Crosbie's mother kept everything shining bright, and the range gleaming. There might be lino instead of carpets, but his family had a piano and in 1928 bought a gramophone. Henceforth, the house echoed with singing and music.

In a world of scrubbed doorsteps where a penny could make the difference between wealth and poverty, the bright atmosphere of the Crosbie household contrasted not only with the tenements, but with the accommodation sought by those pouring into the city seeking work. There were the filthy lodging houses like the one found by Patrick Kavanagh after his arrival in the city from Monaghan; or the ramshackle flats which would remain unchanged for decades. Sean O'Faolain described a typical flat as having 'two rooms (that is, one room cut in two), with the WC on the ground floor and the bathroom on the top floor; and in the bathroom . . . an unpleasant greasy-looking gas stove such as Prince Albert might have unveiled at the Great Crystal Palace Exhibition'.

In sleazy private hotels, 'neither private nor hotels' according to O'Faolain, guests might stay for the greater part of a lifetime. But for those with means, the grand hotels like the Shelbourne (although Virginia Woolf complained that it only served boiled potatoes) and the Russell offered luxury; the latter boasted a telephone and a wireless listening-in set in every bedroom, excellent cuisine, a garage, and moderate winter terms.

The poor or 'plainer class of Dublin folk' could take the tram or train to the nearest stretch of sea. At Merrion Gates, fruit and cake stalls were set up during the summer holidays, while ice-cream carts trundled up and down the sand . . . Hot water for tea-making could be obtained from nearby cottages. Rubbish was a familiar problem. The *Irish Times* observed in 1928, 'Judging by the debris after Whit Monday, crowds must have revelled in the first summer day of the season . . . but it seems a pity the local authorities should not have a "cleaning up" . . . so as to leave it fresh for the next batch.'

The popularity of bicycles brought the countryside nearer, while the nascent tourist industry touted the attractions of seaside towns within reach of the city. Dun Laoghaire was promoted as the Premier Holiday Resort in Ireland; 'bracing, sunny, bright and well equipped – open air music, cinemas . . .' In Bray on the recently re-erected bandstands there were shades of the Imperial past, as 'bands both military and civilian discourse sweet music three or four times a week'. Bray also offered military tattoos, fireworks, cricket, tennis and croquet. Rail and coach tours took Dubliners as far as Avoca and Glendalough with its 'famous Seven Churches – midst that valley of stern and desolate grandeur'.

It is difficult to exaggerate the importance of cinemas in alleviating the bleakness of people's lives. Censorship, which tore out yards of celluloid, never stopped the queues. The great picture palaces were Dublin landmarks like the Capitol 'with its big attractive well-ventilated premises' and its adherence to the principle of the 'mixed shows' – the stage performance which would end with the white screen thundering down to accommodate a flickering black-and-white film. The Theatre Royal, which had a history dating back to the early nineteenth century, was another which supported 'cine variety'. The Savoy, frowned on by the *Catholic Bulletin* as 'an English picture house', opened in O'Connell Street in 1929.

Paddy Crosbie recalled other cinemas outside the heart of the city which promoted the 'penny rush' or offered a choice of seats, either 'woodeners' or 'cushioners'. Cinema-goers could lose themselves in the glamour of Hollywood at the 'Manor' or Broadway in Manor Street, the 'Tivo' in Francis Street, the 'Roto' or the Rotunda in O'Connell Street, the 'Fizzer' at Blackquire Bridge or the 'Feeno' on Ellis Quay. There could never be enough of them; by 1931 the talkies had come in and the queues grew longer.

Writing in *The Bell* in 1944, Marion Brennan remembered the fourpenny flicks and the queues – you queued at the Savoy for an hour. The 'Mayro' specialised in 'follier-uppers', i.e. serials. In the late thirties she would go to the 'Roto' and watch the stage show which included a 'dainty soubrette' – usually a thin Dublin child imitating Shirley Temple who would be pelted by boys with orange peel.

Commenting on the 1930 Budget, the *Catholic Bulletin*, always a killjoy, grumbled about the extra £20,000 raised through entertainment tax, equating the cinemas – sources of untold evil – with the 'promoters of crime from murder to common theft'.

The Abbey Theatre had made its famous decisions, rejecting O'Casey's *The Silver Tassie* and Denis Johnston's *The Old Lady Says 'No'*. The latter play had been called at various times *Symphony in Green* and *Shadow Dance*. Its new name, according to Johnston's wife Shelah Richards, came from Lennox Robinson who 'shook his head sadly and said, "The old lady says 'no'."' In fact, it was not the decision of Lady Gregory alone; it was a committee judgement.

Too many plays with depressing settings such as tenements and peasants' cottages were still being performed, what Honor Tracy described as 'PQ' or

'Peasant Quality'. Audiences tended to agree with Norman Reddin, who became a director of the Gate Theatre, when he deplored 'the endless cottage sets' and 'the purple peasant, who, when he was not cheating his brother out of a field or killing his Da, was whining and philosophising into the mist that does be on the bog'. In the 1950s Honor Tracy saw an Abbey play with a smoky cabin interior and 'an aged crone huddled over the fire, passing remarks of a typically racy kind. Ragged figures came and went: a bottle circulated: there was a struggle.'

In the late twenties the Abbey, with its insistence on showing native drama, was entering a period of doldrums. Then the old lady died. At the same time, Mícheál Mac Liammóir and Hilton Edwards began their Irish careers as actors and producers. They were Englishmen, although Mac Liammóir hid his past, invented a convoluted Gaelic alternative to his given name of Alfred Willmore, and insisted that he came from Cork. The progress of the Gate Theatre, its association with Lord Longford who subsidised it, and the subsequent amoeba-like split into two companies, would make a fine pageant in the manner of *The Hurdle Ford*, which Mac Liammóir wrote about Dublin. Very unlike the timid Abbey, the Gate's early productions (performed at the Peacock, a subsidiary theatre of the Abbey), included *Peer Gynt* to celebrate the centenary of Ibsen and the first public performance in England or Ireland of Oscar Wilde's *Salome*. Because of a lack of funds, many of the parts in *Salome* were played by amateurs who were expected to provide or hire their own costumes; some were scanty. When the first soldier delivered his line 'The Tetrarch has a sombre aspect' in a broad Dublin accent, the audience sniggered.

The Gate took on the rejected *The Old Lady Says 'No'*. Mac Liammóir played Robert Emmet, a role with which he was identified for thirty years until he became Oscar Wilde (in his one-man show *The Importance of Being Oscar*). He declaimed fine lines about Strumpet City. Cathleen Ní Houlihan made yet another appearance, but in spite of that, the play was original, robust and popular. Virginia Woolf saw a revival in 1934: 'The play was good: about Emmet, advanced, pseudo-Auden, I imagine. Three instruments to make music. A curtain that wouldn't close; much satire of the Irish love of bloodshed; satire of the attempts at culture; sudden sense came over me of being in the midst of history – that is of being in an unsettled, feverish place, which would have its period given it in the books; anything may happen.'

Although they lost money steadily, the Abbey with its state subsidy and the divided Gate offering its amazingly varied repertoire and 'air of mouldy arty refinement' in Marion Brennan's opinion, staggered on. In 1931 the sixteen-year-old prodigy Orson Welles arrived at the Gate. 'Tall, young and fat', according to Edwards, with Chinese eyes, he appeared in most of the plays during the winter season of 1931–32. Memorably he played the part of the Archduke in *Jew Suss*; he also appeared in *The Dead Ride Fast*, *Hamlet*, *The Archdupe*, *Mogu* and *Death Takes a Holiday*.

In 1931 the Gate played Mary Manning's *Youth's the Season—?*, set in

Dublin's wealthy suburbs. Manning had written from experience and her boyfriends and cocktail shakers were much appreciated by the section of the audience that came from Ballsbridge and Rathgar. Critics were a little disconcerted by Mac Liammóir, who played the effeminate Desmond Millington in a cyclamen polo-neck jumper. Mac Liammóir, who habitually wore mascara and an ill-fitting jet-black toupee, was tolerated, and in due course loved, by a society obsessed with heterosexual sin.

The conflict between the new enthusiasms and dynamism and the old rigid attitudes intensified. The iceberg of conservatism, reinforced by clerical codes, showed no signs of melting. At its worst, anyone who made a faintly liberal pronouncement might be attacked for 'the use of the muck-rake of malice, detraction and misrepresentation'. Those who questioned censorship or the lack of divorce and birth-control, or who admitted to reading *Ulysses*, could expect to be told that they possessed a cesspool of a diseased mind. 'Disillusionment' was the word much used by impatient liberals. Insularity and prejudice persuaded some to leave. O'Casey had gone, and in 1932, following the election victory of de Valera, George Russell also packed his bags. 'Dublin is depressing these days,' he wrote to Yeats. 'Ireland seems to be in my old age like a lout I knew in boyhood who became a hero and then subsided into being a lout again.'

There were signs of progress. The Irish Hospitals Sweepstake provided a way to fund hospitals. The first 'Sweep' was held on the Manchester November Handicap in 1930. Henceforth, many would benefit – the winners, patients in 400 medical institutions and Joseph McGrath, an ex-Republican who thought up the ingenious and lucrative idea.

Having retired from politics, McGrath became a businessman who acted as Director of Labour for the Shannon Scheme. Through the enthusiasm of Dr T. A. McLouglin, a contract was signed in 1925 with the German firm of Siemens Schukart to undertake the work of diverting the water of the River Shannon and building a power station at Ardnacrusha in Co. Clare. The financial implications were enormous; initially banks refused to lend the capital to set up the state company and had to be threatened with nationalisation.

For four years, knickerbockered engineers were to be seen in the Limerick area. The Germans brought in their own supplies, German bread, sausage and wine. Men who came from all over Ireland to take part in the work included labourers, ex-servicemen laid off from the Free State Army and locomotive drivers from the Listowel and Ballybunion Railway, which had closed in 1924.

Work was arduous and dangerous, starting at 7.30 in the morning and ending at 6.30 with an hour for lunch. Living conditions were rough in the camps at Ardnacrusha, Parteen Weir, O'Briensbridge and Clonlara which accommodated about a third of the huge workforce; the rest sought refuge in Limerick or found housing wherever they could, often in cabins and barns, while some even slept in stables, pigsties and hen-houses. Some of the men from Connemara who had walked to Limerick in search of jobs had only one set of clothing each; they kept themselves clean at the end of the day by wading fully clothed into the Shannon, even in winter. There were riots and much rough and tumble, in addition to the more regular entertainment provided by cinema shows and hurling and football matches.

Sean Keating, who had been commissioned to do a series of paintings, found new heroes; his painting *The Key Men* poses engineers in profile in similar fashion to the revolutionaries he had painted eight years before. *Night's Candles are Burnt Out*, which he painted towards the end of the construction phase showing the great wall of Ardnacrusha in the background, depicts a worker holding up an oil-lamp, which he is about to extinguish, to the old regime which is represented as a skeleton hanging from an electric pylon. But a good deal of time would pass before all the lamps were extinguished.

In October 1929, the power station at Ardnacrusha, 'the nerve centre of the country', was opened. A choir of priests and laymen chanted the *Te Deum* and the Bishop of Killaloe prayed: 'O Almighty and Merciful God, sole source of light and power, Who commandest the winds and the waves and Who made streams run down the rocks in the wilderness, pour, we beseech Thee, Thy all-protecting blessing over this immense aqueduct constructed in Thy Name . . . so that it may eventually bring the waters of the Shannon to the three turbines and generate the mysterious power of electricity for Thy Glory and the benefit of the people of Ireland.'

Before the Shannon Scheme, ninety-eight per cent of electricity was provided from coal. In most towns oil-lamps and candles in shops and pubs were the only sources of street lighting, while in larger towns the coal-run gas house, installed in the nineteenth century, supplied lighting for street lamps. Many churches were lit by paraffin lamps fixed on walls. The installation of electricity had been haphazard. One of the earliest towns to acquire electric power was Bray, lit in 1904 from a generator powered by a head of water from the Dargle River. Bray Electric Company not only supplied light to the town, but illuminated the sea front. In the West, Charlestown in Co. Mayo was one of the first towns to have electric light supplied from its own power house. Most towns had some form of local lighting; in Belmullet at the far end of Mayo, electricity was supplied by Jack McLoughlin who bought a trawler called *Dairy Maid* and used her engine as a generator, lighting the town's hotel and some other premises like Hurst's Ballroom.

In parts of the country the idea of electricity was utterly strange; people learned that they would be able to do without fires, and began to grasp the principle of light without flame. Now the new power was available throughout the country. Already in 1926, in anticipation of the completion of Ardnacrusha, Waterford had been looking for tenders for the installation of street lighting. High-tension wires linked towns and cities; by 1931 W. S. Lawlor, writing in the *Capuchin Annual*, declared that 'today there is scarcely a village larger than 500 which is not supplied with electricity'.

Writing in the anthology *No Shoes in Summer*, Dursie Leonard remembered seeing the electric light switched on in a town in Clare. 'Everyone came out of their houses and shops and stood waiting for the "magic" to happen. There was such an uproar and wonder that some thought the end of the world was near.'

But the use of the new power came slowly; Dervla Murphy remembered the lamplighter as a familiar figure in Lismore, Co. Waterford, in the 1930s. Householders in towns were generally reluctant to install electricity because of the cost, and when they did it was used principally for lighting and radios. There was also prejudice; some middle-class romantics like Pamela Hinkson felt that the new 'cold strange brightness' available by pressing a button was no substitute for the lamps and candles that continued to be in use; one lamp on a wall in the kitchen, and perhaps a fancy one with red-coloured glass for the parlour.

Many big houses did without, although special electric lighting sets supplied by Siemens Schukart were available. Cost was the usual reason given. Francis Hackett was quoted £250 for installation in his fairly ample house in Newcastle, Co. Wicklow; he also had to give a guarantee to pay a pound a week for five years. In addition, electricity was linked to a similar reluctance to install central heating – a feeling that such luxuries were effeminate. There were those like Molly Keane's character in *Time after Time* who were repelled by the new convenience: 'He hated the stuff and never asked for more heat than that supplied by a couple of good logs in the morning-room fireplace.'

Farmers had little interest in removing the drudgery of their lives or easing the hardships which their wives endured. The idea of having a reliable supply of hot water to scour milk buckets and help to remedy the nightmare link between contaminated milk and TB was felt to be outlandish.

For most country people, light still came from candles and the paraffin lamp whose ritual evening lighting was described by John McGahern in his autobiographical novel, *The Barracks*. 'The head was unscrewed off the lamp, the charred wicks trimmed, the tin of paraffin and the wide funnel got from the scullery. Elizabeth shone the smoked globe with twisted brown paper, Willie ran with a blazing roll of newspaper to touch the turned-up wicks into flame.' This was a police barracks; even here no electricity was provided. The house, like most, was also lit with what McGahern called 'the ghastly red glow from the Sacred Heart Lamp'. Elsewhere, peeled rushes steeped in grease were not yet extinct.

The Shannon Scheme was set up with the idea of benefiting the economy, still reeling from the destruction caused during the Civil War and already stagnant with the effects of worldwide depression. In 1928 the agricultural depression had been compounded by the mortal blow dealt to the fishing industry; tariffs in the United States on cured mackerel meant the collapse of the fish market for thousands of small fishermen–farmers along the western seaboard. Overnight the seine boat became obsolete and the bare-armed girls from Donegal, with their slicing knives and repartee, lost their livelihood, no longer pickling mackerel and laying it in barrels.

Fishing from small boats produced little income. (The exception was lobsters; the Blasket Islanders continued to supplement their incomes by selling lobsters to Frenchmen.) The sea was full of fish, although the French trawlers, with their sailors who ate crow pie, were seen as threatening the stocks. Compared with today, every time a net dipped into water it brought up a miraculous draught. A certain number of the hake and cod and bream caught by the hundred on the long line left coastal ports by train for London and Dublin, but that left a lot of fish and few to eat them.

The Irish market was limited in a country where fish was never a favourite item of the diet. In the year of the American tariffs, McCabes, the Dublin fishmonger, advertised a promotion of fish during Lent. 'A boon to country residents . . . Fish by direct post from sea to your door ready for cooking . . . saves trouble as fish is cleaned . . . When ordering please state whether (1) for boiling or frying (2) the day you wish to receive fish.' In summer more salmon was provided than ever was needed; suburban households knew that their maidservants would only eat so much. The yellow ling, hard as a board, was always there as a Friday meal or a Lenten penance. McCabes would never have offered ling or sent its clientele mackerel, as these were not fish for eating in company. On market days in coastal towns, scores of fishermen's wives and boys would be lining the roads selling mackerel and herring, food for the poor. A hundred mackerel would cost twopence and much of it was dumped.

The country struggled with stagnation and poverty compounded by the three horsemen of Republicanism, Religion and Language. It had not taken long for Gaelic to be turned from a patriotic joy into a hated burden. The Gaelic bandwagon rolled on, fuelled by the patriotic middle classes, and what Myles na gCopaleen would call the buck-leppin' antics of the Gaelic League. Soon, the language would be as heartily loathed as ever was the tongue of the conqueror.

Only a decade had passed since the discovery of Irish had been, for patriots like Frank O'Connor and Sean O'Faolain, an emotional strand of their new Republican identity. 'Irish became our runic language,' wrote O'Faolain. 'It made us comrades in a secret society. We sought and made friendships, some of them to last forever, like conspirators in a high state of exultation, merely by using Irish words.' Learning to speak correctly was a worthy obstacle. 'Listen, sister,' says a character in O'Faolain's *The Man Who Invented Sin*, 'I'll show you the way to speak Irish. If you'll pardon the expression, make a great spit inside your mouth and gurgle it out like this . . . "carrwoochhk".'

Influenced by the passion of Daniel Corkery's Nationalist views, O'Connor not only took up Irish, but became a qualified teacher. Austin Clarke went to Donegal to experience his initial contact with a Gaelic-speaking people: 'I heard in the darkness the patter of steps. Half a dozen youngsters ran beside me calling out in shrill tones: "*Tabhair dom pingin. Tabhair dom pingin.*" [Gimme a penny.] It was the first time I heard Irish spoken as a living language – fittingly by bare-footed urchins – and I was thrilled by the sharp syllables.'

For Clarke and others, the inducement of visiting the remote and beautiful areas of the West where Irish was still spoken as a first language more than made up for the drudgery of learning. There were mountains to climb, the sea to swim and people to make you welcome. You did not have to be a scholar or a poet or a civil servant; there were many children like Paddy Crosbie, leaving his school in the heart of Dublin in 1926 and travelling to Ballingeary, to imbibe Irish: 'The countryside appeared as a fairy land to me, while the people were every bit as nice as our own Dubliners.'

Ireland would be Gaelic as well as free, just as Patrick Pearse had wished. The romantic and patriotic passion for the language was enunciated by Eoin MacNeill, the new Government's first Minister for Education, who told the Dáil that once again Ireland would set an example with 'our ancient ideals, faith, learning, generous enthusiasm, self-sacrifice – the things best calculated to purge out the meanness of the modern world'. But MacNeill had also said, 'You might as well be putting wooden legs on hens as trying to restore Irish through the schools system.'

The Government set to work with messianic zeal. Although only seventeen per cent of the population could speak Irish in 1922, the constitution established it as the national language. The new State was to be bilingual, and children would learn it in school. From February 1922 crash courses were introduced to teach teachers Irish. Children under seven in the first two years of national school were to be taught entirely in Irish. In 1924 it was decided that the language should be an essential subject for the Intermediate Certificate and soon after for the Leaving Certificate. In 1928 it was also made an essential subject for entry into the Civil Service, and eventually it became a requirement in the law courts.

One approach to the language was to use Irish names. A simple John Murphy incised across a fascia board above a shop was easily changed into Seán Ó Murchadha. Plenty of little girls were christened Sorcha and Sinéad. Rory was turned into Ruaidhrí, while Turlough became Toirdhealbhach; a batch of post-Revolutionary Pádraigs and Séamuses saw the light of day. Saints' names, Gobnat and Attracta, found favour. Austin Clarke observed that 'one can almost date that generation by its Liams, Seáns and Peaders'.

The occasional gold or silver *fáinne*, a ring indicating proficiency in Irish, sprouted in a buttonhole and millions of pounds were spent on revival at a time when the country was desperately short of money. But the old enthusiasm for the language, now no longer a semi-secret weapon against the English tyrant, soon began to subside. As early as 1924 a member of the Irish National Teachers Organisation in Wexford was complaining how 'Irish-speaking "rodeo cowboys" were lassooing teachers young and old . . . stampeding them into classes where they were drenched with abnormal doses of Gaelic'.

The eager crowds who had flocked to learn the language in Pearse's day were decreasing, their enthusiasm dampened for various reasons – the Civil War, the shortage of literature in Irish and the simple fact that it was a difficult language to learn. No longer did the majority concur with George Nicholls, one of the inspectors in the Department of Education, that 'every dog, hog or devil' would have to learn the language. The restoration of Irish needed public support, good attendance at schools, proper facilities for teaching and co-operation with the inspectors instead of reviling them as ogres. All these factors proved impossible to implement.

The Gaelic League condemned writers like Yeats and O'Casey who wrote in English. The League, according to Sean O'Faolain, wanted 'to abolish utterly all books other than those written in Gaelic and to abolish English utterly as the general, practical language of the island'.

By 1926 books of Irish literature were being sold by the Publications Branch of the Department of Education. Books by Pearse were the most popular. It was difficult to get enough typesetters capable of understanding the setting of Gaelic characters. Apart from school texts, other books in Irish proved a commercial failure and had to be subsidised; native Irish speakers did not buy them and students provided the only market.

The always dissenting voice of Gogarty could be heard with his view of compulsion: 'All that it is doing . . . is bringing the graffiti lower down on piss-house walls.' The Irish were being turned into a race of bilinguals 'ignorant and gullible in both languages'.

In 1932 Joseph Hone stated the obvious: 'An Englishman might be a long time in the Free State, knocking about in trains, in buses, in hotels small and large, in places of public amusement, and he might return to his own country without, except in the Welsh packet to and from Holyhead, having caught a word of any speech but his own.'

Inevitably, compulsory Irish had a detrimental effect on education, although it took the State decades to admit that its 'interesting experiment' was a failure. By 1928 most subjects in primary schools were taught through Irish and the dreaded inspectors toured the country to see that the rule was imposed. An indignant teacher told me, 'I think it was a sin crying to heaven for vengeance the methods we were supposed to use. Imagine young children of about seven or eight trying to write a composition in Irish with the grammar and everything perfect! . . . All the conversations had to be in Irish, and we'd talk about ploughing, harrowing and horses and everything old-fashioned, and it was very slow going.'

Perhaps money spent on the Irish revival could have been better used restoring the fabric of school buildings. The Government supplied a basic fuel allowance for rural schools, but it was insufficient. The small fires in large schoolrooms were inadequate, particularly on wet days when children, having walked long distances, arrived wringing wet. There was the agony of trying to dry scores of wet coats while children took turns to come up and sit by the fire to get warm before returning to their desks. Overcrowded classrooms, incomprehensible Irish, leaking roofs, dry lavatories, no running water (in some schools water would be brought in bowls from the nearest stream) and corporal punishment did not encourage a love of books.

There are many accounts of the misery of country schools which lasted almost to the 1950s. Among those with harsh memories was Donal Foley. 'About a fifth of boys came to school barefooted even in the hardest of winters, boys with pale little faces dressed in tattered rags. On arrival they were always given special places close to the fire and on wet days their clothes would be steaming.'

Bryan MacMahon taught in barbarous conditions in Co. Kerry for years. 'I look at the dim class photographs of that time with misgivings. Disease was implied in the pale faces before me.' He remembered how it was taken for granted that children should have dirty, bloody bare feet and be infected with mites. Noel Browne recalled children from the Gaeltacht who 'in ragged misfitting clothes walked barefooted to school, hair uncombed and laden with lice, unwashed and dirty. Teeth rotten, skin pockmarked by flea bites, they were treated with contempt.'

At MacMahon's school the damp building was without proper heat, there was one tap for 350 children, the place was overrun with rats and the lavatories were 'Augean stables': 'What with faeces, cocoa, soup, rats, mice, crumbs, spiders, crows, gulls and the various insects that prayed on humankind, not to mention inspectors who examined the intellect and clergy who presided over the spirit – ours was a poor example of a centre of learning.'

One of the planks of education were the schools run by the Christian Brothers, noted for harsh discipline and 'angry Nationalism'. Paddy Crosbie attended a CBS in Brunswick Street in the heart of Dublin, which until 1924 had the usual dry toilets and no proper lighting or heating. In one classroom stood an altar to the Blessed Virgin and every time the clock struck the hour the classes stood up and recited a Hail Mary. The strap ruled. Noel Browne remembered 'enthusiastic religious zealots' who used physical violence 'to reinforce the values of a very narrow and introspective green flag-waving Irish Nationalism, a suspicion of the establishment and an antipathy to all things English'.

The 'new and pitiless Free State', as Browne called it, did nothing for the children of the poor. In 1932 almost ninety-three per cent of children had no secondary education; those who wanted it had to pay for it. Primary education was supposed to be compulsory, but the Attendance Act was a farce. All over the country there was a distrust for education among those who had learnt a basic lesson – that sitting in squalid schoolrooms listening to lessons delivered in Irish was a waste of time. Like the young Patrick Kavanagh, they despised learning: 'What good is grammar to a man who has to work with spade and shovel?'

Tens of thousands of young people whom the State had failed took their ignorance abroad to escape poverty and indifference. Between 1924 and 1928 130,000 emigrated, of whom eighty per cent were aged between fifteen and thirty-five. Whole hurling teams would leave. On railway platforms, parents watched their sons depart whom they would never see again. Lennox Robinson recalled the 'shawled women and sobs, a bearded father kissing a young bewildered son; *a caoine, a caoine* [keening] as the train moved away, and at Patrickswell, the station outside Limerick, the porter would half-facetiously call out: Change here for America. And true enough, a train would hurry you from there to . . . Charleville, to Cobh, to Boston and New York.'

It has been said that the 'American wake' was intended to make emigrants too tired and too drunk the following morning to feel grief or fear. By the late twenties these wakes had become a quieter commonplace, since nearly every family had a son or daughter leaving for America. Some emigrants recalled that eventually 'there was no great fuss about emigration'.

'I can remember the day I left very well,' an emigrant who returned to die in Ireland in the 1960s told me. 'It was Saturday 16 August 1929, the day after the fair. A few of my friends came to see me off. I went on the *Franconia*, the Cunard Line ship, and it was grand, to tell you the truth . . . She was packed with Irish from all over the country. It was the last time the Irish could travel like this before the restrictions on emigration came in. It was all dancing, singing and drinking . . . I didn't see many families go. They were mainly single men and girls, and, like me, without any trade or qualification.' When he arrived in New York he never saw his fellow passengers again.

'Who's going today?' people would ask after they had discussed the weather. Along the coast of West Cork they could see the Cunard and White Star liners passing from Cobh to New York and Halifax; the *Cedric*, the *Adriatic*, the *Celtic Sun*, the *Baltic Sun*, all with facilities provided on board for celebration of Holy Mass. Frank O'Connor watched a liner off West Cork 'moving in a series of jerks like the swan in *Lohengrin*'. Some who stayed at home lit bonfires on the hills so that their people could see the smoke from the deck of the ship.

Sons and daughters went out of every family. Those who remained behind awaited those essential remittances known as the 'American post'. Tom O'Flaherty described a village in the West where 'every woman . . . who had a son or daughter in America waited at the top of the hill for the letter-carrier. They were all knitting stockings and pretending not to care whether there was a letter or not. Yet they were burning with anxiety, for on the remittances of their children in the United States depended to a great extent whether they dined luxuriously on bread or tea or existed on a straight diet of potatoes and fish.'

The eighth of December was the big day for the arrival of American money, which came in dollar drafts with the name of payee and sender, seldom accompanied by a letter. As late as 1958 American money constituted approximately two and a half per cent of the national income. Sending back money to relations in Ireland was a holy trust. 'The world will never know,' wrote John Healy, 'how much these scared, brave, sometimes ignorant but always loyal emigrants to the New World sent home in dollars and parcels to the people of the old country. No one will ever know the sacrifices and how much they kept hidden from the old people.'

A common tale throughout rural Ireland was that of people – usually the old – seeing visions of dancing groups – their neighbours who had emigrated.

The man who returned to Ireland to die told me how the first time he made money in the States he sent five dollars to his mother. 'But it came back again because there was no one to claim it. She was dead. I guess that settled me from wanting to return home.'

Families dwindled to nothing. As Patrick Kavanagh wrote savagely in the 1940s, 'a whole generation eliminated itself . . . The Irish form of birth control was a drastic one.' Judge Daniel Cohalan from New York, visiting in 1926, commented that everywhere he went the country appeared to be empty. 'The one thing lacking in Ireland is Irish people.'

So much was dismal. Unemployment was forever on the increase with the cutting down of the bloated Army and the sacking of the men who had mended the railways blown up in the Civil War. Short of money, the Government saved on welfare. Although the old age pension was partially restored in 1928, it remained lower than in 1924. It was given with stringent means testing; appeals were rejected mostly on grounds of falsification of age.

Few new houses had been built to take the place of the tenements; only 14,000 houses were built from public subsidy between 1922 and 1929. In 1931 Cosgrave's Cabinet reduced the salaries of civil servants, teachers and the Garda. One hundred thousand were unemployed. Many felt it was time for a change.

On 11 August 1927 de Valera and the members of his new Fianna Fáil party had entered the Dáil and signed their names in the book containing the Oath of Allegiance which swore fealty to King George and his heirs. Pragmatic and/or cynical, they did not take the 'empty formula'. In 1933 they would abolish it. By then, they had won two elections.

In vain did Cumann na nGaedheal put forth its posters, captioned 'Shadow of a Gunman' and 'His Master's Voice', showing de Valera being propelled forward by a gunman's pistol. De Valera would convince the electorate that Cosgrave's main support came from Freemasons, Rotarians, Imperialists, ex-soldiers of the Great War, graduates of Trinity College, members of the Royal Dublin Society and Unionists in general. Unionists appeared in cartoons as fat, moustached, sinister profiteers. Fianna Fáil election posters read: 'Freemasons vote for Cosgrave's party.' 'You vote for Fianna Fáil. They are to God and Erin True.'

'Cosgrave is a dear,' Signe Toksvig was told by a Unionist lady in 1932. My own relatives certainly supported him, people like my grandfather who lived in Dundrum, near Maud Gonne's Roebuck House. What happened inside his mini-estate with its gardens and dairy herds bore little relation to the world outside its gates. Maids came and went like butterflies, serving us with rich but monotonous food – chicken soufflé, woodcock, fish cakes on Friday, braised steak, huge Sunday roasts, cabinet pudding, marmalade pudding. I remember a garden fête in our fields graced by the Lord Mayor of Dublin, Alfie Byrne, another friend of Protestants, wearing his gold mayoral chain with its medal bearing the likeness of King William.

By then de Valera was firmly in power; the election he won in March 1932 by a narrow majority was bolstered by a more convincing success in 1933. He was seen as the poor man's friend; on the Aran Islands bonfires were lit in celebration. 'The fascination de Valera had, and has over the Irish people is astonishing,' wrote Sean O'Casey. 'There seems to be no streak of joviality, good humour or humanity in him as there is in the warmer natured Cosgrave. His speeches are dull, his voice unattractive.'

In the first Cumann na nGaedheal Government, Ministers who formed the so-called Clongowes Mafia included Paddy McGilligan, Kevin O'Higgins and Marcus O'Sullivan, all men of high ability. Clongowes, run by the Jesuits, was a school whose aim, ever since its foundation in 1814, had been to cater for the emerging Catholic middle classes. During the Great War its old boys had answered Redmond's call and gone to fight; it was said that more Clongowes boys went to the front than Etonians.

Now the Clongowes Mafia was defeated, and the new Government, they said, was overseeing the substitution of Clongowes boys with Christian Brothers' boys. 'Once again the Irish people have proved true to the faith of their fathers,' crowed the *Catholic Bulletin*. Although Cosgrave was a sincere Christian, de Valera and Sean T. O'Kelly out-Christianed him. Before the 1932 election, de Valera had paid a call on Cardinal MacRory, and many clergy remembered the clever boy educated at Blackrock who became a patriot, narrowly escaping execution. The Pope sent a message of congratulation when he was elected.

A few months later Ireland's new leader was offered a brilliant opportunity to display himself as a servant of the Church. When the Eucharistic Congress took place in June, 1932, all the Catholic world came to Ireland, 5,000 priests, eleven cardinals and 160 bishops to celebrate the fifteen hundredth anniversary of St Patrick's landing. Twenty thousand Irish priests participated. Irish Army aeroplanes, flying in the shape of a cross, escorted the SS *Cambria* into Dún Laoghaire harbour where thousands were gathered to greet Cardinal Lorenzo Lauri, the Papal Legate. 'No emperor or king ever received a welcome more sincere or more heartfelt than Ireland gave . . . to the Prince of the Church,' declared the *Irish Independent*.

The city was awash with decorations; the Hibernian Bank in College Street had a large replica of a round tower outside its building. On the quays a number of elegant cast-iron pissoirs were erected that would remain in place for the next thirty years.

De Valera and O'Kelly helped carry the canopy that wavered above the Papal Legate. A garden party was held at Blackrock College, de Valera's Alma Mater, where the headmaster was Dublin's future archbishop, John Charles McQuaid. The embers of the Civil War smouldered with the omission of the Governor-General, James MacNeill, from the list of guests. A few months later MacNeill would be replaced by Dómhnall Ó Buachalla, an Irish speaker and Dublin shopkeeper, who refused to attend any official functions. He avoided the Viceregal Lodge and lived in a modest suburban house in Monkstown, from where he commuted to Phoenix Park by bicycle.

The crowds that watched as the army of priests went by were like those at Daniel O'Connell's monster meetings. On 23 June a mass meeting of men was held in the Phoenix Park; the next night it was the turn of the women. The open-air Mass in the park, which was the climax of the celebrations, was attended by over a million people. Children of Mary processed in the sunshine, little girls in yellow and little boys in white, many dressed by Guiney's in Talbot Street. A choir of 900 children sang; so, inevitably, did John McCormack.

The poor had officially contributed to the cost of the Congress, much of which was paid for during a national collection at all Masses on 30 November 1930. The total cost was over £75,000; a credit balance was donated to Archbishop Edward Byrne's cathedral fund. But this blend of national and religious fervour was most manifestly apparent in the decorations in Dublin's tenements. Banners, flowers, bunting and flags were hung on crumbling brickwork; miniature altars appeared in front of cracked and broken fanlights, while windows were decorated with religious pictures, flowers and the Congress shield. Women in Dominick Street waited until traffic had ceased before scrubbing the footpath. Whitewash was liberally applied and carpets laid before the street altars. GOD BLESS OUR POPE, read the banners, EUCHARISTIC HEART OF JESUS KEEP IRELAND TRUE TO YOU! 'The poorer were the Dublin streets, the richer the decoration; it was like passing through a supernatural toy store,' wrote G. K. Chesterton, who had come over to Ireland once again to take part in the celebration.

CHAPTER 11

The Castle of the Irishman

Did I ever tire of small-town life? In the immortal words of
Eliza Doolittle, 'not bloody likely'. I came to know almost
everything that happened in every house, in every shop as I
came and went during the day – and indeed as an addicted
walker, far into the night as well.

Brian MacMahon

O Christ, Maguire thinks, I am locked in a stable with pigs and
cows for ever.

Patrick Kavanagh

In the countryside the Eucharistic Congress was also celebrated with banners
and shrines all over the place. Where there was a wireless, people gathered to
hear the prayers sent forth from the Phoenix Park and O'Connell Bridge. At
Ferrybank-on-Suir a publican put up a loudspeaker; Donal Foley remembered
how 'we were on our knees for hours in the yard in the open air answering the
responses. It was like Lourdes at home.'

Rural life was idealised, not only for its loyalty to the faith. The rural family
was considered to have all the virtues and was praised as the pillar of society. A
typical fulsome appreciation of country people, simple, hard working, religious
and good, appeared in 1935 in an article in the *Capuchin Annual* by Aodh de
Blacam, an Ulsterman turned fervent Celt.

After praising highland shepherds ('old plain men in homespun garb; men
with rosy faces, keen untroubled eyes') de Blacam turned his attention to the
'virile folk' inhabiting mixed farms and 'wee holdings'. He applauded 'the
woman of the house at the spinning wheel . . . the Irish Penelope makes the
stout socks that keep the menfolk healthy; their bawneen jackets of the natural

wool that throw off rain better than any waterproof are hers; so are the dyed curtains and patchwork coverlets, those things of old-fashioned beauty'.

The farmer 'knows the ways of animals . . . is a gardener, grower of fruit, carpenter, drains fields, fells trees. The wife prepares food for animals, breeds poultry, bakes, spins, sews, knits; she manages a house . . . from dawn to dusk when at last the wall-lamp is lit and the candle gleams red before the Sacred Heart as the family Rosary is said . . .'

In *The Barracks*, John McGahern described the household kneeling on the concrete floor on newspaper. They recited a prayer for the canonisation of the Blessed Oliver Plunkett, followed by the last prayer: 'O Jesus I must die, I know not where, I know not when nor how, but if I die in mortal sin I go to hell for all eternity.'

'Happy children run barefoot on the clean grass,' wrote Aodh de Blacam. 'They learn to love their country and the true ring of words through country ballads . . . Among neighbours they find a true Christian society.' Coming back from school, children would change their clothes and help to work on the farm right through to the evening to the detriment of homework, and often on Sundays.

Politics, religion and the work of artists like Paul Henry, Charles Lamb and Sean Keating, reinforced these rapturous images which reflected de Valera's aspirations. The thatched, whitewashed cottage that looked so well on calendars became a shrine. Pamela Hinkson listed its qualities: 'the whitewashed walls within have always a warm tinge in them from the turf fire, out of sight, which is the life of the house . . . the open door, the shining dresser, the movement about the floor of animals and fowl, are all symbols of welcome . . . That tumbledown cottage with its door open was more truly the castle of the Irishman and woman than any English cottage ever was.'

The lives of picturesque Irish-speaking peasants living in harsh and beautiful surroundings were hard; but since poverty could not be abolished, it was not only excused, but extolled. Work was labour intensive, food and living conditions were of the most frugal kind. 'Our means were little and we were very happy in small things,' nostalgic old people recall today. The old people with their traditional clothes were particularly to be revered; Paul Henry's wrinkled old woman of Mayo in red shawl and bare feet became an icon. Dignified poverty was the ideal, strengthened by family values, the Irish language and simple recreations of fireside stories, cards and Sunday night dancing (although dancing would soon be frowned upon). These, together with the festivals that broke up the year, were the rewards of working on smallholdings.

Above all there was the strength of religious belief. The family that prays together . . . The priest was 'the centre of gravity'. 'If you struck the man who was privileged to hold the body of Christ, your hand would wither.' 'O God Almighty, they thought the priest was king,' I have been told. 'They were a sight to the world . . . If you were seen talking to a girl and a priest came, you'd go through barbed wire – you'd be gone as if you were a hare . . .'

The enemies of such a simple and sinless lifestyle included the talkies and the dancehall. The radio was not liked very much either. Among the many who disapproved of progress was Aodh de Blacam's wife who, during a Muintir na Tíre meeting in Ardmore, Co. Waterford, in 1937, attended by an approving de Valera, deplored all the talk of making country life brighter by bringing to it the radio and the cinema. Country life on the sustenance farm was not monotonous: 'She was sick of the talk of entertaining the farmer who had all the amusements, including riding and shooting, which were only enjoyed by fortune's favourites living in the town.'

It was hard on the young, without 'artificial' amusements. In *Woodbrook* David Thomson observed how 'the life of young people in the 1930s appeared to be senseless, almost loveless. Even students in Dublin would not dare to be seen holding hands and in the country to make love before marriage was to risk banishment.' Naturally, young men and women could not be trusted to dance together, and the lovely crossroads dances were perpetually condemned. I remember watching enviously a crossroads dance on an August evening on the Beara peninsula, boys and girls jigging to the squeak of a fiddle and the hum of the accordion. An old woman recalled to me with joy the boys and girls gathering on a summer's evening: 'See me sitting down on a fence gawking with the other girls at the fellows, and someone would have a fiddle or melodeon and away they would go. And I remember sometimes coming home through the town on a fair day and the cattle were already in the street.'

But such joyous gatherings were deemed sinful. Patrick Kavanagh remembered 'round 1930 how when of a beautiful summer evening a huge crowd was dancing at Annavackey Cross on a wooden deck . . . the melodeons were playing and life itself was dancing, when up the road came a little black priest who could not have been long out of college. This little man got up on the fence and ordered us to disperse which we did and I was ashamed of those young boys and girls who knew so little about even their own religion not to know that this little man was acting from impulses that were pernicious.'

After 1935 and the Public Dancehall Act, outdoor dances had to be licensed. A case brought before a district court in Kilkenny that same year illustrates the difficulties of holding these gatherings. 'Denis Gorman, licensee of a dance platform at Sheepstown, Knocktopher, had not properly displayed his licence . . . Garda O'Donnell . . . found thirty or forty couples dancing, of whom eleven girls were less than eighteen years of age. The committee in charge of the dance band were respectable farmers and the girls were all farmers' daughters . . . The Very Reverend M. Fitzgerald objected absolutely and unreservedly to the licence being granted . . .' In this case the unusually tolerant judge allowed for the defendant: 'This thing of thinking that country people cannot dance in the country air on a summer's evening . . . is nonsense.'

By the 1940s even traditional house dances to the accompaniment of the violin, melodeon, concertina and *bodhrán* were stopped. People used to bring a few pence to pay for expenses, which consisted of little more than tea or barmbrack. But these innocent affairs were considered occasions of sin. The Wren Boys were also deemed to be sinning when they went their rounds on St Stephen's Day collecting money for a little drinking and roistering. Under the weight of clerical disapproval the pagan custom of waking the dead 'wran' was left to children like the boys John McGahern saw in the forties 'in old clothes with blacking and Red Indian daubs of lipstick on their faces'.

One institution had taken the place of old-fashioned dances and all the clerical condemnation in Ireland could not get rid of it. The Most Reverend Dr Morrisoe reminds us of it: 'There is one agency which Satan has set up here. It deserves to be called after his name, for he seems to preside at some of the dark rites enacted there. We have in mind the rural dancehall.'

A dancehall, which had to obtain a licence in order to function, was generally dirty and without the basic amenities, often in some remote spot in the countryside. For those who had to cycle on their own or on a shared bike, or walk along a muddy country road, their glamour increased with the difficulty of getting there. The men would arrive, their hair brilliantined, many having changed their boots for shoes. The girls dressed up and most of them wore lipstick. They danced orderly waltzes and foxtrots, and the occasional set dances, during which the proprietor, sprinkling the floor with Lux Flakes to make the going smoother, occasionally shouted, 'No four-wheeling here!'

Of course there were dancehalls in towns as well, heralding 'a contempt for moral decencies'. In 1932 the Galway Hospital Committee deplored 'the prevalence of sexual immorality as shown by the number of illegitimate births in the Galway Maternity Hospital. The departure of the Gaelic tradition of purity was caused by the lessening of parental control and want of supervision at dances and other amusements.'

The fruits of the dancehall, thundered the *Irish Ecclesiastical Record*, were unmarried mothers (each illegitimate child becoming a charge upon the poor rate) and infanticide. A Judge Kenny in Cork declared that infanticide had become a national industry.

In 1934 an anti-jazz campaign was conducted, with complaints about jazz on radio programmes. The problem was that the young preferred jazz to Irish music and dancing. Leitrim gave a lead to the campaign, with a parade of 3,000 opposed to the decadent American import while messages of support came from Cardinal MacRory and President de Valera. Canon Masterson of the Gaelic League declared that jazz was a menace to the very fabric of civilisation as well as to religion. Irish faith and Irish music – the man who would try and defile these two noble heritages was the worst form of traitor and the greatest enemy of the Irish nation.

The Cardinal said he knew nothing about jazz dances 'except that I understand they are suggestive and demoralising, but, jazz apart, all-night dances are objectionable . . . and . . . a fruitful source of scandal, spiritual and temporal. To how many poor innocent young girls have they not been the occasion of irreparable disgrace and life-long sorrow.'

Among the young and not-so-young there was what has been described as 'an unnatural hesitancy to marry'. In those decades over sixty per cent of males between thirty and thirty-five were still unmarried. The low marriage rate was nationwide, although more acute in rural areas because of a variety of factors. They included the reluctance of older farmers to give up farms to their sons, the assumption that marriage brought the burden of many children, and the increasing refusal of young women to take on the drudgery of life on farms which were too often isolated and wretched.

The matchmaker still had a role. 'Anyone who had a girl was interested in a fellow who had a farm,' I was told by an old married man. 'The matchmaker was a shopkeeper who knew both families. I met my wife, God rest her, at the match. Before that there had been quite a few others, and all the time my father was desperate to get me married because he was losing the old age pension.'

'People are saying that bachelors should have chalk marks on their backs to make them marry,' declared a delegate at the same Muintir na Tíre meeting in Ardmore where Mrs de Blacam had defended the simplicity of farm life. He referred to the old custom of Chalk Sunday, the last Sunday before the beginning of Lent, when two chalk marks were made on the clothes of bachelors to remind them that there were only two days left in which to get married.

Another priestly delegate touched on love marriages and dowry marriages. He had seen too many love matches which meant black eyes instead of cuddling after a couple of months. The love portrayed in newspapers and films was not love, it was animal passion. But there were fewer marriages of either sort, particularly in the country.

The priest in Sean O'Faolain's story 'A Broken World' summed up the sorrows of one parish: 'In the five years I spent there I had one solitary marriage. I had sixty schoolchildren on roll when I went there. I had thirty-five when I left. Last year I heard they were reduced to eleven and five of those were all one family. No wonder the country is full of ruins.' G. K. Chesterton wrote of how he watched 'the Irish nation dying under the effects of her agrarian fallacies and her land going to perdition in the same proportion'.

Without love, few aspects of life on the farm were attractive to young women. James Kennedy remembered his mother at work. She did all the baking and cooking on the open fire. Not only did she cook for the family but she also had to boil pots of yellow meal and potatoes for the pigs and hens. She got up at six and milked half the cows. She did the washing in the tin bath with rainwater from the barrel at the end of the house.

The 1926 census revealed that out of a population of a little under three million, fifty-three per cent of the labour force worked in agriculture, while two-thirds of the population lived outside towns. The Land Commission had divided up many of the big estates and most farmers owned their land – not much. Trying to run a smallholding and earn enough for subsistence living has been described as a sweated industry. A twenty-acre holding was estimated to support two adults and a child, but not a larger family. The income would come to around £56 a year while living expenses amounted to at least £130, 'a nightmare', concluded an *Irish Times* editorial 'to Mr Wilkins Micawber'. When it did not threaten destitution the 'little farm' offered 'the slavery' of 'a lifetime of drudgery with arthritis as an end at the age of fifty'.

The seasonal work of ploughing, planting and harvesting might bring moments of satisfaction, but it required unremitting labour. Potato ridging with the spade was hard work. Pigs and hens helped to bring a little self-sufficiency, but some money was necessary for basics like sugar and tea. For most, in spite of all the labour and hope at Ardnacrusha, electricity was an unimaginable luxury. The general lack of a good water supply was another drawback to the idealised farming life. It was usually the woman's task to take the buckets to the pump or pond or stream. The sour old joke that the farmer was more interested in the well-being of his animals than his wife appeared to be true. In dry weather water often ran out altogether; then there came the problems of 'borrowing' water from a neighbour or travelling miles to a distant source. Sinking a well and purchasing a pump was an impossible pecuniary investment.

The cow – very likely an Ayrshire – the pig and the donkey were still the props of the countryside; most farmers had a horse and cart, or at least a donkey and cart. They still worked with the spade; the other indispensable implement that went back to the Middle Ages was the scythe. Many fine days were needed to cut the hay and fashion it into haycocks, a race with the rain that would bring black rot. Even so, when the mowing machine was introduced many old farmers would not let it into a field in case it disturbed the roots of the hay.

The parallel images of poverty and nobility were particularly associated with the western seaboard. In the rich pasturelands to the east where farmers tended to have bigger acreages, crops were easier to raise on the lush fields of Meath and Kildare and in the river valleys of south Leinster. There was a sense of stability, of landscape under the control of man. Dervla Murphy described the ordered luxuriance imposed by an alien conqueror in her native Lismore: 'Nor in any country that I have visited have I seen a view more noble – parks and rocks covered with the grandest foliage; rich handsome seats, gentlemen in the midst of fair houses and beautiful bright plantations and shrubberies.' But the Blackwater valley where Lismore is situated was untypical of Ireland.

The West was different. Connaught, wrote Stephen Gwynn, 'has always had its double dose of sorrows in a sorrowful land; and the Connaught man's gaiety wears a touch of recklessness which knows some kinship with despair'. In 1931 H. V. Morton posed the question of how somewhere like Connemara could exist in the modern world. The people were 'so poor that no one has tried to exploit them; their land is so poor that no one has tried to steal it . . . there are no railways, no shops, no motorcars, no telegraph poles. There are three things only; the Catholic faith, nature and work.'

'A poor land with poor crops – malnutrition – tuberculosis – barefoot children in homespun shifts – poteen' was Nicolette Devas's less lyrical impression of the same area.

Donegal was equally bleak, little changed since Patrick Gallagher, 'Paddy the Cope', writing of the last years of the nineteenth century, described 'the brown bog, the grey rock and the little patches of green which appear here and there . . . streams with boulders like tombstones under which human shapes are buried. There is not a tree where the earth could shelter from its own storms, and yet if we climb at all we see a multitude of little holdings separated by grey walls of stone built up from the litter of the fields.' In parts of Donegal and the Rosses people could not survive without seasonal migration to Scotland.

Motoring to Glengarriff in April 1934, Virginia Woolf found 'a mixture of Greece, Italy & Cornwall; great loneliness; poverty & dreary villages like squares cut out of West Kensington. Not a single villa or house a-building; great stretches of virgin sea shore; the original land that Cornwall & much of England was in Elizabethan times. And a sense that life is receding.'

In the West, hens walked across the main street of towns like Ballina and the shop windows were full of advertisements for sailings to America. The typical small farmer's house was thatched, with an earthen floor. There was the kitchen with the open fireplace and the seat on either side. Many houses had a loft created by a platform built under the kitchen roof, and some possessed another ideal of de Valera, the west room for a retired couple. Among the utensils bowls were much in use as drinking vessels during the thirties. A wooden chest with a sloping lid would be divided into two compartments, one for white flour, the other for yellow meal. Often it was not until the fifties that yellow meal ceased to be eaten by the family and was given instead to the hens.

The open fire was never allowed to go out. The turf that supplied it was cut from nearby bogs; a good slansman could cut four tons of turf in a day, and the whole family would be involved in the final harvesting, and the stacking of newly cut sods, footed and, if there was no rain, drying in the wind. 'That hard brown turf is won from the bog in the months between spring work . . . and the fall,' wrote Aodh de Blacam, 'and ah! what joy there is in those family gatherings on the plain of odorous peat . . . Well may the old songs be sung, the melodeon make old music for the dance, while the strong race gathers to save the winter's firing.'

The smell of Ireland, thought Nicolette Devas, was the smell of poverty and decay and Guinness 'sniffed with a ray of hope'. Add to that the smoky scent of burning turf, part of the air people breathed. 'Bluey turf smoke rising from the chimney,' enthused Pamela Hinkson, 'no artificial heating or fuel that they can ever give us will produce a smoke like that.' James Kennedy remembered how 'our fire was the only source of heat in the house which was warm because it was thatched . . . The fire was the centre of life for us; for six months of the year – October to March – we sat around the hearth when the oil lamp was lit.'

In his story 'The Silence of the Valley' Sean O'Faolain lyrically described the house in West Cork of Timothy Buckley, the Tailor of *The Tailor and Ansty*: 'Everything in the kitchen had the same worn look of time and use, and everything was dusted with the grey dust of turf – the kettle over the peat fire, the varied pot hooks on the crane, the bright metal of the tongs, the dresser with its pieces of delft, a scalded churn lid leaning in the window to dry. There was nothing there that was not necessary, unless perhaps the red lamp and the oleograph of the Sacred Heart . . . The only light in the cottage came from the turf fire.'

Such detail caught the eyes of painters and writers who tended to ignore the attendant discomforts. The walls were usually damp and so was the clay floor, making mats desirable to protect bare feet. Bedclothes had to be dried regularly at the fire.

In *Tarry Flynn* Patrick Kavanagh described an interior in Co. Monaghan:

> Ten by five
> And a low roof
> If I stand by the side-wall
> My head feels the roof.
> Five holy pictures
> Hang on the wall:
> The Virgin and Child
> St Anthony of Padua
> Leo the XIII
> St Patrick and the Little Flower.

Tarry Flynn's uncle says, 'There's no necessity to live in this sort of place, is there? The best way to love a country like this is from a range of not less than three hundred miles.'

Life in Monaghan was as hard as anything perceived in the West. 'In our house the two most important subjects were saying the Rosary and making money.'

Intensive labour on the family farm was somewhat compensated for by living close to the soil. 'Spring came round again with its magic and innocence. And still I was one of the people. The land, which once gets a grip on a man will not easily let go. The land is jealous of literature and in its final effort to hold a poet offers him, like a despairing lover, everything, everything.'

But the time came when Kavanagh had had enough.

'On the nineteenth of December, nineteen thirty-one I said to my mother: "I'm going on a bit of a journey."

'"Musha, where," she asked in surprise.

'"As far as Dublin," I said.'

He left the stony grey soil of Monaghan and set out with little more than the clothes and boots he walked in, plus three shillings and fourpence halfpenny. The sixty-odd miles were hardly an odyssey. Each small locality he passed was a world in itself, a tight-knit community. For others like himself, making a break with the land was usually a prelude to taking the boat. For him, there would be poverty in Dublin, and eleven years later, the publication of *The Great Hunger*, the antidote to the rural idyll.

Watch him, watch him, that man on a hill whose spirit
Is a wet sack flapping about the knees of time.
He lives that his little fields may stay fertile when his own body
Is spread in the bottom of a ditch under two coulters crossed in
  Christ's Name.

For the most part, Irish towns and villages survived with all their charming features and hideous decay. The luxury of change was beyond most county councils' planning. Large towns had their slums which were without the picturesque qualities of Georgian tenements. When Sean T. O'Kelly visited North Cork in the mid-thirties and inspected Millstreet, Newmarket and Kanturk, he said, 'People are paying rent to landlords for living in byres . . . I thought housing conditions in Dublin were bad, but they are much worse here.'

Sean O'Faolain vented his spleen on many towns, but he reserved particular venom for Rathkeale, Co. Limerick, which he knew well, 'a dead, lousy, snoring, flea-bitten pig of a town . . . Nobody ever came to Rathkeale unless he came there from his mother's womb or for business.'

Not all towns were Rathkeales, inspiring revulsion. In an article in *Country Living*, Dervla Murphy remembered with affection her home town of Lismore which had a population of around 1,200 during the 1930s. The community was largely self-sufficient; the two cobblers not only mended but made boots and shoes. 'There were two tailors, several dressmakers, many carpenters, four stonemasons, three basket weavers, a saddler, two forges, and three butchers as well as four thriving bakers, each of whom employed a boy with a bicycle to deliver his distinctively flavoured loaves, hot from wall ovens.' Three farmers delivered milk in churns, twice daily in summer, once daily in winter. Lismore had two cinemas and twenty-two pubs or 'licensed premises' which included the four bakers, since most 'licensed premises' had other purposes as well as the supply of drink.

A typical pub was half-shop, a dark place lit by oil-lamps and candles, serving mainly porter out of barrels that served as seats. On the shop side drapery would be sold – flannelette shirts and coarse frieze trousers – together with 'American bacon', barrels of pigs' heads and sherbet for the children. Tobacco sales were important: Garryowen Twist, Wild Woodbine, Players and Gold Flake cigarettes and Clarke's Perfect Plug. Much tobacco was supplied by Methodists, who eschewed selling drink in favour of a wholesome trade that provided satisfaction to the working man. Goods on offer would include White Cap snuff, Quaker oats, Van Houton cocoa, Lipton's tea, Kavanagh's marmalade from Dundee and twopenny boxes of Take Me matches. Jam was sold in jugs in country shops during the twenties.

'Oh, definitely the pub and the bar is the place where you get a person's innermost thoughts,' a publican told me. 'Those that he wouldn't reveal to his wife. And he should have to know a friend a very long time before he will open up to him in the same way as the man behind the counter. Every publican in the country is a father confessor.'

To many people, such shops, usually combined with pubs, were seen as a desperate solution to insolvency. There were 46,000 in 1932, mostly family shops, one for every twenty families, almost half of which had a turnover of less than £5,000 a year. John Betjeman would write a panegyric about their 'sense of smell . . . paraffin lamps and a long counter . . . nestfuls of drawers and where you buy anything from sticky and boiled sweets to home cured bacon'. At night the typical village shop was lit by a single lamp hanging from the ceiling behind the glass jars of sweets in the window. 'Round the lamp clustered a conglomeration of boots, hams, tin cans and brushes, all hanging in confusion. The door had a bell that rang with a faint ping. You then made out beyond the zinc covered counter a pile of small dark wooden drawers with glass knobs.' These drawers would contain an immense variety of wares. But in many a shop in a potholed backstreet in a country town, problems with cleanliness, mould and mice might arise. At the very least the concept of a sell-by date had not been introduced.

Bigger shops, general stores often by now deserted by Protestants, with their signs NO SECOND PRICE, offered a better lifestyle. General stores sold most things from country butter to screws, nails and 'delph', or china. When we were children, nothing could equal the magic of O'Brien Corkery's emporium in Kenmare, large as a cathedral, filled with anything from anchors, fishing nets and ropes to tweeds, boots, sides of home-cured ham and rashers of Waterford back bacon which women would select as if they were examining gold leaf. Change and bills travelled in small satchels that buzzed overhead on a network of wire.

The danger for many shopkeepers was the system of credit. Everything was bought on the slate and actual immediate payment, even by those who could afford it, appeared to be an embarrassment. My mother would receive a docket with an air of vagueness; she favoured the traditional Anglo-Irish filing system of placing bills in a Chinese jar. I think she paid O'B C's about once a year. In country areas it was not uncommon for the butcher's bill, unpaid for months or even years, to be sent in after a funeral – sometimes with dire financial consequences. Otherwise the general shortage of money and the system of credit were ever-present problems; ledgers might contain hundreds of accounts for sums down to a penny. In a town with many shops, the crafty impecunious could spread their credit around. A customer might put a penny down on a two-and-sixpenny jug and be paying it off five years later. There were extreme cases of returned emigrants paying bills which were over a decade old. It was better to hope for successful deals at fairs which offered farmers opportunities to pay off their accounts. An old farmer's expression was 'I'll pay you on fair day'. The other source of payment would be the American cheque.

Tailors were kept busy; a master tailor like John Condon of Nenagh would employ up to twenty journeymen tailors during the summer months. In

Ballinrobe, Miley the Tailor had eight or nine assistants to turn out blue–black serge suits for men by the dozen every week. Drapers with their brass measuring tapes stretched along mahogany counters supplied other necessities. A big draper's shop like McCormack's of Ballinrobe sold rolls of white 'long cloth' or linen for handkerchiefs and pillowslips, bleached and unbleached calico for sheets, women's underwear, red doctor's flannel for kidney and back patients, and lace curtains, much in demand at those times when the Stations of the Cross were celebrated.

Báinín, white woollen cloth, was supplied for sleeveless working waistcoats, and homespun tweed lingered on until the fifties, brown and fawn and Thrushes' Breast for gentlemen's jackets. Leather leggings had gone by the late twenties. Now men aspired to have two pairs of shoes, 'kip boots' with hobnails for hard work, which would last for ever, and the Sunday pair of shoes, often the box calf boot, which was worn to Mass together with the blue suit.

In many parts of the country women knitted between household chores to earn a little petty cash; later, outlets like the Country Shop in Dublin would take their work. Meanwhile they sold locally; the women of Tourmakeady would walk into Ballinrobe knitting as they came; each would knit a sock on the way in and another on the way home, the pair to be sold at McCormack's and checked for thorns, since in some cases the wool was picked off the hedges.

The dead were provided with honeycomb quilts; in their spare time salesgirls stitched a picture of the Sacred Heart (for men) or the Blessed Virgin (for women) on the breasts of brown shrouds.

Like the churches, the banks were divided according to religion, the Hibernian Bank being Catholic, the Provincial Bank of Ireland Protestant. Managers had a seven-year tenure, like Methodist ministers before they moved on to another town; William Trevor's father was a bank manager in Youghal, Mitchelstown and Skibbereen, which gave his son a lifetime's material for fiction about Co. Cork.

There was still work for the forge, mowing machines to be fitted and shoes for the horse – in the thirties four new shoes cost five shillings. Certain shops had particular problems before the days of electricity or refrigeration. Without the electric saw or the humane killer the butcher had to be a strong man, killing his bullocks with a fearful instrument that might have been in use among medieval knights. The cleaver, chopper and boning knives all required hard physical strength. Inside the shop the sausages were coiled in an enamel basin together with the tripe; outside, carcasses hung on hooks on which crows would sit and peck their midday meal. On a hot summer's day the flies would be all over the meat, and the butcher and his boy would be slapping them with leather straps, covering the carcass with newspaper or gauze. 'If you killed on a Friday it would be black by Monday.'

In 1937 a guide to good and bad hotels recommended the avoidance of different types of bad hotels:

'Bad Expensive – the whole place is spotlessly clean, but it smells of linoleum. It is the only important available hotel in the town and profits ingratiatingly, obsequiously and without conscience.

'Bad Cheap – fleas, unwashed cutlery, damp beds and dirty bedrooms. For tea oily bacon and eggs.'

Sean O'Faolain visited a number of 'strange relics, these old Irish hotels – *Imperials, Royals, Princes of Wales.* Balzac would have enjoyed describing them room by room: the dark carpets the pattern become indistinct, the edges of the risers on the stairs rubbed to the cord; the rose-patterned ewer and basin and the flowery chamber pots; the electric bulbs plonk in the middle of the ceiling; the blinds that may or may not run up; the invariably friendly servants, the exalted boots, the motherly manageress, the bar which is the town clubhouse.'

Two sorts of guests frequented these establishments. The farmers appeared on fair days in their muddy boots; 'they sit at table, tuck their napkins into their collars and consume the soup with satiated smacks of the lips and noises like train whistles'. The commercial travellers, or 'commercials', many from breweries and distilleries, were known by their smelly mackintoshes, bowler hats, spats and umbrellas. They were the winter mainstay of many a hotel. They would stay overnight, eat their steaks – nothing but a steak would do – and drink much of what they earned. Next day they would take their orders and drive in their little Ford cars to the next town. When O'Faolain visited New Ross, Co. Wexford, a shopkeeper told him that although the town was 'a little pinched', the commercials '"get paid". Emphatically, and with modest bourgeois pride: "They get paid!"' New Ross, at that time, was in decline with 'the air of an old man whose day is over'.

Hotels were considered to have improved. 'Admittedly,' commented the *Irish Times* in February 1936, 'there remain a few hotels which are as dirty and dear and inefficient as ever, but this graceless class is found as a rule in "non-tourist" districts and does not matter immensely. Some are without a telephone . . . some could do with more bathrooms. How many country hotels do not possess a wireless?'

Outside Killarney and places in the West with spectacular scenery like Connemara, tourists were 'rare as Tibetans'. But there were golden exceptions, and the Great Southern palaces like that at Parknasilla frequented by Shaw, or the Eccles Hotel at Glengarriff, would entice the foreigner. I remember visitors arriving at Kenmare station and being greeted by a porter in a bright red jacket with a trolley to wheel their baggage up the town's main street to the glory of the Great Southern Hotel. Most tourists were English, the hated Saxon, the fellow countrymen of the Black and Tans.

From Cork to Glengarriff, from Killarney to Galway, stretching up to Sligo and Donegal, the English tripper was to be found, usually well-to-do, usually driving a car. In 1933 he had to follow the regulations of the new traffic act and pass a ridden horse at a distance of six feet. A person in charge of cattle, sheep or pigs had to make passage for any vehicle coming either way, but when necessary a person in charge of animals could request a vehicle's driver to stop at a reasonable distance by raising his hand. There was more traffic than there had been when Speakman toured in his ass cart, but not much more.

Stephen Gwynn analysed the appeal for the stranger: 'People in Ireland dress the same way as English or Americans; they use the same kind of food, the same kind of drinks and they speak the same language. Yet every English visitor . . . cries out at the unfamiliarity of everything.'

Among the hotels Gwynn recommended was one run by my cousin near Castlebar which 'takes in paying guests, supplies a motor car, arranges for boats and fishing on most reasonable terms and has excellent cock and superb duck shooting'. A note added, 'The normal charge for a boat and a man is now a shilling a day – it is usual to provide the man with a bottle of stout.'

Gwynn records a day in which the visitor's activities did not differ from those of his Victorian predecessor. 'Our programme is as follows. Breakfast at nine o'clock, and then off for a good day's shooting until sunset. We have a rest about noon, and have some sandwiches at some wayside cottage where one is treated to the very best they can provide and there is a great difficulty in recompensing them in any way. Off we go again, until it is impossible to see any more. Back home again, and we are ready to enjoy a great feed, a nice smoke, and a quiet evening talking over the sport of the day in front of a turf and coal fire.' The bag for five days' shooting was '50 snipe, 24 golden and green plover, 2 teal, 2 grouse, 2 rabbits, 1 woodcock and 1 curlew'. The country still quivered with birds, including corncrakes which kept people awake in Dublin suburbs; grouse and snipe were plentiful in the Dublin mountains.

Lynn Doyle was a Northerner whose heart was in the South. In his *Spirit of Ireland* he proclaimed that 'southern Ireland will always be one of the most pleasant places of humanity . . . the future of the tourist's trip to Ireland may be decided by his "good morning" to his taxi man . . . I will presume that the tourist in question is an Englishman and that he belongs to the wealthiest class coming to Ireland to see its "beauties" to shoot, fish or to hunt.'

Among the places visited by the Englishman H. V. Morton was the Claddagh outside Galway. The thatched cottages arranged beside the Garraí Glas – the green open space along haphazard cobbled streets and lanes, strewn with cocks and hens – Dogfish Lane and Rope Walk, had been the homes of a traditional fishing community for generations. But by the thirties the fishing smacks were dwindling as trawlers took over, and photographs of the annual Blessing of the Bay showed a steady decline in their numbers.

Morton peered into the little rooms that belonged to 'primitive' thatched houses; they were clean and comfortable, but minuscule. The houses had to be re-roofed every year, they had no sanitation, and the tiny bedrooms had no windows. According to Nicolette Devas, they were so rotten 'that they lean against each other for support . . . children play marbles with live cockles and tear starfish apart. Young women in shawls whisper in groups while others push carts of seaweed or trudge between stacks of potatoes.' With her father she spent time in cabins drinking poteen by the light of a candle and experiencing the fierce strength of this isolated community.

Irishmen rediscovering their country were less critical and saw its beauty with patriotic pride. An important impetus to the enjoyment of the countryside was the founding of the new Gaeltacht colleges. Native Irish speakers tended to live in remote and beautiful places where enthusiasts, schoolchildren and those for whom a knowledge of Irish was an essential for a job, could go during the summer months to brush up their Gaelic. Tod Andrews took his family to Carraroe and was enchanted by the countryside and its people: 'For a Dubliner Carraroe was a new world.' But he was also appalled by the poverty, a mirror image of the destitution which he had observed in the Dublin slums. 'One family near us had no less than nine children living in a two-roomed *bothán* with a few acres of land.'

Civil servants also flocked to the Ring peninsula in east Waterford, taking notes and talking to the mystified people. They were affectionately treated as eccentrics. Donal Foley lamented how the village of Ring declined and the people emigrated, while their culture was cherished behind the walls of Coláiste na Rinne.

It was an Irishman who wrote 'the past is another country'. There are two ways of viewing it. One old man lectured me: 'Never mind the people who keep telling you how good it was in the old days. It was dire. There were dire standards of living. The children now think torture and hell was the sort of existence I can remember older people having . . . If you throw in . . . a very uninteresting diet, ragged clothes, bad shoes or no shoes – and walking for miles with your cattle to the fair – that was hard, all right.'

In *The Great Hunger*:

> The fields were bleached white
> The wooden tubs full of water
> Were white in the winds
> That blew through Brannagan's gap on their way from Siberia.

Sacheverell Sitwell wrote of his impressions of the Free State in 1936, 'Its shapes and contours make it a paradise that is unhappy. And so it must remain far away from the stream of life with the sadness of all things that are a little remote from reality.' In 1931, however, Evelyn Waugh, writing about Kenya, had observed, 'There is a quality about it which I have found nowhere else but in Ireland, of warm loveliness and breadth and generosity.'

Many who felt the hardship remember the past with nostalgia. Listen to the words of a bedridden old man in a county home, now dead, talking a few years back: 'You might think that an old man like myself is living on borrowed time, and a few more years will see me out . . . I had a jolly life all my life. I was always happy, and I'll tell you I had a great life. I lie here in bed and think of the old times.'

CHAPTER 12

Genie Out of the Bottle

Up de Valera you're the champion of the fight
We'll follow you to battle 'neath the orange green and white,
When next we tackle England we will wash her out of sight
And make de Valera King of Ireland.

Fianna Fáil anthem

To the tune of 'Let Erin Remember':

... while Collins, the lion, looks down from the stars,
Let us swear to be true to his leading.

Blueshirt anthem

In later years de Valera told Robert Collis: 'When I came to power in the thirties by replacing Mr Cosgrave, a very critical moment arose which isn't in the history books. The Chief of the Free State forces approached Cosgrave and said, "We'd better not let the Republicans in. They are bound to revenge themselves ... let's have a coup d'état." But Cosgrave answered, "I am a democrat. I have been defeated at the polls and I am going out."' The Army chief was Richard Mulcahy.

In the same conversation de Valera said, 'I sent for Frank Aiken and said, "Now Frank, we've got in ... no revenge." Cosgrave and I were then not on speaking terms, but we both believed in the same thing. A new Ireland was born that day, though neither of us knew it.'

Aiken was appointed Minister for Justice. He had not been prominent during the Civil War, which made him more politically acceptable to his opponents. On 9 March 1932, a few days after the election, he paid a visit to IRA prisoners in Arbour Hill and next day every prisoner there was released.

Orders proscribing the organisation were revoked. When a member of the IRA was convicted of possessing firearms, he was released without serving his sentence.

In June 1932, when Ireland was celebrating the Eucharistic Congress, 15,000 men and women sympathetic to the IRA were brought down to Kildare in special trains, private cars and motor lorries. Thousands marched in military formation to the graveside of that much-put-upon Protestant, Wolfe Tone. Five Fianna Fáil trumpeters and four drummers lined up in front of the grave.

The IRA could do what it liked. The genie had been let out of the bottle. The early thirties would resound with a low level of violence which reminded people uneasily of the full-scale bloodshed of the past. IRA drilling was ignored by the police, while many new recruits rushed to join up.

De Valera turned his attention to agriculture, defending his role as the friend of the small farmer. 'The land annuities will never be paid to Great Britain; if the British succeed in beating us – then we'll have no freedom.' In June 1932 he withheld annuities due to the British Government of £3 million annually which had been paid by Cumann na nGaedheal, claiming that the financial agreements of 1925 and 1926 to compensate owners of confiscated land had never been ratified by the Dáil. Britain retaliated by imposing tariffs of twenty per cent on Irish cattle and agricultural produce, including eggs and butter entering the United Kingdom. It was the cattle that counted.

De Valera struck back with tariffs on British goods like coal, cement, iron, steel and electrical goods. But Britain was in a better position to sustain the contest, as Irish agriculture plummeted and cattle became virtually unsaleable.

In 1931 livestock exports had been worth £18 million, but two years later this had been reduced to £7 million. The counties most affected by the economic war were those where pasture was the mainstay of farms – Cork, Kilkenny, Waterford, Meath, Westmeath, Carlow, Kildare and Tipperary. The big cattle farmers suffered most; they were described as Irish kulaks. De Valera faced their ruin with complacency, since in general they did not vote Fianna Fáil.

Since cattle could not be exported, their numbers remained constant. The countryside was crowded with unsaleable animals, many dying in their fields. Often the drovers beat their animals along the road in vain, starting at two in the morning, lighting their way with a torch or carbide lamp to get to the fair by dawn. A farmer told me, 'I've seen men go to the fair, their young families at home, and they didn't sell their cattle, they couldn't sell their cattle. The worst situation of all was to take your cattle on a wet morning over the mountain and not to sell them and have to come back again. In very lean and very poor times it was many farmers came home from the fair disgusted. They called it an economic war and there were no economics in it at all.'

Victor Griffin wrote of a farmer taking a calf to the fair in Enniscorthy, having been told by his wife to get rid of it at any price. Unable to sell it, he was returning when he stopped at a local pub: '"Would anyone like to buy a calf for sixpence?" Still no takers. After talking to the boys he went out to find two calves in the cart instead of one.'

In October 1934 only one animal out of forty-four at Cork show was sold. Many farmers butchered their own meat and went around from door to door trying to sell it. The Government's remedy for the glut was the calf-slaughtering scheme introduced in 1934; thousands of calves were disposed of that way. Fianna Fáil's agricultural policy also introduced weird rules to try and regulate the pig trade; if a man had a pig that weighed 175 pounds he might get more money for it than for a 200-pound one.

It was in this atmosphere that the Army Comrades Association came into prominence, founded in February 1932. Its members were ex-officers and men of the Free State Army whose purpose was to commemorate the men who had died during the War of Independence. During the election of March 1932 the Association gave its support to Cosgrave and Cumann na nGaedheal. In August 1932, the ACA was open to others apart from military veterans, and obtained a new President, Thomas O'Higgins, brother of Kevin O'Higgins who had been murdered five years before. It soon claimed to have a membership of 20,000, attracting support which was seen as coming from farmers and farmers' sons who were being ruined by the economic war.

Since cattle were often the only capital a farmer might have, his useless animals would be seized to pay the Land Commission's annuities. After cattle prices collapsed, farmers who were supporters of the new movement began a policy of non-payment of rates. Cattle seizures were opposed riotously; as a matter of principle farmers objected to their property being taken forcibly. Incidents occurred almost daily involving clashes with the police, now under Fianna Fáil leadership.

Sales of confiscated cattle would be conducted under duress. Often they were like the one in Fermoy in March 1935 at which many gardaí were present, fully armed, machine-guns having been brought in to avoid trouble. In a tense atmosphere one buyer from outside the district bought eighteen milch cows for £30, while thirty lambs and sheep changed hands for £10. All business in Fermoy closed for three hours in sympathy with the farmers whose cattle had been seized, and afterwards 500 farmers marched through the town. This was a relatively orderly occasion.

At first, members of the ACA wore a trefoil badge on a white ribbon in their buttonholes. Then they started to wear uniforms. They picked a colour which had not been claimed elsewhere in Europe. Eoin O'Duffy said, 'The blue shirt, like a flag, is not a mere piece of cloth. It is our emblem, our symbol, our idea which may be summed up in three words, Service, Discipline, Country.'

Adopted as the official uniform of the ACA in March 1933, the blue shirt was noted at a convention in Kilkenny early in April. A week later Ernest Blythe was photographed in one; soon young men were wearing them at Cumann na nGaedheal dances and deputies wore them in the Dáil. According to Frank O'Connor, Yeats was seen in one in the Kildare Street Club. Yeats also wrote 'unsingable' Fascist songs to the tunes of 'O'Donnell Abu' and 'The Heather Field'. This was the period when the poet, to the dismay of his later devotees admired Mussolini and his imitators. But soon O'Duffy would lose his popularity, and together with it, Yeats's support. The remarkable William Cosgrave, modest man of peace, never put on a blue shirt.

Together with the shirt went the beret. 'Onlooker', who wrote the ACA's official (and short-lived) magazine, the *Blueshirt*, observed, 'I have seen some men wearing them perched perilously on top of their heads as if they were pancakes. I have seen others wearing them with the bands down so that they were converted into tam-o-shanters. A beret should be worn with about one inch of the band turned in so that when well pulled down, it fits fairly closely to the head.'

From the outset the Blueshirts picked up bad habits. The IRA and many of the new political parties in Europe liked marching in military formation, and soon the Comrades were doing the same. They took to a salute that resembled the one adopted by enthusiasts of Herr Hitler. 'The right hand is to be swung up until it is in front of and higher than the shoulder,' instructed 'Onlooker', 'with the palm facing forwards and downwards until the arm is at an angle of forty-five degrees from the perpendicular. The fingers will be kept together full stretched with the thumb close to the forefinger.'

In the early days even de Valera found something appealing in this type of arm raising. 'I have always thought that it was a manly salute, a much better salute than the mere doffing of one's hat, so if people want to use the salute, I have no objection, not the slightest.'

In July 1933, General Eoin O'Duffy, who had been Commissioner of the Garda until he was dismissed by de Valera, became President of the Army Comrades Association; at the same time its name was changed to the National Guard. Its declared aims were to promote the reunion of Ireland, oppose 'the many-headed beast of communism', which, its members implied, included de Valera and the IRA, and 'to awaken throughout the country a spirit of . . . discipline, zeal and patriotic realism which will put the state in a position to serve the people efficiently in the economic and social sphere'.

For many followers of O'Duffy it was a time of desperation. A young supporter of the movement, Geoffrey O'Shea, wrote how 'the way it was you were a follower of Dev, thought him God, or you were against him and hated him. We were on the hate side . . . When Eoin O'Duffy started the Blueshirts . . . all we youngsters backed him. We wanted to sell our milk and cattle. Survival was what it was all about.'

In August 1933 de Valera banned the Blueshirts. His opponents regrouped. Fine Gael was formed, the name meaning Tribe of the Gaels, an amalgamation of Cumann na nGaedheal, the National Guard and the National Centre Party, which had been founded in 1932 specifically to support the farmers. Unfortunately, its first President was Eoin O'Duffy.

In their uniforms the Blueshirts met, marched, raised their arms, shouted and wrangled with Republicans. Parades, meetings and organised opposition to cattle seizures met with constant clashes; at other times rioting would occur, with weapons varying from sticks and stones to pitchforks. From the outset the movement had been opposed by supporters of Fianna Fáil and members of the IRA who disrupted their meetings with pitched battles, using hurley sticks, stones and hand-to-hand fighting. Blows, scuffles, clashes with hostile opponents and shots fired over the heads of crowds became commonplace. Bailiffs were attacked as cattle were hidden and sales were broken up. Republicans retaliated, tearing up railway tracks and felling trees across roads to impede Blueshirt meetings. In Annagary, Co. Donegal, shots were fired at Mr Cosgrave's car, and nine meetings in Co. Clare turned to rioting.

Geoffrey O'Shea, who attended a rally on a warm day in May 1934, complete with cheering and shouting crowds, booing supporters of de Valera, boys in blue shirts and girls in blue blouses, remembered the occasion as 'a bit of amusement for us . . . Easy to amuse at that time.' At Wexford a crowd of stone-throwing youths were baton-charged by police. In Skibbereen armed men ordered Fine Gael supporters to put up their hands; shots were fired over their heads and an attempt was made to burn the platform on which they were standing. In Drogheda a fight took place between Blueshirts and a hostile mob shouting, 'Up de Valera!' Every now and again someone died, like the elderly woman killed by a bomb in Drogheda. When Hugh O'Reilly died early in January 1934 after a beating he received on Christmas Day, the mourners who gathered at his funeral had their arms raised.

In February 1934 Cardinal MacRory condemned in a Lenten pastoral what had become a campaign of violence conducted by both sides: 'What is one to think or say to these people, mostly young men, who for political reasons are waylaying defenceless men at night or dragging them from their homes and savagely beating or even murdering them? I confess I burn with shame every time I read of such an outrage . . . what right have these young bullies to judge and condemn their neighbours?'

Patrick Lindsay was passionate in his support: 'The Blueshirts were born out of the need for self-defence. No less. No more. As for the charge of Fascism, that's total nonsense. As for Eoin O'Duffy, he was a brilliant organiser and a great Commissioner of Guards, and that was where he should have been left, but Fianna Fáil sacked him.'

Sean Lemass commented that O'Duffy's knowledge of Fascism 'appears to have been acquired during a fortnight's cruise of the Mediterranean'. In a later speech Lemass emphasised his abhorrence of any form of Fascism for Ireland: 'It is not for us to criticise the actions taken in Italy and Germany. The people in these countries are entitled to have whatever type of institutions they like. But we are going to see to it that in this country similar institutions are not going to be imposed upon the people.'

O'Duffy continued to strut about the country. A tour of Munster in September 1934 was described in the *Blueshirt* as a triumphal progress.

Enthusiasm was reported at Waterford, Clonmel, Cashel and Limerick. There were waiting crowds and mention of the New Spirit in Tipperary. But at Fethard, fist fights took place and all roads leading to the town were blocked with stones and tree-trunks to prevent O'Duffy from arriving.

The Fianna Fáil Government sought means to curb the Blueshirts. The Wearing of Uniforms (Restrictions) Bill, introduced in February 1934, was delayed in the Senate so that it would not become effective for eighteen months. But the movement was faltering because of growing criticism of O'Duffy, especially among moderate members of Fine Gael. His admiration for Hitler and support for Mussolini revealed him as progressively more Fascist, while violence followed everywhere he went. He was impetuous and given to extravagant and unpleasant statements. He became stridently anti-British in an effort to attract new recruits to the Blueshirts, calling for the end to Partition. Opposition to his flamboyant pronouncements caused him to resign the presidency of Fine Gael in August 1934, and after that the Blueshirt movement petered out. It hiccuped into a brief revival when, with the blessing of the Church, O'Duffy, together with 600 followers, went to Spain in support of Franco in 1937. But Fascism was not for Ireland any more than Communism. By the election of 1937, normal relations had resumed between Fine Gael and Fianna Fáil.

Meanwhile, the mid-thirties had proved bleak and brutal for Ireland. Because of quota restrictions, emigration to the USA had virtually ceased and for the first time in well over a century more Irishmen returned home than went abroad. The population rose from 2,927,000 in the first half of the 1930s to 2,971,00 in 1935. But this rise covered a very brief period of time and soon statistics resumed their remorseless downward trend. The 1936 census revealed that in the past ten years nearly 167,000 people had emigrated. The population had decreased in that period by 0.1 per cent, in other words, a loss of over 3,500 people. Emigration was highest from Kerry, Mayo, Leitrim and Roscommon. When emigration began to rise again, people went to England rather than to the United States.

Young men were returning to a life of unemployment or exploitation on impoverished farms. The unemployed roamed the streets; at my uncle's house outside Palmerstown two or three unemployed men a day would call in for work – not so much for money, but for the meat and two-vegetable meal the household provided.

Publicly, poverty was fought on various fronts. The Fianna Fáil Government was responsible for the first faltering footsteps towards a welfare state. The dole was introduced in 1934. Pensions were increased. In West Cork Timothy Buckley, the tailor in *The Tailor and Ansty*, was gleeful that he had managed to receive, at a rate of ten shillings a week, a total of £150 from the Government 'free, gratis and for nothing'. In 1935 an allowance was introduced for widows with children; childless widows got nothing until they qualified for a pension, but at least mothers no longer had to endure their children going to orphanages.

The means test limited a widow with one child to six shillings a week, while a penniless widow with three children received twenty-one shillings.

The modest housing programme initiated by the previous Government was extended; its efforts were not always well received. In 1934 the little houses in the Claddagh outside Galway were pulled down and the community was given unpicturesque dwellings instead, 'hideous little modern houses . . . coarse and hateful to the eye', according to the fastidious Morton. But hideous little modern houses were more comfortable than traditional homes with thatched roofs and clay floors.

In Cork Sean O'Faolain, equally critical, condemned 'a rash of red roofs, a slum-clearance scheme known as the Red City. It has begun to empty that lively poor-folk region around the Cattle Markets, Fair Hill, Nicholas Well Lane, Merrypole Lane, Quarry Lane, and all the warrens around and behind Shandon Street; and I have a terror that the poor . . . are going to be made slaves of that curse of all provincial towns, and the blight of this town of all towns, Bourgeois Respectability.' O'Faolain's affection, however, did not waver for the city that his fellow Corkonian Frank O'Connor described as a 'hell-hole'.

The new Government embarked on a policy of self-sufficiency, encouraging tillage and the development of the turf and sugar beet industries under the direction of the youngest member of the Fianna Fáil Cabinet, the Minister for Industry and Commerce, Sean Lemass. When O'Faolain visited Thurles at the end of the decade, he was impressed by the change for the better that had come about since the sugar beet factory was built. In the old days Thurles had been a town of hovels and squalor: 'You could step from dung-heap to dung-heap to the square.' Now, sugar beet had brought prosperity; the square was newly concreted and Thurles had become a modern business town with busy streets and bright shops.

In 1931, Canon John Hayes founded Muintir na Tíre, the community development association which would assume importance in encouraging electrification schemes and the establishment of local industries. Creameries were replacing the old separator and churn, and beginning to supply the monthly cheque; the churns assembled outside them behind ass and cart and horse and cart. Small farmers were given price supports and welfare concessions, including free beef to help them over the worst of the economic war. In Charlestown, Co. Mayo, John Healy remembered 'hundreds of bikes coming down for Free Beef . . . the men wobbling home, parcels of fresh meat under the springs of their carriers, the blood coming through the brown paper'.

In 1933 the Government set up the Turf Development Board, which would evolve into Bord na Móna in 1948. An observer of the thirties, seeing the Bog of Allen, exclaimed that there was enough turf in the country to last a hundred years. Advertisements of the day promoted an Irish fuel: 'Four thousand million tons of turf are spread over Irish soil waiting to be cut and dried, to be transported to every Irish home . . . every penny's worth gives heat because it burns to the very last . . . Turf for Better Heating, for Better Health.' Turf burning was a patriotic gesture among those who believed in the old slogan, BURN EVERYTHING BRITISH EXCEPT THEIR COAL. In Northern Ireland, according to Lynn Doyle, turf was considered a Catholic fuel, 'not quite fit burning for the dominant creed'.

A nationwide programme of road building was started. Stone breaking was still done by hand; large stones were first broken with a sledgehammer and then into pieces with a small hammer. Sean O'Casey, who had done stone breaking as a young man for half a crown a cubic yard, said it was easier than the pick and shovel. In a period when emigration was difficult, payment 'by the yard' was eagerly accepted. Travelling in Leitrim, one of the nation's poorest counties, Norah Munnay commented, 'You hear of the godsend the work on the roads is to some struggling farmers' sons that couldn't get to America.'

In May 1935 the author Francis Hackett, Signe Toksvig's husband, wrote a furious letter to the *Irish Times* indicating that life was hard for the middle classes as well. He listed the irritations a man like himself had to bear: 'the worst radio in the world, the dearest telegrams, the worst telephone development, the worst electric system . . . with our politicians hoodwinking us and blathering to foreign correspondents about our spirituality and our happiness'. Much of the fault lay, he contended, with education being in the hands of 'under-developed celibates'. The Irish language was important, but it was costing millions and was 'a wild goose chase'. He denounced 'fatuous film censorship, press intimidation, book censorship, sterilised education, birth control by infanticide and divorce by strychnine and the hammer'. The last items referred to murder cases, including the sentencing to death of two young sisters, Elizabeth and Rose Edwards, for the killing of Elizabeth's child. An all-male jury found them guilty; there was no sign of the father in the proceedings. The girls were reprieved, but the case left a nasty taste.

The North of Ireland was brutal at the best of times. A report in the *Irish Independent* in October 1936 described the ordeal of a priest travelling between Lisnaskea and Enniskillen in a carriage with some Orangemen wearing sashes and singing 'Dolly's Brae' and 'Derry's Walls'. Shouting in his ear, 'Up Ballinamallard, where a Fenian cannot go through, Up Lisbellaw, where they make the Orange tweed!' they put their sashes around his neck and cursed the Pope. But things were often worse with rioting, arson, murder, sniping and terror. Maud Gonne visited her old friend Mrs Despard: 'Few people realise just what life is like under Orange terror in the North. One time I counted five children on crutches in the garden, recovering from bullet wounds.'

For a time the IRA, having enjoyed almost complete freedom to make mischief, benefited from the island's miseries. But increasingly the Fianna Fáil Government came to recognise a serious threat. The Minister for Telegraphs, Gerald Boland, issued a warning in May 1935: 'They will realise anyway they cannot go around shooting people – that game has got to stop in this country. We tolerated it as long as we could but they have gone too far.' The IRA, however, continued to be tolerated for another year.

In Castletownshend in May 1936 old Admiral Boyle Somerville was shot on his own doorstep. His assailants shot out the oil lamps in the hall behind him. Drishane had no electricity. The note they threw in read: 'This English agent has sent 52 Irishmen to the English forces during the past seven weeks.' At a time when unemployment was at its highest, Somerville had helped local men to get jobs in the Royal Navy.

A month later John Egan was murdered in Dungarvan and Fianna Fáil had had enough. On 18 June 1936 an order was made by the Executive Council declaring the IRA an unlawful association. The Bodenstown Commemoration of Wolfe Tone was suppressed. On Sunday 21 June 1,000 troops with an armoured car and 500 gardaí were in force along the route of Egan's funeral and inside the cemetery. Mrs Hannah Sheehy-Skeffington was forced to read Mary MacSwiney's address by the roadside to a little group of faithful members of Sinn Féin.

Sinn Féin continued to function as a political party. The virus was latent.

Adherents of Eoin O'Duffy with their timid imitation of German Fascism got the bad press – mocked as 'pudgy middle-aged businessmen in blue shirts howling about cattle prices'. Since there was much that was unpleasant in their right-wing attitudes, they deserved some of the scorn. Although they did not follow the Nazis in open anti-Semitism, O'Duffy betrayed his Fascist opinions in the way he loudly condemned the travelling people. 'The spectacle of small farmers giving a half stone of potatoes to an able-bodied muscular tinker who happened to stroll among them contributed to the continued living of idle and dissolute lives by an unworthy class.'

The plight of the journeyman and tinker who slept rough was worse than that of the majority of those caught in the 1930s poverty trap. It was still acceptable to call travelling people tinkers, a word that went downhill. Before the age of plastic, tinkering was their prerogative. Tin smiths worked in tin, beating out sheets of metal, re-rimming wheels, repairing household utensils, mending sieves and putting handles on saucepans.

For many farmers the arrival of the tinkers was a herald of summer. All over the country were scattered barrel-shaped caravans, and humpies or tents with their smoking fires and attendant clothes strewn on bushes. Nearly half the itinerant population lived in tents without any other form of shelter. It was too easy to glamorise the open-air life, the moment when the family pitched their tent, and prepared to boil the kettle and cook the stew over the open fire. Accounts tell of the delight of the open road, the warm fresh air, and the sound of wind and rain beating on the canvas.

The trades the tinkers followed were diverse. Besides that of tin smith, every way of making a living was tried. They sold halters, *Old Moore's Almanacs*, delph, mirrors, pins, needles and household goods; they bought and traded in meat, eggs and milk. They repaired clocks and umbrellas and sold horsehair and rabbit skins. Later when they got motor transport they went into feathers, moving from one chicken factory to the next, buying up feathers for bedding.

Or they sold scrap linoleum and carpeting from door to door. Chimney-sweeping was traditionally an occupation for travellers. The horse trading or the vetting of horses for buyers would continue while the countryside was unmechanised. But begging was often the mainstay of travelling families, the basket women going from one farmhouse to the next hawking their charms, medals and holy pictures with a whine of desperation. 'When the travelling woman called to a house she always stood at the door unless she was invited in. Her greeting was "God bless this house"; then she would ask for charity in the honour of God. "In the name of God, have you a bit of bread or a cup of milk for me poor childer. God comfort you and may he have mercy on your dead."'

The darker side of travelling lives was heightened by illiteracy and ill health. A woman bathing her child in a stream on a frosty morning. A child born between the shafts of a cart with the rain spilling down. The heavy drinking and the old-style faction fights with sticks, stones, soldering irons, iron bars and bare knuckles that could crush bones sickeningly to the sound of curses and shouts. When such fights take place in the 1990s and events happen that reflect that the lot of the travelling people remains unacceptable in a civilised society, we have a continuing guilty link with the poverty of the past.

In the thirties, during the harsh winter months, many tinkers and their families moved into 'spikes' or lodging houses. Many public houses banned them, as they still do, and the familiar complaints about their lifestyle were heard sixty and seventy years ago. Dirt and litter, mangy dogs and piebald ponies were accoutrements of outsiders, increasingly marginalised as their traditional trades declined. Like all nomads, tinkers were a nuisance to the settled people; even the respectable journeyman tailor or cobbler, always on the move, was regarded as unreliable.

There were few fairs that tinkers did not attend, bringing their trades and horses with them. The fair with its ritual of bargaining, reluctant hand claps and encouragement from bystanders to 'split the difference' would continue to be the mainstay of rural life until the coming of the marts and the less picturesque but more reliable methods of buying and selling livestock. There were big and little fairs, sheep fairs, horse fairs and pig fairs. Harold Speakman had encountered a pig fair in Kerry. 'Here are assembled all the youth and beauty of pigdom – pigs and piglets of surpassing porcine loveliness, fairly bursting with breakfast potential . . . *"What makes more noise than a pig under a fence?"* Some may answer, "Two pigs under a fence" but there is a far better answer than that. It is "Three hundred pigs in carts on the main street in Dingle."'

At Ballinrobe, prominent as a meeting point in rural Mayo, besides the four big fairs spaced through the year, a general fair day was held every Monday and a pig market on the first Thursday of every month. Two big sheep fairs were held in September and October and a big cattle fair in November.

On Sundays in summer people would row across Lough Mask with boats laden with flannel, *bréidín* tweeds, knitted goods and pigs. In the town were traditional places for selling goods, just as there had been in the Middle Ages. In the Cornmarket wheat, oats and barley were weighed out on big scales, while in Abbey Street crib carts of turf drawn by donkeys were sold with potatoes, hay, turnips, cabbage plants and poultry. During the economic war bull calves at three and sixpence were on offer.

Noel Browne remembered the Ballinrobe fairs, 'streets lined with huddled horses, cattle, sheep and calves in rough pens, heads all turned away from their tormentors, the road fouled with animal waste, straw and mud. The pungent smells; a pig's scream; the questing moan of a cow newly separated from its calf; the distinctive metallic sound of the solid steel cartwheel shafts on the well-worn oaken wheel hop slowly trundling through the streets . . .'

A great horse fair like Ballinasloe, which took place in October, had up to 3,000 horses for sale. The horse fair at Cahirmee, Co. Cork, was said to be where Napoleon's white charger, 'Marengo', was purchased. Horses were constantly on offer at less spectacular fairs since large numbers were still needed, particularly for Dublin.

Sean O'Faolain recalled the frenzy of a cattle fair in Rathkeale: 'Outside the door the pent cattle thrust their tousled fur through the red bars and the blue bars of the creels under the drizzling rain, their mooing and bleating passing from cart-creel to cart-creel and from dawn to noon, weaving in the wet air with the crying of men's voices, linking cry to cry in ceaseless lament.' Paul Henry took a train to Achill 'crowded with drovers and cattlemen on their way to the great fair at Mullingar. Here the train was invaded by more cattle dealers coming from the fair; many of them had been up all night, they told me; and they brought a whiff of the farmyard into the dining car. They fell to, like starving men, on the breakfast. God! What breakfast! Porridge, fish, ham and eggs, finishing up with beef steaks, one of which would have lasted me for a week: quantities of bread, butter and marmalade, and quarts of tea.' At all fairs catering played an important part; mutton and beef was served in quantities in hotels, and a hundredweight of herring would be gutted for Friday fairs.

Farmers brought their animals great distances to fairs. H. V. Morton wrote of Kerry, 'If your bedroom is in front of a house you will be awakened while it is still dark by a queer, insistent pattering on the road outside. You look at your watch. It's 5 a.m. When you pull the blind, you see herds of cattle going past in the moonlight. The drovers walk behind, bent over their sticks.' He wrote before the impact of the economic war when the drovers would be back again in the hours of darkness with the same animals.

Fairs began at daylight; pubs and hotels would get morning extensions to allow them to open by 7.30. Drinking was part of the ritual, easing the hundreds of little deals that were going on. Drinking habits changed from the leisurely whiskey followed by a pint, to the half-pint of Guinness which could be drunk fast, giving a reason to be at a certain place where drovers and farmers might be, and the excuse to leave in a hurry. Sometimes a man standing at the bar would have a rope in his hand and an animal at the end of it outside the premises.

Small farmers sold cattle to middlemen and the animals were shipped east for fattening. Both dealers and farmers tended to dress down on fair days so as not to appear too wealthy. A two-day growth of beard might appear on an otherwise clean-shaven man, and he might wear a ragged coat tied with a rope. A publican told me: 'I remember a usually well-dressed person coming in on fair day . . . in this torn raincoat . . . I said, "Jimmy . . . am I seeing right?" and he looked at me rather sheepish. "It's the fair . . . you can't afford to put on an image of wealth, and I have to appear poorer than the next man."'

At the end of a fair morning the town would be filthy with straw and manure. Here would be work for the travelling men. Before the piped water and sewage schemes came in, pig dung, cow dung, blood and guts from butchers' yards, and human waste from dry closets would have to be disposed of, often by carters who were travellers. Dirt in Ireland, observed a reporter from the *Australian Sunday Sun*, inevitably condemned as a 'cheap hack writer', 'is seemingly next to Godliness. There is always holy water, but there is rarely soap.'

In addition to sheep fairs, cattle fairs, horse fairs and pig fairs, in the early thirties there were hiring fairs for humans, attended by landless men and unmarried girls. With low wages and scarcity of jobs they still fulfilled a need. In small towns young men would stand with their spades and shovels at street corners or beside landmarks such as the big tree in the main street of Thomastown, Co. Kilkenny, hoping to be hired from February to October. A man with a knowledge of cattle who could milk might receive £20 for summer and £15 for winter with food and lodgings. When Patrick Kavanagh was asked at the hiring fair at Carrick if he could milk, he replied, 'I can milk anything but a hen.' Girls would expect a lot less money for a twelve-hour day of drudgery.

Liam O'Donnell described how prospective employers 'would be gathered in their dozens, having arrived from the adjoining counties. They usually walked up and down the street a bit at a distance from the boys and girls, viewing their future servants, studying their walk and appearance.' In Omagh in the 1930s Benedict Kiely saw 'a strong Presbyterian farmer . . . feeling the biceps of a young fellow, as Georgian cotton planters used to do with black boys and girls in the slave market. The young fellow and his friends . . . talked in the loveliest Irish which further encouraged the farmer and his friends to think they were dealing with animals.'

In the worst of times an alarming and steady growth in lunacy was noted. Cork Lunatic Asylum grew by forty inmates a year, and in general asylums were overcrowded. One reason given was intermarriage in country districts.

There was movement around the country apart from emigration. The towns had all increased in population. With the break-up of large estates and the Land Commission dividing up the land, the Government devised a resettlement scheme in what James Dillon described as 'the pious hope of undoing the work of Cromwell'. Irish-speaking families from the Gaeltacht were persuaded to settle in smallholdings in the fertile lands of Royal Meath, in hopes that they would spread the language. They were known as *culchies*, a word that is said to derive from the name of the Mayo town of Kiltimagh. In 1937 migrants from Kerry, West Cork, South Mayo and Donegal, described as being 'of good type', were encouraged to take the train and bus eastwards. The Land Commission divided 70,000 acres among 5,800 allotted people from Congested District Board estates. The cost was £980 for each migrant. The change from boggy or rocky fields to rich green pasture was not always successful. Many culchies emigrated, although the descendants of those who stayed are still found in the neighbourhood of Athboy and Navan. Others dreamt of the old home left behind in the West. As John McGahern put it, 'These families have been transplanted . . . from the seaboard as part of de Valera's ideas to swamp the country with Irish; lighthouses put out on the plain from which Gaelic would spread from tongue to tongue throughout the land like Pentecostal flame. Used to a little fishing, a potato patch, grass for a cow beneath the rocks, they were lost in the rich green acres of Meath.'

For every 1,000 males there were 952 females – largely because of emigration. Unmarried girls departed in droves. From country areas young girls were perpetually going to England, leaving behind a shortage for doing women's work. Even parish priests, although they offered ten shillings a week, were said to have to cook their own dinners and combine housework with their parochial duties. The parish priest of Aughadown in Co. Cork complained that 'this going to England has become a craze'. He told how parents everywhere were saying, complacently, 'My little girl is going to England', when the girl was offered a respectable and secure job in her own country.

CHAPTER 13

The Lure of Islands

Say your farewell to Ireland, cries one of the rowers, and I turn
and bid farewell, not only to Ireland, but to England and
Europe and all the tangled world of today.

Robin Flower, The Western Island

If I wished to show anyone the best thing in Ireland I would
take him to Aran.

Lloyd Praeger, The Way That I Went

Innumerable islands are located off Ireland. A few are scattered off the east and
south coasts, but most are to the west and south-west. Some are flat as playing
cards, others are splinters of rock cut off from the mainland or cones topped
with clouds of birds. Many have traces of ancient and holy history. In the
twenties and thirties of this century many which are now deserted maintained
lonely dwindling populations.

By contrast, other islands were owned by rich men who could afford an
intermittent passion for solitary living, at the same time making some fine
gardens. Rich men's islands included Lambay, a lump of black rock and turf off
the east coast of Co. Dublin where Sir Edwin Lutyens and Gertrude Jekyll
collaborated in planning a terraced and compartmentalised garden for the
Honourable Cecil Baring. At Ilnacullin, more generally known as Garnish, off
Glengarriff in Co. Cork, the northern businessman Annan Bryce had
employed a huge labour force to lay out a hundred acres in a dream that
combined Robinsonian wild gardening and Italian formality, complete with lily
pool and a temple in which there was a copy of Giovanni da Bologna's *Mercury*.
In the Kenmare River Lord Dunraven owned another Garnish, planted with

rhododendrons, bamboos, tree ferns, azaleas and other hardy exotic plants that flourished in the rain.

In 1933 my father aspired to the rich man's dream of an island kingdom. Like Lord Dunraven, he chose the Kenmare River, where the Great Southern Hotel at Parknasilla owned a stretch of rock and tussocky bog offshore, known as Illaunslea, which it was willing to sell.

The fact that this island was destitute of amenities was a spur to frenetic and expensive endeavour. Every year my father inaugurated some new project. Drains had to be dug. Hundreds of trees were planted, including six apple trees and two little eucalyptuses in pots which when I last saw them were well over a hundred feet high. New Zealand flax with its creaking rustle, a Himalayan forest of rhododendrons and tree ferns that were New Zealand's best soon grew out of the black soil; the rocks were covered with roses. Coral taken from a small beach was carried up in sacks on the back of a donkey, laid on paths hacked through gorse and dumped on the newly laid-out tennis court. A suspension bridge swooped across a muddy creek, piers were provided and boat-houses were fitted with railway tracks as an aid to launching boats.

The house was almost an afterthought. Designed by the architect Michael Scott, who came from this part of Kerry, it was planned around the fittings of a ship which my father had gutted. Pull-out wash-basins, mahogany ship's drawers that fitted neatly into cabin spaces, brass chronometers, teak and mahogany fittings and a ship's ladder created the illusion of an island within an island. The folding ship's bunks were extremely uncomfortable.

At the grand opening for the island in 1935 my brother and I cut a ribbon with silver scissors; a marquee was brought over from the mainland, together with a platform for dancing. According to *The Kerryman*, 'the visitors . . . inspected the house, after which they adjourned to the dance platform where refreshments were liberally served throughout the evening, when dancing and singing and the best of good fellowship prevailed'. People rowed themselves across for a party which lasted a day and a night; there were fiddlers and copious barrels of stout, and miraculously no one was drowned. The event was welcomed locally as some sort of return to normality in an area still wounded after the wars. We were made welcome, and year after year spent our summers in one of the most beautiful places in the world.

We had oil-lamps and candles, and later Tilley lamps. There was no hot water and when the dry lavatory in the soaking bushes was occupied, a railway signal was raised. *La vie sauvage* did not entail living without servants; a couple of men rowed over each day from their homes on the mainland to tend the garden, mind the Kerry cow, pump water and act as crew. Our old-fashioned yacht the *Shira*, with its brass binnacle, teak decks and enormous anchor, needed a paid hand. One of Kiely's duties was squatting in the galley under the muddy anchor chain trying to coax the Primus stove into flame to boil the tea. He had a bad habit of cutting off the tails of dogfish and throwing them back in the sea.

In those days the sea abounded with killer whales, dolphins and porpoises. We caught lobsters until we were sick of them. I remember a hot summer in the thirties when the water was covered with Portuguese men-of-war and deck-chairs were placed on deck for those lazy enough for a fitful slumber, who were advised to be watchful of the boom that might make a sudden sally, scraping their heads. The odd yacht called into the Kenmare River; among those who were invited on board was Conor O'Brien, a fierce-looking sailor who never wore shoes and whose trans-ocean sailing was a pioneering feat; we raced his yacht, *Saoirse*, around Sherky Island and beat him.

For years before the war Illaunslea remained a holiday home, filled with friends and relations who poured down to Kerry every summer. When our fortunes began to decline we rented it out. In 1947 one of the tenants was the newly married Garret Fitzgerald, who tells in his engaging memoirs *All in Life* how his mother won £150 on the Grand National Spring Double, and with this money the Fitzgeralds spent some weeks on Illaunslea: 'It had a house that could accommodate the whole family; my parents, my three brothers and their wives, seven young children and Joan and myself. After we had got over the initial awkwardness on such an occasion, we found life on the island enjoyable. Journeys by boat had to be made to four different points for the post, telephone calls, the bus service (actually a taxi) and to reach my brothers' cars on a nearby pier.' Dr Fitzgerald does not mention any drawbacks to the holiday; presumably his family were used to the same sort of austere regime my father enjoyed.

All that our experience on our holiday island with its artificial discomforts had in common with the Atlantic islands where communities strove to survive was the proximity of the sea in its moods; perhaps we gained a little insight into the particular brand of isolation that comes from living a step away from the mainland.

Each inhabited island offered a home to a tribe that was really a small nation, whose people were dependent on one another to an extent difficult for outsiders to appreciate. By enormous co-operative effort these lonely colonies were able to survive with the potatoes, cattle, pigs and the harvest from the sea that kept them from starving. Salt fish dried on rooftops so that it looked like slates, salt bacon and boiled eggs provided a relatively healthy diet and a houseful of potatoes would last the winter.

Many islands had been owned by landlords to whom rent had to be paid. In West Cork the Bechers had owned Cape Clear and Sherkin. The Aran Islands were in the hands of the Digby family, while Valentia belonged to the benevolent Knight of Kerry. (Even the Skelligs, unoccupied except by seabirds and lighthouse keepers, had been in the hands of a landed family, the Butlers, who paid an annual rent to the Crown of a handful of eagle's feathers.) In 1921 the Congested Districts Board bought out the Arans, which by then had passed into the possession of the Guinness family.

After the Treaty, under the 1923 Land Act islanders became owner-occupiers, paying a small fee to the Free State Land Commission. But although rent was hardly a problem, there was little money in coin. Ferrying their cattle and pigs to fairs on the mainland to exchange them for ready money took an immense effort; tying up a bullock and shifting him over the Blasket Sound in a currach required a quiet day and steady nerves. The collapse of the American market for fish and the incursions of foreign trawlers into Irish waters threatened meagre livelihoods. When the fishing failed, those fishermen who had no land had to rely entirely on outdoor relief.

The small income from summer fishing, seagulls' eggs gathered in June for the English market and lobster trawling had to cover a range of necessities from needles and pins to homespun suits and twine for herring nets. Most islanders could make their own oars and sails, while men could sew and thatch and mend shoes and pampooties, the traditional rawhide footwear. In the south-west, on the Calf Islands, some women had never worn shoes and could walk on broken bottles. But a little money was always needed, and the remittances from America became an increasing necessity. On Inishmore in the Aran Islands, the total Christmas money from America would amount to several thousand pounds. Once a year at Christmas, island children in West Cork might eat a fistful of currants or raisins or an apple or an orange. They were only given sweets when visitors were rowed over. They would eat paper and all.

Traditionally along the west coast seaweed, called the black weed, would be gathered in February after winter storms to coax the potatoes along. After Leon Ó Broin saw a mother gathering up soaking weed for the family potato bed near Spiddal, the scene remained with him all his life; he took it as a symbol of poverty. For islanders without the 'bag stuff' or commercial fertiliser, seaweed was an essential. In his story 'Poor People', Liam O'Flaherty described the weed on Inishmore, 'slime-covered, dribbling in with every wave', and the shivering gatherer with his pitchfork and squelching rawhide shoes working frantically until 'the cloak of red seaweed on the beach shimmered like freshly spilt blood'. In 'Spring Sewing' the seaweed has rotted and Mary helps her husband Martin with potato seed, a line for measuring the ground, and a spade as she confronts 'the pitiless cruel earth that would keep her chained to hard work and poverty all her life'.

Most islands had no priest; he might brave the waves on calm Sundays to come across and say Mass, but in general island communities within reach would struggle to the mainland in fair weather. When islanders from Roaring Water Bay went to Mass, they seldom had a penny to put on the plate. There was no schoolteacher or doctor; home remedies for the sick did not always work, and people would be helpless in the face of a sudden death from an accident or from appendicitis. There might well be no midwife, but the collective wisdom of the women was usually sufficient for a safe birth. Island children were healthier by far than those who struggled for life in city slums.

Islands like the Arans, composed largely of limestone, had to rely on the mainland for supplies of fuel; the hookers with their loads of turf that sailed from stages on the south Galway coast like Rossaveel to Kilronan only stopped their trade in 1972. During the winter, communities would be cut off as white seas, *garraí an iascaire* or fisherman's garden, marooned them. Winter storms were forecast from a circle round the moon or seabirds coming ashore. On Great Blasket, where there was no harbour and the landing stage was a tiny creek between rocks, communication with the mainland could be impossible for weeks during the prevailing south-westerly gales. It was taken as a matter of course that supplies of tea and flour would run short, and the neighbours, closer than most families, lent what they had to each other until the short journey to the mainland was possible.

An island like Tory, seven miles off the Donegal coast, could be cut off by the weather for considerable lengths of time. In the 1920s Arthur Fox was told that as late as May 'one of the Captains . . . had been unable to land any goods for six successive weeks . . . When the sea is rough they cannot fish and the barren soil does not produce anything like enough for their simple needs. It seems certain that many a long dark winter's night they will perforce go supperless and in the darkness to bed.' The isolation of the Tory Islanders resulted in the preservation of their own Gaelic dialect, and farming by the old rundale system of fields laid out in narrow strips which had long vanished from the mainland; when they journeyed there they talked of 'going over to Ireland'.

Islanders were leaving. Long before the emergence of the Free State they had begun the pattern of emigration, mostly to America. The majority of people from the Great Blasket ended up in Springfield, Massachusetts.

In some cases the First World War speeded departure as men joined the British Navy, which broke the links with their homes. Sometimes a catastrophe might make a whole island community depart, like the people of Inishkea who fled their treeless home after a fishing tragedy in 1927. Disaster at sea was always a danger when men set off to fish in coracles like those in use on Tory Island or the currachs which varied in size from island to island, but were essentially canoes made out of wooden laths, tarred cotton flour bags and tarred canvas, rowed with bladeless oars. A bottle of holy water and a St Christopher medal might help. An Aran currach might take twelve people or a ton and a half of potatoes or a cow. The song 'Báidín Fheilimí', which all Irish schoolchildren know, is about a disastrous journey from Aran when an animal on the way to market in Galway put its hoof through the bottom of the currach and all the passengers were drowned. The traditional currach, 'as light as an eggshell', had to stand up to gales, but fog was feared as much as storm. Thomas Mason was told of a tragedy off Inisheer when three men were caught in a currach some miles out to sea as fog came down; they rowed for days trying to find land, and when the boat was washed ashore two of the three were dead.

The young were going, emigrating with the rest of Ireland. Island people were conservative, the last to dress their boy children in skirts (to confuse the fairies who wouldn't then steal them) and the last to be heard keening. A man from Valentia recalled to Daphne Pochin Mould a spring morning 'with birds singing and cuckoos calling as a procession wended its way down to the emigrant ship, men, women and children, the very old and the very young, filling the clear summer air with their wails of lamentation'.

At some moment the people left behind, mainly the old, might get the urge to follow – to find a life on the mainland where storm and isolation were no longer daily worries and they could go to Mass on Sunday. Every island around the coast began to lose people; there were 200 living on Gola off Donegal in 1930; by 1968 there were ten. Even on islands with surviving communities the numbers continued to dwindle; the 1926 census reported 479 people living on Clare Island off Mayo, but by 1956 this had been reduced to 223. One of the most recent islands to be evacuated was Scattery in the Shannon estuary a mile out from the town of Kilrush. The last two people to abandon the holy island and its round tower left in 1979.

When Inishark, the island beside Inisboffin off Co. Galway, was abandoned in 1960, a reporter from the *Daily Mirror* was there to see them go. 'I have watched the last 23 survivors – members of six families – moving out like a garrison surrendering after a lifetime's siege.' They took with them thirteen cows, twelve dogs, ten donkeys, eight cats, sixty hens, a hundred sheep and a stack of hay. They had no regrets. One old man expressed the thoughts of them all: 'Why should I not be happy in going? I'll not be grieving for it. I've wanted it for years.'

During the previous winter, from November to December, it was possible to leave Inishark for only six days. The islanders were without tea or paraffin for five weeks. On the mainland each family would be given a brand new bungalow by the sea and six acres of land. It was cheaper for the Government to give them new homes than to provide them with a pier.

Elsewhere, like the demise of a species, fallen numbers passed the point of no return. An old man who was the last of a tiny community in Roaring Water Bay sat in his comfortable house in the town and told me how it happened. 'Once it starts there is nothing to stop it going down. A lot went to America and others joined the British Navy, for of course, being in the nature of seamen, they were mad for the sea. The youth had gone, no one was getting married and the old people were left behind. My brothers had gone away, my mother was sick then, and my own family had grown up. My wife said, "Try and leave, you're getting old," and then we had the chance of this house . . . It was good luck in a way, and yet the worst. Island people often die after leaving their houses, it's a well-known fact.'

He recalled the day the couple left, having 'packed up everything except the bare necessities for spending the last night. The next morning when we rowed over it was one of those calm mornings . . . I think I'll ever see that picture again, it was so peaceful and everything. I didn't return for about two years and when I did I was on the beer for a week. Everything saddened me. Where we had fine crops and cattle, there was nothing but weeds, and it had all gone very shabby. I missed the people and the old life, and walking there I was remembering the twenty-eight of my class who were confirmed with me and are now all dead and scattered. And I was remembering the life we had in that old house.'

Even the Great Blasket would die, famous though its people became. They envied those other well-known islanders on Aran with their shops, public houses, priests and midwives. Dunquin across the Blasket Sound offered access to all that.

The discovery and romantic exploitation of certain islands and their emergence into fame was a haphazard process; luck, or perhaps ill luck, played its part in bringing them into prominence and investing them with the glow of holy places. The West of Ireland might be exalted for its simple poverty, but these islands were much more so. Here were separate worlds, physically cut off from worldly contamination, as the hermits knew a thousand years before, where the sea kept the people apart from sinners on the mainland to indulge in clean living, sustained by strong religious faith, and zealously maintained traditional values. The myth grew that an ideal could be attained more fully in isolation than at any location on the mainland. But the great plus was that many islanders continued to speak the Irish language.

Fame could be a matter of publicising work by a chance visitor, an artist in the case of Achill, which became well known after Paul Henry discovered its attractions. Reproductions of his paintings of Achill's mountains, coffee-brown stretches of turf and sugar-cube cottages adorned many a doctor's waiting-room or solicitor's office. His depictions of Slieve Mór and cottages on boggy patches of land crouching under cumulus clouds painted in Chinese white were taken up by the Great Southern Railway. When I met Henry as an old man he told me he had received little financial return for the posters that appeared in every railway station in Ireland, and considered that they harmed his reputation as a serious artist.

A Northerner, he went to Achill for the first time in 1912 for a two-week holiday and stayed for eight years. It was the turning point of his career. Critics might dismiss as repetitious his renderings of 'clouds, blue mountains and black bogs' but they have as many moods as Cézanne's Mont Sainte-Victoire. The light and the magnificence of Achill is in them.

His first sight of Keel village with its thatched roofs and brown donkeys with their panniers of turf reminded him of African kraals. He liked that – simplicity was his watchword. When Harold Speakman visited Keel in 1924 he noted 'several automobiles' which had been carried over the water and the little factory built by the Congested Districts Board which employed thirty-five women. Meanwhile, Henry recorded the bare footed and bare legged women in their traditional dress; Speakman considered the red skirts of Achill women 'a richer more militant red than the skirts of the mainland'. Henry revelled in Achill's remoteness. 'There were many folk who had never seen a train. All these things proved attractive and satisfying to me, and the habits and way of life of this remote community surrounded by savage rocks and treacherous seas, provided me with all I required as a painter.' But Achill would soon lose the qualities that arose from isolation when a bridge linked it to the mainland.

Henry's men dressed in *báinín*, toiling on turf bogs in the manner of Millais's peasants, captured the spirit of the West more successfully than the dramatically posed Aran Islanders of Augustus John and Sean Keating. Their work contributed to the fame of the Aran Islands and the emerging heroic myth which depended on the survival of Irish. The Achill Islanders were also Irish speakers.

The chance of whether the population of an island should continue speaking Irish was haphazard, dependent perhaps on the whims and skills of a teacher. Why should Dursey, sliced off from the mainland of West Cork, and difficult to reach before its cable car was built because of strong currents, become English speaking, while Cape Clear, no more isolated, continued to be Gaelic speaking? Many communities that had surrendered to the English language passed their time in quiet desperation unnoticed until the moment of decision as to whether to aim for the mainland or America. Hundreds of sturdy inhabitants of less spectacular and lonelier islands escaped the eyes of artists, scholars and those for whom life on Aran and Blasket offered an unsullied Gaelic society, a rugged garden of Eden.

As uncontaminated survivals, these islands and their inhabitants were respected and cherished by scholars and by the State. The West of Ireland was to be revered, but these islands more so; with their culture preserved by isolation, their primal innocence which remained intact, and the perceived heroic lifestyle of their inhabitants, they took on an aura of symbolism. They were glowing outposts of the Gaelic tradition which the State was trying desperately and expensively to preserve elsewhere. The Great Blasket, visited by a succession of scholars, enjoyed decades basking in fame. In 1936 when Thomas Mason visited Aran he found 'a courtesy that is impossible to describe; the inhabitants may be peasants, but they are the remnants of an ancient race and are gentlefolk in the literal and highest meaning of the phrase'.

Fintan O'Toole has observed recently how 'the Aran Islands and especially the Blasket Islands became for European culture a mythic terrain, a place where Odysseus and Nestor still walked the earth and the older verities still remained true'. However, even in the thirties there were sceptics. Virginia Woolf observed with a cold foreign eye some Aran Islanders in the Shelbourne Hotel. They were on their way home after a trip to London organised by the film-maker Robert Flaherty. They were in thick tweeds and singing what she thought might be hymns. Hearing Irish for the first time, she failed to be impressed. 'I don't believe in the songs of the Aran Islanders or in old men who can't read – that is, they are not of necessity Homer.'

The Aran Islands had been attracting discerning tourists since the mid-nineteenth century when George Petrie went to visit the great forts and little churches. By the time Synge came along he could decry the changes that had taken place and lament the evils imposed by what he perceived as prosperity:

'The charm which the old people over there share with the birds and flowers has been replaced by the anxiety of men who are eager for gain.'

The desire to preserve the men and women of Aran as living fossils persisted over the decades. They resented it; I can remember the annoyance expressed by islanders at the sight of tourists aiming cameras in their direction. It was their own fault for presenting to visitors their grave handsome demeanour which proclaimed a rich heritage and suggested a throwback to a vanished golden age. They lived in a place of strange beauty, where gentians, saxifrages and maidenhair fern sprang up from between the grey slabs of limestone pavement, laid out in a way that seemed to indicate a legendary urban origin; where great hilltop forts built by giants dominated the weird landscape and exquisite churches had patron saints who seemed to be still living nearby.

Above all other islanders, the men and women of Aran caught the imagination of lesser folk. Harold Speakman was impressed by the cleanliness of their houses. 'They are spick and span. The bed linen may be old and worn, but it is clean – a condition which cannot always be truthfully reported of the mainland. The Aran Islanders live frugal, temperate lives . . . A sturdy upright people, these, with a great love for their rugged promontories.' Their lives were without crime. The hardships they suffered, no more than those of other islanders, were immediately visible and spectacular, enhanced by the sight of storm waves breaking under wicked cliffs.

They dressed like princes. Augustus John was glad to paint them in their bright clothes; Sean Keating's pictures would attract more visitors still to marvel and photograph. Orson Welles admired the 'fine Erin men in indigo and homespun and beautiful (I use the word unhesitatingly) and smiling colleens in nice red skirts and sienna jackets'.

Men wore diverse homespun, often dyed indigo with the help of urine, or grey–brown from the wool of 'black sheep', woven into shirts, waistcoats and trousers which were held up with the multicoloured *crios*. These brilliant belts were sought after by visitors who would call at houses in search of them. For footwear both men and women had pampooties ('absurd' in Muriel Gahan's phrase) made of cowhide steeped in sea water. Women still wore thick heavy petticoats, the under petticoat made of white flannel and the outside one of red, blue or black brushed frieze. They wrapped their patterned shawls tightly over their close-fitting blouses and tied them behind their backs.

Women and even small girls knitted as they walked to their tasks, controlling their steel needles, as many as nine, to produce blue knee-length socks with white heels, stockings and the fisherman's *geansaí*, which was dyed navy blue so it did not show the dirt. Sweaters in natural white wool were knitted for the confirmations of young boys and then worn by them afterwards to Mass. The distinctive stitches on these were far more visible than on the dark *geansaí*; Elizabeth Rivers was told that many patterns which seemed to derive from early Celtic design were inspired by the exertions of one man with 'a passion for knitting and a furtive and inventive mind'. When winter came he would go to bed and stay there for weeks at a time, knitting away. 'Many of the patterns that you see now were his at first.'

It was Muriel Gahan, an inspired and dedicated Anglo–Irish woman who devoted her life to the promotion of traditional crafts, who persuaded the women of Aran to knit full-scale off-white pullovers for adults with intricate Celtic patterns. After her first visit to Inishmore in 1931, she offered them a market for their work. Later there would be many imitations, but every white sweater sold at her Country Shop bore a label to say it had been knitted by a woman on Aran.

When Muriel Gahan returned from Inishmore after that first outward journey on a steamer loaded with cattle, the drunken mate and steward who struggled to cut bread and butter and make tea for the seasick passengers had been attending a lively farewell party, a guest at which was sixteen-year-old Orson Welles. Welles had spent some time on Inisheer, 'the most primitive spot in Europe'. The islands still had no radios, and amusements were traditional; he attended a *céilí* in 'the kitchen of, let us say, Maggie Flaherty (dealer in the mountain dew)' and was exhilarated by the dancing and stamping in leathern slippers and the ballads and stories. Such céilídhs continued for decades. Kevin Crossley Holland attended one in 1972 where men and women, carefully segregated, were jammed two or three deep against the walls of a cottage. The dancing was 'an endless succession of jigs, in which the footwork of both girls and men were prodigies, and Viennese waltzes, occasionally broken by an unaccompanied song'.

Welles was ecstatic about island life. 'I know and love every spot and every soul on these isles . . . I spent an hour or so lying in the sand listening to the sounds of the night – afar off the crying of dogs, and donkeys – the mournful note of a Gaelic ballad and nearer me the wailing of the gulls and the "wash-wash of the sea".' Other visitors also mentioned the perpetual clamour of dogs and donkeys. 'Here life has attained a simplicity and is lived with an artistry surpassing anything I am sure in the South Seas . . . a kind of lost Eden rich in romance and of bounteous beauty.'

Most visitors to Aran thought of it that way. In the fifties Hubert Butler could write, 'I am tempted to use the language of hyperbole about Aran. It seems to me one of the most enchanting and interesting spots in Europe since it has held to a precious beauty and simplicity which the rest of Europe is disastrously discarding.'

In *Stranger on Aran* Elizabeth Rivers tenderly described how the crew of a currach endured a terrible sea crossing without making any reference afterwards to the dangers they had endured. There was a palpable sense of discovery about encountering for the first time people who were a race apart. In 1931 Nicolette Devas sailed over in an open, undecked turf hooker, following in the steps of her mentor Augustus John who had painted islanders twenty years before. Little had yet changed; there was the same smell of burning kelp, and the similar women and girls in black shawls and red or saffron skirts standing by the shore. They were as John had found them and as Synge had known them, dignified, beautiful, speaking English reluctantly with an Elizabethan vocabulary.

A good many spoke no English at all. When Terry Trench came to Inishmaan in 1932, he found it difficult to make contact with the inhabitants of the middle and most inaccessible island. 'They had no English; in any case we used no English on the island – except with the nurse when I needed medical attention after . . . maggoty lamb. I suppose I simply failed to bridge the culture gap, and did not, for instance, say the Rosary with them.'

Meanwhile the islanders, most of whom were potential emigrants, had to tackle English. Thomas Mason was told, 'There is too much Irish, sure it is no use in America.' He listened to an emigrant saying farewell, 'a pathetic sight. As the steamer left the quay the last message that I heard was "Goodbye, Tom, and remember me to all the friends in Boston."' But American quota restrictions meant that Irish was becoming useful at home. It was a benefit to those who could go to the mainland and gain coveted jobs because of their knowledge, or who could stay at home and give lessons to the hordes of teachers and civil servants who arrived on Aran seeking to learn Gaelic for the sake of their careers. These visitors were becoming nearly as important a crop as potatoes.

One of the fiercest critics of island life was himself an Aran Islander. Liam O'Flaherty's family wished him to become a priest, but instead he went off to war – the wrong war. After fighting on the battlefields of France, he found his own people shunned him and his father refused to recognise him. In his disturbing account of his return, he remembered how 'when the grey mass of the islands rose suddenly from the white-capped sea, I felt that this indeed was the promised land to which I returned. All the people in the boat looked askance at me, for I had already become a damned soul in their eyes. Immediately I felt an alien among the people who stood on the pier. They spoke to me and shook me by the hand, but their fear was in their eyes. Had it been hatred, I would not have felt so alien; but this mute fear was deeper than hatred and unapproachable.' Later his mother hid away in a cupboard as tainted material the books he wrote in two languages describing the hardships of Aran life.

Another Aran man who came back to his island was Pat Mullen, who returned in 1922 to help his father eke out a living on a bare seven acres of land dressed with soil and seaweed. It was a dispiriting experience for someone who had tasted life in America. His father still treated him as if he were a child. Pat snapped back at him, 'What the hell do you think you are talking to, a pup dog or something? Now listen here to me. I never took kindly to being ordered about by any man . . . Wake up, open your eyes and understand that you aren't talking to one of the boys.' But his father still called him his scoundrel of a son.

Wistfully Mullen wrote how 'on the mainland today there are motor cars and motor cycles, buses and every sort of convenience to take young women into the towns where they can see moving pictures and attend dances. We have no attraction to offer that could induce them to come in and settle among us.'

But Mullen would be involved with the transformation of Aran when he acted as an assistant to Robert Flaherty, the film director who blew apart the traditional island identity. It would be difficult to exaggerate the effect of the making of *Man of Aran*, known locally as 'The Film', on the people of Inishmore. It was said that Flaherty offered them immortality for a keg of porter and £5.00 apiece. Many years later Brendan Behan commented, 'The fact that Flaherty was making the film filled their heads with notions that they were never going to see a poor day again . . . He brought some of them over to London for the showing of the film, and all in all, destroyed many a happy home in the end.'

Pat Mullen wrote that 'Aran people were looking sideways at Mr Flaherty . . . some of them believing at the back of their minds that his talk of a film was only a blind, and there were rumours that he was a socialist.'

But the film would be made, full of great cliffs, booming seas, storm after storm and heroic figures against the skyline. They still show it most days at Kilronan. It might have been condemned by Graham Greene, a film critic at the time it was released, but it was a superb piece of PR for the mythical Gaelic world of self-denial.

I have always felt sorry for the basking sharks. Plenty of those harmless lazy monsters would be floating on the sunlit face of the sea near our own island. But they never assembled in the Kenmare River on the scale of the shoals Flaherty claimed to have seen in Galway Bay – they 'averaged twenty-seven feet – six feet across . . . thousands and thousands of them'.

The Aran Islanders had stopped hunting them for years, and the two-year reconstruction of the old sea forays was conducted with new hand-held harpoons made in Galway, the use of which was preceded by a whaling harpoon in filmic deception, the islanders in their boats, Flaherty following with his camera. Finally they learnt the technique of spearing the poor creatures.

'The shot was a good one,' wrote Mullen in the book of the film, *Man of Aran*. 'The harpoon entered almost two feet in front of the fin and a bit down on one side. Both sharks went down with a great splashing of water. Then, as if sensing its mate was in trouble, the other shark suddenly appeared about two hundred feet astern of our boat and came rushing through the water towards us at terrific speed. The great tail churned the sea into foam and tossed it swirling into the air. With its horrible mouth wide open it came straight for us . . . Its monstrous snout was above the surface, and its evil eyes, as it came closer, glared at us savagely.'

Loitering at Kilronan, Beatrice Glenavy watched the harpooned sharks being towed into the harbour. 'I remember Flaherty trying to get a shot of seagulls in flight. They were all so gorged with basking shark flesh that nothing would make them rise from the water.'

After *Man of Aran* appeared the old secrecy and tranquillity eroded rapidly. Flaherty was far more to blame than the artist Elizabeth Rivers, who lived for nearly ten years in the cottages he constructed for the interior shots of his film.

Rivers was resented as a stranger, an Englishwoman who offended public decency by wearing trousers. The parish priest, Father Kileen, was adamant that she must go, as a corrupter of morals. (He also condemned Liam O'Flaherty and all his works.) But Rivers was liked by the islanders and stayed on, producing her drawings and a slim volume of reminiscences published by Cuala Press which Tim Robinson cattily wrote had 'the feel and look of a delicately flavoured and wholesome biscuit'.

When Thomas Mason wrote *The Islands of Ireland*, which was published in 1936, the threat of tourism already overshadowed the Aran Islands. 'More than one person has expressed to me the fear that the publicity given to the islands in recent years by books and films will make them popular as tourist resorts and destroy the finer characteristics of the people.'

But Mason and others thought complacently that the ethos of Aran would be preserved because only the best sort visited the islands – not vulgar trippers who preferred to go to Blackpool. The right kind of tourist was a benefit, thought Pat Mullen. 'Only a few of the more cultured types of visitors come to Aran each year . . . these travellers are interested in learning all they can about the pagan civilisation on Aran – they like to visit the ruins.' One wonders what he would think today. In the summer the line of people making their way up to visit Dún Aengus resembles the famous photograph of Klondike prospectors, a multiple echo of the silhouettes against the skyline endlessly photographed by Flaherty.

Regrettably, because of Flaherty, the emergence of Aran on to the world scene assumed a note of farce. The fame achieved by the Blasket Islanders came about more soberly. When the Irish Revival was in full swing, language researchers were drawn to isolated parts of Ireland in search of the most unsullied sources of Gaelic speaking – where, preferably, people had no knowledge of English whatsoever. The purest source of all was one of the most inaccessible, an island where a valiant little community, possessed with some remarkable genes, struggled to stay on.

Today the Great Blasket is left to flocks of choughs and pairs of ravens. It is infinitely moving to travel out from the harbour of Dunquin where currachs still linger and reach the northern face of the phallus-shaped island where houses on steep terraces like fulmars' nests, their gables facing the sea, have been deserted since the last islanders left in the early 1950s; their shells are there with their ghosts. Tomás Ó Criomhthain wrote of these minute hovels in a sinuous Irish which, we are told, has suffered in translation: 'There were two beds in the lower portion where people slept. Potatoes would be stored under these beds . . . There was a coop against the partition with hens in it and a broody hen just by it in an old cooking pot. At night time there would be a cow or two, calf or two, the ass, the dog on a chain by the wall or running about the house. The old people used to spend the night in a post bed beside the fire with the old stump of a clay pipe going . . . A good fire of fine turf smouldered away till morning.'

What is left is small. The village had nothing more than a north-facing outlook, sunless much of the time, one little strand of white sand, a stretch of flat land where there was just room to play games or tether donkeys and a harbour that was more hope than haven. The rest of their territory was more or less cliffs, and dangerous cliffs at that, down which islanders fell and died like Tomás Ó Criomhthain's son.

With the encouragement of scholars like Robin Flower, George Thomson and others, the Blasket Islanders were encouraged to record a store of literature which until then had been preserved orally in storytelling and conversation. The resulting books made a remarkable impact. Gaelic scholars put Ó Criomhthain's prose ahead of the others, but it was the autobiography of Muiris Ó Súilleabháin, *Fiche Blian ag Fás*, translated by Moya Llewelyn Davies and George Thomson as *Twenty Years A-Growing*, that gained an international reputation. He wrote it, he claimed, to amuse the few old women left on the island. In his introduction E. M. Forster wrote how the reader 'is about to read an account of neolithic civilisation from the inside. Synge and others have described it from the outside – but I know of no other instance where it has itself become vocal, and addressed modernity.'

Ó Súilleabháin left the island in 1927 to join the Civic Guards. The year before, he wrote, 'a great change is coming to the island. Since the fishing is gone underfoot all the young people are departing across to America, five or seven of them together every year.' He wrote, 'I am for taking the Leap.' A quarter of a century later all those who were left took the Leap and settled in Dunquin, from where they could look across and see their little houses decay.

Besides the scholars, plenty of the usual visitors in pursuit of the Gaelic tongue came over in currachs to make the islanders restless. My brother was one of the last, staying on the Great Blasket a year before the final departure. He, alas, was another of those of whom Eibhlín Ní Súilleabháin complained: 'going in and out of our house, talking and talking, and they on their holidays, and they at home having a comfortable house and no worry, during winter and summer would never believe the misfortunes on this island, no school, nor comfort, no road to success, no fishing – everything so dear and so far away. Surely people could not live on air and sunshine.'

The paradise of Peig Sayers, the queen of the storytellers, was vanishing. 'There are people and they think that this island is a lonely, airy place. That is true for them, but the peace of the Lord is in it. I am living in it for more than forty years and I didn't see two of my neighbours fighting in it yet. It was like honey for my poor tormented soul to rise upon the shoulder of the mountain footing the turf – very often I'd throw myself back on the green heather, resting. It wasn't for the bone laziness I'd do it, but for the beauty of the hills and the reflections.'

When Brendan Behan visited the Great Blasket in 1947 the island population had sunk from a peak of 160 inhabitants in 1916 to just fifty-three, and when, six years later, the island was abandoned there were only twenty for the last boats to carry away. One of the last visitors to give an appraising eye to what remained before its final evacuation was Honor Tracy. Tracy found 'an austere, a bitter world in which everything spoke of poverty. Even the animals looked weary of the struggle to get a living as they hobbled painfully . . . a front leg shackled to a back to prevent them from straying, and pulled hungrily at the meagre blades of wayside grass.'

In this atmosphere the old lived on their memories while the young longed to leave. 'They could hardly wait, those young people, to exchange their simple, wholesome, laborious lives in that lovely corner of the earth for the high wages and debased pleasures, the bustle and confusion of an English and American town.'

The glory clings to the shadowed cliff side. The famous photograph of Tomás Ó Criomhthain standing outside the door of his house in wide-awake hat and ragged jacket tied with a safety pin is that of a proud old man who has achieved success and recognition.

His introduction to *An tOileánach*, translated as *The Islandman*, was prophetic: 'I have done my best to set down the character of the people about me so that some record of us might live after us, for the likes of us will never be again.'

CHAPTER 14

An Old Lady

The city is shabby, shapeless, provincial . . . her citizens are
compelled to make apologies . . . to the German, French or
English visitor . . . Surely it is a sorry state of affairs where a
man cannot take pride in his city?
Letter to the Irish Times, *May 1935*

The slums were still there. In 1938 there were over 6,000 tenements in Dublin,
'human piggeries, rat-infested and without basic amenities'. New housing
legislation had made little impact, and the act which decreed that unfit houses
could be condemned had done little to ease the lives of 100,000 people. On the
north side, in the area around Gardiner Street and Gloucester Street, big old
tenement houses were stuffed with people from attic to cellar. Out on the south
side in Rathgar, regarded as 'one of the swankiest, snobbiest districts of the
town', many of the poor lived underground in basements.

The beauty of dilapidated Georgian buildings, their smashed fanlights,
peeling stucco and broken soaring staircases, gave them a false glamour. As you
passed each scarred doorway you could sense the plight of the inhabitants.
Many writers have commented on the unassailable impression of walking down
some elegant street lined with buildings of a rusty pink. The battered doors
were gaping, some of the jammed windows were held open by brooms like the
window of the Shelbourne Hotel drawn by Thackeray in 1840, and the smell
was inescapable, 'of damp and decay', remembered Bill Kelly, 'of deep-rooted
dust and poverty, of urine and red raddle, and above all, of hopelessness'. An
interior recalled by Helen Lucy Burke 'had a faint disgusting smell of poverty,
a sour compound of unwashed bodies spiked with the elder flower fragrance of
tom cat mess rotting in corners. There, too, that earthy smell which to the
initiate conveys the dismal news that dry rot has taken hold of the timbers.'

Life in these graceful houses was a battle with malnutrition, poverty and disease. One small boy sitting on a tenement doorstep was asked why he was not at school; he replied that it was his turn to go without food that day. Of the diseases that menaced, TB continued to be the most dreaded. Throughout Ireland deaths from TB for 1935 amounted to 3,480, which was a rate of 1.17 per thousand of the population; 2,724 of these were pulmonary. There was a worrying lack of improvement in these statistics. Tubercular meningitis and tuberculosis of the spine and hip killed and crippled and made hunchbacks out of children.

In 1934 Signe Toksvig was shown 'bone cases' waiting for surgery in Steevens's Hospital and was told that they were costing the community £500 per case. 'Clean milk would have been cheaper.' The horse-drawn drays of small city dairies continued to carry handsome brass-bound churns full of poison. The Milk and Dairies Act would not come into operation until 1937, and even then it would be woefully inadequate. Detailed rules concerning hygiene in dairies, involving drainage, water supply and the removal of manure, were simply ignored. As late as 1940 one-third of cows slaughtered in the Dublin Corporation abattoir were tubercular.

The main treatment for pulmonary cases was surgery. It was drastic in the way that surgical treatment of lung cancer still is. Otherwise the sanatorium regime was recommended, the basis of which was rest, which lowered the rate of metabolism and the demand for oxygen. The amount of work to be performed by damaged lung tissues was reduced, and as they healed, the degree of resistance to tubercular bacilli increased. Fresh air and good, plain food alleviated symptoms, but did not cure the patient. Besides, time spent in sanatoria resting was luxury for the working man.

For Elaine Crowley's family, who lived in the heart of the city during the thirties and forties, every day someone they knew died of consumption. Her father would be a victim. Most fatalities were young adults: the maximum mortality for TB occurred among young people between the ages of fifteen and twenty-five. 'My mother and her sister . . . looked for the reasons why. "It was riding bikes, all that bending forwards was bad for the lungs . . . too many heavy wettings . . . dancing too many nights a week."'

A danger on a lesser scale that refused to respond to medical concerns was maternal mortality; in 1936 704 women died from puerperal sepsis. At the same time infant mortality had a grim rate of 74.15 per thousand births, the highest since 1926. The rate was exceptionally high in Dublin – 114 per thousand births – where, owing to the growing urban population, there was a general lack of beds to receive the sick. The Hospital Sweep had not alleviated this problem, and patients, particularly children, were turned away to die because there was no accommodation for them.

Much has been written about life in the Dublin slums, most recently the oral evidence collected by Kevin Kearns and Elaine Crowley's vivid memoir *Cowslips and Chainies*. She tells of the diet of the poor – ham parings, bacon pieces, whiting, herring, mackerel, pigs' tails and backbones, and 'elder' or cow's udder. Shell cocoa was made from husks. The hardware shop which supplied paraffin oil and pot menders for holes in enamel basins, also sold coal by the stone and half-stone, weighed out on big brass scales. Lighting came from paraffin oil-lamps and candles; heating and cooking depended on the open fire.

Religion continued to be the anchor that kept the heroic women of the slums steady with a faith that went beyond reason. For First Communion they beggared themselves to dress daughters like miniature brides and sons in short trousers, shirts and new shoes. Before her First Communion Crowley received daily instructions from a 'sweet tempered old nun' who told the class how their souls died when they committed a mortal sin and if they died before confessing it God would send them straight to Hell.

'"What happens to anyone who commits a sacrilege?"'

'"They'll go to Hell, sister," forty voices chorused.'

We know about the camaraderie of people living on the brink, finding money for the rent, the heavy drinking, the struggles to keep clean and decent and the menace of disease. The weekly visits to the pawnshops were social occasions with women and children and their prams queuing with anything that could be pawned until next week. ('I don't mind taking your pot, missus, but would you wash the f— cabbage out of it.') Pawning was no disgrace; 'the highest in the land had done it'. But Crowley, remembering how her father's best suit and her own coat were regularly taken to the pawnbrokers in a brown paper bag, recalled how 'the clothes smelt of the pawn, a mixture of camphor and of being stored with so many other used garments'. Her mother had her standards; she was never reduced to pawning her bedclothes or her wedding ring. Nor, like some, did she ever have to strip her husband of his working clothes and run to redeem his good suit for Mass while he stood in his drawers and vest.

In the thirties Dublin had over fifty pawnshops. The great day was Monday when suits worn for Sunday Mass went back into pawn. Other props to poverty were the moneylenders and the society-men who took insurance for funerals. Like the pawnshop, the role of the moneylender was considered a safeguard; the 'Jew man' was usually shrewd but fair, demanding interest at five shillings to the pound paid back at two and six a week. More iron-handed were local moneylenders, probably neighbours who demanded far greater interest and were ruthless about collecting debts. For special occasions such as Christmas or First Communion women might save through the 'didley club'. Amateurs would set themselves up as banks, women who would save money for others on a small scale. For a small commission, perhaps two shillings, they would keep the savings safe, refusing to give them up early until the day they were needed, when little bags of money were handed out.

The poor could fall back on the charity of St Vincent de Paul, provided they could prove themselves holy and penniless. Examinations by the 'Vincent Men' stripped people of their pride. A tenement dweller interviewed by Kevin Kearns remembered how 'we'd always had men – you called them the "gentry" and they walked into your home to examine your condition before they'd give you anything. They'd come in and sit down and ask: "Why are you asking for help?" They always had this upper-class attitude – I remember my mother crying.'

A woman interviewed in *The Bell* in 1942 described the methods of the Vincent Men. 'He knocks and I say, "Come in." "You're Mrs So and So?" "Yes." "You wrote for help?" "I did." "How many in family?" "Seven." "What assistance do you get?" "Twenty-three shillings." "What's your rent?" "Six shillings and I'm thirty shillings in arrears . . ." "Do you go to Mass?" Now here's a funny thing about me. I go all of a tremble at that question . . . I just stand dumb and [my man] pinches my bottom . . . and as soon as the pain hits me I rise to it like a bird. "Every Sunday, sir, every Sunday." When he asks if I am in a sodality I tell him at once we are, and that we are in the middle of the Nine Fridays praying for work. He gives me a *Standard* and a *Messenger* and half a dozen dockets for a daily loaf of bread. We both show him out. We carry the lamp to the head of the stairs . . . when I begin hammering my man for pinching my bottom . . . I never once went through the St Vincent de Paul questions without going into a tremble.'

There were other schemes of philanthropy like the Herald Boot Fund formed by Dublin businessmen which provided footwear for barefooted children, especially at Christmas. Throughout the year people talked about those boots and socks. My family were involved in the Mount Street Club (its name a heavy joke contrasting it to the Kildare Street Club). Formed in 1934, it aimed to help the unemployed or 'help the lame dog over the stile'. A derelict house in Mount Street was acquired and refurbished; in 1936 five acres were rented at Merrion for allotments, and later a farm was acquired near Lucan. The club ran on self-help co-operative principles, similar to Robert Owen's Lanark, although I doubt if my uncles knew much about Owen. It was 'based on the assumption that decent men wanted to work'. Any unemployed man could enrol; he was paid in 'tallies' which he could spend on the product of other men's work. He could exchange his tallies for potatoes and vegetables grown on the farm or use them to obtain his needs from the kitchen, baker, tailor or boot repairer. At first the club was considered a 'philanthropic freak' but when its methods were seen to work it came to be regarded as a philosophy in action.

More remarkable as a private experiment for alleviating poverty was the Marrowbone Lane Fund which was set up during the years of the Emergency. The genesis was a play called *Marrowbone Lane* written by Robert Collis, a Dublin paediatrician. Having seen the conditions of the slums in his role as physician to the National Children's Hospital, Collis was encouraged by Frank O'Connor to dramatise his observations. 'I wrote as fast as I could; I wrote all night. At last as the dawn began to lighten the sky I found the story of the play was finished. This was the only time in my life I have experienced something completely outside myself, containing emotions of which I had no previous knowledge.'

After the Abbey considered it 'too controversial' the play was put on by the Gate under the auspices of Mícheál Mac Liammóir and Hilton Edwards. The plot concerned the doom of a country girl, played by Shelah Richards, who comes to live in Dublin's slums. Although it was described as 'a social tract in dialogue rather than a piece of theatre', nevertheless it had passion and truth that its audiences recognised and it led directly to the founding of the Marrowbone Lane Fund.

Long before *Marrowbone Lane* was staged, Collis had written in a letter to the *Irish Times* in October 1936, 'Dubliners are wont to describe their city affectionately as "an old lady"; when visitors admire her outer garment – the broad streets, the 18th century houses . . . they smile complacently and feel proud. Lift the hem of her outer silken garment, however, and you will find suppurating ulcers covered by stinking rags, for Dublin has the foulest slums of any town in Europe.'

Collis was described by one Catholic doctor as 'a slumming medical publicist' for his insistence on socio-economic conditions in the spread of TB. His ideas met with much opposition, particularly from religious sources who were reluctant to place the problems of TB and disease in any social context that might come into conflict with the teaching of the Church. In particular, statistics and common sense might promote the spectre of birth control.

A serious problem of tenement life was huge families. Collis, who befriended the handicapped writer Christy Brown, pointed out that Brown's mother was not unusual in giving birth to nineteen children. In fact the final tally of Brown babies was more; later Christy wrote, 'I was born in the Rotunda Hospital on June 5th, 1932. There were nine children before me and twelve after me, so I myself belong to the middle group. Out of this total of twenty-two, seventeen [plus himself] lived and four died in infancy.'

The *Irish Ecclesiastical Record* condemned birth control as 'a foul and filthy way of denaturalising the Divine Command to man to fill the earth'. When Dr Halliday Sutherland published *Laws of Life* in 1935, which had some reference to this subject, his book was denounced as indecent and obscene.

Dr Sutherland, a Scotsman who had received his medical training in Ireland, was a convert to Catholicism who considered himself a good friend of the new State. After he had travelled around the country lecturing extensively, he felt he had the goodwill of politicians and clergy. But his book was banned in Ireland, even though back in England it had been given the imprimatur of the Archbishop of Westminster. What did an English archbishop have to do with Irish clericalism? A friend telephoned. 'Have you seen what Professor Magennis says about you in Éire? He says you will be known as the author of the Fornicator's Vade-Mecum or the Harlot's Handbook.' Professor Magennis was Professor of Metaphysics at UCD and a Dáil senator.

Dr Sutherland's crime in Irish eyes was that he wrote not only about love and marriage, but mentioned contraception – by the rhythm method, which was approved by the Catholic Church as being an acceptable aspect of natural law.

He should not have been so unpleasantly surprised. Any book hinting at birth control was automatically prohibited in Ireland. In 1930 Marie Stopes's *Married Love* was one of the earliest books to be banned; it did not have a snowball's chance in hell.

In his defence Halliday wrote with a trace of ill temper, 'I believe *Laws of Life* was banned because I had written in the cold language of psychology an account of the function of sex . . . In Eire too many people, including clerics, regard ignorance synonymous with innocence. These people should enquire how many Children of Mary are now prostitutes in Piccadilly.'

There was probably some truth in the point made by Professor Michael Tierney who spoke up in the Senate about 'this unfortunate book' and 'the tendency to debate it from the standpoint that on our side is virtue and Erin, and on the other side the Saxon guilt, or something of that sort'.

Dr Sutherland should have recognised how censorship was thriving, and how the Censor was having a busy time banning books published at home and abroad. Most contemporary Irish writers of quality were indicted for trading largely on lust and 'working with one eye on England and one on America'. Those deemed guilty included Shaw, St John Irving, Shane Leslie, Sean O'Casey, Liam O'Flaherty, Frank O'Connor, Lord Dunsany, Kate O'Brien, James Joyce and James Stephens. The Censor was aided by amateurs like those who gathered outside the cathedral at Thurles to burn a bundle of irreligious publications in the presence of the Confraternity of the Holy Family singing the old standby, 'Faith of Our Fathers'.

For all his setbacks with *Laws of Life*, Dr Sutherland's opinions of Ireland were amiable. He was in broad sympathy with de Valera whom he met during a visit in 1935. He had pleasant things to say about Dublin. Away from the horror of the slums the capital was becoming home to a new moneyed middle class as the Catholic bourgeoisie was moving into newly built housing estates on the outer reaches of the city. The more prosperous chose the south side, which had hitherto been dominated by comfortable Protestants. Garret Fitzgerald's family – his father had been a Minister in Cosgrave's Government – moved house to what had been 'an exclusive Protestant upper-middle-class area, only the third Catholic family to do so'. Similar areas around south Dublin were changing in a generous swathe of fashionable areas from Foxrock and Dalkey to Monkstown.

New houses were being built for the rising middle classes. A house at Mount Merrion costing £920 in 1935 offered a lounge, kitchen, four bedrooms, large bathroom, separate WC and outside larder, in addition to a coal and tool house which could be converted into an outside WC at a little extra cost. A garage was included, since this was the top of the price range of suburban houses.

'All-electric' houses were also for sale in Deansgrange and Sandymount, and Glasnevin on the north side. At Highfield Road, Rathgar, within reach of the number 15 tram, new houses were 'situated in the most healthful and exclusive part of Dublin's suburban residential quarter within easy reach of the city and convenient to churches and educational colleges . . . They are surrounded by a good deal of timber which protects them from north-easterly winds.' The trees were leftovers from the original large walled demesne that occupied the site of the big house and estate, which would probably have been the home of a departed Protestant. 'The air is balmy and exhilarating owing to the close proximity to the mountains . . . and the view of the surrounding gardens is simply charming.'

In a serial that appeared in *The Modern Girl and Ladies' Home Journal* in 1935, the heroine, Anne, and her mother move into 'Newlyn' on a new estate which is still full of 'builders' rubbish, concrete mixers . . . beginnings of red brick front walls . . . lines of twine fastened to white deal pegs'. Like the houses advertised in Highfield Road, Newlyn has a view of mountains 'in a blue mass at the end when you looked up from the bus stop'.

Who would be living in a thousand-pound house in Mount Merrion or Terenure? Those who aspired to be upholders of domestic bliss are described in an *Irish Times* article, 'Where Modern Housewives Shine'. 'Let's take a peep at these up-to-date housekeepers in their homes and see how they set their well-trained intelligence to combat that undeniable lack of domestic experience which is their biggest liability.' They would ideally bring to their new role their business-training assets – tidiness, cleanliness, alertness, bookkeeping methods and a true value of money. Business training would have no other use for them, since they would have given up their jobs on marriage.

A housewife might have a sitting-room like that recommended in an article in *The Modern Girl* entitled 'A Room You'd Love'. The wallpaper would be deep-flecked with tints of brown and blue. Beige Chinese curtains would be striped horizontally with yellow and flame. ('Newlyn' had 'neat little Madras curtains'.) In addition, she would still have net curtains, which had not yet taken their social downward plunge.

She was encouraged to maintain an old-fashioned fire burning Irish turf. Other rooms might be fitted with 'panel' gas fires. A dining-room and three bedrooms could be equipped for £40. In the kitchen the 'Regulo' controlled cooker and coke boiler would take care of meals. Coke from the Dublin Gas Company was thirty shillings per ton, delivered free 'from seller to cellar . . . No smoke, soot or smut . . . Irish made.' Alternatively, gas was even cleaner. 'She hasn't got a Gas Fire!' exclaimed the advertisement which was illustrated with a black hand print.

By the mid-thirties there should have been 'gleaming snow white' refrigerators in the kitchens of most middle-class homes. 'It's so nice to KNOW that the children's food is safe and pure!' The housewife was told that 'actually this refrigerator will pay for itself in a few years in money saved through food being kept fresh'. The milk her children drank would be certified Tubercule Free from a reputed dairy like Craigie's or the one in the Howth demesne, 'Best by Test':

> I Invest in Milk the Best
> I Insure in Milk most Pure
> My Children's Health that is my Wealth
> Milk of Purity is my Security.

Among the gifts advertised for Christmas 1937 were conveniences like an electric hair-dryer, 'a safeguard against chills after washing'; an electric clock and a Pilot 5 Wave Radio Model, 'American Reception Guaranteed'. You could buy a Philco famed for 'quiet crystal clear reception' or the expensive 'Empire 8' which cost £35 and offered 'shadow tuning, glowing beam tuning indicator and automatic bass compensations'. Radios were ubiquitous among those who could afford them; in 1937 the committee of the Kildare Street Club sanctioned the purchase of a 'wireless'. Local programmes were becoming more adventurous; at the Easter Week Commemoration in 1935, during which the statue of Cúchulainn was unveiled in the Post Office, a special broadcast featured only men who were out in Easter Week. It would not have appealed to members of the Club.

Both on radio and gramophone Count John McCormack continued to be a top favourite; at Christmas 1934 you could buy 'Friend of Mine', 'Poor Man's Garden', 'A Little Prayer for Me' and 'Green Pastures'. Many householders would have attended the concert McCormack gave in October 1935 at the Theatre Royal which was so packed there were even seats on the stage; they would have listened to Ireland's tenor singing Handel's 'Caro Amor', 'Oft in the Stilly Night' and 'Song of the Seals'. The Count would retire with a similarly packed farewell concert, also at the Theatre Royal, in 1938; before he died in 1945 he came out of retirement to tour on behalf of the Red Cross and other charitable organisations.

In her new home the housewife could entertain. She would have bridge parties with card tables which looked 'gay with little blue dishes of Irish pottery for ash trays and bon bon dishes . . . and brown wooden match stands painted in Celtic colours'. Bridge scores would be written with pencils in dainty sugar-stick colours. Sandwiches would be spread with celery and Galtee cheese sliced to a paper-like thinness and cut into dainty pieces. Galtee and Three Counties, made in Mitchelstown, Co. Cork, where the Castle once stood, were – and are – cheese ground down and treated with chemicals so that the finished product remained soft and formed no rind. No tradition of farmhouse cheese-making existed in Ireland. When *The Bell* wrote of Mrs Crichton, a cheese-maker in Sligo in 1940, she was considered a phenomenon.

The housewife or her daughter might give a party like The Party That Wouldn't Go Right described in *The Modern Girl* where guests assembled for Excuse Me dances and Paul Jones dances, which were for the benefit of girls who tended to be wall flowers. Men and women faced each other in two circles and gyrated in opposite directions; when the music stopped they danced with the partner in front of them. 'The one thing we had forgotten was to bring in a stock of cigarettes and with so many girls smoking, the private supplies soon began to thin out.' 'Raymond's friends from University', presumably UCD, were 'louts'. 'There was one bit of luck, the Fortesques couldn't come – their freckly maid brought the note to save the postage.' The Fortesques must have been Protestants.

Aspiring members of the middle class – a solicitor, perhaps, on £500 a year – would have a gardener and a maid. The readers of *Dublin Opinion* had maids like the one in the joke: 'We've only had her three weeks and she's broken everything except the connection with England.' From 'Newlyn' Anne sees next door a 'healthy'-looking maid with a clothes peg in her mouth. Elsewhere in *The Modern Girl* 'a mere man' scolds his girlfriend, 'It's that outrageous air of superiority you all adopt when you order them around. Why don't you *ask* them nicely to do things? Why have you to impress upon them in every intonation of your voice that you are the Great White Queen? . . . A woman hires another woman to do all the rough work of the house at a fraction of her husband's income . . . I know being a maid is a good job . . . she has her keep and her wages are pocket money . . . A man doesn't order a gardener about the way a mistress does a maid.'

In *An Irish Journey*, written at the end of the decade, Sean O'Faolain saw the new houses and their furnishings in a different light. He described the smallest sort located on the north side of the Liffey, on Griffith Avenue, in Phibsboro, Drumcondra or Raheny. 'Behind the hall door is a badge of the Sacred Heart to which the home is dedicated. A tiny wick in colza may burn behind a red globe to a large picture of the same symbol in the main bedroom. In the little parlour or sitting room you will be pleased by the good taste – not original or personal but still good . . . There is almost certain to be a reproduction of a Paul Henry painting. There may well be an original Sean Keating or Maurice MacGonigal.' In 'A Room You'd Love' the recommended wall decorations are 'a couple of watercolours, an etching, a tiny reproduction of *The Fighting Temeraire* and some happy little Mallorcan tiles.'

The north-side family, wrote O'Faolain, had books of Irish interest, together with religious books, including a Chesterton or Belloc 'and there may be a book by one of the English Dominicans or Jesuits such as Father Vann or Father d'Arcy or Monsignor Knox'. In 1937 *The Modern Girl* considered that 'Dubliners are reading more than formerly . . . This week we have what I am sure will be a thrilling tale by Frank O'Connor – *The Life of Michael Collins*.'

Householders in Raheny or Drumcondra read the *Irish Press* or the *Irish Independent*, never the *Irish Times*. Their gardens were rarely cultivated. They had two or three children, limiting the number through chastity, and might or might not say the family rosary at night. Holidays were spent in the South or West of Ireland, but later, after a spell in Blackpool or the Isle of Man, at Dún Laoghaire, Bray or Greystones. According to O'Faolain, this lifestyle produced the IRA and the Legion of Mary 'and both of these bore me. They are unoriginal, unpersonal, part of the dead tradition of nationalism gone stale and religion gone sour.'

In the more affluent south-side suburbs the houses also had religious symbols. The householders were always in debt, they ran a car, played golf, drank whiskey and soda and bought English magazines. They, too, spent their holidays in the West of Ireland; 'everybody in Ireland who can afford it has sipped with greater or lesser appreciation at those well-springs of national tradition'. Later they would go off to London and perhaps to Paris after the children grew up. O'Faolain hinted – 'families are carefully smaller here' – that such people might be using birth control.

His assessment of Dublin society omitted the middle-class single woman. *The Modern Girl* catered for her, encouraging her to wear lipstick, whatever the clergy might say. 'Go gay . . . and use enough to well accentuate the outline of your lips. Then with your finger tips covered in brilliantine, smooth very lightly along the lips to make your mouth look slightly shiny and more inviting . . . dowdy faces are a state of mind.' Hair was as important as make-up. 'The right haircut has been known to lead to a June wedding.'

The Modern Girl used its preferred vein of fantasy to describe the single girl's office life. Neither she nor her companions were given Irish names. The men who worked with her included fifty-six-year-old George, Cecil the office wit, Cyril, the (mild) philanderer, and Ken who lived for his boss. Girls included Sally, the 'It' girl of the office, and Muriel, weak-minded, fussy and depressing.

One would imagine that any office would contain a number of Muriels. In late 1935 *The Modern Girl* untypically ran a series of practical articles about jobs open to the single woman. Naturally it was taken for granted that as soon as she married she would relinquish employment; since 1931 even female schoolteachers were required to be unmarried. Prospects were relentlessly discouraging. A woman who knew Irish might still find opportunities in the minor grades of the Civil Service, although such positions were increasingly hard to come by. A cartoon in *Dublin Opinion* showed a huge crowd: 'A demonstration?' 'No, applications for ten civil service jobs.' *The Modern Girl* considered that 'a Civil Service post is still a plum for the girl who seeks an office career, though pay standards have been cut . . . Work in Civil Service offices . . . is onerous and exacting and poorly paid for its quality and responsibility.'

Welfare work also had 'scores of applicants for one job'. To become a nurse a girl had to bring along a dowry which varied between £30 and £50. For free hospital training it was necessary to go to England. Pay in Ireland was 'definitely low'. After eleven years' work as a fully trained nurse a sister in hospital started at £75 a year rising to £95 with room and rations.

Banking might offer a place as lady superintendent at the Bank of Ireland or the National Bank once the obstacle course was overcome. 'You need a nomination or a substantial banking account or the assistance of someone who has one is an agreeable factor.' 'A girl's best hope is the Bank of Ireland' where she could enter as a temporary clerk, a position which meant she could be dispensed with at short notice. She had to be prepared to go anywhere. Interviews for permanent female staff, conducted by directors assessing deportment, appearance and general intelligence, were known as 'Beauty Shows'. 'As a career for women banking is very limited. Women in banks do not reach the higher executive posts.'

Why not become a librarian? Irish, of course, was necessary; so was a BA degree, preferably with honours in psychology. For the diploma you needed some subsidiary studies; the choice included History or Philosophy, Logic, Aesthetics, Sociology, Bibliography and Book Selection, Paleography and Archives. Without the diploma you could become a library assistant as long as you knew Irish. Your salary would be £45 per annum with cost-of-living bonus raising it to £100.

Opportunities in law, medicine, horticulture and art were equally dispiriting. Better perhaps to dream of becoming a flying hostess on some foreign airline, 'an Ultra Modern Career . . . Air hostesses must be under 25, unmarried, have some knowledge of nursing and be able to make up a four at bridge'. Ireland was about to have its own airline, Irish Sea Airways, which launched a flight from Baldonnel to Bristol on May 1936 in a de Havilland Dragon named *Iolar* or *Eagle*. It carried five passengers.

Soon there were flights to Berlin – nine hours; Copenhagen – eleven hours; and Hamburg – eight and a half hours; flying to London took under three hours. By 1938 the airline, now rechristened Aer Lingus, could advertise how 'the O'Laughlins had a date for lunch in London. They left yesterday on the 9 a.m. plane. Lady O'Laughlin was surprised to find in the comfortable cabin of the airliner that sound-proofing made light chat a simple matter . . . In two and a half hours they landed in Croydon. After lunch they caught the one o'clock plane back to Dublin in nice time to change for dinner.' The lunch must have been a lightning snack.

Not many could afford a flying London lunch date. But by the late thirties there was a reaction to the old Republican doctrine that 'frugal sufficiency' should be the highest attainment. People who could afford it, wished to have fun – even those closely associated with de Valera's Government. They included Mrs P. J. Ruttledge wife of the Minister for Justice, a die-hard Republican who opposed any restrictions being put on the IRA. Mrs Ruttledge, who lived in Clyde Road, always wore Irish-made clothes and her children had Irish names. She hunted with the North Mayo Harriers and was well known in coursing circles and on the golf course. Her daughter Máiréad, aged six, had a greyhound called Rebel Beauty. Her husband was the only member of the Cabinet to have his colours registered on the Turf. She found time to assist him at his work: 'I sometimes read and discuss books which my husband reads before they are banned in the Free State.'

The old guard, like Alderman Tom Kelly, talking to Sean O'Faolain, might regret that the young preferred jazz dances and cinemas to going to the Gaelic

League. (Opposition to 'jazz' continued into the fifties, when Radió Éireann banned it on the Hospital Sweeps programme.) But conservative puritanical Republicanism was relaxing. Tod Andrews recalled that 'within ten years we had all played golf and tennis. We had worn black ties and even white ones. We had joined bridge clubs, we had sampled alcohol and even modified our views on cosmetics and women's dress. We had visited France.'

A trip to the centre of Dublin offered varied entertainment. If the car was preferred to the tram, problems might arise. *The Modern Girl* complained that 'parking facilities in Dublin are not improving. There is still a daily source of irritation . . . in particular for lady owners arriving in town in the afternoon who are . . . generally at a despairingly isolated distance from shopping centres.' In 1931 Dublin Corporation decided unanimously to remove Nelson's Pillar since 'the flower sellers and loungers as well as the ordinary crowds were always in danger of traffic'. Besides, 'the figure of Nelson on top was out of sympathy with the city and its people'. It had survived the Rising, the bombardment of 1922 and the wishes of the Corporation and would remain an impudent relic of Imperialism and a traffic hazard for another thirty-five years.

The lady who ventured downtown might enjoy a coffee at Mitchell's in Grafton Street, or the Monument Creamery with its thick Dun Emer carpets, or the Patisserie Belge and the Café Belge started by Bob Geldof's grandfather. She might lunch at the Country Shop with its bright rugs and crafts made by country people, straw *súgán* chairs, scent of tweeds, home-made jams, and drawings by Elizabeth Rivers on permanent display. Not for the lady was the public house, even such a mecca as the Palace Bar in Fleet Street, patronised by writers and artists where porter could be obtained in tankards. *Dublin Opinion* published a cartoon of its customers and there is not a woman in sight. But she might get a drink when her husband took her to Jammets, the Dolphin, the Red Bank or the Shelbourne. The first Continental Bar opened in 1935 at the Royal Hibernian Hotel in Dawson Street and became known as the Buttery.

Plenty of formal dances formed an alternative to the lofty high jinks of the Horse Show balls. The Metropole and the Gresham were locations for staff dances like those given annually by Messrs McBirney and the Electricity Supply Board. At the Royal Hibernian Hotel during the Christmas season of 1937, 400 guests attended the Fine Gael dance which included almost all the deputies of the Opposition. 'Mrs Cosgrave who came with the President of the Party wore a dress of handsome black satin . . . Mrs Mulcahy . . . favoured an embossed black evening dress while Mrs O'Higgins had a smart green lace gown.'

Sean O'Faolain wrote that Drumcondra householders occasionally went to the theatre, although they were suspicious of the literary movement and 'its disturbing list of banned and so-called anti-clerical authors'. They would have copies of the *Capuchin Annual* on their bookshelves in which they would have read about Cieran, the civil servant who 'read poetry, prose and drama in which writers, mostly of alien race, misinterpreted Irish faith and Irish vision in a literature that delighted the world'. Readers were warned against 'a movement by some Anglo-Irish dramatists and littérateurs to restore paganism in thought and in action and to rob the land of Erin of its Christian religion'. As a result of reading about dangerous revivified Celtic myths, poor Cieran nearly lost his faith; he 'suffered from intellectual pride . . . despisal of ordinary mortals . . . he pitted his finite mind against the Mind of God'.

It was much safer to go to the cinema. Having endured the queue and seen the show, perhaps afterwards one might try for a hamburger at Billy's Snack Bar at the side of the Capitol Theatre. The big cinemas with their hybrid entertainments were at their height of popularity, offering their blend of Irish Tinseltown and Hollywood. At the end of the decade 'Stanelli', the Dublin-born musician noted for his radio 'stag parties' and the invention of the 'Hornchestra' which favoured ranch rhythm, was playing at the Theatre Royal. After Mr Stanelli and the Rockettes had disappeared from the stage, the screen came down and the audience would prepare for something like Mickey Rooney in *Judge Hardy's Children*.

By 1938 Jimmy O'Dea was established in the Gaiety Theatre; that year he played Buttons in *Cinderella*, 'the world's most romantic story . . . Lyrics by Harry Donovan – over Fifty Artistes a Real Crystal Coach – a Team of Beautiful Ponies . . . the kind of laughs that only JIMMY O'DEA can raise!'

According to Christopher Fitz-Simon, the social scene which met up at the Gate Theatre in the thirties consisted of 'the unusual mixture of ancien and nouveau regime, the Anglo-Irish nobility, the Protestant middle class, the rising commercial sector, newly elected deputies of the Free State parliament, the Dublin arts circle . . .' But social functions attended by the aristocracy and intelligentsia were depressing affairs, according to Signe Toksvig.

'May 1931. Dinner – Dermod O'Brien *dull* – His wife nice and intelligent. Lord Monteagle, gentle, nice . . . Lady Desart . . . very fresh-looking with her white hair and emanated kindliness.

'. . . September 1931. Went to Walpoles for dinner . . . They were cordial and kind but very dull. Like their dinner of cream soup, mutton, celery . . . beans drowned in white sauce, choice of chocolate pudding. For drinks – lemonade and coffee – water.

'. . . Jan 1933. The Longford party . . . the artistic monde – Keating, Whelan, Kernorff, Gate actors, Abbey actors, Glenavys, MacNeills – always the same people in Dublin – that will never keep me here.'

Another Longford party was 'crowded, unreal, banal, undistinguished'. Increasingly, she and her Irish husband Francis Hackett felt isolated; the Keatings 'poetically told us the Fitzgeralds were shocked at our destructive and subversive ideas, also thought we were corrupting the young. *Soit/soit*.'

By 1936 Toksvig considered:

'There is no intellectual sustenance.

,,   ,,   emotional   ,,

,,   ,,   sensual   ,,

,,   ,,   financial   ,,   '

In December 1936 she wrote, 'Ireland, a withering mediocrity, kindly at best, loutish and malignant at worst.' A year later she was sharing with Halliday Sutherland the distinction of having a book banned. The Hacketts left the country, never to return. 'I am as one awakened from a nightmare, from a heavy and bad enchantment. Eleven years. Purifying and penitential and instructive, but no joy.'

Was Ireland really as bad as she made out? It is tempting to put alongside her depression the view of another foreigner, Virginia Woolf, who in 1934 was equally trenchant in her criticisms of Irish life. 'At last I gather why, if I were Irish, I should wish to belong to the Empire; no luxury, no creation, no stir, only the dregs of London, rather wishy washy as if suburbanized.'

But there was idiosyncratic varied and energetic life stirring among Sean O'Faolain's suburban neighbours whom he eulogised affectionately at the end of the decade. 'To my left is a retired British Army Captain. To my right a retired Colonel. Up the hill is a Protestant jeweller. Next to him a Schools Inspector with a Gaelic name and a Gaelic name on his gate . . . Below . . . lives my friend Robert Childers, the son of Erskine Childers. Across the road lives Mr Patrick Belton, creator of the ill-fortuned Christian Front which sent an Irish Brigade to fight for Franco in Spain. Behind me . . . the pub . . . Two brothers from Mayo who spent ten years in America own it . . . one of them . . . is an omnivorous reader. In the next house I know lives my friend Joseph Hone, the biographer of George Moore and Yeats. Close by lives a man who is said to have walked in his bare feet to Lourdes. The gardener in another house is a native Irish-speaker. Most of the village people have connections with the British Army and Navy, but the last two men I had working in my garden left to join the Volunteers. An (Irish) Army doctor drives past my gate every morning in uniform. There is an Orangeman, a Scotsman, a family of Austrian refugees, including a Jew. Two Abbey actors are in digs around the corner . . .'

CHAPTER 15

Guilt is Very Vulgar

There is more of Chekhov here than . . . Kipling. Irish
landlords were often eccentric, sometimes demented, seldom
romantic . . . If ever there was a Raj, it was a Raj left out in the
rain.

Conor Cruise O'Brien

The Anglo Irish . . . the only children of Irish history . . . spoilt,
difficult, unable to grow up.

Elizabeth Bowen

The Conor girls were Protestant but well thought of – they
spoke in haughty accents, they rode horses and followed the
hunt in winter time. When they went to race meetings they had
walking sticks that they could sit on. They never spoke to me.

Edna O'Brien

In 1932 David Thomson, an eighteen-year-old Scotsman, came to Co.
Roscommon to a house called Woodbrook as tutor to the daughters of the
Kirkwood family. The Kirkwoods belonged to the middle gentry, typical of the
surviving Anglo-Irish. Their house had been raided during the Civil War, but
they had stayed on. For such people who lived in remote parts of the country,
getting a live-in tutor was a common experience.

Thomson's account of his sojourn at Woodbrook combined a haunting view
of a vanishing lifestyle with a treatise denouncing the Anglo-Irish as responsible
for Ireland's evils. No Irishman could have done it better.

Although much of Woodbrook's land had been confiscated under the Land

Acts or sold to pay off debts, the Kirkwoods still attempted to carry on in the same carefree manner as their forebears had done during the nineteenth century. Major Kirkwood bred racehorses, an occupation almost guaranteed to lead to penury. One lucky winner, a famous animal named the White Knight, kept the estate going for a time. But now money was in increasingly short supply; in lieu of servants' wages small items vanished without comment.

The Major wore a monocle dangling from his collar on a black cord. His English wife found little pleasure living in Roscommon; this was a common situation among the Anglo-Irish. In West Cork Lionel Fleming's English mother devoted what she regarded as years of exile to the creation of an enormous garden. At Woodbrook every time it rained the roof leaked, a situation which had become a Big House cliché. Caroline Blackwood pointed out how 'the roof has always had an almost mystical importance in Ireland because of the incessant rain'. It has been said that there were two sorts of Irish country houses, 'the sort which has a roof and the sort which has not'. Thomson was put to work positioning jam jars under the drips. 'I knew every chipped slate, every crack in the lead valley – I had patched it so often.'

'What can you do when you have no money – practically?' says a character in Molly Keane's *Taking Chance*s, 'Not enough, not nearly enough to pay your debts – all of them screaming on different notes of intensity to be paid.'

Protestants were shrinking like a balloon with the air going out of it. Between 1926 and 1961 the Protestant population of Northern Ireland increased by 92,000 or eleven per cent, while that of the Republic fell by 75,000 or thirty-five per cent. *Ne Temere* has largely been blamed; one figure estimates that because of that Papal encyclical each generation lost twenty-five per cent of its people. But there were other intangible factors that included a disinclination to survive as if they were under a voodoo curse. Perhaps the conviction held by Catholics that Protestants were damned had a slow poisonous effect.

Most Protestants retaliated with an equally fervently held view that they were superior – indeed, not a petty people. The gentry – colonists, colonels, minority, Ascendancy – went under different labels, all of which implied alien superiority. Jack White, whose *Minority Report* was astute about his tribe, admitted that 'underlying all Protestant attitudes – the very tap root of prejudice – was a belief that religion was the mould of character. Catholics were dirty, lazy, thriftless, unreliable and ignorant.'

This led to a certain detachment as far as the new State was concerned. The problem of forming new allegiances once the old ones had been shattered was not solved with any enthusiasm. Caution, and perhaps a genuine fear of expressing unpopular opinions, kept Protestants unwilling to participate in the new order. Joseph Hone observed how 'from an embarrassing situation the ex-Unionists tend to withdraw and cultivate their gardens' – or to hunt or go fishing. They also chose to withdraw from cultural activities. Garret Fitzgerald has noted mildly how 'the attitude of southern Protestants in the Republic has been throughout the whole history of the Irish State rather passive'. He himself has a special interest in the minority. He tells how as a child he had once made a derogatory remark about the Protestant religion of their family friend, Ernest Blythe (whose wife, Anne, spent much time praying that Ernest would be converted to the true faith).

'My mother eyed me sternly and responded quietly, "You do know that I'm a Protestant, too, dear, don't you?" . . . Her remark came as a shock. The religious bigotry that had somehow begun to stir in me inculcated from God knows where (I hadn't yet started to go to school) was suddenly halted in its tracks.'

Arland Ussher scented ingratitude among the Anglo-Irish: 'That the Colonels did not all have their throats cut was entirely due to the innate decency and forbearance of the Irish people.' But Ussher was *déclassé*, the man who had written that de Valera was 'the noblest Roman of them all'.

The Kirkwoods belonged to a class that was becoming history, but not quite yet. They faced penury, but it was relative penury; their people were divided less between the haves and have-nots than those who had a lot and those who had not so much. 'The Protestant God', wrote Terence de Vere White, 'practises the rule of double entry. His accounts are strictly kept. And there are other reasons; an awareness of priorities in which the substance preceded the shadow. School bills – for good schools – must be paid, buildings and capital investments kept in repair. All this is true; but Protestants when they die, are usually richer than they appear to be; Catholics are not so well off.'

Typical of those who had not so much were the Glenavys. Patrick Campbell remembered how 'for as long as I can remember the family lived in considerable comfort – on the very edge of bankruptcy. An unnecessary shovelful of coal on the fire, or a stove left on in an empty bedroom would bring on the Lord's grim look and the statement: "You simply don't understand the value of money."'

A pocket of have-a-lots lived in Malahide practising their small snobberies, referring to RCs and *le nez du Pape* when discussing the anatomy of a chicken in the presence of its maids, paying its cooks ('treasures') £29 a year, and continuing wistfully to play 'God Save the King' after tennis and golf dances. Hubert Butler thundered that such attitudes were 'sad cinders of a once blazing enthusiasm'. According to Patrick Campbell there were numerous 'over-dressed and over-painted Protestant ladies who seem to decorate the Dublin social scene for ever'. These were the people whom Bertie Smyllie, the new editor of the *Irish Times*, sought to wean from die-hard Unionism, making deathless decisions in his paper like printing 'Dún Laoghaire' instead of 'Kingstown'. Even Tod Andrews approved of Smyllie for blowing a fresh wind into a hallowed corner of the old order; he 'brought tolerance to the *Irish Times* and the paper offered the only forum available at the time where free discussion of ethics and religion could take place'.

Meanwhile the country have-a-lots like the Kirkwoods' neighbours, the King-Harmans of Rockingham, treated kindly by the State, lived very comfortably, if not ostentatiously. They maintained their estates and had fun in their own way, enjoying hunting, shooting and fishing. They fished for salmon, often on their own private river banks. While the State may have taken most of their land, it neglected to confiscate stretches of bank beside Ireland's great rivers which remained in private hands.

Newspapers and magazines like the *Irish Tatler* had regular photographs of moustached figures in tweed hats standing by rivers with large dead fish at their feet. If they belonged to the Kildare Street Club, and most of them did, they could bring the fish they caught there and it would be cooked and served up to them. (But fish stocks were already declining; T. Kingsmill Moore who fished on Lough Corrib wrote that 'the great days of Corrib were over before 1926 . . . According to the old boatmen the decline started about the turn of the century and had been going on ever since.')

In addition to the booty gathered on the first day of the salmon fishing season, shooting triumphs were chronicled as part of the year's cycle: 'Cahir Park Covert Shoot.' 'Covert Shoot at Rockingham.' 'Irish Peer's Shoot – The Earl of Bandon – A Bag of 85 Birds was Secured.' Grouse and snipe were abundant, even close to the city; my uncle regularly went shooting in the Dublin mountains. Any large estate provided its own shooting with farm workers brought in as beaters while their employers banged away from dawn to dusk.

But far more important were pastimes associated with horses. In *Taking Chances* Molly Keane wrote how 'all thoughts of spring were shunned with loathing by the greater proportion of the community who thought in terms of hunting, and then in the greatest possible number of days which could be fitted into the five possible months of the year'. Dedicated hunting folk liked to hunt four days in the week. Their houses, attended by harness rooms smelling of soaped leather, were adorned with Snaffles prints and decapitated foxes.

'The Sweet Cry of Hounds,' trilled the *Irish Tatler* in February 1937. 'Hunting folk who are still enjoying the glorious runs over the countryside are having an excellent season . . . And they meet everywhere at the Hunt Balls.'

'Mrs B. Lawlor and Sons, Naas, catered for the following Hunt Balls: the Duhallow, the Longford, the Westmeath, the Ballymacad and the Island . . .'

The *Irish Tatler* wrote of '. . . The Royal Meath Hounds at Killeen Castle. Miss Eva Watkins . . . Miss "Babs" Watkins . . . The Misses Watkins are daughters of Colonel C. F. Watkins, late Scots Greys, who holds the record for having caught the largest salmon with rod and line on the Boyne.'

'At the Killing Kildares – Miss Rosalind Mansfield, who is the youngest race horse owner in the Irish Free State, was presented at Court last year.'

Members of this society included the Pond's beauties. 'Lady Ainsworth – divinely tall and most divinely fair . . . interests, hunting, shooting, fishing and gardening . . . and her beauty care? "Since I was seventeen I have used Pond's Cream."' For several years the portrait painter Sean O'Sullivan earned his crust by sketching such society beauties as Anita Ainsworth on behalf of Pond's – as late as 1941 he was caricatured in the *Irish Tatler* with his paintbrushes in a Pond's Cream pot.

'What do the hunting set do when they are not hunting?' Signe Toksvig asked as the season drew to a close in March 1931. She was told, 'O, they walk the puppies and they cross the days off the calendar till cubbing.' 'Horses, hunting and to a lesser extent racing,' wrote Patricia Cockburn, no mean huntress herself, 'were like a drug addiction . . . They worshipped them with a religious intensity . . . they talked of little else and perhaps would turn against their children if they disliked hunting or were bad horsemen.'

After the hunting season was over came Punchestown. 'The Countess of Enniskillen was in a tweed suit with a small hat of the beret variety . . . Mrs Gerald Dunne wore a becoming brown straw hat with a brown flecked tweed suit and fox furs . . . Viscount Milton escorted Viscountess Milton who wore a grey flannel suit with brown fox furs and a navy hat trimmed with two upstanding quills.'

The Horse Show, run by the Royal Dublin Society, flourished in the face of criticism from the likes of the *Catholic Bulletin*. On one occasion the *Bulletin* got support from an unlikely quarter: '29 August 1931 . . . The Longfords are delightfully mad this year,' wrote John Betjeman in a letter. 'Edward (L.) struck a man in the face at the Dublin Horse Show because he was a hearty and sang "God Save the King" when people were not supposed to. There was a free fight all over the stand and Edward had to leave.'

Not quite everyone was devoted to horses. In the 1930s Lord Castlerosse took up golf instead and determined to turn part of the land of Kenmare House, his Killarney estate, into an internationally famous golf course. It was not an idea that found favour with the Catholic Bishop of Kerry:

'"Do you realise what you are saying, my son . . . You are suggesting that we should turn this lovely, lonely place into a bedlam of English people, all equipped with smelly motorbikes, and there will be air planes overhead and girls in bathing costumes."

'"My dear Bishop . . . you talk as if golf were a cannibalistic orgy. It is a game, sir, and a damned serious one . . . Why, even the Pope, God bless him, has been known to handle a golf club. For two hundred years Killarney has been a private domain of my family. It is too lovely to remain private property. I want to make it a resort to which people from all over the world will come – but it must be the loveliest golf course the world has ever seen."'

Unlike my uncle, who regarded people who played golf as having nothing better to do, Lord Castlerosse was a pioneer; he was also a have-a-lot, able to continue opulent traditions. There were others. No Dublin Horse Show was complete without the reassuring figure of Lord Powerscourt standing in one of the enclosures, 'known to the public chiefly as a tall figure in a grey top-hat, short black coat and sponge bag trousers welcoming dignitaries . . .' Out at Powerscourt the lavish life continued, although its owners complained of financial gloom and uncertainty. The occupants of great houses like Powerscourt, Killruddery, Rockingham, Curraghmore and Castlecomer kept up the old standards. They employed butlers and liveried footmen, whose uniforms, complete with waistcoats with buttons stamped with the family crest, were supplied by Callaghan's of Dame Street. One of the footman's duties was to carry up the food from the kitchen; it was imperative that no smell of cooking should reach the dining-room. Lesser houses like Woodbrook also had servants, but they made do with a selection of women, cooks and maids who worked long hours from seven in the morning to late at night. At Woodbrook only the upper servants were allowed to use the bathroom.

In West Kerry, Patrick O'Sullivan, who lived in a house without running water or electricity, observed without rancour the routine of his neighbours, the Leeson-Marshalls. 'Mrs Marshall played the piano before dinner and spent a great deal of her time arranging the flowers for the drawing room.' At tennis parties maids in blue and white uniforms carried out trays of drinks between games. Round about the Marshall estate, shooting pheasants and woodcock after they had flown in during the November full moon took up more time. O'Sullivan's mother had worked at the house as general kitchen maid, milking six cows morning and evening and boiling water for the Major's shaving water.

In the evening not only did the family change for dinner but the butler, too, changed into a swallowtail black suit and white shirt to serve dinner, much of it made up of produce from the estate and garden. Together with the game birds and salmon there would be home-grown potatoes and vegetables, grapes from the greenhouse, figs from the tree in the back garden, bottled fruit from the walled garden served with cream from the herd of Kerry cows.

The obsession for changing for dinner remained strong, a vestige of old custom and entrenched ideas of civilised behaviour. At Powerscourt, according to Sheila Wingfield, 'if fate was capricious, certain things in life, thank goodness, were immutable. Such as changing for dinner and the times of meals.' In Glaslough, a house where electricity had not yet been installed and only candles were used for illumination, after the gentry had changed for dinner they carried hot-water bottles and fur rugs to the dining-room. My mother changed for dinner (usually something like a poached egg) until she died in 1980. In 1936 Lionel Fleming, a connection of the Somervilles, was sent to Castletownshend by the *Irish Times* to cover the murder of Admiral Somerville: 'What I most remember about the shooting is this – that the old man, though dining alone with his wife, was wearing his dinner jacket . . . For him, the old outlook and customs were things that remained unaltered.' This observation caused great offence among the Somervilles.

There were straws in the wind like the quills in Viscountess Milton's hat. Many Anglo-Irish continued to leave Ireland, or did not go back. 'Ireland?' queries one of Molly Keane's characters. 'Would you go back . . . Would you care to? Such a hopeless country and everyone one knows has had to leave . . . it's a great pity [the house] wasn't burnt. Then you'd have some compensation from the Government, instead of a house you can't live in and can't sell.'

Years after the Civil War broken gates were still an indication of decay. 'It's funny how we all forget how time passes,' wrote Sean O'Faolain, 'but there they were – the gateposts falling. The lodges boarded up. Notices for sale. Fifteen years of grass on the avenue.'

What was there to keep them in this new country? Especially the young? Hubert Butler felt that 'for our parents of the Ascendancy it was easy and obvious to live in Ireland, but we of the "descendency" were surrounded in the twenties by the burnt houses of our friends and relations . . . England beckoned us and only an obstinate young person would wish to stay at home.' Common sense dictated departure, and many fitted into Joseph Hone's category: 'the Treaty was only a pretext for carrying out a long-cherished design to taste of the life of South Kensington, Cheltenham and Bournemouth.'

Among those who departed was the head of the ancient Norman family of Butler which had lived in Ireland since the twelfth century.

By direction of the Right Hon the Earl of Ossory
Kilkenny Castle,
Kilkenny, Ireland.
Catalogue of the valuable antiques and interesting contents of this historic mansion. To be sold by Auction. Commencing Monday, 18th day of November, 1935.

This was a memorable country house auction; there would be many more during the coming years, most of them a lot less splendid, like those attended by Signe Toksvig. 'The same shabby tristesse and Victorian grandeur . . . The same awful furniture mixed with a few ill-cared for good bits. The sugary Victorian prints, the army calendar, sporting books, Zulu cowhide shields on the wall . . .'

The auction of the goods of Kilkenny Castle took the best part of a week. Among the hundreds of items sold was a pair of massive antlers belonging to a great Irish elk, which were bought by my father, always with an eye to the practical. For years afterwards the castle stood in melancholy dominance over the Marble City, empty as the elk's ribcage, a perpetual reminder to the citizens of change and decay. 'Ossory's white elephant', Sean O'Faolain called it. Only a series of fortunate accidents saved it. Elsewhere historic and beautiful mansions were being abandoned to their fate. Some were rotting, others were too cold. Others were situated in the wrong places, in the rushy Midlands, perhaps, too far from towns, cinemas and churches. Some owners made desperate attempts to salvage their homes, like Miss Kathleen French, who in 1938 bequeathed Monivea Castle to the Irish nation as a 'home for Indigent Artists'. The Irish nation rejected it, and in due course the castle was demolished.

Not everyone abandoned the family home. The compulsion to keep an estate going, to pay 'a crippling debt to those limestone shrines' was fuelled by tradition and a sense of duty which tied many impoverished owners of big houses to their crumbling heritage. They were also swayed by a genuine passion and affection.

Elizabeth Bowen inherited Bowen's Court on the death of her father in May 1930. Even as late as this the traditional mourning for a former landlord united North Cork. 'A great sea of people,' she wrote with satisfaction, 'so many hundreds of people that it looked like a dream, people from all over the county, from the most mountainy places, stood on the gravel and on the lower avenue, their faces fixed to the house.'

Her inheritance was half poisoned chalice, half beloved burden. Her love for the tall square three-storeyed eighteenth-century house built by her ancestor was sensual: 'In fine weather the limestone takes on a warm whitish powdery bloom – with its parapet cut out against a bright blue sky this might also be a building in Italy. After a persistent rain the stone stains a dark slate and comes out in regular black streaks – till the house blots into its dark rainy background of trees. In cold or warm dusks it goes either steel or lavender; in full moonlight it glitters like silvered chalk.'

Without Bowen's Court she could not have written with the same confidence and perspicacity of the Ireland she knew. Edward Sackville-West believed that 'the rich background of Anglo-Irish life from which she springs must be presumed in the main responsible for her extraordinary gifts'.

But there was not much money, and only by scraping and saving and cutting down staff to the minimum was she able to keep up the house and entertain. The *Irish Tatler* pictured her with her guests at a meet of the Duhallow Hunt in 1935 – 'Co. Cork Authoress Entertains – House Party at Bowen's Court, Kildorrery, Co. Cork.' For her guests 'beds and even a room in a neighbour's house were borrowed, washstands, blankets (we really did need new ones), cans . . . local bath towels and four small new tea pots bought'. The old tin baths were replaced with modern plumbing, but there was no electricity until 1945.

A critic of Bowen's Court condemned 'a great barrack of grey stone 4 storeys and basement, like a town house, high empty rooms and a scattering of Italian plaster work, marble mantelpieces inlaid with brass and so on. All the furniture clumsy solid cut out of single wood – the wake sofa on which the dead cat lay – carpets shrunk in the great rooms.' But Virginia Woolf had little sympathy for the Anglo-Irish and their houses; Adare Manor, which she was shown by an ex-RIC man who had lost his arm in the Troubles, and misnamed Dunraven Castle, was 'a French Château in grey stone costing a million & better razed to the ground'.

For those like the Kirkwoods with little money, life was a struggle. Woolf observed a couple in similar circumstances. The Rowlands of Ballincurra House near Midleton in Co. Cork had not changed their Loyalist opinions. '"But I love my King and country. Whatever they ask me to do I'd do it", this with great emotion. "Oh yes, we believe in the British Empire; we hate the madman, de Valera."' Woolf concluded, 'Yes I felt this is the animal that lives in the shell. These are the ways they live – he hunting all day, and she bustling about in her old car, and everybody knowing everybody and laughing and talking and picnicking and great poverty and some tradition of gentle birth and all the sons going away to make their living and the old people sitting there hating the Irish Free State and recalling Dublin and the Viceroy.' Such people were dull, Signe Toksvig declared after a session with the three Tottenham sisters, people of 'real character and real breeding' who were 'stone deaf, middle deaf and non-deaf'.

Not all of that society was so unexciting. In 1930, Elizabeth Harmon, the future wife of the present Earl of Longford, travelled to Westmeath. 'The glitter of my first visit to Pakenham Hall will never be effaced. It was the glitter of eccentricity, not luxury; but eccentricity that was intellectual, high-spirited and comical – the evenings often ended with hymn singing from the Church of Ireland hymnal' – not everyone's idea of comedy. John Betjeman records the guests staying in 1931: 'Maurice Bowra ... David C[ecil] (who is off his rocker), ... Henry Lamb [the painter] ... and Evelyn Waugh with his eyes blazing with religious fanaticism ...'

For Betjeman, Ireland was love at first sight. 'Ireland seemed to me Charles Lever and aquatints come true. I thought it was the most perfect place on earth. In a letter to T. S. Eliot in July 1938 he wrote, 'Do you know Oireland? It is what England was like in the time of Rowlandson with Roman Catholicism thrown in ...

'There aren't any aeroplanes.

'The roads are too small for many motors.

'The Church of Ireland is 1835 Gothic and 1835 Protestant.'

He unearthed a rich vein of dim Irish peers – 'Cracky' William Clonmore of Shelton Abbey, later Lord Wicklow; Lord Dunsany, called 'Lord Insany'; and 'Little Bloody' Ava at Clandeboye. 'Really what I liked was the Ireland of the Ascendancy and I liked particularly people who had gone rather to seed.' There were high jinks at Pakenham Hall, later rechristened Tullynally Castle, and at Birr, and tennis at Lord Farnham's where the lord – 'just like a pear. Very tall and slim' – did the umpiring. Of the house, Farnham, Betjeman wrote, 'He has had to sell most of the furniture, it is a little bare, but the acetylene gas makes a brave show.'

With Betjeman one is with people who have lost all semblance of influence and power. The grasping landlords have been exchanged for jokers. The Leslies at Glaslough took themselves more seriously, welcoming visits by Yeats, while Shane Leslie pursued the problems of reconciling two cultures, 'the English culture evoked by Eton and Cambridge and the old Irish culture which he had found for himself and loved so dearly'. Could the Leslies consider themselves Irish 'after three hundred years sitting by their lake'? Yes, thought Anita Leslie, 'we belonged to this earth, to these trees, to this rushy lake. We were part of the landscape.'

At Bowen's Court Elizabeth Bowen also continued to entertain. 'She wasn't just a brilliant writer,' Molly Keane remembered. 'She was a proper countrywoman, she rode beautifully and gave great ordinary hunting parties.' Among her guests was Sean O'Faolain who could not understand why she wanted to keep such a large and cumbersome house against the odds. He analysed the society with which she was identified. 'Its fatal weakness was that the Big House people felt themselves here, not merely of a different class to the worker and farmer – which was natural, since it happens to be true – but of a different race, or religion or life mode, and they took their political philosophy from England whose problems were of a quite different nature.' Not that Bowen cared; she is reputed to have said, 'Guilt is very vulgar.'

For many Protestants outside the Ascendancy, such as the future Dean of St Patrick's, the term 'Anglo-Irish' sounded as distant thunder to their ears. In Carnew, Co. Wicklow, Victor Griffin felt that the couple in the Big House lived in another world: 'Only the shining ones up at the Castle, Captain Woodhouse and his wife, Beatrice, had dinner at 8 p.m., announced every evening to the Carnew townsfolk by the ritualistic ringing of the castle bell. Lords of the Manor or the Ascendancy . . . always referred to the locals by their surnames, "Griffin" or "Molloy", not even prefixed by "Mr". His female partner was simply called "wife" never "Mrs".'

Arland Ussher found a collective noun for those associated with the Big House – 'the Colonels'. The Earl of Wicklow reproached him for using 'the Anglo-Irish colonels amongst whom he spent his childhood as Aunt Sallies for his wit'.

This term excluded society in Malahide and Foxrock – Dublin Protestant families lacked the fighting spirit and had no military traditions. But so many who lived in big houses actually were colonels, or ex-officers of the English Army, that military rank came to be associated with a vanishing class. *Dublin Opinion* was forever caricaturing military men with moustaches in the Kildare Street Club, where buffalo heads were displayed on the wall, together with portraits of W. G. Grace and much reading of the *Poona Times*, *Darjeeling Echo* and *Tanganyika News*. M. J. MacManus wrote a poem entitled 'The Colonel':

> Last of the local gentry
> Last of his name and clan
> Huddled up in an armchair
> Alive beyond his span.

Ussher came to feel fondness for Colonels: 'When I meet any of them today, I love them tenderly, but only because their circumstances are reduced.' Part of his affection arose from the way many of them lived in discomfort reminiscent of their military campaigns. Caroline Blackwood described a fictitious house in Northern Ireland, based on her memories of her family home, Clandeboye, 'a grey and decaying fortress beleaguered by invasions of hostile natives'. She listed its drawbacks, including sketchy plumbing and vegetables boiled together in iron pots on Monday and reheated later in the week, and concluded, 'It seems no wonder that people brought up under these conditions should have produced such a glittering array of field marshals and generals.'

Since an army career tended to exclude any sort of financial acumen, the

Colonels' lack of financial success cursed this generation whose ancestors had grown fat on expropriated lands. They had developed a distaste of the vulgar occupation of making money, and Major Kirkwood was not the only military officer who grappled with penury.

A particularly bleak example of a military man who lost a spectacular amount of money was Colonel Alec King-Harman. Having returned to Ireland after the Troubles following a distinguished military career, he found that Mitchelstown Castle, which he had inherited, had been burnt and its furniture and paintings destroyed. Mitchelstown had been one of the largest and grandest castles in Ireland, built by the King family; a succession of Lord Kingstons had acquired a reputation for extravagance and eccentricity. One branch of the family, the King-Harmans of Rockingham, continued to live splendidly as David Thomson saw them. But Alec King-Harman found himself in a different situation as he tried to gain compensation for the burning of his castle. In due course, rather than attempt to rebuild with inadequate funds, he decided to invest the small amount of compensation money in building seventeen new houses in Dublin with the idea of letting them out. These proved to be an unsound investment, and he lost heavily.

He was fortunate enough to own another property. In 1919 he inherited Newcastle, a substantial early eighteenth-century house and estate near Ballymahon in Co. Longford. In 1900 a visitor to Newcastle had seen 'a well-run great house . . . a masterpiece of smooth and intricate organisation . . . The place was self-supporting to a degree which even then was passing out of England, but which was absolutely necessary in the solitudes of Ireland. Twenty men and maids sat down to dinner every day in the servant's hall, and that did not include all the gardeners and stable hands who mostly had their own cottages.' The coach-house had a variety of 'shining and burnished' carriages, while the harness room was filled 'with what seemed to be enough saddlery to equip a cavalry regiment'. The beautifully kept demesne included a mile-long avenue of limes and another avenue of beeches known as 'Lady Ross's Drive'.

By the time Alec King-Harman came into his inheritance, much of the land had been taken by the Land Acts, but with careful management there was enough to provide him with a good income. However, he made an immediate and unwise decision. He sold off 800 acres, including the land right beside the house, to the Forestry Commission, which immediately covered its acquisition with conifers. In one stroke he rendered the house virtually valueless – a large unwanted mansion in an inaccessible part of Ireland with no land attached.

The few thousand pounds he received from the sale he invested in an elaborate central heating plant which was soon deemed too expensive to run. He showed an eighteenth-century generosity to any passing beggar with a hard-luck story. His large staff included Henry Elliott, a Northerner, of whom it was said 'he was quite fearless, loyalist to the core and outspoken in his contempt for the Republic and Republicans'. The Colonel's secretary and friend, Robert

Montgomery, betrayed him; 'this unmitigated scoundrel' used his guns and took his car unasked, with which he ran down a woman and killed her, a crime for which he received five years in jail for manslaughter. When he got out he returned to Newcastle and rifled his old employer's safe.

King-Harman continued doggedly to waste money on a large scale, not because he was a spendthrift, but because he had no sense of the economic spending of his income. He kept up what remained of his estate, grumbling that he was a poor man on the way to the workhouse. He survived the war without a telephone or car, but his zeal for doing the wrong thing survived into old age. Six months before his death he decided to install electricity in the house and employed a cowboy electrician, 'half-ignoramus and half-rogue', who worked at intervals, being paid £200 altogether. After the Colonel's death the basement was found to be full of wires; when the 'half-rogue' was sacked a qualified electrician did the work for £20.

King-Harman's record of his decline was meticulous; he kept his financial affairs in the most careful order. When he died his lawyers remarked that his books of accounts were as good as any kept by a professional accountant. For a lonely old man one thing was still of supreme importance in his eccentric life – the ownership of a family home. Having lost one, he struggled to hold on to another. Without one, he believed passionately, a family would inevitably disintegrate. In the context of what survived of Anglo–Irish life, time proved him right. Today fewer than forty inherited big houses where generations of one family have lived are in the hands of those destined to inherit them.

When I saw Newcastle a few years ago it was up for sale, forlorn and empty, surrounded by a dark and almost impenetrable forest of Norwegian spruce. The house had gone through various terminal experiences. After time as a religious institution it had become a hotel whose main focus was an enormous bar installed in the drawing-room; on the ceiling above was some fine provincial plasterwork with musical emblems. Outside, lying half-submerged in weeds, was the large stone coat of arms of the Kingston family which had been rescued from the burnt-out ruins of Mitchelstown Castle.

In Kerry Patrick O'Sullivan mused, 'It is perhaps hard for people today to appreciate the importance of the country house to its immediate neighbourhood ... The Leeson-Marshalls were ... the setters of standards, the arbitrators of taste, the landlords, employers, benefactors, law-enforcers, and often the only refuge of the poor and needy.' But more often the presence of nearby landlords was resented as much as it had been in the bad old times. Marie Walsh was indignant about the way her village in Mayo was hemmed in by the local landowner: 'We were not allowed to fish the river, even from our own land. It was the property of Captain Berry who lived in the big house ... A vast acreage ... belonged to this landlord; lands that were taken from the original owners.'

That colonists had usurped land which rightly belonged to native Irishmen has been a theme held through many generations. The concept of becoming a landlord by cheque-book was still a couple of generations away. Old memories had not died. H. V. Morton was told of a certain Colonel Buckley who during the Troubles declared that his land belonged to him. The man who disagreed told him, 'Take a good look at it while you can; that demesne belonged to me before you came over with Cromwell.' After his house was burnt, Colonel Buckley 'retired to an English cathedral town'.

Recently, when a crusty old farmer asked me if I was a Cromwellian, I felt stirrings of uncertainty and displacement. At Woodbrook David Thomson made friends with the Maxwell brothers who worked Major Kirkwood's land. '"Woodbrook belongs to us,"' one of them said to him, 'as naturally and quietly as though the whole world knew.' The Kirkwoods had owned the place for many generations, but Thomson felt it was fitting that the Maxwells should become the new owners when Major Kirkwood had to sell up.

When justice was done, the results were often unsatisfactory. In 1937 Colonel Head, the intransigent old Loyalist whom Kevin Fitzgerald had met during the Troubles, and who had praised the Black and Tans, came back to Kings County, now renamed County Laois, to see what had become of his old home. It was an unwise decision. He lamented that what had once been a well-managed estate and family home had been transformed by the division of his land among neighbouring farmers. 'It was a picture of dilapidation and neglect.' The house was a heap of rubble covered in briars except for the kitchen yard, the end of which was converted into a labourers' cottage. Horses and cattle browsed in the shrubs and many trees had disappeared. The demesne had been divided into seven or eight small farms. All of the tenants except the pair that had got the farm buildings 'were in a state of abject poverty, fast reverting to the primitive state of manhood. Their so-called freedom had meant only a change of masters, which they did not greatly appreciate.'

CHAPTER 16

Hedgehog

At the first sound of war we have seen the small modern state abjure all the enlightened sympathies of its citizens, contracting into a tight ball like a hedgehog at the bark of a dog, seeing nothing, hearing nothing, smelling nothing.

Hubert Butler

The neutral island facing the Atlantic
The neutral island in the heart of man
Are bitterly soft reminders of the beginnings
That ended before the end began . . .

Louis MacNeice

As Church of Ireland clergyman in Castletown Bearhaven in West Cork, my Uncle Billy took the Sunday service on one of the two British destroyers which were anchored in the protected sound between Bearhaven and Bear Island. Sometimes he would motor out into the sound in his own launch named *Heather*; on other Sundays the destroyer's jolly boat would fetch him. Either way, in due course he would stand on the gleaming deck in his flowing robes, his First World War medals pinned to his cassock, and Matins would be held in front of ranks of sailors.

Bearhaven was one of the three Treaty ports, the others being Cobh and Lough Swilly in Co. Donegal. Under the terms of the 1921 Treaty, the British retained rights to these ports and to depots at Rathmullan and Haulbowline which they continued to exercise until the agreement that ended the economic war in March 1938. In spite of strong opposition from Winston Churchill, all three were returned to Éire on 11 July 1938 and my uncle's duties in connection with the British Navy ceased. Negotiation with foreign powers was not one of Neville Chamberlain's skills.

De Valera's settlement has been described as an achievement almost equal in importance to the Treaty itself. The return of the ports gave him essential manoeuvrability in the struggle to remain neutral during the coming world war.

Among those who believed he should give them up to England was George Bernard Shaw. A long stay in England had made many of the old playwright's views untenable to Irish patriots. He had supported Irish conscription in 1918, and now he backed Churchill. 'If I were in Churchill's place . . . instead of saying I will reoccupy your ports and leave you to do your damnedest I should say, "My dear Mr de Valera, your policy is magnificent, but it is not modern statesmanship . . . The ports do not belong to Ireland: they belong to Europe, to the world, to civilisation, to the most holy Trinity."' But later Shaw would admit that Dev's neutrality had been the right thing; he admired his ability 'to get away with it'.

The year before the 1938 agreement, de Valera had reconstructed the country and affirmed its new identity in a document known as *Bunreacht na hÉireann* or the Constitution of Ireland. This was ratified in a referendum held on 1 July 1937 which was won by 685,105 votes to 526,945.

Article 44.1 of the Constitution gave special recognition to the Catholic Church as the church of the majority of the State's population. Among de Valera's advisers was Dr John Charles McQuaid, President of de Valera's Alma Mater, Blackrock College, soon to be appointed Archbishop of Dublin.

A note in 'An Irishman's Diary' told readers, 'I hear a rumour that the name to be given to the ceremonial head of the Irish Free State in the new Constitution will be *An Taoiseach* which means The Leader.' The country itself would be renamed Éire, while the office of Governor-General, which had been allowed to fall into ridicule through the extreme Republican behaviour of de Valera's friend Dómhnall Ó Buachalla, would be abolished.

Now the new office of President was created. Appointing Douglas Hyde as first President was a shrewd move, aimed at diluting the impact of Article 44.1. For David Thomson the choice embodied 'the almost perfect social and religious toleration that had allowed a Protestant minority to live in peace in the twenty-six counties since the foundation of the Irish Free State'. But many Protestants considered the old walrus-moustached Gaelic scholar, who had founded the Gaelic League which had led to all their woes, a turncoat. They saw him as George Moore did, as having crossed over to become 'the archetype of the Catholic Protestant, cunning, subtle, cajoling, superficial and affable'. On his way to the Viceregal Lodge, which the new broom had rechristened *Áras an Uachtaráin*, the new President stopped opposite the GPO in respect for those who had fought there during the Rising.

The year that Hyde was inaugurated President, W. B. Yeats left Ireland for the last time, to die in France. Gogarty departed for America. Of the old Dublin socialites of the twenties, one of the few left was Sarah Purser. In March 1938 the Friends of the National Collection of Ireland held a party in the Shelbourne Hotel to celebrate her ninetieth birthday. The menu heading was designed by Jack Yeats, while Professor Thomas Bodkin recited a rhyming toast he had written himself. In flowered chiffon and velvet coat, the old lady cut the huge cake on which stood ninety flickering candles.

That year Lord Wicklow was reassuring fellow members of the Kildare Street Club. 'Austria-Hungary,' he told them, 'has learned her lesson from the last war. If Hitler were to attack Austria, Hungary would take him in the rear, and he knows it.' When his friends reminded him of more recent changes, and that much of the territory of Austria-Hungary was already in Hitler's hands, the Earl considered, 'Hitler will not dare to act. He has to reckon with the Serbs.' His friends told him that Serbia had merged with Yugoslavia. 'In that case the whole thing is reduced to an absolute farce.'

We were on our island in Kerry on 3 September 1939. The small battery wireless was perched on a table in front of the great views of the Kenmare River as, amid squeaks, Chamberlain's gravelly voice announced that Great Britain was at war with Germany.

Shortly after Chamberlain's speech the Dáil unanimously declared Ireland neutral while authorising the Government to proclaim a state of emergency. It would not take long for the term 'Emergency' to become a loaded one.

In the next few days hundreds of people returned to Ireland from London. On 4 September the SS *Athenia* was torpedoed off the west coast of Ireland en route for Canada with a loss of 112 lives. 'Is this the war?' asked a little girl as she was handed down into a lifeboat. On 7 February 1940 the passenger ship MV *Munster* was sunk off the British coast; it might have been a ghastly repeat of the loss of the *Leinster* in 1918, but fortunately all were saved.

Within weeks every adult and child was fitted with a gas mask, and a sort of carry-cot was provided with a cover and air pump for babies. Blackout was imposed and black blinds and curtains for windows had to be bought.

On 14 September 1939 Sir John Maffey, the newly arrived United Kingdom Representative in Éire, had a meeting with de Valera. At Irish insistence he had travelled to Dublin under the pseudonym of Harrison and was told to report to the Department of Agriculture; at that time the Department of External Affairs was housed on a floor in the same building. Such secrecy indicated the nervousness felt by the Government about contacts with Great Britain. De Valera said that two-thirds of his people were pro-British or at least anti-German. But there was an active minority. Personally, he had great sympathy for England. But Partition was in the way of any understanding; it was a subject he mentioned a number of times during the two-and-a-half-hour meeting.

Those in the British Government who immediately opposed neutrality were in a position to put pressure on Ireland. Their intentions were made morally easier by the Irish Government's refusal to sign the Anglo-Irish Trade Agreement in August 1940. Talks had broken down as prices which the British offered for butter, cheese and bacon were considered too low. Then the British proposed that the difference could be made up by the price paid for cattle imports. But the Irish Government refused the offer because of a clause giving the British storage and port facilities in Ireland which were considered incompatible with the policy of neutrality. This breakdown was kept secret from the Irish public, so that the British were blamed and a section of public opinion was given another reason to sway towards Germany.

Since imports into Ireland depended on British and American goodwill, in February 1941 the Government decided that it was imperative to establish a deep-sea fleet in order to bring supplies into the country. Irish Shipping Ltd, which consisted of representatives of three Irish shipping companies, bought eight ships with great difficulty – there was a world shortage and prices were high. In addition they chartered five more; the whole fleet eventually totalled fifteen ships. They had varied fortunes. Two chartered American liberty ships, the *Irish Oak* and the *Irish Pine*, representing twenty per cent of the whole fleet's carrying capacity, were torpedoed. Other independent merchant ships were also lost at a cost of 128 lives, the heaviest losses occurring among the coasters who made the Dublin–Lisbon run; one or two even went as far south as West Africa. Most sinkings were the result of German action, although one ship at least, the *Kerlogue*, was bombed by an RAF plane. During the hostilities twenty Irish ships and seventeen foreign ships on charter bringing goods to Ireland would be sunk. The gallant efforts of this medley of merchant vessels kept Ireland alive. Other ships were vulnerable, like the Irish Lights relief vessel *Isolda*, bombed by a German plane in December 1940, which sank in fifteen minutes off the Great Saltee with the loss of six of her crew.

Meanwhile, thousands of Irishmen went off to fight for the Allied cause. Fifty thousand men from Éire serving in the British forces won between them a total of 780 decorations, including eight Victoria Crosses – twice as many as for Northern Ireland and nearly as many as Canada, which had three times the population. War workers also contributed to the huge numbers who were involved in the war: one estimate gives over fifteen per cent of the eligible population travelling to England to help in the war effort. Following the trend of other silences, the endeavours of these people, who believed that what they were doing was right in the world situation, have received no official recognition from any successive Irish governments.

Naturally the Anglo-Irish were rushing to join the British forces with great speed. Within months my father and one of my uncles (I had several) were in the British Army and I would not see them except during the occasional fleeting leave for the next five years. At the Irish St Leger at the Curragh in October 1939 it was noted that 'Mrs Denis Daly, whose husband has left to join his regiment, was not there to see her horse arrive second in the big race'. For a few months the actions of those who had crossed the sea to join with Britain in her hour of need were recorded in newsprint by the *Irish Times*. 'Irish Beauty for War Work – Lady Maura Brabazon, daughter of the Earl of Meath who is going to do war work in England.' In January 1940 the newspaper carried a photograph of five Irishmen in the RAF 'at a west of England Flying Station'. Afterwards there were no more news items of this nature; censorship had been imposed.

At home, the departure of so many Irishmen to play their part in the global conflict did not diminish the support for neutrality which increased as the war went on. Recent research suggests that the majority of those who joined the British armed forces still believed that Irish neutrality was the best policy for their own country.

James Dillon, the deputy leader of Fine Gael, was the only TD to oppose the policy of neutrality and denounce the evils of Nazism. As a fervent Catholic he based his plea for aid to the Allies on moral and spiritual grounds, and was thrown out of the party for his pains. Another member of Fine Gael confided in Harold Nicolson that he thought neutrality was not worthy of Irish ideals and he hoped that Ireland would be on the same side as 'our ancient enemy and our present dear friend and neighbour'.

These politicians were exceptions in their opposition. Even Loyalists supported de Valera's view and liberal Protestants like two ex-journalists were more equivocal. In 1940 Brian Inglis joined the RAF, but when he heard a rumour that Churchill might take over the Irish ports, he knew what he would do in such a case: 'Two of us were Anglo-Irish – there was no doubt in our minds that we could not continue with our flying programme if England and Ireland were in a state of war ... we knew which side we would be on, Ireland's.' Lionel Fleming, who was working at the BBC, faced a similar dilemma. However, their ex-boss Robert Smyllie, the editor of the *Irish Times*, disagreed. Throughout five years of global warfare Ireland's position revolved around the burning issue of neutrality. Smyllie deplored it. The policy of the *Irish Times*, he once declared, was 'to advocate the maintenance of a strong Commonwealth connection, while insisting no less strongly on Irish political independence'. But neutrality was going too far.

Another journalist caught up in such arguments was Lord Castlerosse who worked for Lord Beaverbrook on the *Daily Express*. In the summer of 1939 he had just completed laying out the world's most beautiful golf course on his family estate, Kenmare House in Killarney. 'They can have their bloody war if they insist upon it,' he kept saying, 'but please let them hold off until October.' They did not. Chamberlain's solemn announcement of hostilities was a month old by the time the rotund figure of Castlerosse was seen taking up a golden club on 2 October 1939 and hitting a ball into one of Killarney's rhododendron bushes.

Perhaps he was annoyed about the way the war had interfered with his plans for Killarney when he wrote an article supporting neutrality in a style that Synge might have been proud of: 'I am telling you that the rushing wind of disaster will pass Ireland by, for there is peace in her heart and geography is on her side. Ireland will be an oasis where the cows will be giving of their milk and the sheep their wool, while men and women in London, Paris, New York, Berlin, Rome and Moscow, red-eyed with hate, will be destroying the accumulated labours of two thousand years.'

Jack White observed that '"the pro-British group" men who had fought for the Crown and are anxious to be called up again, men whose sons are at the front today . . . generally agree in supporting the policy of neutrality'. An unexpected ally of neutrality was Elizabeth Bowen, who was doing some quiet intelligence work for the British. She felt that neutrality arose from a fear of repeating Redmond's mistake in the First World War, and a suspicion, perhaps a hope, that England would lose the war. 'This . . . is Éire's first *free* self-assertion; as such alone it would be a great deal to her. Éire . . . sees neutrality as positive, not merely negative. It is typical of her intense and narrow view of herself that she cannot see that her attitude must appear to England an affair of blindness, egotism, escapism or sheer funk.'

Neutrality was generally seen as best suited to Ireland's interest. The country had no military defences. The Army had to build up strength. The Irish Navy and Airforce were miserably small. The Navy consisted of two ancient fisheries protection vessels, the *Fort Rannock* and the *Muirchú*, formerly the British gunboat *Helga* that had shelled the rebels from the Liffey during the Rising in 1916; these were commissioned in January 1940 as Public Armed Ships. In addition, a fleet of six motor torpedo boats was built up during the Emergency, boats which were unsuitable for patrolling except in fairly calm weather. These were backed up by a naval reserve, consisting of amateur seamen and a coast-watching service whose lookout posts on virtually every headland were linked by telephone with command headquarters.

The Air Corps was equipped with a squadron of Hurricanes and another of Hawker Hectors, an assorted group of bombers and Avro trainers, and three Gloucester Gladiators nicknamed, like their counterparts in Malta, *Faith, Hope* and *Charity*. Those based at Baldonnell aerodrome south-west of Dublin were under Army command, and there was little idea of how they should be employed if needed. Once when a German invasion was thought to be imminent the planes were placed on the runways as obstructions, while the pilots were ordered into slit trenches with rifles to pick off descending parachutists.

There was a sneaking belief – hope, perhaps – that Britain was losing, and then what would the Germans say if Ireland had been on her side? But there was emotion as well as logic in support for the policy that the British considered cowardly and loathsome. 'Most of it,' observed Harold Nicolson, 'is attributed to the genius of de Valera, who has already gained enormous prestige and many new adherents. "Neutrality" has thus taken on an almost religious flavour; it has become a question of honour; it is not something to be ashamed of, but tremendously proud.'

Through an appointment made by John Betjeman, the British Press Secretary in Dublin, Nicolson, paid a formal visit to de Valera. 'In the waiting room there is a statue of Lincoln and a copy of the American Declaration of Independence. His own room is ill-designed with cold, high windows . . . there is a thick Hibernian carpet and a clock that strikes the quarter hours with a loud noise. On his desk he has a telephone box which buzzes occasionally and to which he talks in Gaelic.'

To his surprise, Nicolson, like other visitors, was charmed by the leader of the Irish nation who was not the grim-faced man he had come to expect: '. . . an admirable smile, not showing teeth, but lights up the eyes and face very quickly like an electric light bulb that doesn't fit and flashes on and off. Yet not an insincere smile. A happy smile.'

It was said that this tall, distinguished, semi-blind leader had a way with women. Patrick Campbell reported how 'the other evening at the Mansion House, when he told them about the *Fáinne* embroidered on his dinner jacket, he held them spellbound and starry-eyed.'

But de Valera had many critics, one of the fiercest being David Grey, the American Ambassador, who wrote of the Taoiseach that 'he has the qualities of martyr, fanatic and Machiavelli. No-one can outwit, frighten or blandish him. Remember that he is not pro-German nor personally anti-British, but only pro-de Valera.'

In 1941 Grey arranged a meeting between de Valera and Wendell Wilkie, the American Secretary of State, one of a number of foreign diplomats who beat a path to the Taoiseach's door to try and persuade him to modify his policy of neutrality. The painful subject was broached; partition was used as a justification. The exchange was reported to Nicolson. De Valera brought out in his defence the thorny old Nationalistic argument of the occupation of Northern Ireland by England. Wilkie said, '". . . but we know all about that. That doesn't count anyway. You want Britain to win?" De Valera assented to this. "And yet you are making it more difficult for her." So in the end that fine obstinate Spaniard was obliged to say that if he leased the bases, Dublin might be bombed. Wilkie (having been at Coventry and Birmingham) did not conceal his contempt. "American opinion," he repeated, "will not be with you."'

In de Valera's Cabinet, Frank Aiken, Minister for External Affairs, was doggedly anti-British although, according to Maffey, not pro-German. Joseph Walshe, Secretary of External Affairs, never failed to make his support for a German victory known. Not only did he express his admiration for German achievement, but he also claimed that no one outside Britain believed that Britain was fighting for anything worthwhile. In the 1930s Charles Bewley had been Irish Minister in Germany. Although he had retired to Italy by the outbreak of the war, his loathsome anti-Semitic views during the thirties had influenced the Government in its refusal to admit ever more desperate refugees into Ireland. William Warnock, then Irish First Secretary in Germany, applauded Hitler's Reichstag speech in July 1940 and expressed admiration of Hitler's 'international justice'.

In England such opinions brought bitter reaction, including the remark of an MP who snarled that 'a dose of Nazism would do Southern Ireland all the good in the world'. Churchill had attacked neutral countries generally in a broadcast: 'Each one hopes if he feeds the crocodile enough the crocodile will eat him last. All of them hope that the storm will pass before their time comes to be devoured.'

Undoubtedly the pro-German 'substantial minority' among the general population mentioned by de Valera was a large one. Many Irishmen looked forward to German victory as a settling of old scores. A huge radio audience listened gleefully to the speeches of Lord Haw Haw. At school in Wexford Nicholas Furlong remembered how 'taunts of . . . German atrocities . . . were met with a query about Amritsar, a million murdered Zulus, Bloody Sunday, Macroom, India, Kevin Barry, the Six Counties . . . and "What about the Black and Tans?"'

Furlong was present at the funeral in Wexford of five German airmen killed over Carnsore Point in June 1941. The Irish Government contributed military of every service, cavalry, infantry, regular army, Volunteers, navy, Local Defence Force and a military band to accompany the coffins draped in their Nazi flags. Two Church of Ireland clergyman were there to pray for the Lutheran dead. After the Secretary to the German Legation had laid a laurel wreath wrapped in a scarlet and swastika-stamped flag, he made a speech with much mention of Führer and Reich, as many of the Irish civilians present, both men and women, joined him in outstretched salute.

Mr Burke in Belfast spoke for many in Brian Moore's *The Emperor of Ice-Cream*: '. . . the German jack boot isn't half as hard as the heel of John Bull. All this guff about Hitler being a menace to civilisation is sheer English hypocrisy.'

Hugh Leonard's father held similar opinions: he was, 'according to himself . . . pro-German, holding that Hitler was the greatest man barring de Valera that ever trod shoe leather. The truth of the matter was that he was anti-English and pro-nobody, but he could never grasp the distinction. "Hitler," he would say. "Oh he's the boy to give them whackery" – at which he would trot out his litany about the Black and Tans.'

As a child and teenager throughout the war, Dervla Murphy was 'straighforwardly pro-German in a light hearted sort of way, as one might be pro-Scotland or pro-France at a rugger match. While reading such patriotic stories as the Biggles books, I automatically transposed names in my mind to make the British the baddies and the Germans the goodies.'

Rumours abounded of U-boats landing at small ports and being provided with food and supplies by local people. The desire for further revenge among those who had fought with Tom Barry and Liam Lynch was combined with admiration for German technical ability fuelled by memories of German involvement in the Shannon Scheme. 'Neutral against whom?' asked a wag in *Dublin Opinion*.

In many parts of the country much pro-German sympathy was felt among those who relished the thought of the Colonels, generally believed to be spying for the Allies, having a bad time if Hitler won. In the election of 1944 members of Fianna Fáil took time to upbraid Irish Protestant voters for their 'sullen hostility' to Éire's achievements and ordered them not to be 'fifth columnists' at that critical time. Ill will lingered long after the Emergency was over; in 1975 John Ryan was writing scornfully about 'aggressive little ladies of the Anglo-

Irish persuasion who let the air out from the tyres of the Japanese Ambassador's car – these diminutive little Amazons would save their tea and sugar rations from the F and M café or Mitchell's Tea Shop to send to the boys in blue'. Probably this category included the woman who went out to Irishmurray island and used the cursing stones there to curse Hitler.

The Gaelic scholar Professor Daniel Binchy talked to Harold Nicolson in 1942. 'He says that a visiting Englishman is taken in by blarney to imagine that the feelings of this country towards us [the English] are really friendly. Not in the least; at the bottom of almost every Irishman is a little bag of bile, and although the hatred of us may die down at moments, it is there, even as our Protestantism and Puritanism are there subconsciously.'

Support for Germany and her allies ranged far and wide, and among the highest in the land. In conversation with Elizabeth Bowen the new Catholic Archbishop of Dublin, Dr McQuaid, defended both Pétain and Laval. McQuaid had grown up in Cavan, and the proximity of the Border had some effect on his opinions. Some Catholics whom Bowen met criticised the Church for its failure to pronounce on current events. 'This ranges from criticism of the parish priests for their lack of outlook, their ambiguous . . . attitude . . . to criticisms of the Vatican's political feebleness.' There was no condemnation by the Irish clergy or hierarchy of Nazi persecution of the Jews, although American bishops and an English cardinal did so in statements that were published in Irish papers. Nor did the hierarchy publicly condemn the bombing of Belfast.

When Count Balinski of the Polish Research Centre came to Dublin in 1941, he found that Dr McQuaid and the Papal Nuncio, Monsignor Paschal Robinson, were 'well acquainted' with the facts of religious persecution carried out by the Germans and the Russians. He was frequently irritated when speaking of the persecution of the Poles to be told by Irishmen that they knew by experience what persecution meant. 'I reacted with some heat to such assertions . . .'

Among the stubbornest opponents of England was one who had every reason to hate her. In June 1939 Kathleen Clarke, Tom Clarke's widow, was inaugurated the first Lady Lord Mayor of Dublin. As an old Republican she refused to wear the mayoral chain which bore King William's profile; another had to be provided. Her first action on taking up office was to remove the paintings of English monarchs that still decorated the Mansion House. One of the largest was of Queen Victoria. In her haste to get rid of these odious reminders of Albion, she had them placed outside just in time to be seen by passengers of an early morning tram in Dawson Street.

One of those who applauded her was an Irishman living in America. 'I was delighted when I read of you putting that old b— out of the Mansion House. Many a time I walked down Dawson Street and saw her looking out of the Hall and wished I could put her out, but why in hell didn't you burn her?' Queen Victoria may have been evicted from the Mansion House, but her massive statue was still to be seen round the corner in front of Leinster House where it would remain until 1948.

Life had been hard on Mrs Clarke, and soon she had further reason to grieve. The most stubborn opponents of Britain, the IRA, including young Brendan Behan, had begun a bombing campaign in England in January 1939 which during the year claimed seven dead and nearly 200 wounded. A number of the bombers were caught, including Peter Barnes and James McCormick who were executed in February 1940 as accessories to murder. This provoked strong anti-English feeling in Ireland, particularly as Barnes had not been in Coventry on the day of the explosions there. On the day the men were hanged, cinemas and theatres in Dublin closed and sporting fixtures were cancelled.

Six weeks before, on Christmas Eve 1939, fifty armed IRA men in lorries raided the magazine fort in the Phoenix Park, taking away a million rounds of ammunition, almost all the country's stock. The Irish Government took harsh measures. It had already passed the Offences Against the State Act in June 1939, which allowed for internment without trial. When IRA prisoners went on hunger strike in February 1940, in protest at being treated as common criminals, two were allowed to die before the strike was called off. Ultimately, 500 IRA men were interned during the Emergency and six were executed.

The terrible irony was felt by Mrs Clarke. 'I could understand the British Government with a war on their hands punishing the IRA – what I could not understand was the action of the Irish Government in punishing men for what they themselves had been doing in opposition to the Cosgrave Government.' When Patrick McGrath was executed in 1940, she ordered the blinds of the Mansion House to be drawn and the flag flown at half-mast.

The Emergency continued. In case Hitler or Churchill invaded the country, all road signs were removed. The German-style coal-scuttle helmets of the Irish Army were replaced. Among the new defence forces was a cyclist squadron known as the Pedalling Panzers or, to schoolboys like myself, the Piddling Panzers.

In 1940 I was sent to a prep school on the north side of Dublin attended by sixty-odd boys, all of whom were Protestant to the core. Most of them came from old Loyalist families and many of their fathers, like mine, had joined the British forces.

We played rugby and cricket and learnt the classics; I have a memory of lying sick in the sanatorium while the headmaster sat beside me reading Horace's *Odes*. Very soon we were made aware of the war. There was rationing of food and petrol; our parents could not collect us in their cars, and strange taxis from a firm called Dubtax with gas bags floating over their roofs appeared on the school avenue. When fitted, our gas masks erupted delightfully with fart-like noises.

In all Ireland you could not find a more English-orientated group of boys. We knitted scarves for the troops and collected silver paper with which to make Spitfires. We sang 'Run Adolf, Run Adolf, Run, Run, Run'. We jeered at dwarf-sized Goebbels and Field Marshal Goering with his chest full of medals. When we were driven past the German Legation in Northumberland Road, outside which hung the flag emblazoned with the swastika, we booed. No wonder the IRA sought to attack us when we walked in crocodile for our Sunday service at Raheny; that was who those rough-looking men were, we were told. Perhaps they wanted money, not guns, from little boys with skinny legs showing beneath their shorts. Our headmaster, with his experience of quelling tribesmen on the North-west Frontier, sent them packing.

Later in the year he assembled us in what was grandly called the great hall. Flanked by the matron and an assistant master, a youth without a degree who had been hired at a cut price, he announced, 'Gentlemen, the *Hood* has gone down.'

We all knew about the *Hood*, one of the great battleships of the British Navy. Now we were individually made to share the suffering of hundreds of drowned sailors: 'Gentlemen, I have decided that for the next few months we shall all abstain from cream.' Our personal experience of war would not come until May 1941.

So far Ireland had felt little of the violence beyond its shores. In December 1940 three people were injured when bombs fell in Sandycove, Co. Dublin. A farmer was injured by a bomb at Carrickmacross, Co. Monaghan. Bombs killed people in Co. Carlow and Co. Wexford.

In early 1941 came the bombing raids on Belfast when more than 700 lives were lost in less than five hours on the night of 15 April. The poet Robert Greacen heard 'the crunch of bombs that meant torn flesh, blood, death, rubble in the streets, women's tears, children's screams'. Belfast suffered a second bombing raid on the night of 4 May when eleven more bombs were dropped; the death toll was one hundred and fifty.

Were these raids, as was widely believed, choreographed by IRA agents sending useful information of defences through the German Legation in 'collaborationist Dublin'? Most probably not. De Valera's immediate response was humanitarian, ordering fire tenders from Dublin, Drogheda and Dundalk to speed north to fight the blazes. This annoyed the Germans, particularly when he used the old Partition argument as a justification; he blandly told them that his Government was entitled to act in what it regarded as a breach of neutrality because it claimed sovereignty over Northern Ireland.

Up in Belfast, Brian Moore had been an air-raid warden, whose grisly duty, described in his autobiographical novel *The Emperor of Ice-Cream*, was to put bodies into coffins. He recalled how the city was alight: 'All around the night bowl of sky, from Cave Hill to the Lough, from Antrim to Down, a red glow ebbed and sank, the reflected light of hundreds of burning houses, shops, factories and warehouses.'

It was not like that on the North Strand, on the night of 30 May, only tragedy on a far smaller scale, touchingly illustrated in news photographs of firemen and ARP workers saluting each body as it was brought out of the rubble.

In our dormitory we were watching the searchlights playing on the sky, the usual nightly display. The fat boy beside the window heard the drone of aircraft: 'Jerry!'

The curious sound of the engines was not the usual roar of a passing plane, but what Robert Greacen elsewhere described as 'the purr-purr-purr of those aerial ships of death'. There was only the one plane, but we heard it long enough to hold a shouting discussion of whether it was a Heinkel or a Dornier – it was the latter. Then came the two colossal explosions which rattled the windows of Green Dorm and killed thirty-four people in the locality, injuring ninety others. Twenty-five houses were destroyed and 300 made uninhabitable.

Alex King, the Chief Air Warden, recalled how 'the whole place was a shambles. There were cries for help, people running here and there – the North Strand people were absolutely out of this world . . . "You want a cup of tea, so?" There was always tea going. They had sandwiches, all kinds of sandwiches which they kept handing out.'

As our headmaster, carrying his ear-trumpet, chivvied us back to bed, the Dornier continued on its mission. The bomb destined for Dorset Street fell into the Liffey, while artillery fire prevented the plane from reaching the Phoenix Park. It turned for home, but never got back to base. An Irishman serving in the RAF, Pilot Abercorn, reported to his commanding officer that he had shot down a lone plane in the Irish Sea.

A few weeks later the German Government expressed its regret, saying the raid 'may have been due to high wind'. The compensation it promised was eventually paid by the West German Government, which handed over £327,000 in 1958.

Much about the raid on Dublin remains unclear. Although the Germans always claimed it was accidental, recent research in German archives has suggested that the raid, code-named Operation 'Roman Helmet', was planned as a response to Irish sympathy over that in Northern Ireland. The crew of the Dornier were directed to bomb the North Strand fire station, then the Dorset Street station, and afterwards to go off to the Phoenix Park and bomb poor old Douglas Hyde, who as a Protestant was perceived to be in sympathy with the Allies.

The detritus of the Battle of the Atlantic was appearing on the coastline, while German or British planes crashed on Irish soil. Dead bodies were washed ashore and debris from sunken ships became a familiar sight. By June 1940 British shipping losses stood at 282,560 tons. The old convoy route of British and Allied ships around the south coast was changed to the North Channel above Donegal, but the huge losses continued. By May 1941 more than 400,000 tons of Allied shipping had been sunk, a total of 120 ships. Many in England, and in Ireland, too, believed that hundreds of lives would have been saved if they had been able to make for the Treaty ports.

It was a time of invasion scare which included a rumour of the landing of 3,900 German troops along the south-west coast. The Germans had every intention of including Ireland in the empire of the Third Reich. They knew all about the country and its people through their intelligence reports. One under the heading 'Militär Geographische Ausgaben' told of how 'the great mass of the population consists even today of small tenant farmers who often work insufficient allotments of land . . . hence, poverty was and still is a general thing . . . the houses, especially in the West, are often extremely primitive of rough stones with straw roofs and with a few badly aired and lighted rooms in which large families huddle. The possibilities of billeting troops are, therefore, apart from larger towns, to be described as bad . . .'

German intelligence had also gathered that Irish characteristics included 'a lively temperament, good nature, cheerfulness, a talent for music and dancing, educational and social entertainments. The Irishman supports a community founded upon equality for all, but associates with this an extraordinary personal need for independence which easily leads to indiscipline and pugnacity (*Streitsucht*) . . . A profound piety characterises these people who have defended their Catholic beliefs with fanaticism, and the authority of the priest, sprung from the ordinary people, is enormous.'

De Valera ignored the menace, unaware that Churchill had sanctioned an RAF plan to use poison gas on Ireland if invasion went ahead. He continued to feed the crocodile, and his relations with Hempel, the German Envoy, were excellent. The swastika continued to fly in Northumberland Road; you didn't see any Union Jacks. 'The Germans,' William Warnock recalled long after the war, 'expressed their appreciation that Ireland had managed to assert and hold on to its neutrality.' Any fear they might have had would have been of Ireland's invasion by Britain.

My mother disagreed with de Valera about invasion. Europe was falling, and it was only a matter of time. When the Nazis came, she decided, we would hole up on our island, cut ourselves off from surrounding humanity, and survive like the Swiss Family Robinson. We would lay down secret stores of anything that was available at the time. This must have been before petrol rationing became absolute. We rounded up cans of paraffin oil, tins of peaches, rice pudding, Carnation Milk, tinned salmon and anything else the shops in Kenmare and Sneem had on their shelves. They were ferried over to the island where we buried them at dead of night so that the men we employed did not know the exact locations. They were marked down on a map but unfortunately this was lost. Long after the threat of invasion had receded, and the Emergency was over, rusty tins would emerge from the dark soil.

We returned to Laragh House, yet another demonstration of my father's propensity for playing ducks and drakes with money. This was an estate of about 800 acres in Wicklow which he acquired in the early thirties with the purpose of turning it into a country hotel. A ballroom was built and an annexe added, together with a hard court for tennis, a golf course and a sun deck overlooking the freezing lake where guests were expected to swim.

The army of staff included riding masters, golf professionals, a White

Russian countess and an English manager who was at 'varsity' and had started the Coconut Grove night-club (which was later destroyed during the Blitz with heavy casualties). Was it Mr Melville-Barker who vanished with the till? Was it the former head chef of the South African railways who stabbed a kitchen maid with a boning knife?

'A hotel with such enterprise must certainly be on the high road to success and fame,' mused the *Irish Tatler* in 1939. Alas, it was not. The unavailability of petrol did nothing for a hotel thirty miles from Dublin; guests could no longer use their cars to drive out and enjoy the 'fully licensed dance every Saturday (band)' or the 'golf, shooting etc.' at 'the perfect place for the perfect party'.

Amazingly, the place continued running during the war, giving some much-needed employment in the area. People would come down by St Kevin's bus, the one constant motor link between Dublin and Glendalough, or they were met at the railway station at Rathdrum. There were horses for guests, one hard and two soft tennis courts and a croquet lawn which was mowed by horses. Many English guests came over, probably to enjoy meat; and Catholics, too, I have been told, came down to Laragh to eat meat on Fridays.

Next door to us was Laragh Castle, a castellated 1798 blockhouse where German Abwehr military intelligence, which was responsible for contacts with discontented foreign minorities, had been at work. The castle had been bought by Maud Gonne in 1929 and given to her daughter Iseult and her husband Francis Stuart. Stuart, who declared himself 'completely fired with enthusiasm' for Hitler, had left Ireland and travelled to Germany in 1940 to take up a position as lecturer in modern English in the University of Berlin. In addition, he broadcast regularly for *Irland-Redaktion*, the radio station headed by Hans Hartmann, a Celtic scholar who had lived in Ireland, which sent out propaganda over the air waves throughout the war. Most of it, sweetened with promises about a united Ireland once Germany had won, was aimed at keeping Ireland neutral. The Irish Government only twice objected to the broadcasts; once when Stuart protested about the execution of IRA men in Belfast, and again when he advised voters in the 1943 election not to vote Fine Gael.

Besides giving scores of broadcasts over German radio, Stuart wrote some speeches for 'Lord Haw Haw', but William Joyce did not use them. Stuart also seems to have been involved peripherally in the sending of German agents to Ireland – at least, he gave one of them his wife's address. Iseult Stuart had inherited the strong anti-British opinions of her mother, as Stuart recounted in his massive self-justification *Black List – Section H*, the style of which suggests to some readers the rhythm of jackboots.

In May 1940 a German secret agent, Captain Hermann Goertz, parachuted into Meath with orders to contact the IRA. He hid his parachute under a hedge and started to walk southwards, swimming the Boyne. He wore a black beret and carried US$20,000 in his pocket, together with his First World War medals.

Four days later he reached Laragh in a state of semi-starvation. He came to our back door and asked the way to Mrs Stuart's house. After my mother was told, she telephoned the Garda, with what results she never knew. Years later I met an ex-employee of the hotel. 'Did I know that a German had a hut in the rhododendron wood near the avenue?' The avenue was two miles long. She had looked into the hut and there were clothes hanging up to dry and a few tattered possessions lying on the ground.

Today it is not possible to piece together the full story. Goertz had little luck; he was captured and interned after Mrs Stuart tried to buy him new clothes in Switzer's, the shop that supplied the dreadful herring-bone suits we wore at school. Hempel did not acknowledge him, the IRA did not trust him and he committed suicide after the war. He wrote, 'Although I have nowhere found better friends than in Ireland, I have sometimes had the feeling that I might perhaps have carried out my task better if I had by chance been born a Catholic.'

In the other direction from our hotel was Glendalough House, which belonged to Robert Barton, de Valera's comrade-in-arms and a cousin of Erskine Childers. Here a secret meeting took place in March 1941 between General McKenna, the Irish Chief of Staff, and Brigadier Gregson-Ellis from Northern Ireland, which resulted in agreement about liaison arrangements for combined Anglo-Irish resistance in the event of a German invasion of the South. The meeting was arranged through Bobby Childers, Erskine Childers's son, who was McKenna's staff officer. This liaison, which, in spite of all the rows and incidents, was effective until 1944 when German invasion was no longer feasible, was kept secret by both the British and Irish Governments both during and after the war.

Meanwhile, my uncle christened his good-natured gun dog Maffey after Sir John Maffey. His later dogs were Hankinson, Clutterbuck and Tory – all with the same whirling tails and gentle expressions, all called after leading British diplomats and ambassadors. The tease evolved from the fact that from 1939 until 1956 my grandfather's estate, Farmhill, on the outskirts of Dublin was leased as the official British Residence.

Sir John Maffey was very tall, the tallest diplomat in the world, with a record of Imperial service. When he came to Ireland on 22 September 1939 there was disagreement over his title; the British would not describe him as ambassador to a country which in theory was part of the Commonwealth, while to the Irish title 'High Commissioner' was equally repugnant. So they compromised on 'United Kingdom's Representative to Éire' and for the next ten years Maffey, who later became Lord Rugby (taking the name of his old public school), would play a crucial role in Anglo-Irish affairs.

De Valera would have an excellent relationship with the ex-Governor-General of Sudan, as good as the one he had had with Hempel. In those difficult times both Maffey and de Valera appreciated each other's qualities in spite of their many differences. It was to Farmhill that Sir John would retire to brood and worry about the latest impasse in Anglo-Irish relations. Here Lady Maffey entertained, as reported in the *Irish Tatler*: 'Lady Maffey AT HOME . . . one meets everyone from Ballsbridge to the Curragh. The house, which was formerly the residence of Canon Somerville-Large, is not extensive, but as the rooms are all connected, the visitors had the comfort of moving freely around and chatting to their friends.'

Farmhill had gardens and paddocks, a laundry room and a billiard room. There was no central heating. When Harold Nicolson arrived in Dublin in the winter of 1942, 'the High Commissioner drove me out here where he lives . . . a country house of small dimensions with trees and cows and fields. Crocuses among the rock work and some daffodils showing their long buds.'

It would be pleasant to conclude that Sir John found Farmhill congenial to his difficult task. Probably not; a later ambassador, Sir Walter Hankinson, considered it 'a most depressing and inadequate house, especially in the winter, being dark, cold and sunless'. Hankinson insisted that the Residence should be moved; after a long and frustrating search, which included the rejection of Abbeville, now Charles Haughey's estate, the Ambassador's Residence was moved to Glencairn near Carrickmines. This had once been the home of 'Boss Croker', Richard Welstead Croker, 'boss' of Tammany Hall, USA, who returned to his native Ireland in 1904, bought Glencairn and remodelled it so that it became a mixture of baronial and American colonial designs. As far as British diplomats were concerned, it turned out to be even less attractive than Farmhill: 'a failed Balmoral . . . with a nightmarish quality and the appearance of a horribly nouveau riche type of house'. Serve them right.

CHAPTER 17

The Eye of the Storm

Yes, it's been a hard year. Sacrifices have been made by rich and poor alike. Nobody has minded that. No sacrifice, nor hardship can ever be too great when the reward is our own homeland.

Irish newsreel, December 1942

Bless de Valera and Sean MacEntee,
Bless their brown bread and their half ounce of tea.

Traditional

Air-raid shelters were constructed in O'Connell Street while banks of turf lined the roads in the Phoenix Park. The polo ground was ploughed up and people were encouraged to cultivate allotments. But neither the Commissioners for Public Works nor the Corporation would fence off these vegetable patches, whose gardeners complained, 'We patrol our land at night and chase away the deer. But they always come back.'

The absence of petrol was soon felt. On 28 October 1939 the new oil refinery at Alexandra Basin in Dublin was ready to begin operations. The oil it produced would not be for domestic consumption. On the same day a petrol ration of eight gallons a month was introduced for private motorists. At Christmas there was no petrol whatsoever, and by January 1940, when some returned, the ration was cut in half. Soon there would be none at all for private consumption and precious little for those with essential needs like doctors and taxi men.

The *Journal of the Medical Association of Éire* complained in March 1941 that 'nothing is more calculated to cause adverse public criticism than the sight of petrol being used to convey people to and from cinemas, racecourses and other places of amusement . . . while . . . medical men have to reduce the volume of their work to the detriment of their patients'. Rural doctors were hardest hit.

The writer of 'Motor Matters' in the October 1939 issue of the *Irish Tatler* lamented how 'the rationing of petrol also affects hunting, as hounds always travelled in the hunt motor van . . . and now they will have to walk. Motors will no longer be able to motor round with horse boxes attached after the hunt, as they would use in one day what ration is being allowed for one month.' In November he still showed optimism, with reports on traffic 'jambs' (*sic*). But gradually as the months went by realism stepped in, although it was not until February 1941 that 'Motor Matters' was discussing petrol substitutes. 'Diesel oil and coal gas and tar oil – there is the initial difficulty of not knowing the precise duration of the shortage and the not unnatural hesitancy of embarking on the expense of changeover, alterations and adaptions . . . The gas bag . . . candidly there has always been a prejudice against what many regard as the somewhat unsightly cumbersome equipment.' After that the 'Motor Matters' column was dropped altogether from the *Irish Tatler* for the duration of the Emergency.

In spite of the reservations of 'Motor Matters', the gas bag became a familiar sight and other alternatives would be used with ingenuity. Commercial vehicles which used petrol were encouraged to fit themselves with gas producers. In 1943 a scheme was introduced for commercial companies which had three or more vehicles to fit at least one lorry with gas or face a reduction in petrol rationing. Reaction to the scheme was 'slow'.

Hugh Leonard had a friend who was given ten shillings to dismember a Rolls-Royce and throw it piecemeal into the sea. But others were less despairing. My uncle had a large American open sedan called a Terryplane; he carved out the boot and placed a home-made charcoal burner inside, looking like an old stove entangled with pipes. At regular intervals the car was stopped and fed with nuggets of charcoal; if the fire in the burner went out it was relit with a rag covered with paraffin which was placed in a pipe; the whole contraption would give off a reassuring steady roar. If the wind blew the wrong way any passenger in the back seat was in danger of being asphyxiated. At a time when cars were almost non-existent it had the monopoly of those empty roads; it might be challenged by a donkey and cart, or occasionally a gas-filled car with a swaying canopy on its roof might pass the belching vehicle.

The bicycle helped to keep the country going. We once made an expedition from Wicklow down to the island in Kerry by bike; I carried the Persian cat in a basket behind me. Otherwise in country and town, ancient broghams, Victorias, side-cars, traps and even a stagecoach which took guests to and from the Shelbourne Hotel were dusted down and brought into service. Viscountess Powerscourt was seen in her smart Ralli trap drawn by a beautiful piebald pony; the Earl of Meath boasted a four-wheeled vehicle drawn by 'a fine moving horse'. We used to journey the thirty miles to Dublin in a dogcart which we stabled in Goffs in Merrion Square. This was nothing compared to Patricia Cockburn's mother who drove 170 miles to Dublin from her home near Cork in a pony trap, a journey that took her five days. In *Dublin Opinion* an old man says, 'It's just what I said way back in 1903 . . . these motor cars are only a passing phase.'

Dublin was full of horse-drawn vehicles; a horse dealer in Stonybatter remembered how 'they were coming to our place same as a supermarket looking for horses'. Among the assortment of laundry and bread vans, brewers' drays pulled by Clydesdales, and milk floats, it was startling to see the van belonging to the Swastika Laundry with its large symbol of a swastika painted on its side.

Eamonn Mac Thomáis tended his horse lovingly. 'In the morning the first thing you do is to let Daisy out for a drink, clean out the stable, put in fresh straw for the bedding and lock the stable door. The next thing we do is to currycomb and brush Daisy, oil her hooves, put on her harness and give her a nose bag. On Thursday we oil and Brasso the harness and wash the van.'

It was said, 'Oh, during the war there would have been no Dublin, only for the horses and horsemen.' But the city was rattling with bicycles and the trams ran until 1944, emitting their ping-pong noises to warn pedestrians of their approach. People doggedly made their way into the centre of Dublin by one means or another to avail themselves of the entertainment offered. In October 1943 they could queue to see Tyrone Power in *Crash Drive* at the Metropole or Judy Garland in *Presenting Lily Mars* at the Adelphi. At the Olympia, Anew MacMaster dressed in ruffles as *The Scarlet Pimpernel* while at the Gate Mícheál Mac Liammóir rolled his eyes and carried a head in a hatbox in *Night Must Fall*. The Abbey took no chances and offered *The Playboy of the Western World*.

Some preferred the rink in Duke Street which offered roller-skating at its best. But for most it was the cinema, especially for the young. Out in Dún Laoghaire Hugh Leonard remembered 'any summer evening after the light came up and the "Soldier's Song" blared out, the record cracked and hissed while we stood to attention, cigarette butt cupped in our hands, and saw with surprise that never lessened the dinginess of the cinema; the bare walls, the upholstery dribbling from the seats, the yellow pall of smoke'.

A reward for a cinema-absorbed nation was the filming of battle scenes for Laurence Olivier's *Henry V* outside Dublin. In 1943 Powerscourt became Agincourt; 500 officers, NCOs and members of the defence forces, together with hundreds of unemployed, were conscripted as English and French knights, foot-soldiers, and archers with longbows and crossbows.

From early on, Dublin became a place of rest and recreation for war-weary England, attracting her careworn citizens with its lights. The anti-aircraft searchlights on Dún Laoghaire pier were visible in Wales. They shone from a world where, in spite of shortages, the good things in life continued. In 1941 Elizabeth Bowen thought that 'Dublin seemed as dazzling and legendary as New York'. Robert Greacen found it 'the most fascinating city in these islands, an oasis of light in the surrounding gloom'. Louis MacNeice was less impressed. 'Dublin was hardly worried by the war; her old preoccupations were still preoccupations. The intelligentsia continued their parties, their mutual malice as effervescent as ever.'

Within days of the outbreak of war, hundreds of people returned to Ireland from London. They were known as Blitz Gaels. Others who came included wealthy Englishmen who managed to obtain travel permits and those who wished to avoid the harshness of war – conscientious objectors, artists and musicians. The White Stag group of 'young moderns' who gave their first exhibition in May 1940 included a number of refugee artists. There were no Jews among them; only sixty Jews were allowed into the country during the whole war. Censorship concealed unpleasantness happening abroad, and few felt guilty.

The White Stag artists, among them Thurloe Connolly, Ralph Cusack and Basil Rákóczi, met regularly at the Country Shop in Stephen's Green with its scent of home-made tweeds, its straw *súgán* chairs and drawings by Elizabeth Rivers on the walls. 'Tis cheap and tis dainty,' Patrick Kavanagh, another regular, said of it. The Shop not only provided good food, but it also acted as an important outlet for countrywomen to sell their goods and for artists to hold exhibitions. The Royal Hibernian Academy had become increasingly conservative, refusing to hang the pictures of Louis le Brocquy; hence the establishment of the Irish Exhibition of Living Art in 1943 which more closely reflected trends in European painting.

The art world provided plenty of entertainment, like the Nine Arts Ball in 1940 at which Mr Desmond Leslie, 'kinsman of the new British Prime Minister, Mr Winston Churchill', appeared dressed as a gaucho. In August the artist Mainie Jellett threw a party in her home in Fitzwilliam Square which brought writers and artists together; the reporter for the *Irish Tatler* met 'Miss Purser, Mr J. Hone, Mr Jack Yeats, Mrs Walter Starkie, Major and Mrs Kirkwood. Mrs Sean Purser, Mrs Phillips and Miss Bay Jellett acting as hostesses, made everyone welcome to the recherché tea.' Sarah Purser, who had continued painting well into her eighties, died aged ninety-five in August 1943. A Dublin story claimed that 'Miss Purser was killed by a stamp.' When she saw a bad portrait of her friend Douglas Hyde on a stamp, she went into a rage that led to a stroke, dying two weeks later. Appropriately she was buried on a second Tuesday.

After her death the auction in Mespil House offered wartime bargains – a Gainsborough for £45, a Hogarth for £35. Later the house and the rus-in-urbe garden would be turned into flats, while the delicate plasterwork ceiling in the drawing-room would go to Áras an Uachtaráin.

Mainie Jellett's party was the sort that John Betjeman disliked. Betjeman served in Dublin from 1941 to 1943 as Press Attaché to Maffey. One of his tasks was to persuade the Irish that the German new order was anti-Christian, but he reported in March 1941 that he found 'even amongst the most sincere Catholics a refusal to believe in stories of German persecution'. Part of the trouble was that Irish people with long memories remembered how Allied propaganda about German atrocities during the First World War turned out to be untrue.

Those were not easy years for someone whose love for Ireland was expressed so joyously in a wartime bicycle ride (no cars) across the country with Emily,

Lady Hemphill. He was startled by the opinions he encountered. He wrote, 'We are at the mercy of a people who are either anti-English, anti-German and pro-Irish (faintly a majority) and there are pro-Irish and pro-German (about forty-eight per cent) and two per cent pro-German above everything. The Irish papers are all anti-British and the best selling writers are pro-German. I am beginning to hate Ireland and the Irish.'

In his first months in Dublin everything seemed to go wrong. The Betjemans stayed in the freezing house belonging to the artists Eva and May Hamilton near Lucan. Penelope Betjeman wrote to a friend, 'We are both badly homesick and loathe all the social life here. We have to go to large cocktail parties, dinner and lunch parties and, worst of all, a special brand of Dublin party when you arrive after dinner: about nine p.m. and are expected to stay till at least two a.m.'

However, Betjeman's natural ability to make friends prevailed. The writers and artists he helped included Patrick Kavanagh and Jack Yeats. Soon he was engrossed in a whole range of social activities and immersed in the life he and his wife had earlier deprecated.

'12 October 1941 . . . I opened an Art Exhibition in Dublin today. A fat lot I know about Art. It is ridiculous. This is the second time I have done it. A young priest artist, under the influence of Dufy, called Fr Hanlon . . .'

By the time he left Ireland in June 1943, his resentment towards Irish neutrality had vanished. His departing address to a meeting of clergy gave some indication of his quixotic attitude to a country and a people he never ceased to be fond of. 'After more than two years' residence here, I shall return to England with the profoundest gratitude to Ireland where everyone – Roman, Anglican, Non-conformist believes in another world, and where everyone goes to church.' In 1944 Betjeman had lunch with James Lees-Milne. 'Said he loved Ireland but not the Irish middle class . . . When the Betjemans finally left Ireland, Penelope Betjeman . . . offered to plan an equestrian tour for de Valera and her last words to him were "I hope you won't let the Irish roads deteriorate. I mean I hope you won't have them metalled and tarmacked."'

After Pearl Harbor an increasing number of Americans stationed in the North of Ireland came down to Dublin. Patrick Campbell 'trailed a tall olive-green American Air Force Lieutenant down Dawson Street and caught up with him asking for gum. "Gaash," he said, "that's baad, but baad. Look I gaat no gum by me, but . . . Lootenant Taans, in the Hibernian Hotel, he's got a stack. You call him up."'

The Lootenant was permitted to wear his uniform. So were the young servicemen from Canada, New Zealand and Australia who came and stayed with us on leave through an organisation called the Dominion Hospitality Trust. They had a brief respite from fighting, plenty of steak and the opportunity of playing the Andrews Sisters on our wind-up gramophone. They, too, walked through the streets of Dublin in their uniforms of fighter pilots, soldiers and sailors.

This privilege was not permitted to those who fought under British command. De Valera came to an agreement with Maffey that the thousands of Irishmen who had joined the English forces should wear civilian clothes when they returned home on leave. 'You would help us and help yourselves.' So a depot was established at Olympia in west London where Irish servicemen, who were given an extra day's leave, divested themselves of uniforms and donned civvies before they were permitted to return to the land of their birth. Officers, too, put aside their uniforms, but in cold weather wore their khaki overcoats with epaulettes adorned with pips and crowns. These insignia had to be removed after complaints from the German Legation; it was assumed that as part of their spying operations, members of the Legation staff waited at the gangplank to gather information about the movements of British forces.

In 1943 Sean O'Faolain's magazine *The Bell* brought out a series of articles on people's incomes which demonstrated how even during the worst days of the Emergency life was pleasant for the affluent. A solicitor was cited, with an income of approximately £800 a year. Although his car was up on blocks for the duration, he and his wife made regular trips to the opera and to the Gaiety. In addition, 'an RDS [Royal Dublin Society] badge dangles from an ornament'. In his household, for breakfast there was bacon and eggs; for other meals, meat, including the Sunday roast, brown stew, and steak and kidney pie, featured largely. Perhaps the family followed the advice offered in an advertisement in December 1941: 'Give the festive meal a happy ending. Dainty foil-wrapped sections of Galtee cheese – After a succession of rich sweet foods . . . be sure you have a box of Galtee Cheese sections on the Christmas table.'

The solicitor ate out regularly. The Gresham, Hibernian and Shelbourne Hotels offered their meaty meals; so did Jammet's and the Dolphin where it was said the best steaks in the world were cooked over charcoal. Dublin restaurants and bars were never fuller. 'The English refugees lined up the bottles and we brought our friends along to drink them,' Patrick Campbell recalled. Pubs flourished; Brian O'Nolan, the world's expert on Dublin pubs, wrote of them lovingly under one of his pseudonyms, Flann O'Brien (his other was Myles na gCopaleen) – Barny Kiernan's on the quays, with its collection of glasses from which hangmen had drunk their pints of stout; Fanning's, centre of intellectual sodality; Grogan's of Leeson Street; Higgins's of Pembroke Street for UCD students; Davy Byrne's for Trinity students; Mulligan's by the Theatre Royal for theatrical people; the Scotch House, which served whiskey to civil servants; and the Brazen Head, where 'the most random spit will land on ten centuries of antiquity'. The Palace Bar catered for writers and journalists. John Betjeman brought Cyril Connolly there who found it 'as warm and friendly as an alligator tank.'

O'Nolan mourned the demise of the old-fashioned curate in his apron and deplored the increasingly popular lounge, 'the Lounge Bar, the Select Lounge, the Oak Lounge . . . and still more refined booze-shops called brasseries and butteries'. Women were beginning to appear in pubs; cartoonists in *Dublin*

Opinion joked about their presence. A decade later Honor Tracy could write about the frequenters of the Pearl Bar in tedious detail from personal observation.

In November 1940 the Gate Theatre put on a play named *Roly Poly*, adapted from de Maupassant's *Boule de Suif*. De Maupassant's French refugees during the Franco-Prussian War were set in a modern context; Christopher Casson considered it 'so topical it was as if it happened in the next room'. The French Minister thought similarly, complaining that his countrymen were being traduced, while Dr Hempel protested strongly, saying that 'no Nazi officer would behave like the Lieutenant in the play'. As a result of his objections and under pressure from de Valera, *Roly Poly* was withdrawn after its second performance.

Ireland was well used to censorship. But now there was a new variety which not only imposed a news blackout, but also insisted that nothing should be printed or broadcast that might disturb the nation's tranquillity or annoy the Germans. Charlie Chaplin's film *The Great Dictator*, considered particularly offensive to the Germans, was condemned by Dr Hayes, the film censor, as 'blatant and vulgar propaganda . . . if the picture had been shown in this country, it would have meant riots and bloodshed'.

The Emergency Powers Order meant a crackdown on war pictures and newsreels generally. The *Irish Times*, which was disliked by Frank Aiken who controlled censorship during much of the Emergency, had to submit even small ads to the censor. Any news item that revealed the presence of Irishmen in British forces had to be suppressed. Death notices of Irishmen killed in action could not mention military rank or how they died. Once, someone tried to include 'Greater love than this no man hath than that he lay down his life for his friends.' The second part had to be removed.

Weather conditions were censored; when de Valera's private secretary fell and broke his arm while skating on the lake in the Phoenix Park, this item could not be published lest unfriendly sources should learn about the ice. And yet at the same time the Irish Meteorological Office was sending vital weather reports to London, sometimes in a code supplied by the British Commonwealth Office, a practice that must have been sanctioned by de Valera.

Although Smyllie at the *Irish Times* got around the censor on a number of famous occasions – referring to the torpedoing of a ship as a 'boating accident' and arranging photographs on the front page in the form of a V on VE Day – he had little chance of regular evasion while Aiken was emboldened to attack and censor the princes of the Church. A bishop in whose diocese several deaths had occurred as a result of German bombs had to remove the phase 'accursed bombers' from his pastoral letter. Another bishop who criticised the policy of neutrality was suppressed.

The object of such censorship was to prevent the suspicion that either deliberately or inadvertently Ireland was taking sides. It led to the mistaken practice of suppressing all accounts of Nazi atrocities as propaganda. As a result, in the words of G. K. White, 'Ireland during the war suffered little physically, but spiritually . . . she was corrupted by existing in something like a state of suspended animation, cut off by her own free will from the tortured world around her.'

The nation turned in on itself, ignoring the turmoil outside its wave line. *The Bell* complained of the priorities of Radio Eireann with regard to news. On the Sunday night news at the end of July 1943, when Mussolini had resigned and the battle of Sicily was being waged, the news items in order of priority were:

1. Pilgrimage to Croagh Patrick. Sixteen Masses said on the summit. The sermon of the Archbishop of Tuam.
2. Conference in Cork of Muintir na Tíre.
3. Sicily.

News items describing bread queues in Dublin were suppressed lest the public should become panicky and the news only extend the queues. In 1942 the Bishop of Ossory was prohibited from publishing a letter in the *Irish Farmer's Journal* criticising the prices of growing foodstuffs and suggesting that farmers deserved more. The letter had already been read out in every church in his diocese. Aiken said that anything that discouraged wheat growing was 'as treasonable as advocacy of the disbandment of the army'.

Compulsory tillage forced us to grow wheat at Laragh. Bureaucracy chased us. *Dublin Opinion*: '"How many do you employ on your farm?" "Ten. Four labourers and six clerks."' We ourselves employed about a dozen men. The ploughing and seeding by Johnny Byrne, behind the horses, was followed in late summer by the reaper and binder slowly working its way around the golden heads of grain. The steam threshing machine came up the long avenue billowing out clouds of smoke. Owners of threshing machinery were given a coal allowance of up to ten tons; otherwise they were told to use turf or timber which, if kept under cover, was deemed quite suitable.

Plant more potatoes! urged the Department of Agriculture. Self-sufficiency was vital; in 1943 when the carrying capacity of Irish ships had been reduced by half with the loss of two merchant vessels, precious space for imports was taken by 100 tractors, 100 reapers and binders and 2,000 tons of binder twine from the British Ministry of Agriculture.

The plan was to bring 300,000 acres under tillage by 1944. Farms that did not comply could be fined or taken over. The lack of fertiliser – 30,000 tons per annum were used instead of the prewar 250,000 tons – meant wretched crops; so did the ploughing up of unsuitable terrain, like our hilly land where the wheat and oats we planted tended to shrivel.

The efforts required by compulsory tillage went towards producing the notorious wartime bread. 'If you bring home a dozen loaves nowadays, the smell of them in a car would knock you sideways,' declared a TD. Not that there were many cars. Bread varied from grey to black. 'At first we ate it with our eyes shut,' Eamonn Mac Tomáis remembered. 'It was a funny sort of bread, it didn't go stale. It went green.' *Dublin Opinion* had a man gasping like a

Bateman character as he ate it. Before baking, many housewives would illegally separate the bran from the white flour by sieving it through a silk stocking. According to Hugh Leonard, bread became darker and coarser and acquired laxative powers 'which increased as the war went on; until by D Day it had the efficiency of an enema'. Propaganda urged, 'Buy today what you need today . . . bread will not keep . . . don't feed wheat flour or bread to animals.' That was 'not merely an offence against the law, but an offence against humanity'.

Leon Ó Broin recalled the panic in a remote Irish-speaking village in the West when flour did not arrive. Flour was carried round the country in travelling shops, and this time, in order to conserve their petrol stocks, they had omitted this district. Women carrying empty sacks were fearful of some sort of recurrence of famine, of which there was a lively folk memory.

Quantities of tea imported ranged from 6,110,000 pounds in 1942 to 6,125,000 pounds in 1944. Only in 1946 did imports begin to improve, when nearly 16,000,000 pounds of still-rationed tea were brought in. During the worst days of the Emergency it was reduced to half an ounce a week per person. Tea-leaves that had done duty for one pot were dried and reused; one of the images of the time is of tea-leaves laid out on a window-sill. Substitutes were tried like cocoa husks, seaweed, carrot tea, ash tea, dandelion tea and herb tea. A bottle of whiskey or fifty cigarettes or a gammon of ham were considered fair exchange for half a pound of tea. Myles na gCopaleen made the best of it. 'The brother was saying that he has eighteen pounds of tea stored up above in Finglas. He knew the war was coming five years ago. He said the thing couldn't last.' *Dublin Opinion*: 'Champagne! Tut tut, Jeeves. My daughter's wedding is an occasion that calls for TEA!'

If they made such a fuss over tea, when the rest of the world faced starvation, things couldn't be so bad in Ireland – or so her enemies thought. But many factors contributed to the atmosphere in Dublin described in a letter by the actress Betty Chancellor. 'Life is so drab here and the country does get one down a bit. Things like scabies . . . The gas goes off at 7 at night. The buses stop at 9.30. We have barley flour which is . . . madly constipating' – an opinion that differed from Hugh Leonard's. 'This city is dying. The frightful censorship and narrowness is sapping the life out of everything.'

Clothes rationing was introduced in June 1942; a month later footwear was rationed – boots would remain scarce until well after the war. Dublin women like those elsewhere took to painted stockings. 'Look girls, I've got liquid stockings. Miners Liquid Stockings. Looks like gossamer . . . doesn't streak, is waterproof. No more ladders or holes. Shades: Grape Mist, Gold Mist.'

In peacetime twenty-five tons of newsprint and 16,000 tons of cardboard per annum were imported. Now under the Emergency Powers Orders it was illegal to throw waste paper or cardboard into public bins. Scrap paper was recycled into ration books. No paper for sweet wrappers was available, although sweets themselves were plentiful. People were eating more sweets because of the shortage of tobacco. Paper drives resulted in many big houses sacrificing –

willingly in many cases – centuries of estate accounts, to the frustration of later historians. The 'Irishman's Diary' reported, 'Some days ago I was offered a loaf of bread wrapped in a copy of the *Freeman's Journal* dated to the beginning of this century, while last Sunday in Wicklow I was offered a loaf of bread wrapped in a copy of *Punch* published in the summer of 1905.'

One or two enterprising farmers tried to grow tobacco. Mild profiteering was illegal. 'Ballinrobe District Court – July 8, 1942. James Scahill, Ballinrobe, for selling cigarettes in quantities other than five or lots of five and charging one penny per cigarette fined £2 plus expenses. Emily O'Connor, Cong, fined for selling a 6d packet of cigarettes for 7d.' By 1943 the 'black market', still within inverted commas, had been firmly established.

'Keep the Home Fires Burning' urged an insurance advertisement in June 1941. 'There is great activity in the Turf acres today . . . The despised fuel of yesterday has now assumed a vital importance due to the restrictions imposed by the present emergency.' At Laragh, our men used to walk up to our patch of bog to cut turf, reluctantly because the area was haunted by a spirit known as the Great Boo. Billowing turf smoke poured out of Dublin chimneys, while the banks of turf lining the roads in the Phoenix Park were robbed by thieves with prams. The turf, which had long been promoted as the fuel of patriots, was now found to be a poor exchange for the coal on which industries, factories and hospitals depended, as well as most households.

From 1942 fuel ration cards were distributed and gas was available for only a few hours a day. The acute shortage of coal and other suitable fuel led to restrictions that wavered throughout the period with various increases and reductions as were warranted by coal supplies. The worst time for gas users came in October 1944 when 600 Gas Company workers went on strike, leaving the city without any gas at all for a whole weekend.

The Glimmer Man became a newly invented villain, empowered to enter people's kitchens and check if the burners on the cooker were hot with illegally lit remnants of gas. In April 1944 Lemass threatened that the use of gas in 'off' periods would be made a criminal offence. After the Emergency it was acknowledged that the efforts of Glimmer Men were relatively ineffective.

Oranges, lemons, bananas, coffee, candles, chocolate, paint, wallpaper and pots and pans became unavailable. On Inishmurray shortage of sugar meant abandoning the traditional distillation of *poitín*, the first glass to be offered to the fairies. This has been given as a reason why the island was abandoned soon after the Emergency.

Economy on beauty preparations was recommended, with tips on spraying on lotions using old scent bottles and scooping out the surplus at the bottom of lipstick containers. 'Put in a little pot – use for rouge or apply to your lips with little finger.' Soap was recommended instead of cleansing cream. But there was a shortage of soap.

Shortages added to the problems of the poor. In the Dublin slums there was an increased incidence of scabies – the old 'Republican itch' – because of the lack of soap and of fuel to heat water. Impetigo induced dry scaly patches and cracks around the mouth. In Cork the usual health menace was compounded in 1941 by a polio epidemic in which sixteen died. Doctors noted that there was still a certain amount of rickets among children.

In 1943 *The Bell* interviewed a Mrs K who had six children and lived in a two-roomed flat in a Dublin tenement without gas, or water, which was carried up two flights of stairs. The WC in the yard was shared by five people. Mrs K's expenses included the usual burial insurance, rent at seven shillings a week, and one shilling and ninepence for cigarettes for himself – perhaps he had his own supplier. Since himself was unemployed she received food vouchers, home assistance and various charities including the St Vincent's men. She attended the Centre for Expectant Mothers three months before and after a baby was born, where she received a regular good meal and a layette. Her chief worry was clothes; the Parish Clothing Guild dressed the children for their First Communion. The children themselves, noted the interviewer, were bright, healthy and happy. 'She asks nothing but that her family shall not go to bed hungry.'

In winter the family used one candle a week.

With the increased use of bicycles, a shortage of tyres, for which the black market demanded huge sums, became a problem. Dunlop's of Cork offered a reward to anyone finding bales of rubber washed in off torpedoed ships. Other trophies could be found on the sand. Over the war years walking on Rossbeigh Strand in Co. Kerry, Patrick O'Sullivan picked up a wallet containing $50, a suitcase filled with sailor's clothes and a small table marked '*Capitaine*'.

Now that trains were fuelled by wood and turf, railway travel became increasingly erratic. *Dublin Opinion* showed a lady being tied to a railway line by a moustachioed villain: 'You can't leave me here, you beast – I'll starve!'

Travellers without motor transport – the vast majority – relied completely on the uncertain train services. A journey from Dublin to Killarney, a distance of 210 miles, took a mammoth twenty-three hours. Often trains were cancelled, which meant waiting for the milk train at four in the morning. There were many stories of how pedestrians overtook trains or how passengers were invited to step down and search the neighbourhood for turf or timber before they could continue.

The country was quiet. Edward O'Brien remembered wartime Durrow in Co. Laois where there was no motor traffic apart from two bread delivery vans and the Cork to Dublin bus. Children played all day in the main street. The little shops were almost empty apart from the occasional delivery of unrationed cigarettes and snuff, kept under the counter for special customers. Often men would walk five miles to Ballyragget in the hope of finding cigarettes there for sale. The bare shelves of shops revealed large areas of mildewed wallpaper and cracked distemper. 'After dark, lit by the glow of a smoke-stained light bulb the shop took on an eerie desolate appearance.' The customer felt his way home in the dark.

In remote country villages shopkeepers would cycle miles to the nearest town for supplies which they would sell to country people at grossly inflated prices. Black-market tea at £1.00 a pound was common – about £40 by today's prices.

Not all was gloom, however. Milk, eggs, potatoes and vegetables were plentiful. In 1944 an editorial in *The Bell* commented on the prosperity arising from the war, writing of 'plenty of money in circulation, internal trade flourishes, hardly any unemployment, pastoral trade flourishes because Britain needs wool and mutton'. Poultry was also sent profitably to England. Then there were the rabbits. By the end of the war rabbits had risen from one and sixpence a pair to four and sixpence each; since workers' wages were thirty-eight shillings and fourpence, a week's wages was equivalent to nine rabbits. Two rabbits represented a day's wage or twelve pints of beer. Scores might be caught at night, lamping with electric lamps and greyhounds. Rabbit-hunting expeditions were arranged out to the Saltees where they hopped about helplessly in their thousands. At Laragh, Billy Connolly did nothing else but snare rabbits or flush them out of their burrows with his ferrets and send them to the hungry English for profit.

England offered even more money than rabbits. The demand for workers in English factories was denuding the Irish countryside. Few wished to stay behind as labourers working from five in the morning until nine at night for low wages and meals taken apart in farmhouses. Patrick O'Sullivan remembered one farmhouse in the forties where a single plate was provided for every two labourers, each portion on either side.

Many labourers were recruited by agents for McAlpine and Wimpey who got £2.00 for every able-bodied person they signed on. An emigrant would go to Dublin by train and be marched off to a doss-house opposite the Iveagh Baths where he would be bathed and his clothes disinfected for lice. Then it was off to England on the crowded mail-boat.

It was said that infanticide in Ireland increased during the Emergency since girls could not get the restricted tickets to go to England and have their babies there, far from local disgrace, often at the expense of English Catholics. Other women flocked to England to enter the services or do war work. Back home, a shortage of domestic servants developed. Girls no longer wanted to be owned body and soul by mistresses paying ten shillings a week. In many households their conditions were appalling; their letters were read and their rooms were searched when they were out. Sometimes there would be pork chops for the family and two sausages for the maid; Fridays offered fish for the family and a fried egg for her. Many girls endured freezing kitchens and one half-day a week, when they often did not get off until five in the afternoon. Some had the audacity to ask for a thirty-six-hour week with two and a half days off and evenings free after eight o'clock. But many more fled to English factories.

After the sinking of the *Munster* at the outset of the Emergency, mail-boats travelled in darkness to escape the attention of U-boats. When Donal Foley took the boat in 1944, 'the other emigrants . . . were in the main poorly dressed.

A ragged penniless army with nothing but their health and strength to hurry them on their way.' 'They went in droves like cattle,' wrote John Healy, 'often with no education – a Rosary in their pocket – biased history which said that England always did us down.' Thomas McCarthy's poem 'The Emigration Trains' recalled how 'I owned a suitcase of card, while others carried mere bundles of cloth'.

Foley remembered the ship 'like a travelling Irish town, moving slowly and darkly across the water – all the lights blacked out, the first grim reminder that we were travelling to a country at war'. Down at the bar hundreds were thronging around the serving hatch for a drink. In the darkness a voice began to sing 'Kevin Barry'.

'A primitive feeling of fellowship with that young defiant voice welled up in my breast. The song was taken up by hundreds and when our ship landed at Holyhead, that strange chorus filled the dark air – that night we were conscious only of the sharp wind, the dark and dreariness of Holyhead, surely the unfriendliest spot during those years in the whole world.'

But there was money to be made at the final destination, whether it was in a factory or laying an airfield over a cabbage field in East Anglia. John Healy wrote of men regularly wiring back money orders of £20 and £30, of the heaps of money that came back to Charlestown and were put in the post office, in the town's only bank or stacked away under a thousand mattresses. He noticed the men in new suits and flashy ties coming back, descending from buses and lurching into bars with full wallets 'who would drink until the buses pulled out again . . . on to the next town'. They had been making more than the school-teachers and the sergeant in the barracks.

In Limerick, according to Frank McCourt, 'families up and down the lane are getting telegram money orders from their fathers in England – they have electricity now so they can see things they never saw before, and when darkness falls they turn on the wireless to see how the war is going. They thank God for Hitler because if he hadn't marched all over Europe the men in Ireland would still be at home scratching their arses in the queue at the Labour Exchange.'

The Labour Exchange offered ten shillings a week and a voucher for tea. There were many who took it, the new short-lived prosperity having passed them by. An editorial writer in the *Irish Times* felt that 'no words are strong enough to describe the destitution which is the lot of thousands of Dublin families . . . the men (with sallow pinched faces) resentful of their lot, the women resigned to it . . . above all the little children, their young bodies disfigured already by hunger and disease'. For the first time a Children's Allowance Bill would be introduced.

The unemployed could always join the Irish Army. Recruiting literature made little appeal to patriotism.

THE ARMY WANTS MEN.
YOU WILL LIKE LIFE IN THE ARMY.

As well as training you, the Army will look after your health and comfort. There are Physical Training Instructors to build up your muscle and bone, to say nothing of three good hot meals a day, a bed in warm comfortable quarters and enough pay to keep you in cigarettes . . . There are books to read . . . and hurling, boxing and other athletics to keep you fit. Besides, there are doctors and dentists . . . WHAT MORE DO YOU WANT?

In 1942 Garret Fitzgerald joined the Local Defence Force or LDF and his brother, Fergus, the Irish Army. The Army was a great healer of Civil War divisions. Sons of Republicans could parade beside the sons of Fine Gael families; Vivian de Valera, Liam Cosgrave, Eoin Ryan and Fergus Fitzgerald were comrades together.

Hugh Leonard joined the LDF, whose duties were those of a Home Guard; the uniform was green with boots and leggings. 'We were a lethargic group, and the army sergeant who taught us small-arms once a week in Dalkey town hall endured us as if he were on Calvary and we were his cross.' Later Leonard joined the Local Security Force as an auxiliary policeman with a navy-blue uniform; he learnt, as part of his training, how to work a stirrup-pump.

Patrick Campbell joined the defence forces in Ireland, instead of going to England like so many of his peers. 'You don't know what suffering is until you've been the one Protestant among 32 Roman Catholics in the Dublin Bay Port Authority.' After being drilled in English for a couple of weeks the group was told by the NCO, 'From now on youse bowsies'll be doing it in Irish.' There was 'a roar of outraged complaint: "Sure we can't even do it in muckin English yet."'

The Army was uncertain whom it might have to fight. Men in the 1st Division in the South prepared for a German invasion while others near the Border expected the British. At one stage Hempel was sounded out about possible German help if the British came South.

Ireland's most painful awareness of war had been the bombing of the North Strand. Otherwise, physical reminders of conflict came with aircraft which crashed on her soil. One hundred and five British planes crashed with 182 men killed, sixteen German aircraft with twenty-six killed. The bodies of Germans who died on Irish soil or were washed up on beaches were later collected and buried in the beautiful war cemetery at Glencree in Co. Wicklow. Hermann Goertz is also buried there.

Thirty-nine American planes crashed with fifteen killed. The most dramatic crash occurred on 27 February 1944 when a Navy Liberator clipped the pinnacle of the sheer island of Skellig Michael off the Kerry coast before plunging into the sea with all its crew. At the request of the US Air force, to help straying American aircraft from bases in Northern Ireland keep off Southern soil, the word ÉIRE was written in stones thirty feet in length on eighty-four headlands around the coast. Some are still to be seen.

For farmers and their families, the sight of a low-flying plane circling their fields caused panic. 'They were terrified,' remembered Marie Walshe, 'as were the animals . . . Pigs . . . ran amok . . . they jumped stone ditches at heights that would do justice to a racehorse.' Children crowded round the grounded plane to 'marvel at this German vehicle of war that could unleash weapons and create havoc by the mere press of a button'.

Trophy hunters gathered beside the wrecks. A crashed plane could offer a wide range of salvaged articles impossible to obtain otherwise – pieces of perspex, engine fittings or tyres. Martin Morrissey remembered 'Peter on his donkey and cart . . . like a king on his throne . . . His throne was the well-padded high-backed pilot's seat from the aircraft, now securely tied to the cart with *súgán* ropes. Behind him were four or five concrete sheets of aluminium which had been part of the fuselage.'

I was told of the aftermath of a plane crash on Mount Gabriel in West Cork. A man came down the mountain with his trophy. '"I have a boot, man, a German boot." . . . So he handed it to me . . . and the next thing I saw was a fellow's shin bone at the bottom of it . . . so he looked. Oh God! and he threw it away as far as he could . . . For all I know it's still lying where he threw it on the mountain.' A few aircraft came down in one piece, and if they were Allied, they were sometimes dismantled and sent to Northern Ireland.

Life was fairly pleasant for the internees in the Curragh camp for crashed airmen, both German and English. They were paid sustenance pay and allowed considerable freedom. Some RAF engineers were set to work repairing Irish planes. With parole granted, internees could follow university courses or go to dances. They could travel up to Dublin. On at least one occasion, three different groups were sitting apart in the drawing-room of the Shelbourne Hotel – officers on leave from the British forces, British and German prisoners of war from the Curragh.

There were three major escape attempts by British internees and of the twenty-two involved, eleven got away. For three years Maffey negotiated with de Valera who finally agreed that only pilots and crew on operation flights should be interned, while those who crashed on training flights could be repatriated. In October 1943 twenty-one British airmen were discreetly released. Americans who landed in the South were never interned.

German prisoners took jobs outside the camps. Patrick Campbell reported, 'How do the people of Newbridge feel about these 250 Germans? They're agreed that the German is an amazing worker. One man said, "I saw one of them ploughing in a hailstorm. He took off his coat and rolled up his sleeves. I'm tough enough, but I wouldn't do that."' Enough to make Sean Lemass wistful as he continually urged the country to greater effort towards self-sufficiency. He complained how 'Irish farmers looked for a certain income, and when they reached that they slacked off in their work and went for more leisure than a bigger income'.

CHAPTER 18

Merlin's Cave

Ireland became a drop-out from the rest of the world – a sort of
Merlin's Cave.

David Thomson

The power of the Church continued to wax strong. Faith was unshaken. The
red light glowed under the Sacred Heart and the Infant of Prague stood nearby.
A family would never go broke if a coin of any kind was placed under the Infant.
Often Blessed Martin of Porres would be nearby. Honor Tracy overheard a
woman buying Blessed Martin's statuette: ' "He's not very black." "That's the
blackest we can do for three and six." ' Collection boxes for missions and black
babies were much in evidence. A bottle of holy water was part of the household
furnishings. In the evenings mothers would sprinkle it near their children's
beds, asking God's protection during the night. Men would pour it on their
fields before ploughing and harvesting.

George O'Brien remembered a neighbour's room in Lismore. 'An Infant de
Prague stood pertly to attention in his tight-fitting tunic, the cross-topped
globe in his hand no more a burden to him than a ping-pong ball. The holy-
water font . . . was a memento of Lourdes. The figure on the heavily varnished
crucifix at the head of the bed was as naked and as abject as a scavenged bone
. . . The Sacred Heart . . . wore a slightly anxious look, proffering his velvety
valentine with its accessories of flame and fletched arrows.'

Patterns of saint's day rituals, holy wells hung with cloths and crowded trains
to Westport for the annual climb up Croagh Patrick on Garland Sunday had
their place in country life. Such traditions have kept a stubborn hold on
tradition in the 1990s even as Christianity weakens. Making the cure with a
combination of pagan and Christian ritual has almost vanished in the face of
modern medicine; no longer are children with whooping cough passed under
the belly of a stallion in the name of the Father, Son and Holy Ghost. But

whatever the current state of Christianity, tens of thousands of pilgrims continue to climb Croagh Patrick; thousands of others persist in suffering barefoot discomforts on Lough Derg.

George O'Brien recalled that pilgrimage during the forties. 'First there was the trial by land, the bus. For people unused to venturing beyond their own parish, two hundred miles of twisty roads by bus was a right stomach turner, especially since all aboard were smoking . . . trying to get enough nicotine put by to survive the three smoke-starved days ahead. Then there was the trial by water . . . And finally the place itself, unalterably devoted to retaining the stars it had earned in mediaeval Michelins: dry bread, black tea, water.'

During the Emergency shortages might diminish the stock in the shops that sold statues, rosaries and holy pictures; the clerical tailors that made up plain soutanes, Roman soutanes, tonsure suits and other clerical suiting; the statues in all sizes – cribs, Holy Families, Lourdes and Calvary groups for inside and similar in solid Portland cement for outside – guaranteed to stand the weather of any climate. But West and Son could still supply solid silver church plate – chalices, ciboria and monstrances with Celtic designs. The manufacture of Irish rosary beads continued to give employment.

In summer the flowers and banners of Corpus Christi processions filled streets emptied of motor traffic. Wakes lingered on decorously with whiskey and hard-to-obtain tea served to mourners along with equally scarce tobacco and snuff. At funerals there were many more horse-drawn vehicles following the hearse than cars in low gear, but all vehicles were carefully counted to assess the importance of the deceased.

The priest might be aided in his duties by the local branch of the Legion of Mary which John McGahern described as a 'kind of legalised gossiping school to the women, and a convenient pool of labour that priests could draw on for catering committees'. Confraternities flourished; the big one in Limerick was memorably recalled by Frank McCourt: 'Our Confraternity fills the Redemptorist church five nights a week, three for the men, one for the women, one for the boys. There is Benediction and hymn singing in English, Irish and Latin and . . . the big powerful sermon Redemptorist priests are famous for. It's the sermon that saves millions of Chinese and other heathens from winding up in hell with the Protestants.'

Passionist Fathers held the attention of George O'Brien. '"Did you ever hit your fingernail a blow with a hammer? Well, consider, dearly beloved, what it might be to hammer a nail into your hand. Not just a tack, but a big six-inch nail." Or the hand would be described, its nerves, its moving parts, its delicate, God designed tissue. "Think what it would be to do that to your worst enemy. Then THINK what it was to PUNISH the SON OF GOD who LOVES you."'

'Priests are as much "news" in Ireland as are film stars in America,' wrote Honor Tracy at the beginning of the fifties. Every Catholic bishop was a Most Reverend to distinguish him from a Protestant bishop who was a Right Reverend. The Most Reverends and other princes of the Church were celebrities. When in 1944 Cardinal MacRory paid a visit to Bewley's Café he was mobbed. After he clambered out of his car in his flowing ecclesiastical dress, he had to run the gauntlet of a huge crowd; many were kneeling on the pavement, others jostled to kiss his ring. He had to be smuggled out of Bewley's by the Fleet Street entrance.

When we were selling up Laragh some years later, we witnessed a similar star performance when Archbishop McQuaid, his chiselled face like a medieval image, paid us a visit to see if the hotel was suitable to be turned into yet another ecclesiastical institution. Crowds gathered and the ring was kissed a good deal. McQuaid was not only staunchly conservative but a deeply private man suspicious of the media. As a result he has often been portrayed unsympathetically. After he became Archbishop of Dublin in November 1940, he ruled the city from the Palace in Drumcondra to beyond the Residence in Killiney. During the Emergency he organised the Catholic Social Service Conference, which set up twenty-seven food centres, arranged for ambulances to transport the poor to hospitals and founded a maternity welfare unit. He was responsible for remand centres for juvenile delinquents, founded homes for unmarried mothers, and arranged for screening for venereal diseases. He was quietly generous, receiving thousands of begging letters and giving money out of private funds bequeathed by pious parishioners. Among those he helped was Patrick Kavanagh who wrote that without money from the Archbishop he would have gone to England long ago. There 'must have been special grace attached' to the gift which made him stay in Ireland. But McQuaid's good deeds are less well remembered than his annual Lenten rant about Trinity College.

Censorship flourished, not only the kind that imposed silence on war news, but the kind everyone was used to. Among the films hacked to pieces by the film censor was *Gone with the Wind*, so mutilated that the distributors would not allow it to be shown. Church and State combined in banning Shaw, Beckett, O'Casey, Frank O'Connor; banned foreign books ranged from *Mildred Pierce* to Proust's *Sodom and Gomorrah* in translation.

A librarian, writing in *The Bell*, remembered objections to Winifred Holtby's *South Riding*, Kate O'Brien's *Without my Cloak* and Somerset Maugham's *The Moon and Sixpence*, all of which were withdrawn from circulation. Someone objected to John Donne: 'I'm not saying he's not a great poet, but some of his work is certainly offensive.' As a result Donne was only available on request.

A mystery was the banning as indecent of *The Tailor and Ansty*, which perhaps more than any other publication gave voice to de Valera's ideal. 'Across the door of Garrynapeaka there is another world, where values are different; where there is still a zest for the details of living, where time no longer matters; where there is much laughter and little harm.'

It would be hard to fault the Tailor and his wife not only for following a traditional lifestyle, but also for using Gaelic as a living language. Eric Cross's loving portraits came from almost daily observation of the couple. 'Ansty has a hard life made even harder by her own nature. Most of the work of the place falls upon her, and her overture to most of the day's reminiscences begins with "Wisha! when I got up this morning, very early entirely, to let out the cow, and himself shn-o-ring away on the bed like an ould pig, or a gintleman . . ."' You can turn page by charming page and remain puzzled as to why the book should evoke such repellent reaction from a prurient society behaving badly. Surprisingly, Patrick Kavanagh's *The Great Hunger*, published in 1942, escaped the ban.

Churches, together with the bloated buildings of institutions, dominated every town with their crosses and silver railings. In 1940 Sean O'Faolain listed some of the numerous churches and religious institutions in Kilkenny – Loreto Nuns, Presentation Nuns, Sisters of Mercy, Sisters of Charity, De la Salle Brothers, Capuchin Friars, Dominicans, St Joseph's Asylum, St Kieran's College, St Patrick's Parish Church, the Church of the Butts, of St Johns, St John of God's convent. 'Living or fallen, the Church intervenes at every hand.'

Convent schools offered 'a world of women, nuns, lay nuns and little postulants – sins got committed by the hour, sins of thought, words, deeds and omission'. Tormented by the lack of privacy, Dervla Murphy was a pupil in an establishment which 'reeked of Jeyes Fluid and boiled onions . . . in the icy, barn-like whitewashed dormitory there were no cubicles, but only rows of beds with vociferously broken springs and unclean mattresses'. She remembered 'Sister Andrew . . . with . . . eyes that seemed to give off forked lightning in her rages. Verbally she swayed me and physically she battered me – often across the back with a stout wooden pointer.'

Caroline Blackwood, with years of convent education behind her, looked back with loathing on 'long cold corridors punctuated by tormented bleeding plaster Christs. Those nuns with their child-like skins, their canes and their crucifixes.' Her fellow pupils devised an unusual torture: 'They made the new girls hang their breasts over a towel rail and then pricked them with safety pins. Any girl who screamed they pricked much harder, right on her nipples.'

Corporal punishment was freely used in a society where sadism was no sin. No one objected to instruments of torture used on children. In Limerick Frank McCourt remembered the seven masters in Leamy's National School with their leather straps, canes and blackthorn sticks. At Synge Street, Dublin, Gay Byrne was taught by a brother 'who would hit us with anything he could find'. And yet the education the Christian Brothers 'bet into you', biased though it might be, still commanded much of the respect that it had known since the days after the Famine when Father Rice organised teaching for poor boys.

The Emergency mildly aggravated the miseries of school life with the 'grey bread, grey writing paper, sandy sickening cocoa, rations books, scratchy school jumpers' recalled by Pauline Bracken of her Dublin childhood. At the basic primary schools the physical standard of school buildings was still disgraceful. The one-teacher school with its average of thirty pupils attended by Edward O'Brien in Durrow during the early forties was typical. It had a turf fire lit daily by a pupil; there was no electricity or running water. The outside latrine was a tar-covered structure over a pit where three holes were cut. When in summer it was buzzing with flies, a man was employed to sprinkle a few shovelfuls of lime on to it.

Reports of inspections by county medical officers during 1939 confirm O'Brien's description. The custom was general that pupils, inevitably the poorest, should sweep and dust. The inspectors found that lighting was often substandard, leading to visual problems. In Co. Roscommon, out of thirty-four schools inspected, only fourteen were deemed satisfactory. Of the others, it was concluded that twelve required additional accommodation, three required extensive repairs and five should be demolished altogether.

There was one great improvement – since the School Meals Scheme gave children one good meal a day, few were malnourished. But throughout the country children's teeth were rotten – fifty-four per cent of children in Co. Galway and sixty-nine per cent in Co. Longford had caries in their teeth which called for treatment. Most country children were clean, a fact carefully noted by inspectors. In Co. Sligo, out of 3,489 children inspected, only ten cases of uncleanliness were remarked.

Schools varied from those run in Victorian times only in the fact that the children were taught in Irish; the only substantial money invested in education continued to be in the promotion of the language. In 1939 de Valera had declared in the Dáil, 'We have in regard to certain appointments that have been made . . . said that where a person has a competent knowledge of Irish, if he is otherwise qualified, he has to take precedence over those who have even a better technical knowledge . . . If you do not do that you make no progress.' In 1943 he led the opposition to the appointment of W. J. Williams as Professor of Education at University College Dublin after the Gaelic League deemed that the new Professor had insufficient knowledge of the native language.

Remembering his school-days in Lismore, George O'Brien comments that 'to some extent . . . all of us at school were bilingual thanks to compulsory Irish. But everyone thought Irish was useless. It didn't tell us anything we didn't know. The textbooks dealt with sheep, fields, hills and children . . . for reasons best known to our lords and masters the rattling old far-fetched stuff of the sagas was kept from us.' So the boys of Lismore remained ignorant of the vigour of *An Táin*.

The Christian Brothers taught their old-fashioned fierce Nationalism, while other teachers made little attempt to be impartial about the injustices of the past. Writing in *The Bell* in 1942, Eileen Webster complained of textbooks 'concocted in modern times by well-meaning but over-enthusiastic patriots'. In exaggerating the virtues of robust Gaelic chieftains and asserting that every villain was a 'foreigner', they were not always truthful. 'There is a great danger in Irish history . . . the biased propagandist attitude of so many Irish history text books. Ireland's grievances have been bad enough . . .'

Those who were considered to have fallen outside the confines of normal society were the chief victims of institutional conformity. In Magdalen Asylums penitents served out their sentences washing and mangling and praying several times daily for their benefactors, living and dead. In Dublin there were two Magdalen Homes, Gloucester Street and St Mary's Donnybrook. Girls could leave them, but efforts were made to retain them when possible lest they went to the Bird's Nest or the Bethany Home which were run by Protestants.

In the 1950s Halliday Sutherland visited the Magdalen Home Laundry in Galway which was in the charge of the Sisters of Mercy. The Mother Superior received him with every courtesy; her predecessor, he was told, came of a country family. 'She was a grand girl. She used to thrash the inmates of the Magdalen Home, but they loved her.'

He learnt that the home had seventy-three girls, of whom about seventy per cent were unmarried mothers, the rest an awkward category – backward girls whose families had not claimed them, who had been forwarded from the Industrial School in Galway. The uniformed inmates earned their keep by working unpaid in the laundry. They were not forced to work, but neither were they allowed to leave unless they could prove they had a suitable place to go. 'Last week one girl made such a row that we let her go. That night she was ringing the bell and begging to be readmitted.'

The Mother Superior said that discipline was imposed either by 'a good scolding' or a meal being stopped: 'Only one meal and we know that the other girls feed them.' Some girls stayed for life. Most of these were consecrated penitents, which meant that when they died they were buried with the nuns. If they had not achieved this exalted category, they were buried in the common burial ground.

Sutherland was shown over the chapel, the recreation hall with its polished floor on which the girls could dance, and a stage with cinema screen and projector. The last film shown had been *The Song of Bernadette*; the girls preferred religious to secular films. In a room upstairs he saw many of the inmates. 'A small elderly woman had a small black cape round her shoulders and from the front of the cape hung a large crucifix. She was a Consecrated Penitent. I asked her how long she had been here.

'"Twenty-five years."

'"Are you happy?"

'"Yes, very happy" – and she smiled.'

Orphanages kept up their miseries; recently, a series of disturbed middle-aged women who were former inmates have insisted that there was a reign of terror in the Dublin orphanage of Goldenbridge as late as the seventies. Sutherland visited the children's home in Tuam run by the Sisters of Bon Secours of Paris, each of whom was a fully trained nurse and midwife. An unmarried girl who had her baby here worked unpaid for a year, after which she could leave, either taking the baby with her, or leaving it behind in the hope that it would be adopted. But orphanages were filled to overflowing.

Sutherland wrote, 'In the garden at the back of the Home children were singing. I walked along the path and was mobbed by over a score of the younger children. They said nothing, but each struggled to take my hand. Their hands were clean and cool. Then I realised that to these children I was a potential adopter who might take some boy or girl away to a real home. It was pathetic.' He noted a paradox: 'For every Protestant unwanted child there are ten applications and applicants may wait two years before a child is available. For every ten unwanted Catholic children there is only one application for a child.'

My mother was on the Board of a home that looked after Protestant Magdalenes – 'first falls'. There was little problem in finding homes for their babies.

On the night of 23 February 1943 a fire broke out in St Joseph's Orphanage for Girls in the town of Cavan, killing thirty-three girls and one old woman. While the rest of Europe was burning, this was a minor and horrible tragedy whose details were obscured by confusion and cover-up. Flames and smoke billowed out of the building. 'The children were screaming, calling out that they were burning, begging to be taken out.' No nuns were injured.

St Joseph's was under the control of the Poor Clares, an enclosed order which kept a strict regime. When the nuns went into retreat, there had to be total silence. The girls wore the uniform of poverty, a rough blue serge dress, thick black socks, knickers made out of flour bags and hobnailed boots. A former inmate remembered how 'we got up at 6 a.m. and then a line of us would say our prayers over the wash-basins, then the next line would come. Then over to the chapel where we had communion every day – and a lot of us would fall asleep there. Then back to our duties, the breakfast which was shell cocoa made of water and a round of bread and margarine. There would be wriggling things on top of the cocoa, but the boiling water would have killed them.'

After the fire a Tribunal of inquiry revealed that the first reaction of the sisters before they realised the seriousness of the situation was to ensure that they themselves and the girls would not be seen in their nightclothes. Local opinion was that the doors of the dormitories were locked. In the climate of the day the sisters could not be blamed and the conclusions of the Tribunal were fudged. Its secretary, Brian O'Nolan, or Myles na cGopaleen in his role as civil servant, who is believed to have drafted the report, wrote a bitter limerick:

> In Cavan there was a great fire;
> Joe McCarthy came down to inquire
> If the nuns were to blame
> It would be a shame
> So it had to be caused by a wire.

Dr Lyons, the Bishop of Kilmore, spoke of 'Dear little angels, now before God in Heaven . . . taken away before the gold of their innocence had been tarnished by the soil of the world'. Enraged by this sickly example of spiritual heartlessness, Austin Clarke wrote his 'Three Poems about Children':

> Those children charred in Cavan
> Passed straight through Hell to Heaven.

Clarke was a far more trenchant critic of the Catholic Church than any Protestant. The insecurity of Irish Protestants has never ceased. Throughout the twentieth century there has not been a book of reminiscences by any without at least a paragraph proclaiming the Irishness of the author.

In February 1944 Archbishop McQuaid announced in his Lenten Pastoral the closing of Trinity College to all Catholics in the Dublin diocese. He insisted that he was applying a statute adopted by the Maynooth Synod in 1929. But until he intervened, the statute was never implemented and the decision about a student's entry into Trinity was (in practice) left to his parents. But now the college's aura of sin was official. One story was told of a Catholic who defied the episcopal ban; he graduated, only to be killed in a road accident a few days later.

McQuaid hated Trinity for being a bastion of Protestantism. In the 1920s and 1930s, before he became Archbishop, he was involved in a number of extreme right-wing Catholic groups whose purpose was to check Protestant influence in the professions, particularly in medicine. Now he reintroduced the ban with an enthusiasm that even shocked de Valera.

Following the ban, the Trinity classicist W. B. Stanford issued a furious pamphlet entitled 'A Recognised Church', which questioned the view that Southern Protestants had nothing to complain of. On the contrary, he claimed, they had been shabbily treated in the matter of public appointments and pushed out of the way ('a fate incidentally, which many Catholics might sometimes envy', commented Sean O'Faolain). Stanford put forth old arguments. Protestants had gone off to France to fight at an unfortunate time, so that few were there to join the Rising and benefit from its aftermath. The class left behind were 'the old, the cautious and the conservative . . . ill-suited to decide or advise when the Treaty of 1921 altered the Church's political status'.

Stanford blamed the absence of Protestants in public life on obstruction and deliberate exclusion. He condemned the 'drifting element' of his people going over to Catholicism. Naturally he had hard words to say about *Ne temere*; this obsessed Protestants of Southern Ireland because it provided an easy explanation for their dwindling numbers. But what particularly incensed him was a matter of attitude: 'It is fashionable . . . to use phrases like "his mother, tall and hard as a Protestant spire" or "a voice like a Protestant clergyman's". [The spire simile occurs in *The Great Hunger*.] A popular Irish novelist's favourite plot describes a Protestant family's association with RCs ending happily in conversion of good members and the lunacy or despair of the rest. Conversions from Romanism are referred to in the Press as "apostasies" while conversions the other way are plain Acts of God's Grace.'

When 'A Recognised Church' was published it was condemned by a number of Protestants all too keen to follow the unofficial policy defined by Stanford 'to lie low and say nothing'. Among his critics was Lennox Robinson: 'I am sure that Dr Stanford speaks from facts, but I cannot support him.' Robinson had been attending weekend parties at Blackrock College where propagandist lectures and demonstrations were given to 'interested parties'. 'I came out a blacker Protestant than when I went in.'

Sean O'Faolain also had harsh words for Stanford. 'I am not sure that *as a religion* Irish Protestantism was ever as strong as it should have been, but I am quite certain that . . . what keeps it weak is that it is sulking in the vestry.'

O'Faolain was writing an editorial in *The Bell*, which was displaying a wonderful vigour in those torpid times, free of cant, prejudice and hypocrisy. *The Bell*'s attitudes expressed by its editor, 'a rock in foaming seas' according to Honor Tracy, were comprehensively liberal. It wrote on national and international affairs, commented with humour and insight on social issues and published good poetry. Contributors included Frank O'Connor, Brinsley MacNamara, Louis MacNeice, Cecil Day-Lewis and Jack Yeats. The magazine was all things to all Irishmen and women, and O'Faolain was generous in allowing Protestants their voice; the inaugural issue of October 1940 contained an article on the Big House by his friend Elizabeth Bowen. ('To the keeping afloat of the household not only the family but the servants contribute ingenuity and good will.')

Although only 3,000 copies were printed each month, about a third of which went overseas, *The Bell* was hugely important in Irish life at a time when physical barriers were imposed by the Emergency and mental frontiers were raised by religious conservatism.

O'Faolain's role was that of crusader, using the word in strictly non-Christian terms. 'Whenever you see something fine that any of our people are doing anywhere, tell us about it,' he urged his readers. 'Wherever you see anybody creating something cheap and ugly and a large number of people being deluded by him, tell them and tell us about it. Only in that way can we build up real standards worthy of our dreams about a great modern Ireland.'

The Bell's wide-ranging choice of material included an article on tuberculosis by Robert Collis, author of *Marrowbone Lane*. ('"No thank God, there is no delicacy in *our* family." Every Irish doctor has heard this phrase.') An interview with Dr Hayes, the film censor, revealed much that was wrong with censorship: 'There is a simple moral code and there are principles on which civilisation and family life are based.' This made him hard on films in which divorce was mentioned: 'Each film in which divorce is a feature ought to be judged by one standard alone; is it an incentive to divorce, or does it condone it?'

A regular contributor was that troubled, multifaceted genius Brian O'Nolan. The outbreak of war had stunned his novel *At Swim-Two-Birds* (published under the name of Flann O'Brien), which would not be revived for decades. Meanwhile he worked in the Civil Service and wrote under various pseudonyms. His novel in Irish, *Au Béal Bocht*, satirising Tomas O Criomhthain's autobiography, was popular among those who were tired of humourless language enthusiasts.

In the *Irish Times*, as Myles na nCopaleen, he wrote an eccentric column called 'Cruiskeen Lawn' which featured Keats and Chapman.

'Keats and Chapman were once discussing their ancestors. One of Keats's had been Lord Mayor of Port Said.

'. . . Chapman: . . . while he had no dislike of Germans as such, he could not bear the sight of elderly grizzled Germans and did his best to banish all such from the town.

'. . . Keats: Here is [his picture] – he was fifty when it was taken.

'Chapman: He looks very young for his years.

'– He hadn't a grey Herr in his Said – Keats replied.'

As Myles na gCopaleen, O'Nolan defended expenditure of public money on the Irish language at a time when £100 million a day was being spent elsewhere on destruction. 'It is surely no shame for our humble community of peasants to spend £2,000 a day on trying to revive a language . . . and what is half a million in relation to slum clearance?' De Valera continued to think in similar vein, touring the country in the grimmest days of the Emergency, urging people to use Irish Christian names, to learn to say prayers in Irish and to say *Dia dhuit* instead of hello and *slán leat* instead of goodbye. 'As it gives great joy to see things for which generations of Irishmen had died realised bit by bit, so please God, we will have the joy of seeing accomplished the other part of the work for which they died – the restoration of the Irish language.'

In 1944 O'Nolan tackled a subject in *The Bell* which continued to enrage the Church and moralists as well. Dr Hayes had said in his interview that a frequent reason for banning films was 'lascivious dances. There's an appalling spate of this kind of dancing in most of the big American "musicals". Appalling . . . Simply appalling.'

O'Nolan wrote that there were 1,200 dancehalls in the Twenty-six Counties licensed under the 1935 Dancehalls Act. Tennis clubs, golf clubs and Volunteer halls needed no licence. Dances differed according to the cost of admission. Over five shillings demanded 'immaculate evening dress'. 'You are on the borderline when you come down to 3/9. The lighting is poor and the place is too hot . . .'

'You are asked to dance out the Old and dance in the New to the haunting strains of Mulvany's Rhythmic Swingsters . . .' A dance was regarded as successful according to the distance a band had to travel. Nearly every male going to a dance liked to drink. 'An odd accomplishment . . . the craft of going out for 20 separate drinks to a pub four hundred yards away without ever appearing to have left the dancehall at all.' Alternatively, a man could make use of a hip flask, although scenes of drunkenness were rare.

Perhaps William Trevor read O'Nolan, or perhaps he relied on memory when he wrote of 'the dancehall . . . miles from anywhere, a lone building by the roadside with treeless bogs all around and a great expanse in front. On pink pebbled cement its title was painted in an azure blue . . . proclaiming "The Ballroom of Romance".' Certainly the dance he describes confirms O'Nolan's research.

At cheap dances where the prices of admission ranged from threepence to one and sixpence, light was provided by large paraffin lamps suspended from the ceiling or on walls. Music came from a melodeon or piano accordion with possibly a fiddle or some drums. Irish airs were bashed into a desultory 3/4 time, while modern dance tunes were played straight with no attempt at syncopation. Among the dense crowds, the girls who always paid their way dominated. 'If the hall is small and the crowd enormous (the normal situation) the parties quickly lock themselves into a solid mass and keep shuffling and sweating for ten minutes in the space of a square foot, like a vast human centipede.'

How much less of an occasion of sin was a crossroads dance like that in the summer of 1940 reported by E. M. Wells. She was recommended to wear serviceable dress and heavy shoes. Dozens of bicycles were stacked by the road and the entrance was fourpence. Couples danced to concertina and fiddle on a board ten or twelve feet square and waltzed, foxtrotted and did set dances until darkness fell. Dances like these were becoming rarer, although they lingered into the fifties.

There was an air of quiet paralysis about the countryside that characterised the Emergency and became increasingly oppressive. We wondered how different things were in the North. Ulster was perpetually at the corner of Érin's eye. Was the Province an intolerable mixture of boredom, bigotry and violence? Was it true, as Caroline Blackwood made out, that people there felt they were 'interned . . . by the gloom of her industrialised provinciality, by her . . . bigotry and her tedium'?

In the depths of the Emergency my mother suggested that we should visit relations near Eglinton, a few miles outside Londonderry or Derry. We were delighted to have the opportunity of leaving Merlin's Cave and experiencing a modicum of proper war.

The journey did not disappoint. For a schoolboy, crossing the Border was the first excitement. The Border was always a contentious issue; Joe Walshe, the Secretary of External Affairs, would have liked to use the German victories early in the war to deliver the North to Dublin. If that had not happened, at least the Emergency had given momentum to the traditional pastime of smuggling. Cattle were driven across, customs' officers bribed, petrol and cigarettes came over, and there were stories of funeral cortèges composed of smugglers with coffins full of illicit liquor.

We were constantly being told of how Dublin was a magnet for those who were enduring the proper war. Visitors came in droves down from the city of dark to the city of light. Children accustomed to blackout would exclaim that night-time was like daytime. In one weekend in 1943, according to the *Irish Times*, they came from Northern Ireland 'down to the land of butter and fruit – over five thousand down by train. They wanted to walk beneath lighted street lamps after dusk, to eat by the pound delicacies which at home they can only buy by the ounce.' They paid around £5.00 for a weekend in a Dublin boarding house. But alas, some hotels could not resist the temptation of raising their charges, which brought complaints about departures from decency, not to say about Southern dishonesty.

We were going the other way. In Belfast, shop windows were blacked out, and although Union Jacks fluttered, there were no Christmas decorations. Streets were filled with uniformed men, white and black. According to Caroline Blackwood, American troops did not enjoy their sojourn in Northern Ireland. 'I remember one of them saying . . . that he . . . would rather . . . be sent to the front and lose his leg than be stuck away in this god-forsaken fucking back of nowhere . . .'

We saw traces of the devastation of a bombing raid compared to which our bomb on the North Strand had been a firework. In one night more people had died than in any raid on a city in the British Isles apart from Liverpool and London. We saw tanks and armoured cars, and the grey silhouettes of warships in Belfast Lough. Here, we felt, was the real world.

It was disappointing that when we reached Willsboro, we were thrust back into a world of old-fashioned doom and fantasy. My mother's cousin lived on an estate on the banks of Lough Foyle with its own railway station. I remember a lofty hall with family portraits, a pair of duelling pistols, numerous Protestant servants and a table that had belonged to Governor Walker, the hero of the Siege of Londonderry.

In the forties, Protestants ruled in the North without question. Denis O'Donohue, whose childhood was spent at Warrenpoint, wrote that 'like a bird watcher' he 'could spot a Protestant at a hundred yards – in the North a Protestant walks with an air of possession and authority . . . he walks as if he owns the place, which indeed he does. A Catholic walks as if he were there on sufferance.' Professor O'Donohue would have had little difficulty in identifying the religion of my relations.

We returned by way of Lough Erne and had a glimpse of flying boats. Back home, the most important thing that had been happening was that the IRA had beheaded the equestrian statue of General Gough. Later he would be blown up altogether. A song was written about the headless horseman:

> Have you heard the story, it happened in the Park
> The Christmas bells were ringing, the night was never dark.
> And there near the depot of the law
> Without a flaw
> They used a saw
> On Gough's immortal statue up near the Magazine.

Elsewhere the Allies were preparing to invade Europe.

CHAPTER 19

White Bread

From tomorrow Dublin housewives, for the first time since the rationing of gas in March, 1942, will enjoy a full 24 hours supply.

Irish Times, *14 January 1948*

Sir – May I appeal to your readers to remember the birds?

Letter in Irish Times, *February 1947*

The loaves in the shop window were dazzling, snowy, pipe-clay white; a crowd collected outside just to look at them. The year was 1948 when I bought white bread in the bakery and ate the food of the gods, tearing it to pieces in Kenmare's main street, without benefit of butter.

For many who recall that time, the return of white bread is one of the most vivid post-Emergency recollections. Long before that happened a series of events revealed some of the torment of the national psyche.

At the end of the war separate groups in Dublin tried to have Masses said for the repose of Mussolini and Hitler. The former went ahead; the latter was stopped. But de Valera did not hesitate to arouse the wrath of the victorious Allies. There is a story by G. K. Chesterton about an honest man who insists that a debt owed him in gold is paid for in full by cutting the gold-leaf halos from saints in an illuminated manuscript. De Valera was just as over-scrupulous. Ignoring advice from his officials at the Department of External Affairs, he paid a formal call to the German Legation in Northumberland Road to offer Dr Hempel condolences for the death of Hitler. Afterwards he wrote to Robert Brenan, 'I could have had a diplomatic illness, but as you know I would scorn that sort of thing.'

Frank Edwards was among those who condemned the action. 'Not since

Padraic Pearse and James Connolly were forced to surrender the Dublin Post Office at the conclusion of the 1916 rebellion did the Irish people live through a darker day or suffer such a great shame as they did on May 2nd 1945.' But Edwards's sympathies were with Communism and his opinions were not worth much. Potentially more effective was the opposition of Andrei Gromyko, the leader of the Soviet delegation to the United Nations, who in 1947 opposed Ireland's entry: 'We all know Ireland was on very good terms with the Axis powers and gave no assistance whatsoever to the Allied Nations in their struggle against Fascist states.'

On VE Day bonfires blazed on the hills in the North of Ireland. Above Trinity College Dublin students hung flags, British, American, Russian and French. They set an Irish Tricolour on fire and threw it into College Green. The mob that gathered included the young Charles Haughey who claimed later that he removed the Union Jack which got burnt in retaliation. Afterwards the crowd went on the rampage and threw stones at Maffey's office, the American Legation, the Wicklow Hotel and Jammet's Restaurant, both of which were considered 'West British'.

Churchill had the visit to Northumberland Road at the back of his mind in the ill-considered speech he made a month later: 'We left the de Valera Government to frolic with the Germans and later with the Japanese to their heart's content.' More remarkable than the point scoring made in de Valera's broadcast reply – 'it is, indeed, hard for the strong to be just to the weak, but acting justly always has its own rewards' – was the public reaction to it. When he left the Radio Eireann studio beside the GPO after he had finished, there were cheering crowds gathered in the streets. Afterwards, copious letters, telegrams and telephone calls supported him. When he went to the Dáil the deputies rose to their feet and clapped. *Dublin Opinion*'s cartoon showed Ireland shaking hands with him in the broadcasting room and saying, 'Thank you, Dev.' He had soothed her conscience.

George O'Brien's grandmother was among those caught up in the surge of the Chief's popularity: 'She admired Dev's stiffness, his ability at sums, his answer to Churchill, his guts for sticking to his guns with his back to the wall. She also admired his spectacles . . . Dev's glasses made him seem kin to that other bespectacled arbiter of Mam's known world, Pius XII.'

Because of the policies and exertions of de Valera and Sean Lemass, the country had exchanged potential destruction, massacre, starvation and suffering for inconvenience. The fact that imports depended entirely on British and American goodwill could be ignored by those who agreed with the Fianna Fáil slogan during the election of 1943: IF YOU VOTE FIANNA FÁIL THE BOMBS WON'T FALL.

There would always be those who considered that the wrong side had won, eager to equate Dresden and Hiroshima with Auschwitz. Robert Fisk has unearthed a reader of a Kilkenny newspaper in 1945 who declared that newsreel films of Belsen were 'all propaganda' and had been faked by the British using starving Indians. At a fancy-dress ball in the same town first prize went to 'the Beast of Belsen'.

The price which had to be paid was spelt out by Sean O'Faolain in 1945: 'We have suffered by the prolonged suppression of our natural sympathies with tortured humanity, our admiration for endurance and courage; our moral judgement has been in abeyance; our intellectual interest in all the ideas and problems which the rest of the world is still straining to solve has been started.'

Writing of the uneasy literary and artistic movement that was struggling to make its mark, Anthony Cronin reflected that 'Dublin in the late 1940s was an odd and in many respects an unhappy place. The malaise that seems to have affected everywhere in the aftermath of a war took strange forms there, perhaps for the reason that the war itself had been a sort of ghastly unreality. Neutrality had left a wound, set up complexes in many, including myself, which the post-war did little to cure.' There were those who justified it by a sense of detachment. They stubbornly believed that the war was merely a conflict between major powers fighting for world domination. The evils of the Nazi regime and the Holocaust were elements in a struggle that had nothing to do with Ireland.

Throughout the Nazi era a pitiful handful of Jewish refugees was allowed to enter Ireland. Among those who were refused was the aunt of the politician Robert Briscoe; in spite of this awful rejection – she died at Auschwitz – he would remain faithful to Fianna Fáil and become the first Jewish Lord Mayor of Dublin. This cold policy of repudiation contrasted with the humanitarian effort demonstrated by Operation Shamrock in 1946 which brought deprived German children to Ireland to escape the misery of Germany's bombed cities. Five hundred were assimilated into Irish homes – almost ten times the number of Jewish refugees allowed into Ireland at the worst of times.

For farmers the situation had become a mirror image of the economic war. Now, because all their produce could be shipped to hungry Britain, they were better off than they had been since the State was founded. The good times would not last long, however, and the old deprivations continued; most farmhouses would continue to lack electricity and running water. In rural towns the pump at the crossroads continued to be the only source of water for whole communities. In Durrow there were six which had been installed in 1936; a proper sewage system was not established until 1950. Raw sewage polluted the River Nore, slop buckets and wash-day water were thrown out on the streets, and dry toilets were still the norm.

The post-Emergency Irish town had changed little. Marigold Armitage remembered a Tipperary town with a 'main street impressively and excessively wide, however it might crumble at the edges, however locked it might be with donkey-cars and conversational men with bicycles . . . Here were the usual mouldering rows of little stucco-fronted houses, some grey, some white-washed, one or two painted pink and green in an attempt at gaiety that had soon been allowed to lapse again into dirt and crumbling plaster; here was the draughty garage . . . the Garda Barracks where law kept happy company with disorder . . . thé little shops, each selling everything, and each – as advertised in the *Tipperary Star* or the *Nationalist* – the finest business in the South . . .' Another important landmark was the cinema, perhaps like the Eureka Cinema in Charlestown where the machinery and the reels of film came in a van, and John Healy fought with other boys to carry in the reels and help with the projection machine in the hope of being allowed to stay inside.

Ethel Manning ventured into a Connemara pub in 1946. 'Behind the counter was a bar with a good show of bottles and a beer cask. A number of men in cloth caps huddled together sombrely drinking. Inside the shop it was almost too dark to distinguish the faces. The men drank without conversation.'

William Trevor recently recalled the Skibbereen of his boyhood, centred around the statue of the Maid of Érin. For decades after the Emergency the vistas of the twenties and thirties continued unchanged: 'horses and carts in the narrow street with milk churns for the creamery . . . A smell of whiskey and sawdust and stout and dung. Pots of geranium among chops and ribs in the small windows of butchers' shops. A sun-burnt poster advertising the arrival of Duffy's Circus a year ago.'

The winter of 1946–47 reflected the frozen moral and social atmosphere. In central Wicklow people were stranded for a month. Hospitals were full of people who had fallen in slippery streets. During snowstorms trams had to stop every few yards to have the snow cleared off their fronts. The cold killed off the larger apes in Dublin Zoo.

The bad weather began on 9 January with high seas and trees blown down.

'January 13 – heavy snows in the north-west. Six inches in Co. Sligo. Floods in Tipperary.

'Jan 15 – snow, hail, thunder, lightning and sleet.

'January 29 – heavy snowfalls. Flocks of wild birds driven from the mountains.

'Jan 29–30 Night – twenty-three degrees of frost in Dublin, eleven in Cork. Killybegs Harbour frozen, also the lower lake in Killarney.

'February 3 – heaviest blizzard recorded for decades, accompanied by sixty mile an hour winds.

'February 22 – more heavy snow falls.'

When the thaw came in March it was overnight, and heavy floods resulted.

The snow brought about a fuel crisis. Throughout the winter Fuel Coupon Books were delivered to hundreds of households in non-turf areas. Gas rationing was reduced and trees were felled for firewood. Turf on the bogs was sodden and flooded and lorries could not reach it. Cattle trains ceased to run, endangering the trade once more.

The city poor were hardest hit; all over Dublin queues formed for timber and rationed turf. Women and children carrying baskets crowded Cuffe Street trying to get turf, which at the worst time cost a shilling a stone. Old people, who had to buy fuel by the stone because they could not carry any more, had to pay a pound a ton or thereabouts more than those who could buy it in bulk. Bread, butter and margarine were rationed. Archbishop McQuaid granted a dispensation from Lenten fasting among his flock because of undernourishment.

The use of electricity for all signs and outside lighting was prohibited. In O'Connell Street in the coldest weather people still queued in snow and city wind to get into the Capitol where Alan Ladd and Veronica Lake were playing in *The Blue Dahlia* and the Savoy which was showing Ingrid Bergman and Gregory Peck in *Spellbound*. Alongside the queues went the 'kerbside black market', boys and girls offering bars and boxes of chocolate for sale.

The fuel shortage would carry on through the following winter; in February 1948 an American visitor, watching women and barefoot children pushing broken prams up Richmond Hill for turf supplies, compared the scene to chain gangs he had seen in North Africa. Sometimes poverty was as bad as anything experienced in post-war Europe. In 1947 a farm labourer and his wife and three children were reported to be living in a house near Athlone whose only furniture consisted of an old bedstead without a mattress, a dresser and a table; their diet was hot water and potatoes.

In 1946 the Department of Health issued a pamphlet which made a good many people angry, although there was need for it: 'Louse Infection: How to Treat It and How to Avoid It'. 'Your child may become infested as a result of sitting beside a verminous child or if any of his clothes are placed in contact with those of other children.' Many suburban and rural cinemas had a permanent smell of Jeyes Fluid; some sprinkled DDT on the ground to kill parasites.

Shortages lifted gradually. In January 1947 during the deep midwinter, although bread rationing had been imposed, bananas from South America appeared for the first time in many years. In February, the *Irish Elm* docked with generous supplies of tinned salmon and agricultural machinery, as well as several hundred bags of gift fuel from the United States.

Clothes rationing ended a year later, together with duty on personal clothing and footwear – the shortage of boots would ease. Supplies of tomatoes as well as bananas were shipped in from South America, together with 35,000 cases of Jaffa oranges, grapefruit and lemons from Haifa on the cargo ship *Domino*. But tea was still rationed and sold on the black market for ten shillings a pound. 'Ireland is a profiteers' Paradise and a poor man's Hell,' said Tom O'Higgins.

During the Emergency Ireland's isolation had been seen as an opportunity to rejuvenate the Irish language. In vain: now its decline was beginning to be acknowledged. A letter in the *Irish Times* stated, 'In 1919 . . . I stayed in Connemara . . . I heard little else than Irish spoken by those gathered at cottage doors or working in the fields and bogs . . . In 1949 I toured for six months – a week on Aranmore Island, Donegal, a fortnight in Connemara and some time in Kerry . . . listening to school children, men and women conversing. With the solitary exception of an inspector of schools . . . I never heard one word of Irish spoken.'

A scheme suggesting that Irish only should be spoken in the Dáil was declared impractical. Even de Valera, speaking in Irish, said he did not think that there were sufficient deputies fluent in the language. James Dillon said it was common knowledge that when business was conducted in Irish in the House ninety-five per cent of the deputies could not take part. Another deputy protested, 'Not ninety-five per cent!' Perhaps fewer than that number of deputies were excluded when Irish was spoken, but certainly most business was conducted in English.

There were a few signs of change, including a relaxation of the censorship laws by the establishment of an Appeal Board. In 1948 the Censorship Board lifted a ban on thirty-three books, including Shaw's *The Black Girl in Search of God*, O'Casey's *I Knock at the Door* and *The Tailor and Ansty*. Sean O'Faolain sneered, 'We can only hope that the poor Tailor has been duly informed in Heaven.' He himself had resigned as editor of *The Bell* in 1946 after it had served its purpose during the dark times. His place was taken by Peadar O'Donnell and an honourable liberal voice was maintained; *The Bell* ceased publication temporarily in April 1948, but reappeared in 1950 and continued for another five years.

Petrol was once more freely available, and cars were making their comeback – between 1939 and 1950 the number of motor cars, lorries and vans increased by eighty-four per cent, almost entirely since the end of the Emergency. But plenty of horse-drawn traffic was still in evidence. Drivers were told, 'As slow vehicles tend to obstruct traffic, you should keep well to the left, and give way to fast vehicles . . . Always keep your horse under control.' In 1946 horse-drawn vehicles were involved in thirty-four fatal accidents.

Trains still carried people on pilgrimage and to hurling and football games, and the trains to the fairs continued. They operated for an average of twenty-seven fairs every Monday and twenty-six every Tuesday to places as far apart as Ballina and Cahirciveen. But often they pulled ten to eighteen per cent more carriages than they needed. Rail transport was already yielding to lorries; revenue for transporting cattle on the hoof, beet and grain was steadily declining.

Air travel expanded. In March 1948 direct flights were inaugurated between Shannon and both Boston and New York with the stated aim of encouraging tourists. An advertisement described the flight in cartoon pictures: '1. Ready for the takeoff at Shannon. 2. Enjoying a perfect meal. 3. Time passes quickly in pleasant company. 4. Sunrise and the hostess announces your arrival.'

The rural electrification scheme progressed in fits and starts with a few moments of glory – 600 homes in Patrickswell and Mungret, Co. Limerick, receiving electricity following the canvassing of parishioners; switching on of electric current at Kilsallaghan, Co. Dublin; demonstration of electricity in the home and on the farm at Oldtown, Co. Dublin, with a grain grinder, a water pump, an incubator, a portable electric motor for churning, root chopping and separating cream.

In spite of the reservations of the tight-fisted, the arrival of the first electricity pole in an area was a cause for celebration. In small towns the parish priest was nearly always the instigator of progress. In one Waterford village an initial poll returned a negative vote. That Sunday the priest gave a sermon: 'There are children of light and children of darkness, and you lot are children of darkness.' A few months later the village had the new amenity.

The arrival of electricity in Bansha, a small village in the Glen of Aherlow, was greeted by the Bansha Fife and Drum Band; in his address the priest, Father Hayes, declared, 'It is more than an amenity, it is a revolution which will sweep away inferiority complexes.' At Abbeyshrule in Co. Longford a supper was prepared by members of the Irish Countrywomen's Association in a temporary electric kitchen installed in a van lent by the ESB. In the *Irish Times* Patrick Campbell wrote, 'Somebody – I cannot remember who . . . switched on the lights in some village . . . and rural electrification took her bow. And if that does not mean more to the country than all the rest of the year's events put together, I shall be very surprised indeed.' But electricity for all was far in the future.

Building supplies were beginning to be imported once again, and building programmes were being put in place. In Dublin the Corporation Housing Committee constructed nearly 900 two-room and three-room tenement flats at Rialto at a cost of £450,000. The city boundaries were being extended and new housing estates at Ballyfermot and Cabra were planned. But in 1948, 81,000 people in Ireland still lived in one-room dwellings, 23,000 in Dublin alone, the same number calculated by James Connolly in 1912.

The census of 1946 revealed that sizes of families had fallen from an average of eight children in 1911 to five children in 1946 – double that of Great Britain. The highest average of children in a family was among farmers; the lowest among professional groups. Writing about this census some years later, Peter Kavanagh complained how 'two pages and a half are devoted to an analysis of the number of lavatories in Irish houses. Of what use is it to anyone except a dealer in chamber pots to learn that there are 310,265 houses in the Twenty-Six Counties without any sanitary facilities, or that County Cork with 34,908 is the least sanitary county in Ireland? Undoubtedly it is a little bit of a shock to learn that Co. Cork is so primitive; Mayo only comes second – 26,550 without any sanitary facilities. Galway County of course comes next with 24,388 and then Kerry with 21,167. I can see no point . . . in giving these numbers unless it be a warning to tourists visiting ruined Abbeys . . . There are 55,052 houses in Dublin that have no bath but then you haven't to read through a lot of statistics to know that.'

In spite of the national problems of sanitation, Ireland was a magnet for English people who had forgotten the taste of meat. *Dublin Opinion* had a cartoon showing Joe's Café with two doors, one narrow, the other wide; the caption read, 'Visitors trying out big juicy steaks.' For those who were semi-starved after years of rationing in England, a meal in Jammet's or a steak cooked over the open grill at the Dolphin was an unforgettable experience. Elsewhere, standards of cooking were low. Honor Tracy complained of 'plenty of food – the trouble was to find someone with more than the vaguest idea of how to cook it . . . the austere and puritanical Irish are as indifferent to good cooking as to all the arts of a civilised life'. Some visitors from England, used to wartime diets, were unable to deal with the lavish helpings. 'What we found . . . rather unexpectedly, was that the food was much too rich and the portions too large . . . We couldn't get through the courses. The waiters seemed to know the symptoms. They called it "Englishman's stomach".'

It was not only meat that brought the English to Ireland. Fulsome travel books began to reappear; 'The heart of Ireland is the heart of a woman. It will give everything in response to love but yield little to force,' wrote Robert Gibbings. Here was a country which had escaped the horrors of war, where picture-postcard visions were on every side. Here were traditional fairs, traditional dress – even if the women who wore it were getting very old – freckled red-haired children and thatched cottages with their drifts of blue smoke, still lit by lamps or candles. Here were charming fishermen and silver-tongued rogues, all friendly, civil and willing to talk to strangers.

A few visitors were more realistic about the post-war melancholy. Settled in Tipperary, Marigold Armitage noted in her sharp English way, 'Even in the richest grazing lands where the fattening bullocks move gravely about the fields . . . there are the broken-down never-to-be-built-up walls; the blackthorn running riot in the rotting banks; the iron bedstead stuck in the gap; the unopenable gates propped with stones, sagging on rusty hinges; the dusty pot-holed little roads, the rush-choked ditches and the lame, straying donkeys.'

In November 1945, Ethel Manning returned to her small three-roomed whitewashed cottage which she had left in 1940. Confronted with the condition of the interior, as recorded in her *Connemara Journal*, she knew she had made a mistake. 'Many things like kettles and oil-cans have rusted into disuse, and what the rust did not get at, the moth did. A house unlived in for a long time gets a kind of sickness, like an unloved person. The unrelieved damp has caused distemper to flake, paint to crack in the little . . . porch . . . there is actually green moss on the walls.' After a year's struggle she gave up and returned to England for good.

But others were pouring into Ireland. They included a number of Hitler's old admirers like the SS officer Pieter Menton, Otto Skorzeny who had rescued Mussolini in 1943, and Oswald Mosley, all of whom bought large properties. Few raised objections, although there was embarrassment some years later when Menton was convicted in Holland of war crimes.

Most newcomers, however, were rich Englishmen who were fleeing Mr Attlee and his new Labour Party, which had won the election of 1945. Nothing scared the privileged more than the thought of having to live under a socialist government and pay super-tax. What became known as the Retreat from Moscow, during which wealthy English families bought gentlemen's properties in Ireland, was a godsend for many Anglo-Irish who had had enough of their freezing mansions and longed for the comfort of bungalows. By an irony of historical perspective they were rescued from their poverty by their estranged English kith and kin.

The impression the Anglo-Irish made on the newcomers was not flattering. An English woman told me, 'I came over here after the war and found they were all living in a time warp. We had been liberated by joining the ATS and being bombed – bombed properly.'

Elizabeth Bowen thought briefly that she might live permanently in Bowen's Court after the war. This idea, she wrote to William Plomer, 'owed something to a flight-from-Moscow reaction'. She added, 'I have adored England since 1940 because of the stylishness Mr Churchill gave it, but I've always felt "when Mr Churchill goes, I go". I can't stick all those little middle-class Labour wets with their Old London School of Economics ties and their women. Scratch any of these cuties and you'll find the governess.' But she could not bring herself to come back to her old family home for good.

Another who considered escaping the British welfare state was Evelyn Waugh. Having been entertained at Tullynally Castle before the war, he now determined to have an Irish castle of his own. His wife hated the idea. He recorded his Irish adventures in his diary: '30 November 1946. We travelled in smoky, dirty, ill-lit carriages to Liverpool and boarded the boat – the usual St George's Channel personnel – colonel's wives covered with regimental badges, priests, drunken commercial travellers. This time a number of Jews, probably tax evaders.'

Gormanston Castle, north of Dublin in Co. Meath, was for sale. '. . . 3rd December. At 11 started for Gormanston. It was a fine solid grim square half-finished block with tower and turrets. Mrs O'Connor, Lord Gormanston's widow, opened the door, young, small, attractive, common. She had lit peat fires for our benefit in the main rooms – pictures by Lady Butler everywhere.' Lady Butler, famed for her Victorian battle scenes, was Mrs O'Connor's mother. 'There were countless bedrooms, many uninhabitable, squalid plumbing, vast attics. On the whole I liked the house. The chapel unlicensed and Mrs O'Connor evasive about the chances of getting it back to use.'

In spite of Gormanston's drawbacks, Waugh was determined to bid at the auction. Just in time he discovered that Billy Butlin was about to open a holiday camp in nearby Mosney which would accommodate 2,000 people.

A year later Waugh was back. He looked at Lisnavagh, 'a large prosaic Victorian house' in Co. Carlow with twenty-two bedrooms, five bathrooms, twelve acres and a 'luggage entrance'.

He also inspected a Victorian house called Viewmount, a castle in Kilkenny, and another vast pile in Tipperary called Kiltinane, 'a mediaeval Tudor and Georgian castle of great beauty . . . the owners . . . mother and daughter, living in dire poverty and squalor, twenty-seven dogs in the house. Mrs de Sales la Terrière has lost all interest in life, she and her mother told me. The whole place was romantic and inconvenient.'

Between bouts of castle hunting he enjoyed good food at Jammet's and the Dolphin, 'an inn frequented by jockeys, which reeked of whiskey and wine'. He dined with Lord Moyne, 'very barmy, consumed with parsimony, but rather gay in his attire and attending a hair specialist to prevent baldness'.

But his love affair with Ireland was drawing to a close. In 1952, long after he had given up his romantic venture, he wrote in his diary, 'Among the countless blessings I thank God for, my failure to find a house in Ireland comes first. Unless one is mad for fox hunting, there is nothing to draw one . . . the houses, except for half a dozen . . . are very shoddy . . . the peasants are malevolent. All their smiles are as false as hell. Their priests are very suitable for them, but not for foreigners. No coal at all, awful incompetence everywhere. No native capable of doing the simplest job properly.'

At much the same time, Nancy Mitford wrote in a letter to Waugh, 'Total to me is the mystery of why you don't live in Ireland. Never have I seen a country so much made for somebody as *it* is for *you*. The terrible silly politeness of lower classes, so miserable that they long for any sort of menial task at £1 a week, the emptiness, the uncompromising Roman Catholicness, the pretty houses of the date you like best, the agricultural country for Laura, the neighbours all low brow & . . . all 100 miles away, the cold wetness, the small income tax, really I could go on for ever.'

Waugh's conclusions were similar in spirit to those of others who had embarked on the Retreat. According to Marigold Armitage, their comments included, 'You'd almost think the damned fellers were *foreigners*'; 'I'm never quite sure if their hands are clean'; 'The thing is, they're just like the wops – if you treat them as if they were English you're bound to be let down'.

From our island we watched the activities of a super-rich Englishman who, when he was not hoisting the blue ensign on his yacht, was rebuilding a derelict house. Perversely, the fact that so many of these big houses were semi-ruinous added to their desirability, since the new owners felt that by restoring them they would eventually make a financial killing.

In Tipperary, according to Marigold Armitage, 'the Big Houses . . . slid gently into ruin – until, as was happening so often at this time, they were rescued by the refugees, disappeared for long months behind a network of scaffolding and re-appeared rain-proof and centrally heated'. Patricia Cockburn observed the new English buying 'dilapidated mansions, mending the roof and putting in central heating and three or four new bathrooms, papering the dining room with striped Regency wallpaper, adding a crystal chandelier and settling down to what they imagined would be a certainly pre-war and possibly Edwardian gentleman's country life'. A fertile ground for buying furnishing for newly acquired houses was the Dublin auction room where, according to Sheila Pim, 'you have oil paintings and wine coolers and candlesticks and moustache cups and coasters and soiled china sets, but not golf clubs or motor mowers'.

Ethel Manning met 'an upper class Englishman over here looking for a house. It was all one to him where he found it; he knew nothing of Ireland, its history or its people; he had never been here before; he simply had a feeling that he would like to get out of England. He told me that if he lived here for a hundred years he would never understand the Irish neutrality.'

All too soon, the majority of those who had taken part in the Retreat grew disillusioned. Ireland bore little resemblance to Edwardian England. The Labour Party in England gave way to the Conservatives whose brand of government favoured the rich. Having conceded that they did not fit into the Irish life they had imagined for themselves, all over the country those who had fled socialist England made plans to return to familiar territory. The newly renovated house would be sold at a loss, sometimes back to the original owner. Or, if the place proved unsaleable, which was often the case, the roof would be stripped off to avoid tax and the house would become yet another Irish ruin. Our neighbour did this, before hoisting the blue ensign and going back to his native land.

A few succeeded in their quest of finding a permanent home in Ireland. Peter and Christabel Bielenberg decided to settle here after dreadful years spent in wartime Germany. Their first glimpse of their new home in Co. Carlow was not reassuring. It 'was larger than we anticipated, and also nearer to disintegration'. There were two kitchens in shambles, one of which had 'the wreckage of a huge black range which looked as if it had been hit by a hand grenade'. But 'I thought to have seen a certain beauty hidden somewhere beneath the dust and decay'. For the Bielenbergs and their young family that was enough to be getting on with, and the house became a permanent home.

Another newcomer who stayed was the American J. P. Donleavy, who entered TCD immediately after the war under the GI Bill of Rights; when I went there a few years later it was still filled with American ex-servicemen. When Donleavy told a friend that he was going to Trinity instead of some Catholic university, 'it was unequivocally pointed out to me that not only was I to attend the most important and revered of all Irish institutions, but even by being so much as a student of Trinity, upon me a social entitlement was bestowed second to none in the city of Dublin'.

But Trinity was at a low ebb. A letter in *Envoy* in 1950, which gave the college as an address, stated that 'it is singular to find a college with the tradition of Trinity which had fallen into such sterility and decay. It seems to have reached the age of Lear, gone grey and lost its mind, its kingdom gone, its underlings blind – yet it has not even the energy of Lear. The students reproduce neither the high jinks and silliness, nor the wit and brilliance of college periodicals in England.'

Because of McQuaid's ban, most of the brains of the country were going to University College. The ban, which the Archbishop repeated annually in his Lenten pastorals, would continue until June 1970, three years before his death. When Garret Fitzgerald was offered the post of Junior Rockefeller Research Assistant at Trinity, Dr Michael Tierney, the Provost of UCD, 'to my surprise

. . . was deeply upset. I was not prepared for his intense, irrational dislike of Trinity College.' But plenty of students managed to get dispensations to attend the old corner of a foreign field that was forever England. In Honor Tracy's words: 'When is a grave sin not a grave sin? When the bishop says so.'

The Protestant preserve in the heart of the Catholic city had its effect on Donleavy. 'It was in this English–Anglo-Irish atmosphere that my earliest point of view of Ireland was obtained.' He would incorporate the atmosphere in his books, creating a fantasy Anglo-Irish world as unreal as that inhabited by P. G. Wodehouse's Bertie Wooster and Lord Emsworth. He put his money where his pen was, bought a mansion in the remotest part of Ireland, and stayed on.

CHAPTER 20

Faith of Our Fathers

Faith of our fathers, living still . . .

Hymn

In 1949 Douglas Hyde died full of years and dignity. His funeral service was held in St Patrick's Cathedral, but the new Taoiseach, John Aloysius Costello, and his colleagues would not go inside. They sat outside in their official cars in the cathedral close.

Austin Clarke, who claimed that he and the French Ambassador were the only two Catholics inside, watched the coffin:

> . . . trestled in the gloom
> Of arch and monument
> Beyond the desperate tomb
> Of Swift . . .

He described the scene outside:

> Costello, his Cabinet
> In Government cars hiding
> Tall hat in hand, dreading
> Our Father in English. Better
> Not hear that 'which' for 'who'
> And risk eternal doom.

There was no public comment on this behaviour, since religious laws still forbade Catholics from entering Protestant churches. When Hyde had been inaugurated President in 1937, de Valera had rather spoilt the ingenious and reconciling tone of the appointment by his own non-attendance at St Patrick's; he and his Cabinet went off to a Mass at the Pro-Cathedral instead. When de Valera became President himself, one of the main tasks of his Protestant ADC,

Colonel Bunbury, was to represent him at non-Catholic funerals; grieving congregations watched out for the familiar military figure striding down Protestant aisles.

No Catholic was excused the prohibition. When Donal Foley summoned up the courage to enter a Protestant church for a funeral it was partly out of curiosity: 'Of course we did not recognise it as a church at all, but as a kind of mumbo jumbo museum.' George O'Brien peered inside Lismore Cathedral: 'Not a lick of paint in the whole place, just walls of undressed stone which wept, scenting the air with clay. Not a holy picture, not a blessed statue, not a candle, not a Station of the Cross. If they were holy, they kept mightily quiet about it.'

When Sean Dunne daringly entered the Protestant church in Dunmore East, he took note of the cushions and soft kneelers, and the damp smell that 'was an absence of other smells like wax and incense'. There were no statues on the walls, but the memorials to those who had fought in the British Army were a revelation. In St Patrick's Austin Clarke's eye was caught by 'Imperial flags . . . their pride turned to rags'.

The year before Hyde's death, de Valera and Fianna Fáil had been replaced by the first Interparty or Coalition Government, an all-sorts collection of politicians made up of five parties with only one thing in common – to oust Fianna Fáil. Costello, the leader of the Fine Gael party, was a compromise Taoiseach, who made an extraordinary decision almost immediately after he came into power – at a press conference in Ottowa in September 1948 he declared Ireland a republic. Many claimed this had already come about with the Constitution of 1937, when the country ceased to be a dominion. Now it was to become official.

The change was quickly bundled through without any formal decision in Government, and on Easter Monday 1949, the thirty-third anniversary of the Rising, the new President Sean T. O'Kelly signed the bill by which Éire officially became the Republic of Ireland. The move was not greeted with any enthusiasm; many were indignant and it did nothing for Anglo-Irish relations. 'The process . . . was irresponsible, incredible and ludicrous,' wrote Dr Noel Browne. As an insider – he was Minister for Health in the Coalition Government – he repeated the generally accepted version of how the change had come about: 'Costello on a visit to Canada felt he had been slighted . . .' The story goes that when Costello dined with the Governor-General of Canada, Field Marshal Alexander (an Ulsterman), Alexander placed on the table a replica of Roaring Meg, the cannon used against Catholic forces of King James at the siege of Londonderry. This, together with other perceived insults, enraged Costello, and drove him to make his decision.

The minority felt that cutting ties with the Commonwealth was a betrayal. Some, like Dean Griffin, were also uneasy about Costello's message to the Pope confirming the power of the Catholic Church in the State which was sent immediately the Coalition came into office. De Valera had done the same thing sixteen years before. Griffin 'was prompted to write a letter to the *Irish Times* protesting that the Government of a state which professes to be democratic and Republican . . . should not, on election, set about publicising their subservience to a foreign pontiff'.

The Coalition's treatment of the black sheep of their Cabinet, Dr Noel Browne, was unsurprising. Nor was it unexpected that Dr Browne did not conform with his colleagues. In the politics of the day he was a misfit; his enemies accused him of paranoia.

Tuberculosis obsessed Browne as a result of his tragic childhood; few who saw it can forget how he wept when interviewed on television as he remembered the deaths of his relatives. 'It is difficult now to comprehend the sense of shocked disbelief with which one heard of a friend's misfortune in contracting TB,' he wrote in his autobiography *Against the Tide*. A boy of charm and intelligence, he was raised from total poverty by a wealthy Dublin family which paid for him to go to an English Catholic public school. Later he was helped to attend medical school at Trinity; he qualified as a doctor, although a tubercular illness interfered with his studies.

'Because I was a "Trinity Catholic", he wrote, 'I was suspect and unwelcome within the State medical service. To admit a medical training in TCD was an automatic disqualification from posts in any of the local authority sanatoria.' However, after he had joined the new Clann na Poblachta Party, created by Sean MacBride in July 1946, his appointment as Minister for Health in the new Coalition Government was fluent and easy. He accepted the position 'with a mixture of innocence and naïveté'.

Browne's predecessors in Fianna Fáil had set in motion a process of change with regard to the problem of TB. During the Emergency, sulphonamides were introduced and David Grey, the United States Minister in Dublin, undertook to bring in some penicillin from America. By 1947, streptomycin was generally available and deaths were declining. The fall in the death rate was dramatic; in 1948, mortality from childhood tuberculosis in Dublin had fallen by half in one year.

When Browne came into the Health Department in 1947, 900 tubercular patients were on sanatoria waiting lists. In that year the Department of Health was established and a special unit within the department began acquiring land for new sanatoria.

Browne brought in a new dynamism and what his more staid colleagues regarded as a frenetic energy. He raised the profile of the Blood Transfusion Service and instituted BCG tests for children. Impatient with civil servants, he set in motion a reform which liquidated around £20 million in investments – all the Department of Health's assets – and took out a mortgage on the next £10 million due from the Hospital Sweepstake.

His ministerial room in the Custom House had a huge wall chart listing various hospital projects in the planning stage of construction. A system of coloured discs indicated the exact stage each project had reached and the architects involved. A red disc meant that movement had stopped because of decisions to be taken by the department. A red disc made Browne furious.

Civil servants of the day have been critical of him and defensive of such politicians as Dr James Ryan and Sean MacEntee, both Fianna Fail ministers for health, who were just as concerned about the abolition of TB. Browne got the publicity and the public on his side because of his personal experiences and his emotional approach.

'I hate the smell of hospital,' patients used to say, commenting on the distinctive blend of ether and Lysol that pervaded wards and theatres. Those were the days when each hospital did its own sterilisation of sheets, towels, gowns, dressings and instruments by boiling; plaster-of-Paris bandages were prepared by hand, as gauze bandages were impregnated from eight-stone sacks of plaster amid clouds of white dust. An old man told me of his experiences in a big Cork hospital at the end of the war. 'The nurses were not allowed to talk to the patients. You'd be lying there, and they couldn't give you the time of day. I was there three months, and my God, the cold and the hunger . . . The Sister came in one day, and she said to the nurse, "Turn on the lights to keep the place warm."'

Even with Sweepstake money hospitals were grim places, and the atmosphere of many institutions was Dickensian. In his role of Minister for Health, Browne inspected numerous county homes, general hospitals and workhouses surrounded by their prison walls. Straw palliasses were still in use as mattresses, and appalling food was cooked in enormous vats. At a workhouse in Cork children, segregated by sex, wore numbers on their backs 'like old style criminals'. At Longford County Hospital, which had an open sewer, patients lay in long wards with stone floors and no carpets. At the Pigeon House and Newcastle Sanatoria buckets were placed on the floors to catch drips from the roofs. For decades the Pigeon House and its coffins had been notorious as the destination of dying TB patients. Once the disease, which was known back in the time of the Pharaohs, took hold, there was no hope. If you had TB and you had no money, you were sent home to infect other members of your family.

It was admitted that the incidence of TB in the Republic of Ireland was worse than in Northern Ireland or Great Britain. One of the main problems continued to be the reluctance of patients to come forward when symptoms first showed; a large number, perhaps the majority, were first diagnosed when the disease was far advanced. Radio and press propaganda offered a little help, and something about it was mentioned in the school curriculum. But to be infected with tuberculosis continued to be a terrible secret, a sin and a shame. When patients were sent to the Newcastle Sanatorium in Co. Wicklow, their relatives and friends would not write directly to that address, but to the nearby Anchor Hotel instead.

New regional sanatoria were planned for Dublin, Cork, Galway and Waterford and by the end of 1949 1,200 beds were provided. Single-storey buildings were set in wooded estates where patients could benefit from pure air. The first of these opened in 1953 after Browne had left office. By that time, however, the decline in TB cases had been so dramatic that they were already out of date. They came to be known as 'White's elephants' after Norman White, the Department of Health's chief architect. There was irony in the subsequent conversion of many redundant sanatoria into psychiatric hospitals.

The new drugs had done their wonderful work. The impact of such drugs as penicillin and streptomycin was astonishing. Browne described his own amazement when a woman came to see him with her dying husband, whose X-rays showed white clouds where lung tissue was being devoured. He tried one of the new drugs – at that time experimental and expensive – on the patient; in a fortnight the menacing white had diminished and over a short period the lungs had become miraculously clear.

The drama of Browne's departure from the political scene was the most notorious example of the way religion interfered in matters of health. The two continued to be inextricably linked in the way Gogarty had described: 'there are Protestant diseases and Catholic diseases'. The conflict over the term 'ethics' continues today. One example of such problems was the conscience of the Protestant Adelaide Hospital. Under the provision of the Public Hospital Acts of 1933, funds for hospital care had been dependent on money from the Irish Hospital Sweepstake which was distributed to voluntary hospitals through the Minister for Local Government (before the creation of the Department of Health) and the Hospitals Trust Fund. But the constitution of the Adelaide Hospital prohibited it from participating in a scheme in which money came from gambling; as a result that hospital was kept perpetually short of funds.

In 1942 an 'Anti-Tuberculosis League' was proposed; it was to be a voluntary organisation, a broadly based body including, according to David Mitchell, 'veterinary surgeons, clergy, nurses, health workers, workers' organisations, employers of labour, health insurance societies, educational authorities and other groups interested in the health of the country'. But the Catholic Church considered that such an organisation had a decidedly secular, if not Protestant tinge. As its launch was about to take place at the Royal Hibernian Hotel in February 1943, the proceedings were suddenly interrupted when Monsignor Daniel Maloney rose to his feet and read out a letter from Dr McQuaid stating that any anti-tuberculosis campaign should be placed solely in the hands of the Catholic Irish Red Cross.

Among the most dramatic medico–ecclesiastical confrontations was the displacement of the Joint Committee of the Meath Hospital, which, like the Adelaide, had a Protestant foundation. In 1949 a group of newcomers, said to be members of the Knights of Columbanus, took over the annual general meeting. In the words of David Mitchell, 'instead of the few regular attenders, neat elderly ladies in hats with tweedy spouses, the smoke-filled room was packed with blue suited middle-aged men'. The ensuing ballots ensured that the Meath no longer remained a cosy Protestant enclave. Even de Valera, then in opposition, called the proceedings a 'coup', while Browne described them as an 'ambush . . . to swamp the Board of Management of the predominately Protestant Meath Hospital with Catholics and convert it into a Catholic

Hospital'. After the Meath takeover, the Board of the Adelaide, we are told, took great care about full attendance at general meetings. Today the Adelaide, moved to new premises in Tallaght, struggles to maintain 'a Protestant ethos' which seems to be code for performing sterilisation operations.

Browne's discomfiture over the Mother and Child Scheme is the best-known of these conflicts because he took care to make the details known to the public at the time. It demonstrated how politicians and Ministers were as afraid of the Church as the most abject sinner trembling outside a confessional. Even the Taoiseach, Costello, was proud to declare that he was a Catholic before he was a politician: 'I will obey my Church even if I lose votes by it.'

The Mother and Child Scheme was originally a Fianna Fáil proposal to provide free material care for mothers and full medical care for children up to the age of sixteen. There would be no means test, no insurance contribution, no charges and no compulsion to use the services provided. When de Valera was told that the idea was unacceptable to the Catholic Church, the scheme was shelved. Noel Browne revived it.

The Government was for it. The Trades Unions were for it. The doctors were bitterly against it because it affected their pockets. The Catholic hierarchy found itself on the side of these medical gentlemen.

Browne organised a huge propaganda campaign with advertisements, coloured photographs and drawings. He made a public speech once a fortnight during which he mentioned no more doctors' bills, no more chemists' bills. He was negotiating a proposal that the Government should buy off the doctors for a guinea a patient, an enormous sum of money.

On 10 October 1950, Browne was summoned to the Archbishop's Palace at Drumcondra where he was confronted by Bishop Browne of Galway, the Bishop of Ferns, Dr Stanton, and Dr McQuaid. In *Against the Tide*, his autobiography, published in 1986, Browne compared the Archbishop of Dublin with a Spanish inquisitor, an analogy that had occurred to others at the time. Honor Tracy wrote that 'somehow in the uneasy, haunted atmosphere of Ireland one could fancy oneself away in Madrid'.

Remembering that meeting, Browne wrote of McQuaid, 'A broad white silk shawl covered his frail bent shoulders . . . His dark eyes glittering in a mask-like face . . . long straight thin nose and a saturnine appearance with his fixity of expression and the strong mouth of an obsessional.' Two obsessionals confronted one another.

The Bishops' fears were not easy to analyse, but it seemed that information on health which was a factor in the new bill would compromise faith and morals. They declared that the bill was anti-family and could lead to the intrusion of the State into matters like sexual relations and marriage. This was their way of saying that the old bogey of birth control and its means might become common knowledge among their flock. Browne took the wind out of their sails by conceding completely on the promotion of educational literature. There would be none. But the Bishops were still against him; it seemed that they objected to the absence of a means test, which might give dangerous freedom of choice, particularly to women.

When Browne published the Scheme in March 1951, the Bishops declared that none of their objections had been met and that it was 'opposed to Catholic social teaching'. The Coalition caved in and Browne resigned as Minister for Health on 11 April 1951. The Government fell two months later.

Browne's colleagues turned on him, Costello saying that he was incapable of negotiation, Sean MacBride saying that he was not normal and was constitutionally incapable of listening to criticism. When his more tactful and ostensibly more pious successor, Dr James Ryan, introduced a watered-down bill offering free services for mothers and children which aroused no clerical opposition, it was clear that Browne himself, rather than means testing, stuck in their Lordships' throats. Patrick Kavanagh described the new bill as 'a typical grey-coloured compromise striving to be born after a previous false labour'. Some years later in 1956, free or subsidised hospital services were made available for the first time to those on low incomes.

Frank Duff also clashed with Archbishop McQuaid, who considered the founder of the Legion of Mary to be a loose cannon. Duff declared bitterly, 'Anyone who wants to work in Ireland will be cribbed, cabined and confined . . . A terrible conservatism exercises relentless sway and tells the Irish people that they must walk by outmoded ways . . . even when the world has more or less taken up the Legion, Ireland looks at it suspiciously.'

The Church ruled triumphant in most secular matters, however trivial. This could lead to some spectacularly silly rows, like the one ensuing from the appointment in 1948 of Mrs Hanbury, a divorcee, as Joint Master of the Galway Blazers. This was objected to by the clergy, in particular two reverend gentlemen who regularly rode with that hunt. An organised opposition was mounted during which the Church insinuated that farmers of their own volition refused to allow the hunt to enter their lands and coverts. The western bishops, headed by Dr Michael Browne, made a statement declaring that farmers were fully justified if they resented the appointment of a Master who was living in a state of sin.

It was the beginning of the last golden age when the Church held sway not only over those who governed Ireland, but over the Irish populace at large. In the *Furrow*, a leading ecclesiastical magazine, the Reverend Christopher Lee described the popularity of one rural confraternity which met on Sunday evenings like a parish social: 'In the long evenings of spring and summer the menfolk ambled towards the church after their tea.' Younger men and girls came on bicycles or in traps. 'Sometimes for the boys it means a dash home from the local hurling team in time to milk the cow and be back to the chapel.' In autumn and winter the attendance was less good, but people still came to the church lit by oil-lamps and altar candles. By 1950 a Windcharger lighting set had been installed, shedding its light on men and boys, women and girls, grouped in guilds according to their townlands, listening to talks on devotion to the Sacred Heart, Our Lady's feasts, great Irishmen, local history and the life of Our Lord. From time to time there was a Holy Hour.

1950 was marked with Holy Year. Tears were shed on 1 November when Pope Pius XII proclaimed the Assumption of the Virgin Mary into Heaven and the bishops unnecessarily reminded their flock that it was the solemn duty of all Catholics to give their sincere and full assent. Four years later in 1954, when the Marian Year commemorated the centenary of the proclamation of the Dogma of the Immaculate Conception, huge numbers of pilgrims made their way to Knock, numerous new grottoes and wayside shrines sprang up and many girls were christened Marian.

Purgatory awaited every sinner. To avoid prolonged suffering it was as well to avail oneself of the sacraments and holy dispensations, and to perform salutary practices as well as acts of charity; frequent confessions would also help. Most important were prayers to help the souls already suffering there. A hand should be offered to Protestants. The wheel had turned full circle since the days when they were condemned for offering Catholic bowls of soup. Conversions went the other way.

In his pamphlet 'A Formula for Conversion' Frank Duff recommended that 'in our approach to non-Catholics we must study simplicity. Protestants are not impressed by close-knit logic on religion. "Theological" is a good word to us but to them a slightly sinister one – so do not beat about the bush, but state the claims of the Church in a direct concise way.'

Others suggested more furtive methods. An ingenious American idea might help some wretched non-Catholic friend or relative to avoid damnation; he could have placed 'in his hands . . . a little ornamented prayer card . . . which contains all the "acts" necessary for salvation . . . The card is of a very attractive design . . . not "religious". There is no mention made of Catholicity and even the imprimatur is omitted. The prayers are so arranged that all attention is centred on the Act of Contrition . . . a sincere way to save souls by using a new method of approach.'

Duff considered that Protestants, if approached in the right way, should be easy to persuade. 'Protestantism has become an almost total negation. It is a good working rule to reason that Protestants are all painfully aware of this, are unsatisfied with their position, and would seize anything which appealed to them as truth.'

The easiest method of catching them, or at least their children, continued to be via the mixed marriage. This had to take place in a Catholic church, not at the main altar, but miserably in some side chapel. In order to obtain even this second-best ceremony the old rule had to be followed; the Protestant partner signed a paper guaranteeing that any children of the marriage would be brought up in the Catholic faith. Supine Protestants accepted this outcome with continued squeaks of protest. Annabel Goff's father told her sadly, 'I have four children. The odds are that at least one of you will marry a Catholic.' Not until 1966 did the hierarchy decide that a mixed marriage could share the same blessing from the Church as a marriage between Catholics. The term fell into disrepute; henceforth they were referred to as inter-faith marriages.

It was all right to snigger at the Church of Ireland, but not to laugh at the Church of Rome. By now the Church of Ireland, with its ironically triumphalist title, seemed to be in terminal decline. In his story 'Of the Cloth', William Trevor mused: 'while Church of Ireland notice boards still stood by old church gates, gold letters on black giving details of what services would be offered, there was a withering within that Church that seemed a natural thing'. Risen from near-suppression, the great Church of Rome inherited all Ireland.

So there were relatively few Catholics interested in Protestants and their immortal souls. But already some considered the Catholic Church itself at risk, for all the visible trappings of the faith. A letter to *Envoy* attacking Patrick Kavanagh as being an 'anti-Catholic fifth columnist' declared, 'Catholicism is a besieged fortress – the energy of every Catholic who has the God-given gift of words ought to be directed towards the massing enemies without.'

The old litanies continued – denunciations of divorce, the dancehall, the lending library, Trinity College, lewd books and films, jazz on the radio and English Sunday newspapers. After August 1949 these arrived by air in time for 8.00 Mass in major towns. They offered dangers, not only in their sordid details of sexual crimes and misdemeanours, but in the ramblings of 'theological quacks' like Beverly Nichols or Evelyn Home.

The *Furrow* did a survey which revealed that in March 1950, in a working-class suburban area of Cork, out of fifty-five families fourteen read the *News of the World*, which was banned, twenty-four favoured the *Sunday Dispatch*, thirty-one the *People*, while only twelve read the *Universe* and the *Standard*. Elsewhere, the *Empire News* and the *Sunday Express* found favour, and the same proportions of readers were found in an unnamed rural town. In a factory with twenty-eight girls, eight received the banned *News of the World*.

So girls went astray, often after attending the dreaded dancehalls. Austin Clarke identified 'the hasty sin of the young after a dance, awkward, in clothes against a wall or crick-necked in a car'. Such moments still led to places like the Convent of the Sacred Heart in Castlepollard where girls were destined to 'cook, sew, wash, dig, milk cows, clean stables' and twice a day feed their babies with 'milk that cost them dearly'.

Worries about the wavering faith of the flock troubled some priests like the Reverend Seamus McLoughlin who may have had an inkling of the crisis of belief that would take place decades after the time in 1950 when he was lamenting the erosion of Sundays and holy days. He condemned those who sought out the shortest possible Mass. He deplored Sunday activities, lorries driven, greyhounds exercised or the participation in sport. There was a craze for amusement, the 'fan' mentality. Sundays spent on allotments or turf banks were also criticised: 'Any excuse at all, or even no excuse – will send men into the fields . . . Thirty years ago the Sunday worker was regarded as a "half natural" in the countryside, one who would have no luck.' Father McLoughlin blamed the war: 'When emergencies pass, it is often hard to get back to former observance, to get rid of a lax outlook that has come into being.'

But Mass remained a constant. Latecomers, mostly men, stood outside the church door as the murmured Latin floated out to them, which counted as attendance. New churches were being built to accommodate huge congregations. The spread of electricity meant that they would be warm with floor heating, panel heaters or storage heaters at work for twelve hours a day.

The authorities favoured modern designs like that of Our Lady of Fatima in Limerick with its steel roof, timber stations of carved wood and life-sized statue in teak of Our Lady of Fatima by Oisín Kelly. But congregations preferred traditional designs, like the Cathedral of Our Lady Assumed in Heaven and St Nicholas built in Galway between 1957 and 1965 – Dr Michael Browne's dream, stubbornly old-fashioned and beloved by the people of Galway. Even more emotionally unifying would be the restorations, under the supervision of Percy le Clerc, of abbeys blighted in evil times by Cromwellians and others of alien faith – Ballintober, Holy Cross and Graiguenamanagh.

Churches had to have priests. The popularity of St Patrick's College, Maynooth, the biggest seminary in the world, had never been greater. From pagan England Christopher Hollis mused, 'Nowhere is Victorian England more at home than at Maynooth – and with every year that passes in this revolting century, that becomes a higher and higher compliment.' It was considered that 'the average curate comes out of Maynooth and goes into the old structures – keep your mouth shut, keep your ears and eyes open, you'll get the respect of your people and you'll make your money'.

Among Maynooth's most gifted graduates was Bishop Eamon Casey who typically came from a prosperous farming family; his father was manager of a creamery. There had never been a doubt that he would enter the priesthood; having a priest in the family was a form of social nobility. He was a good, if not outstanding priest; but Maynooth failed to teach him how to grapple with the problem of celibacy and the sin of hypocrisy.

Like old army recruiting sergeants, members of clerical orders would scour the countryside in search of conscripts. They would give their lectures at schools, pointing out the attractions of their own particular branch of religion, and visit the parents of any boy who had expressed interest. Then some huge building would swallow up the child. 'The direct aim of Rochestown College is to educate boys who wish to become priests in the Capuchin Franciscan Order. During an ordinary secondary school course the boys are brought into intimate contact with members of that Order, their vocations are tested and developed.'

Francis Xavier Carthy went by train to a seminary. 'I did not like that journey because I was feeling so self-conscious in my black coat, hat, suit and tie . . . Thirty of us arrived that day – we led our parents around the place and some were frightened and sad – all visitors or "weeping parents" . . . were gone by 6.30.'

Catholics might be sorry for doomed Protestants, but we felt just as sorry for the crocodile lines of boys no older than ourselves dressed in black with black fedoras on their heads, each carrying an umbrella, walking Ireland's streets and lanes. In theory a seminarian was not obliged to have a vocation. He could use the knowledge of Latin, Greek, Irish choral music and Gaelic games bestowed on him to go to university and then elsewhere.

According to Patrick Kennelly, who poured his memories of seminary life into a novel, *Sausages for Tuesday*, no stress was placed on recruitment to the priesthood until the fourth year. Before that persuasion consisted of copious sermons from different orders full of information about pagan Africa and the Blacks' fierce thirst for the Truth. 'Should you decide . . . that you will be a priest . . . I have here some leaflets.' When the boys became seniors, more subtle pressure was put on them. 'Remember, my dear boys, that it is very easy to turn a deaf ear to the gentle but insistent calling of Our Lord . . .'

The Superior of a Presentation College confided to Hugh Leonard the steps that led him to the priesthood. The free secondary education of the selected bright country boy ' "nearly not able to walk with the weight of the holy medals from every house in the village" lasted six years. "During my last term the Superior sends for me . . . 'Have you decided to stay with us?' It seemed a little ungrateful to say 'no' right into his face . . ." And so the spell at university, also paid for, was followed by ordination almost as a result of good manners. ". . . my final vows were three weeks off and I still couldn't get up the nerve to tell them that I hadn't a notion in the wide world of becoming one of them. Of course I never did. And here I am now."'

Patrick Kennelly and his fellow seminarians were told of the three things required for ordination. 'Have you a true love of your Creator and Redeemer? Have you average intelligence? Are you free from all bad habits?' Hours were spent each day in the oratory, while retreats and sermons directed the students to become holy, pray often, offer up each minute of the day and give up telling vulgar jokes. In the wings parents waited; potential disappointment was another pressure.

The way was hard. 'Sometimes you would get thirty slaps from [Father] Kelly during his two classes . . . pink eyes shining behind the glasses, broad friendly grin on his face when he would be flailing his cane, and the contented weary look when it was over.' Kennelly was also beaten by 'Father Ryan' who was a demon during Lent because he had given up cigarettes.

The clerics with the worst reputation for beating continued to be the Christian Brothers. They were in charge not only of much of the nation's schooling, but also of penal institutions for delinquent boys. As a legacy of Victorian thinking which postulated that wicked boys should be kept in isolation, industrial schools were often sited in remote and beautiful places like Glencree and Letterfrack. Glencree had changed to other uses, but Letterfrack still functioned.

> One, two, three, four, five, six, seven,
> All good children go to Heaven.
> One, two, three, four, five, six, seven.
> All bad children go to Letterfrack.

St Joseph's in Letterfrack, wildest Connemara, offered a regime in which the brothers were strict and they had no inhibition about beating boys who were not ordinary schoolboys. Mannix Flynn had a spell there and remembered in fiction 'the cane leather, the strap, punch, clatter, kick, tears, hatred, pain' and the smiling brother who had shown him sin and punishment.

The Christian Brothers also ran the Industrial School at Artane with the purpose of giving boys, many of them orphans, a viable trade. It was well known to the wider public for the Artane Boys Band, the silver trumpets and the jaunty rebel tunes; less well known was how the boys were housed in huge dormitories each containing 180 iron beds. Every brother carried a blackjack made up of two pieces of leather stitched together by a bootmaker, often with keys, lead or metal sewn inside.

The orphanages filled with children that could not be adopted kept their secrets longer. Because the revelations of abuse are so recent, they are particularly haunting and accusations and denials ring in our ears: 'I can say before my God I never put anyone in the tumble-drier.'

In 1950 an alien English newspaper tried to harm the reputation of the parish priest of Doneraile in Co. Cork. Honor Tracy published an article in the English *Sunday Times* called 'Great Days in a Village', accusing Canon O'Connell of building an expensive new priest's house in Doneraile while he was living in a perfectly adequate Georgian house and his parishioners lacked running water and electricity. When the Canon protested and threatened to sue, the *Sunday Times*, terrified of possible damages, apologised and paid £750 to charity. The loyal parishioners of Doneraile were delighted and gave their priest a civic reception, singing 'Faith of Our Fathers'.

Furious, Tracy herself took an action against the *Sunday Times*, claiming that their admission of responsibility libelled her; she was awarded damages of £3,000 by an English court. Although her accusations were undoubtedly true, she did not escape censure. Hubert Butler, a doughty opponent of humbug in Irish life, criticised her stand: 'She is like a miniaturist trying her hand at murals. Her generalisations are often so lacking background knowledge and experience as to be ridiculous.' But they hit bull's-eyes on a number of occasions.

Butler's accumulation of background knowledge made him wise and often witty. In recent years he has become St Hubert, spokesman for beleaguered Protestants and their traditions. In going some way towards making them feel important once again, he has done more than merely recite the mantra of Emmet–Tone–Swift. His friend Victor Griffin wrote, 'He believed as I do that the Irish at heart, both Catholic and Protestant, are a tolerant people. They are made intolerant by religion masquerading as Christianity.'

In the fifties Protestants in general were in a particularly bad way; there was a real feeling that they were passenger pigeons on the edge of extinction. Jack White wrote a play about them which he called *The Last Eleven*. They suffered a couple of grotesque injustices, the Baltinglass Post Mistress grievance and the Fethard-on-Sea unfairness. Butler himself underwent mild persecution. In 1952 he criticised in a public lecture the forced conversion by the Croatians of many thousands of orthodox Serbians to Roman Catholicism; for this he received some abuse and was forced to resign from the Kilkenny Archaeological Society, which had been brought back to life by his efforts.

Some considered that the role of prominent Protestants in Irish life was reduced to that of lending their names as directors of companies. Hugh Leonard saw them as on their way out. 'There were the Jacobs and their like; the Quality; sliding away and leaving the field and the croquet lawn to the runners in; the gombeen men and their wives with backsides that sang of soda bread and spuds; advertising men called Brendan or Dermot, puff adders who wore blazers with braided crests that were Gordian knots . . . builders and tearers down, hunters and chancers . . . They were in charge now.'

The general sense of defeat among the Anglo-Irish turned into a rout. Tracy observed 'a downhill trend. A fence has fallen down and not been put up – a window has been broken and starkly boarded over – on the front door the bell no longer rings and has been replaced by a trumpet.'

After her husband died, Elizabeth Bowen struggled for a few more years to maintain Bowen's Court before selling it in 1959 to the farmer who destroyed it. Some do not regret the extinction of that lovely limestone mansion. A recent letter in the *Irish Times* declared, 'When Bowen's Court was dismantled . . . and the foundations dug up, the difference that it made to Irish life was the addition of a good agricultural field to a stock of land.'

At Woodbrook David Thomson observed Major Kirkwood coming to the end of his resources. 'Theirs is the usual story of decline of fortune.' The Maxwells, who had worked for the Kirkwoods and considered that historically they were the rightful owners of the place, bought the house and one of them made changes. 'The yard seemed derelict – the ballroom windows broken . . . the two wings of the house incurably leaky . . . had been a continual nuisance to him, especially as he did not use them nor any of the main rooms, and he had pulled them down, restoring the house to its original shape.'

Thomson considered the extinction of the Big House a satisfactory conclusion to centuries of oppression. 'One might think that the departure of so many influential people with money to spend locally would turn out to be harmful to a rural society. It was not so – the demesnes of Rockingham . . . and French Park had been divided by the Land Commission and parcelled out among small farmers. The huge wall that surrounded Rockingham in time had been knocked waist-high like others all over the country.'

The pulling down of French Park and the accidental destruction of Rockingham occurred within a few years of each other. The fire that destroyed

Rockingham took place in 1957; John McGahern saw it as symbolic: 'The burning of Rockingham House stood out from all else in the still-emptying countryside . . . In that amazing night all was lit up, the whole lake and its islands all the way across to Rockadoon and the forest slopes of the Curlews, the great beech walk going towards Boyle, the woods behind the house, and over them the high plains, the light leaping over to great meadows. The glass of the three hundred and sixty-five windows shattered. The roof came down.'

Thomson wrote that 'the last vestiges of the Anglo-Irish landlord system had passed away'. This was not quite true. Those Anglo-Irish who lingered on, according to Patricia Cockburn, were 'mostly elderly, who maintained their old exclusiveness, became more and more isolated, living like a small endangered tribe, ripe to be studied by visiting anthropologists'. Like the rest of Ireland they could adhere to the old ways. During the 1950s Patrick O'Sullivan observed from his cottage in Co. Kerry life in the big house at Callinafercy. There were still servants living downstairs producing elaborate meals. 'I remember the massive open fireplace surrounded by a gilt-edged mirror, an upright harmonium, the spreading antlers of the giant Irish elk over the door, the sombre portrait of the first Earl of Milltown which hung on the wall above the floral chaise longue.' Someone could write a paper on the significance of elk horns in Anglo-Irish life.

CHAPTER 21

Brown Bag Bulging

Brown bag bulging with faded nothings;
A ticket for three pounds one and six
To Euston, London via Holyhead.

Brendan Kennelly

That man went blind through working for Ireland. Three shifts
of us he would see off and he would still be working at
midnight.

Jimmy Kenny, de Valera's bodyguard, at Dev's funeral

What had gone wrong? On the face of it life should have been full of happiness. In a changed world the period has been recalled with nostalgia and many reminiscences are filled with a sense of exhilaration and joy. Patrick O'Sullivan remembers 'a marvellous coloured way of life that in the space of thirty years had become little more than a memory'. Alice Taylor's account of 'a world of simplicity untouched by outside influences' in her book *To School Across the Fields* attracted a wide readership among those who talk about the good old days. But Bill Kelly insists that 'in fact they were mostly bad old days. Memory tends to be selective and to go for the soft option; to hold on to the good bits and bury the bad ones.'

Much had improved. The diseases which were killers less than twenty years before were being brought under control. The children who still went barefoot in summer no longer had legs twisted by rickets. Gastroenteritis, the killer of babies, was far less of a menace. Scarlet fever and diphtheria were virtually eliminated because of immunisation, vaccine would soon prevent polio and typhoid had become a rarity. The newly built fever hospitals were becoming almost as redundant as the emptying TB sanatoria.

Rural Ireland was as near as it ever would be to de Valera's dream. It charmed foreign visitors, the way Third World countries attract tourists today. A *Sunday Times* correspondent, Elizabeth Nicholson, who toured Ireland at the end of the 1950s, recommended her readership to come and discover a peasant lifestyle and beautiful countryside that was nearby; English travellers did not have to go to Greece to discover such delights. Staying in Tipperary in the summer of 1960, Nancy Mitford wrote to Evelyn Waugh, 'I'm stunned by the beauty, emptiness & *pure* pre-new-world atmosphere of Ireland.' But more perceptively another Englishwoman, Marigold Armitage, wrote how 'the spell of the land . . . owes much to the enormous, the subtle and speculative magic of the unsuccessful'.

The English judge summing up in the case Honor Tracy brought against the *Sunday Times* concluded, 'What is really said by Miss Tracy is this: the majority of the parishioners of this parish – yes, and in many other parishes in the twenty-six counties – are desperately poor, poorly housed, lacking proper sanitation and electric light. They don't have to consider whether they have cigarettes. They can't even afford meat.'

When Eileen O'Casey, visiting Ireland from England, walked through Athlone watching people going to Benediction at the Cathedral, she noticed how 'most of them seemed so poor that I could not help thinking about the pennies they had probably contributed to the Cathedral building fund and wondering whether the money might have been better spent . . . in improving their lives'.

Unemployment was universal. In Lismore George O'Brien remembered those who had regular work, a few postmen, a handful working at the castle, and a very small number of tradesmen. 'As for the rest, grave digging, clearing up after a storm, helping out at threshing and beet-snagging, a day here, a day there, filling in their time with Public Assistance and begetting children.' There were few with money to spend in the pubs. The poor boys of Lismore played handball or soccer with a rubber ball that was cheaper and lasted longer than a hurley stick. 'It made good sense to favour soccer. Sooner or later . . . every youngster in the lane was bound for the boat.'

Driving around the hills and lakes of Cavan, Hubert Butler noted the isolation signalled by letter-boxes on trees, lonely petrol pumps and small shops in boreens selling 'boot laces, aspirins, doses for bullocks and long Cavan spades . . . more exotic commodities like chocolate creams are soft and blotchy with age'. Butler was too glib in blaming the 'stampede' of emigration on foreign influence; he accused not only everybody's target, the British Sunday newspapers, but also the seductive propaganda of 'Mrs Dale's Diary', which told of a paradise where 'everyone has a car and refrigerator and nobody has to struggle with rushes'.

Rural life was not only depressing and poverty-stricken, it was also boring. Patrick Kavanagh wrote how 'the people in the country don't want their own drab life and the old dead balladry tossed back at them'. The dismal nature of small towns was evident in the views of the Publicity Manager of Thomas Cook who motored around Ireland in 1961. 'We found the amenities were exactly the same as they would have been in 1914 . . . the dirty, grimy little bars into which you daren't take a lady, which break up the monotony of grey, humdrum shops, the complete lack of public lavatories, the limitations of entertainment to one-horse cinemas, the limitations of eating . . .' The *Tipperary Star* reported a meeting of the local town council: 'Regarding the question of erecting two public lavatories in the town . . . Mr Cahill said: "I don't know of any urban area in the county with a ladies' and gents' lavatory. You cannot have a low rate and go in for these high-brow schemes."'

Small farms, particularly in the West, were increasingly unviable. Agricultural output stagnated as methods changed infinitely slowly. Hay and oats were harvested with a scythe and when the weather permitted, the pretty handkerchief-topped haycocks were painstakingly built. Patrick O'Sullivan watched his father cutting hay with a scythe, carefully leaving a patch uncut around a corncrake's nest. There were still farmers who threshed their oats with a flail.

Such farms were on the decrease as uneconomic holdings were abandoned or consolidated by larger farms. In towns like Bantry the weekly markets and monthly fairs declined as cattle were taken to larger areas like Skibbereen and Bandon. Around the coast fishing was beginning its dramatic decline.

In 1954 Heinrich Böll spent some time in Ireland and recorded his impressions in a journal. Thirty years later he would reflect that he had seen the county 'at that historic moment when it was just beginning to leap over a century and a half and catch up with another five'. His Teutonic eye observed much that was primitive and backward. Ireland in the mid-fifties, caught between the impoverishment of the old world and the expectation of the new, was contrasted in his mind with the rapid post-war development of Germany.

In Dublin, he wrote, 'in the slums around St Patrick's squalor still huddles in many a corner . . . dirt sometimes lies in black flakes on the window panes. In the dark yards, the ones Swift's eyes saw, this dirt has been piled up for decades – in the windows of the shops lay a confused variety of junk.'

Throughout his journey Böll noticed the desolation of the villages with their barefoot children, and the sense of despair which he found everywhere. Emigration was talked about feverishly. For tens of thousands there was little else to do except follow Shaw's advice: 'Leave Ireland.' Some boys dreamt of staying behind and finding a vocation; for girls the ambition was to become nurses in English hospitals where their training would be paid for: '. . . favourable terms, vacations with pay, and once a year a free trip home'. They would take with them the morals that would create problems in the fields of midwifery and gynaecology.

Nancy Mitford spent time in Tipperary in a 'dark green velvet land . . . dotted with small house like the ancestral home of President Kennedy, the whitewashed box with two tiny windows'. Noting how 'the plan on which the villages are built, one long immensely wide main street which can be used as a market, bordered by tiny houses, accentuates their emptiness', she added, perhaps with some exaggeration, that 'every village, however small and poor, has a luggage shop'.

She found the countryside 'beautiful beyond words and empty'. Roads, too, were deserted, 'bare of traffic except occasionally an enormous man spanking along in a donkey cart or a Rolls-Royce with American tourists buried in white satin luggage. The cottagers' dogs are so unused to motor traffic that they crouch and spring dangerously at passing cars.' Few besides the doctor, priest and vet had cars.

Even for those in employment there was little inducement to stay. While the average labourer in Ireland earned £5.00 to £7.00 a week, in England he could earn £20 working for McAlpine's Fusiliers. Böll wrote, 'At times one would like to believe that this emigration is some sort of habit, a duty they take for granted – but the economic situation really makes it necessary . . . One thing is certain, that of Mrs D's nine children, five or six will have to emigrate.' He was touched by the scenes which had been part of Irish life for so long, 'those farewells at Irish stations, at bus stops in the middle of a bog when tears blend with raindrops and the Atlantic wind is blowing'.

Bill Kelly remembered how 'uncertainty stalked the countryside like a plague. Overnight you could lose almost everything, your father, your girl, your best friend. Everything worked in reverse to the way it should have been. Summer and Christmas were the worst times.'

Recently I met an elderly Irishman in London who had emigrated around this time; he told me in a hesitant cockney that when he left an Irish-speaking village in a Connaught Gaeltacht, whose people shared one bicycle as a means of transport, he could not speak a word of English. He had never gone back.

Dónall Mac Amhlaigh, another Irish speaker, prepared to leave his home: 'Monday 13.3.1951. This morning I signed on for the last time and then carried a hundred weight of coal home for my mother. I have every thing done for her now, the garden planted and cleaned and the old house spruced up a bit on the outside. I'll be able to help her a bit more than that from now on when I'll have a few pence to send her from England. The old lady kept up her courage wonderfully until the time came for me to set off. The tears came then, I didn't delay too long bidding her goodbye. I hugged her once, grabbed my bag and off with me. Indeed you'd think that even the cat knew I was going, for she followed me out mewing piteously.'

With droves of others Mac Amhlaigh set off to become a navvy. After the acquisition of a sailing ticket the emigrant could expect the bleak cross-Channel voyage on a crowded mail-boat like the *Princess Maud* which would be smelling of vomit. Stairways became blocked with people, just as they had been during the years of the Emergency, and songs still echoed around the bars. There followed the long misery of the midnight train, comfortless since callous shipping and railway companies did not care. In the first light of dawn haggard faces looked out at the miles of walled suburbs speeding by 'and suddenly', wrote Mac Amhlaigh, 'I felt lonely all over again. I started thinking about the old house with the pots of tea we'd drink before going to bed, and my heart felt like a solid black mass inside my breast.'

When Mac Amhlaigh found work in the English Midlands, he encountered 'a little jackeen working here and he'd make you feel right ashamed. He started off at dinner-time in front of the English about how little work there was in Ireland and about the poverty. I was about to give him a puck in the gob, but I knew that if I did, the others would know that he was speaking the truth.'

Among those who worked to relieve the lot of the Irish in England was Bishop Casey. He helped to set up the organisation 'Shelter', which catered for many homeless Irish people. In Ireland he had noticed how the young were leaving in droves. 'I was visiting homes . . . and suddenly Jimmy was gone, Mary was gone, Joe was gone. I asked what had happened to them. Did they get a job? Did they get digs? Were they practising their religion?'

In many cases they were not. A letter to the *Furrow* in 1950 read, 'Dear Reverend Editor – While staying in a hotel in England whose staff included nearly two hundred Irish girls and not a few Irish men . . . not more than 2 or 3 per cent ever go to Mass on Sunday even when they have all Sunday off. And they have a saying among themselves: "God is only in Ireland."'

At the highest levels emigration was sanctioned, playing its part in government policy-making. It was feared that if too many stayed at home the unemployment situation would become so much worse. About 400,000 emigrated during the decade at a rate that had not been seen since the 1880s. The vast majority of those who left were young and most of them went to England. Many emigrated from working-class Dublin. Towns and villages in the West reached a stage where they appeared deserted. Böll wrote: 'None would tell us exactly when and why the village had been abandoned; there are so many deserted houses in Ireland, you can count them on any two-hour walk.' In the sixties John Healy lamented the emptying of his home town, Charlestown in Co. Mayo: 'John Yes-Boy Durkan's is closed. No one knocks on Teresa Cassidy's counter any more . . . jovial Jim Gallaher's is no more. Jack O'Donohue's is closed . . . And Tom McCarthy's place. And James Parson's place. And the saddler Vesey . . .'

When Mac Amhlaigh returned home to eat 'a fine Irish dinner, bacon, cabbage, roast and boiled potatoes with a nice sweet to follow . . . I was the only one of the family present. Kevin was in Coventry, Neil in Hampshire, Brian in Sussex and Dympna, our only sister, in London.' He saw the poverty around him. 'You'd be hard put to counting how many people passed you in old worn clothes. Most of them are in threadbare overcoats and their shoes are badly worn down – you don't see people like that in England at all nowadays.'

Paradoxically, as the flight from the land continued, changes were taking place that were bringing the country into the mid-twentieth century. The use of the telephone was increasing amid ample numbers of complaints about the quality of its service; between 1939 and 1953 the number of telephones had risen from 50,000 to 100,000, 40,000 of which were in the provinces. The opening of the Store Street bus station in 1953 emphasised how the country was networked with buses.

Farms were being mechanised and the horse's function dwindled to appearances at race meetings or its export value as steaks for Continentals, the cause of a long-standing row at that time. I can remember our first small grey Ferguson tractor. But mechanisation meant that larger farms employed fewer people, another factor in the emigration statistics. The switch-over to combine harvesters meant that straw was cut into small pieces; people in thatched cottages found it difficult to get straw of suitable lengths for re-thatching.

Electricity brought churns, separators and milking machines to farmers who could afford them. Throughout the decade the drive towards universal rural electrification continued. In 1953 the hydro-electric scheme on the River Lee was launched, bringing power to the south-west. The old days of damp beds and tilley lamps were to depart at last, although caution still tempered the acceptance of electricity. Around Durrow rural electrification was completed by 1956, but it was not until the early sixties that every house in the town was electrified.

The daily routine of women's lives began to change. The range replaced the open fire and electricity brought what were still considered luxuries. Another change was in clothing; instead of every garment having to be made at home, a woman could avail herself of cheap mass-produced clothes. Running water offered an essential improvement, but its general installation was painfully slow.

Caution hampered water and sewage schemes, which, without the glamour and less of the priests' say-so, proceeded at a much slower pace. While towns and cities were beginning to take water on tap for granted, even by the late sixties eighty per cent of those living in rural areas relied on water from the roof tank or the daily trip to the old-fashioned pressure pump with the lion's head. In Kerry, Patrick O'Sullivan and his mother walked every day to a well which was located in a field about half a mile away, years after electricity had been installed in their house. For most of the fifties when his mother washed the floor, she boiled water in a big pot on a pivoting crane over the fire before kneeling down to wash the cement section by section.

In 1966 I visited a small group of houses with a population of sixty people stretching down a steep hill; the water supply was at the bottom so the daily journey was more difficult than in most places because it meant going down and then up again with the full buckets. The water came from a spring which poured across a muddy field where cattle grazed; the residents collected it early in the morning or late in the evening, when they considered that the supply would be less polluted. No strong-minded person among them gave the people the drive to help themselves in the face of indifferent bureaucracy. This community lived only twenty miles from Dublin.

Self-help could be a hazardous business, as became evident in the story of Canon James McDyer. When he arrived in the remote parish of Glencolumbkille in Co. Donegal in 1961, he found one of the dwindling communities which were spread all over isolated places in the West. A despairing number of his parish had emigrated, amounting to almost eighty per cent in an area where small farmers were earning £14 a year. 'Here I saw it happening before my eyes, for Glencolumbkille was dying and the killer disease was emigration.'

Canon McDyer canvassed his parishioners, and like so many other rural priests persuaded them to go for electricity. For the occasion of switching on he organised a pageant. 'First came the bearer of a rush light, next an ordinary candle, then a hob-lamp, the hurricane lamp, the wick lamp with a globe, the tilley and Aladdin lamp, and finally the electric torch . . .' Then the main switch was pulled and the whole area was illuminated with electric light. McDyer followed this triumph by persuading his parishioners to take on a water scheme. Although many of his subsequent ideas of co-operatives, factories and the folk village to draw tourists, invited financial disaster, his energy and drive induced a permanent sense of pride among the people of Glencolumbkille and they were all the better for it.

During the economic downturn, Córas Iompair Éireann, the national railway company, was foremost among organisations who were constantly losing money. By 1958 drastic measures were called for and Tod Andrews was appointed its chairman with the brief of making CIE pay its way within five years. The solution was a savage cutting of branch lines throughout the country. Among the casualties was the Harcourt Street line which ran from Dublin through the inner suburbs and out to Bray; it ran its last train on 31 December 1958. My uncle was the only senior member of staff who opposed this decision. With the subsequent development of the city, the closure proved disastrous. When my uncle retired, not only was he able to include the words 'I Told You So' in his retirement speech, but he also produced a photograph album of the railway lines and bridges which he had helped to repair after they had been destroyed during the Civil War by Dev's people.

In Dublin in 1953 the first of the An Tóstal celebrations took place. The word means a pageant or muster; the Fianna Fáil Government of the time thought that it would cheer people up during a period of severe economic gloom. It did not, although some laughed when a Trinity student threw its symbol, the Bowl of Light which had been installed on O'Connell Bridge, into the murky waters of the Liffey.

An Tóstal's lasting legacy was the Dublin Theatre Festival, which went through some stormy patches, particularly in 1958 when the committee proposed productions of an adaptation of Joyce's *Ulysses* and the world première of O'Casey's *The Drums of Father Ned*; unsurprisingly, Archbishop McQuaid stood with the moral majority. Censorship was having a final fling and the suppressed 'evil literature' included works by George Orwell, Noël

Coward, Simone de Beauvoir and Margaret Mead as well as local pornographers like Brendan Behan, John McGahern and Edna O'Brien. When a priest said in public that he liked O'Brien's early books which were imbued with gentle sexuality, his provincial promptly received an angry letter from Dr McQuaid condemning such views.

In the capital, affluent home buyers were being enticed to the Ideal Home Exhibition where new designs were on display. 'You walk from the kitchen through an opening without a door ("the open plan") into a spacious dining alcove . . .' Soon new suburbs would spread over the Liffey plain. Tenements were being slowly abandoned for new housing estates at Crumlin, Ballyfermot Donnycarney and Inchicore. The rotting Georgian buildings remained: 'you are looking at a lovely shell; the old glory has departed, a new one is not yet in sight', wrote Honor Tracy. She could not prophesy their substitution with substandard ill-designed office buildings that greed and profiteering would bring about in the next decade.

Vanishing landmarks were still there, shops like Cassidy's, Kellett's and Pim's, as well as the Capitol and the Theatre Royal, which would be knocked down and replaced by a huge office block dominating Hawkins Street, considered by some to be the ugliest building in Dublin. Around Grafton Street espresso coffee had made its appearance and the coffee shops mingled with the pubs: Fuller's, Mitchell's, Bewley's, Robert's, el Habana, the Gaiety, F.M.'s, the Palm Grove, the Zodiac and others. Near O'Connell Bridge flashed the Bovril sign and the neon Donnelly's sausage flying out of its pan. The Pillar stood in the centre of O'Connell Street, strung with its cinemas and the new ice-cream parlours; a wire cage to prevent suicides surrounded the weather-worn figure on top. When Böll was in Dublin the newspapers were filled with the familiar argument as to whether the old sailor should be replaced by the figure of the Virgin Mary. He did not have much longer up there.

Up from the provinces, Edna O'Brien's country girls enjoyed the new freedom – 'lights, faces, traffic, the enormous vitality of people hurrying somewhere'. It was said that the boom in ballroom dancing meant that every night 4,500 people in Dublin enjoyed this form of relaxation. Those were the great days of the Crystal and the Four Provinces with their circulating lights made from pieces of mirror. Not until the sixties would the era of show bands get under way, when Albert Reynolds started his new improved string of dancehalls beginning with Cloudland near Roosky, Co. Roscommon. Meanwhile, the staider dancers in Dublin could dance Saturday night away at the Gresham Hotel for eight shillings and sixpence. They could attend the Sunday afternoon dance at the Metropole and then go on to another one in the evening. 'We'd dance, dance, dance!' Dancing continued to be one easy way of defying the clergy.

In 1952 Honor Tracy published *Mind You, I've Said Nothing*, which was spiced with malicious observations that annoyed her fellow countrymen. She noted the way acquaintances took pains to avoid people they recognised: 'A walk in Dublin is full of such encounters. They explain the wary look in the eyes of Dubliners and the strong crab-like sidle of the more nervous among them.'

Among her targets was the ordeal of St Patrick's Day: 'Nothing . . . but hurling and football matches and the dog show at Ballsbridge.' Everything was closed out of respect for the saint. Christabel Bielenberg noted the dreariness of the procession passing by the row of top-hatted figures outside the GPO: 'A few drab floats moving down O'Connell Street followed by a motley procession of – to me – very old men in caps and raincoats, who never seemed quite able to march in step. A saffron kilted band thumping out patriotic airs with bagpipes and drums . . .' No wonder, thought Tracy, 'people walked drearily through the streets with dull Sunday faces longing for it to be over . . . *Ennui*, which is always just around the corner in Ireland, now openly stalked abroad.'

She worked for *The Bell*, now edited by Peadar O'Donnell who kept up the standards imposed by O'Faolain, who would become head of the Arts Council in 1956, much to the displeasure of Archbishop McQuaid. O'Donnell, according to Tracy, 'never allowed the depressing state of affairs in Ireland to weigh on his spirits. He was fully alive to it, of course: a favourite comment of his was, that the young men who formerly came to him with manifestos now only wanted a fiver.'

Other magazines made their contribution to Irish life – religious ones like *Studies*, the *Furrow* and the old friend, the *Irish Capuchin Annual*, and such influential voices as *Envoy*, edited by John Ryan, *Poetry Ireland* and *The Dublin Magazine*. This had been founded in 1923 by the poet Seamus O'Sullivan, the pseudonym of James Starkey. The times were against the success of a literary magazine – the Civil War was raging – and no one, including the editor himself, expected it to survive the year. But it continued over the years, in spite of the editor's reputation for booziness, publishing almost every Irish writer of merit. After Starkey's death in 1958, it was revived as *The Dubliner* and subsequently took on the name of its distinguished predecessor.

In 1952 there occurred the meteor of *Kavanagh's Weekly*, which lasted for thirteen issues before sinking into insolvency. Using his brother Peter's money and some of Peter's opinions, Patrick Kavanagh displayed some of the malaise of the time in bad-tempered attacks on life in general and de Valera, whom he called the Undertaker, in particular. 'Undertaker's harvest . . . Mr de Valera is acknowledged by much public consent as a decent man and an outstanding Irish patriot. Actually it is very hard to find evidence that will sustain this view.'

The social column of *Kavanagh's Weekly* was entitled 'Graftonia':

'Graftonia. Dreary pictures, dreary people, dreary weather. Nothing changes at the RHA exhibitions. They could have put the pictures of 1941 on the walls and the 1941 audience on the floor.'

'Graftonia. Dull people. At State functions the company is composed entirely of the most unimaginative . . . politicians, bishops and business men. Nobody there to give a note of distinction.'

Kavanagh attacked the Mother and Child Scheme – 'it stank a little'; doctors

– 'the doctor is a technician and no more'; and compulsory Irish, to which Brian O'Nolan as Myles na gCopaleen responded in an elegant letter. Myles also condemned the adherents of the Irish programme, although 'one should not abstain from champagne simply because the upper flight of prostitutes drink it'. Myles's conclusions are those of any sensible enthusiast. 'Any notion of reviving Irish as the universal language of the country is manifestly impossible and ridiculous, but the continued awareness here of the Gaelic norm of word and thought is vital to the preservation of our peculiar and admired methods of handling English.'

The Kavanaghs also ran a column that copied the *New Statesman*'s 'This England'. 'This Ireland' reflected some preoccupations of the time:

'Sixteen girls at Shannon are making enough leprechauns to net the airport hundreds of dollars this year.'

A breach of promise case in the Midlands involved a plaintiff jilted at the age of thirty-seven. 'He . . . said: "Would you not be happy with me at Shanvous?" He took out his Rosary beads and she said she would not doubt his word. He said he would put the price of a good bullock into a ring. He gave her a Rosary as a present but subsequently he could not afford to get married until his brother, the priest in England, had been made a parish priest . . .'

Kavanagh's Weekly reflected not only personal bitterness and humour but also the uneasiness among writers and artists of the time whose talents were all too often doused in booze. They have been called a tragic generation who found little outlet or reward for their work. They were perpetually short of money and in their own land they were not appreciated. If censorship did not hamper them – Brendan Behan's *Borstal Boy* was banned in 1959 – many of their countrymen agreed with the Reverend Felim O'Brien of UCD who described Irish writers as 'an insignificant minority who put dirt in their books because they are not good enough to sell on their merits'. Kavanagh thought that 'sentimental pietism sold better'.

Before the pubs opened, the poet from Monaghan would be in Bewley's Café drinking Jersey milk, flailing his arms around; acquaintances would take cover behind their newspapers, hoping that they would not be approached for half a crown. Otherwise it was the pub. The *Irish Statesman* described him as 'hankering on a bar-stool, defining alcohol as the worst enemy of the imagination. With a malevolent insult . . . the Master orders a further measure . . . His acolytes, sylphlike redheads, dewy-eyed brunettes, two hard-faced intellectual blondes, three rangy university poets and several semi-bearded painters . . . "Yous have no merit, no merit at all," he insults them . . . they love it. He suddenly leaves to get lunch in the Bailey and have something to win on the second favourite. He'll be back.' On the strength of these comments Kavanagh issued a writ for libel.

Much has been written of that penurious time, of the feuds between Kavanagh and Behan, the squalor at MacDaid's and around the Catacombs where, according to Ulick O'Connor, 'the open necked shirt revealing the navel clogged with fur, the unwashed body . . . and the overcoat with its aroma of spilt Guinness was a standard outfit for many writers and artists of the time'.

Those who were not recognised geniuses had to tread warily. When Patricia and Claud Cockburn came to Dublin they tried to mingle with the impoverished intellectuals. 'The chief characteristic was petty jealousy and to be really popular you had to be a failure.' Claud Cockburn attracted abuse: 'Time server, hypocrite, West Briton were some of the epithets by which he was denounced before Flann O'Brien . . . fell down on the pub floor and continued to rail further insults.'

Not every writer or artist regarded the Dublin pub as a sanctuary. Joseph Hone, Monk Gibbon and Jack Yeats did not consider a tipple as very important in their lives. Was it significant that they were Protestants? Probably not. The writer and artist Ralph Cusack, associated with the White Stag movement, possessed, according to Anthony Cronin, 'the usual Anglo-Irish ambiguity, hating the English for their dullness and hypocrisy and yet not feeling at home among the Catholic Irish either'. Cusack was our neighbour in Wicklow, living near Annamoe in a house which is said to have the steepest drive in Ireland. Among his many interests was selling rare flowers whose beauties he described in fulsome catalogues. His parties were wild even by the standards of the time. I used to give him lifts when I came across his lonely figure striding over Calary bog; he thought nothing of walking ten miles and more homeward after an evening's carousal.

One signal that an era was ending came in 1953 with the death of Maud Gonne at the age of eighty-seven. To the last she was a determined revolutionary, and had recently been supporting her son Sean in his attempt to make his brand of Republicanism respectable by embodying it in a constitutional party. To the end of her life, amid all the drama and setbacks, she shared some of de Valera's dream that Ireland would enter a new age adapted to Pearse's ideas; the golden age that eventually came was very different. Mícheál Mac Liammóir, her fellow convert to Catholicism, used to meet her regularly: 'Tea with Madam Gonne MacBride. This ceremony, however frequent, has an invariable effect on my romantic pleasure. Her heroic and now cavernous beauty, made sombre by the customary black draperies she wears, is . . . illuminated by an increasing gentleness and humour; she has now what seems a faint far-away amusement at life.'

Three years earlier, another handsome and equally maddening old icon died from the consequences of falling out of an apple tree. Shaw left a third of his estate to the National Gallery of Ireland in recognition of the time he had spent as a young man wandering around the gallery gaining knowledge. Soon *My Fair Lady* would produce royalties of £500,000 to be spent on fine paintings like the gold altar cross of Giovanni di Paolo and the Avignon *Annunciation*. Shaw's money was the impetus for renewed interest in an institution which now attracts hundreds of thousands of visitors annually. In the fifties I enjoyed what must have been a rarity for a major gallery – absence of people. The rooms with their polished floors and attendants deep in their newspapers appeared to be hung with paintings just for me. It must have been the same for Shaw. Some maintain that the spiritual nourishment we gain from looking at paintings is related to a decline in religion.

One room in the National Gallery is now devoted to Jack Yeats's glowing mystical paintings. In the early fifties it was still possible for ordinary people to buy them by visiting Victor Waddington's gallery in Duke Street where they were priced by size. To his surprise, Yeats was beginning to make some money. 'Graftonia is becoming self-conscious,' reported Kavanagh. 'There's a Jack Yeats painting in Davy Byrne's and a Le Brocquy tapestry in the Monument Creamery.'

In 1953 Yeats had an exhibition as usual in Waddington's gallery. He called it 'in all sorts of happy ways the best I ever had'. A show in Belfast the following year was his last. In old age he spent winters in the Portobello Nursing Home, whose rooms were filled with watery light diffused from the Grand Canal. The English art critic John Berger was moved when he visited Yeats: 'His face is that of an old, tall, upright man; no literary image should be used to describe the face of this life-long image maker.' The image maker died on 28 March 1957.

When Sean Lemass came into power in 1959 – full of vigour to attack unemployment, inflation and emigration – poor beautiful simple dismal candlelit Ireland flew out of the window. De Valera was safely put away in the Park; he was twice elected President, winning the second time by the narrowest of margins – even his symbolic leadership was too much for many people. Now Lemass was in charge and a new concept of what it was like to be Irish was set in motion.

Lemass had come a long way from his original adherence to protecting native industries. His achievements during the thirties in encouraging some sort of economic stability during the years of depression, and his efforts during the Emergency as Minister of Supplies, were preliminaries to the transformation he was to bring about. He has been described as a typical product of the twentieth century with his ad-hoc socialism, his state planning and his habit of dividing the economy into a public and private sector. Such a combination of realism and energy had not had a previous outing in Ireland.

Before de Valera's departure Lemass had been at work. As Minister for Industry and Commerce he commissioned T. K. Whitaker at the Department of Finance to outline the first Programme for Economic Expansion; he put this into operation as soon as he came into power. Foreign companies were given generous tax incentives, new bodies were created, existing bodies updated and an export drive launched.

The results were startling. Economic output increased by almost a quarter between 1958 and 1963 and, as a result, unemployment fell sharply. The decrease in emigration was dramatic, a reduction of forty per cent in five years. Lemass laid the foundations for Ireland's entry into the European Economic

Community, although because of de Gaulle's intransigence towards Britain, Ireland did not join until 1973, two years after Lemass's death. De Valera outlasted him by four years.

As agriculture stopped its medieval practices overnight, the small farmer was no longer seen as the backbone of the countryside. The flail and the scythe were hung up; there was no more stooking corn and turning hay with a fork. Labouring ceased as a way of life as the keeping of accounts took over. Going to the creamery with the bulk carrier took ten minutes and was no longer the social occasion it had been when the churn was carried behind the donkey. Marts took over from the fairs and their attendant filth, excitements and heartbreak.

Changes came tumbling in: economic transformations, the coming of television and the pill. The Catholic Church's power had amazed outsiders. Christabel Bielenberg 'could only wonder at the trivialities of such authoritarian rules and regulations designed to keep the people of Ireland on a straight and narrow, but utterly cheerless path'. But such power was on the wane and ultimately the Church would be weakened by a series of grotesque scandals. Ironically, the first blow to its authority came from the Vatican itself with the encyclicals *Mater et Magistra* and *Populorum Progressio*, which both stressed the value of the sort of social democracy the Irish Church had always feared. How could ecclesiastical power belong to the Irish nation? The Vatican Council, with its emphasis on the modernisation of ritual and its intention to usher in the age of the laity, was like the iceberg that sank the *Titanic* – little difference was noticed at first. But Archbishop McQuaid, who was unable to absorb the new sweetness and light among Catholics which reflected the spirit of the times and acknowledged that Protestants were Christians, would be proved right.

The current decline of faith is reflected in the lack of new priests. In 1997 the Dublin diocese desperately initiated a promotional campaign entitled 'Who are the men in black?' As a result, eighty hopefuls attended the seminary open day, out of whom there were 'three or four' possible recruits. In 1965 the seminary of Holy Cross College, Clonliffe, ordained eighteen priests; in 1998 three were ordained. At the same time the college had only eleven seminarians, with no new entrants for 1998.

In the North of Ireland, where religion is a badge of tribe, congregations have not dwindled. Here Lemass failed; the cup of tea at Stormont on 14 January 1965 with Captain O'Neill was meant to express common sense but it only displayed dangerous complacency. The meeting was not only a false dawn, but it also heralded a plunge into darkness. The North of Ireland could never be ignored; it is always a menace at the side of the Republic like a raging Siamese twin.

In 1966 the fiftieth anniversary of the 1916 Rising was celebrated with gusto. The festivities were initiated unofficially with the blowing up of Nelson's Pillar on 8 March. On the following day, Nelson's battered old head was displayed on the stage of the Gate Theatre where the musical group, The Dubliners, were playing. The cheers of the audience rang to the roof. Today it is on display in the Civic Museum.

Did the triumphalism of the official commemoration contribute to the violence that followed in the North? Not according to anti-revisionists like Declan Kiberd, furious at the subsequent miserable toned-down celebration of the seventy-fifth anniversary that took place in 1991. On that occasion five surviving veterans attended; a sixth stayed away as a protest at the betrayal of the ideals of 1916.

This does not please anti-revisionists; nor does the playing down of the past and the ferocious glamour and achievement of the heroes of the Rising and the Troubles. There is an awful logic in the proposition that if a small band of men and women could bring Britain to its knees in the years between 1916 and 1921, why should it not happen again? There is a belief that the recent bloody stretch of Troubles in the North has brought Ireland full circle since the Rising.

In an essay published in *Revising the Rising* in 1991, Kiberd wrote, 'The notion that a glorification of 1916 in poems or ballads leads to recruits for the IRA is insulting to the intelligence of the general public and of the IRA. What created the modern IRA was not any cultural force but the bleak sectarian realities of life in the corrupt statelet of Northern Ireland . . . The idea that IRA violence is rooted in the Christian Brothers' teaching of history is far too simple to account for today's complex and cruel world.'

The anger of anti-revisionists arises largely from the continued reluctance of people in the South to become involved in the Northern conflict in spite of ghastly provocation. In 1937 de Valera thrust into the Constitution two statements that have inflamed Northern Unionists ever since. Article 2 (which was rescinded by the referendum of May 1998) affirmed that 'the national territory consists of the whole island of Ireland, its islands and the territorial seas', and Article 3 that 'pending the reintegration of the national territory' the laws enacted by Dáil Éireann would apply only to the Twenty-Six Counties. But the country seems to have slowly evolved towards the position that a United Ireland should be no more than an aspiration.

Meanwhile, as the sixties advanced, the country moved at her own pace towards the form of prosperity initiated by Lemass. The pretty world presented in the film *The Quiet Man* and illustrated in John Hinde's bright postcards was disappearing. Thatched cottages gave way to bungalows, boreens turned into motorways. In the early sixties a few shawlies were to be seen among the mini-skirts in Cork, but the old women of Kinsale, Bandon and Clonakilty who wore their magnificent cloaks died. The much-derided age of mohair suits, Mercedes cars and jiggery-pokery was in place.

People were becoming more sophisticated and needed guidance about how to behave. In 1968 Martin Mulloy's *Book of Irish Courtesy* was an indication of how far Irish society had changed in a decade. Mulloy instructed and recommended:

Eating out . . . two types of menu – À la Carte and Table d'Hôte . . . the
Ladies invariably take sweet . . . Coffee may be had white or black . . .
Liqueurs very small and rather special types of drinks . . . they are
helpful to the indigestion . . .
Drinking . . . must be done noiselessly. A tea cup is held between the
thumb and first finger only . . .
Lounge suit . . . for informal dinners and weddings, cocktail parties,
funerals, receptions, christenings . . . openings of Church and Schools.
On all these occasions it is bad taste to appear in sports clothes . . .
Eating . . . It is very rude to fill the mouth with food, above all when it
causes the cheeks to bulge. Masticating is done noiselessly and with the
lips closed. To speak with food in the mouth can be very objectionable . . .
Mode of Speech . . . A 'grawnd' accent because of its association with the
foreigner and the Ascendancy is regarded with some suspicion . . .
Certain phrases such as 'D'ye understand?', 'Ye Know', 'D'ye get me?',
'Yer man' and words such as 'God', 'Hell', 'bloody' and 'damn' are
never used in polite company . . .
Wine . . . Ask the Waiter – you will find he is quite human . . .

Up in the Phoenix Park, the tall sombre courteous patriarch presided over the
initial stages of the transformation. No longer did he wear the cloak with the
silver clasp, but the undertaker's overcoat. It was deeply ironic that during the
last part of his life de Valera was blind. How much did he recognise that his
dream was fast fading? He had thought that the new country would lead by
example. When he first came to power he broadcast from the new Athlone radio
station on 6 February 1933: 'You sometimes hear Ireland charged with a narrow
and intolerant nationalism, but Ireland today has no dearer hope than this: that
true to her own holiest traditions she may humbly serve the truth and help by
truth to save the world.'

He had these ideas in mind during those strange moments of the Emergency
when, in the midst of the world's agony, he toured Ireland reclaiming his dream
and begging his people to call their children by Irish names. In its innocence,
his much-derided St Patrick's Day speech ignored the thin line between
frugality and poverty. In fact the dream was beautiful, a redefining of Parnassus
in the romping of happy children, the contests of athletic youth and the
laughter of happy maidens. His mistake was to believe with the greatest fervour
that in this 'dreary Eden' (O'Faolain's phrase) people would be 'satisfied with
frugal comfort'.

Before he retired from office in 1973 he was the oldest serving Head of State in
the world. He died on the last day of August 1975 aged ninety-three. His funeral
took place on 3 September. The Mass in the Pro-Cathedral was conducted by his
grandson, An tAthair Sean Ó Cuiv, who wore the white vestments which had
been given to him by his grandfather two years before at his ordination. The Mass
was conducted in Latin and Irish; not a word of English was spoken.

Those in attendance included the President, Cearbhall Ó Dálaigh, and Fine Gael Taoiseach Liam Cosgrave, son of William Cosgrave who had been the Free State's first President and founder of the pro-Treaty Cumann na nGaedheal. Jack Lynch headed the Fianna Fáil mourners, who included old veterans holding their rosary beads as well as Frank Aiken and Sean MacEntee, the two surviving members of de Valera's first Government of 1932. Princess Grace of Monaco was there and so was the Protestant Archbishop George Simms; in the latter part of his life de Valera had been a good friend of the Church of Ireland.

Mozart's *Ave Verum*, which could be interpreted as a refrain of de Valera's Athlone speech, was sung by the Palestrina Choir and Our Lady's Choral Society. The sermon in Irish by Monsignor (later Cardinal) Ó Fiaich spoke of Dev's deep daily spirituality, a life full of natural dignity which required no conscious effort on his part and of a humility which recognised that everything was in the hand of God.

The coffin was slow-marched down O'Connell Street past crowds six and seven feet deep as the Army Number 1 Band played 'Wrap the Green Flag Round Me, Boys'.

At Glasnevin cemetery more veterans waited, including Michael Merriman who had been in Boland's Mill with de Valera; Tom O'Reilly who had been in the GPO and had earlier heard Pearse's speech at the graveside of O'Donovan Rossa; and Vinnie Byrne who had been a member of Michael Collins's 'squad' dealing with assassinations. None of them would talk about the Civil War.

The playing of 'The Croppy Boy' announced the arrival of the cortège at Glasnevin. The last lament was 'Go dTéighe Tu, Mo Mhuirnín, Slán', 'May You Go Well, My Love, Safely'.

Select Bibliography

Books

Aalen, F. H. A. and Brody, Hugh, *Gola: FHA* (Cork, 1969)
Abbeystrewry: A Parish Memoir (Cork, 1991)
Andrews, Tod, *Man of No Property* (Dublin, 1982)
Arensberg, Conrad, *The Irish Countryman* (Illinois, 1988);
Arensberg, Conrad and Kinnall, T., *Family and Community in Ireland* (Oxford, 1940)
Armitage, Marigold, *A Long Way to Go* (London, 1952)
Arnold, Mavis and Laski, Heather, *Children of the Poor Clares* (Dublin, 1985)

Barry, Tom, *Guerrilla Days in Ireland* (Cork, 1955)
Beagh History Project, *Beagh: A History and Heritage* (Athlone, 1995)
Bence-Jones, Mark, *Twilight of the Ascendancy* (London, 1987)
Bennett, Richard, *The Black and Tans* (London, 1960)
Betjeman, John, *Letters Volume One: 1926–1951* (London, 1994)
Bew, Paul, *Sean Lemass* (Dublin, 1995)
Bielenberg, Christabel, *The Road Ahead* (London, 1992)
Böll, Heinrich, trans. Vennewitz, Leila, *Irish Journal* (New York, 1983)
Bowen, Elizabeth, *The Shelbourne* (London, 1951)
Bowyer Bell, J., *The Secret Army of the IRA* (Dublin, 1970)
Broderick, John, *Fall From Grace* (Dingle, 1992)
Brody, Hugh, *Inishkillane: Change and Decline in the West of Ireland* (London, 1973)
Brown, Christy, *My Left Foot* (London, 1954)
Brown, Terence, *Ireland: A Social and Cultural History* (London, 1981)
Browne, Noel, *Against the Tide* (Dublin, 1986)
Butler, Hubert, *The Sub-prefect Should Have Held His Tongue* (Dublin, 1985);
   Escape from the Anthill (Dublin, 1986)

Callow, Simon, *Orson Welles: The Road to Xanadu* (London, 1995)
Campbell, Patrick, *My Life and Easy Times* (London, 1967)
Carroll, Joseph T., *Ireland in the War Years: 1939–1945* (Newton Abbot, 1975)
Carson, Julia (ed.), *Banned in Ireland: Censorship and the Irish Writer* (London, 1990)
Clarke, Austin, *A Penny in the Clouds* (London, 1968);
   Collected Poems (Dublin and Oxford, 1974)
Clarke, Kathleen, ed. Litton, Helen, *Revolutionary Woman* (Dublin, 1991)
Cockburn, Patricia, *Figure of Eight* (London, 1985)
Collis, Robert, *Marrowbone Lane: A Play in Three Acts* (Dublin, 1943);

To Be a Pilgrim (London, 1975)
Comerford, James, *My Kilkenny IRA Days* (Kilkenny, 1980)
Coogan, Tim Pat, *De Valera* (London, 1993);
    Michael Collins (London, 1994)
Corkery, Daniel, *The Hidden Ireland* (Dublin, 1925)
Costello, Peter and Farmer, Tony, *The Very Heart of the City: The Story of Denis Guiney and Clery's* (Dublin, 1992)
Cronin, Anthony, *Dead as Doornails* (Dublin, 1976);
    Samuel Beckett: The Last Modernist (London, 1996)
Crosbie, Paddy, *Your Dinner's Poured Out* (Dublin, 1985)
Cross, Eric, *The Tailor and Ansty* (Dublin, 1942)
Crossley Holland, Kevin, *Pieces of Eight* (London, 1972)
Crowley, Elaine, *Cowslips and Chainies: A Memoir of Dublin in the 1930s* (Dublin, 1996)
Crowley, Flor, *In West Cork Long Ago* (Cork, 1979)
Crozier, Brigadier General, *Ireland for Ever* (London, 1932)
Cusack, Ralph, *Cadenza* (London, 1958)

Danaher, Kevin, *Irish Customs and Beliefs* (Dublin, 1964)
Delany, Ruth, *Athlone* (Athlone, 1991)
Devas, Nicolette, *Two Flamboyant Fathers* (London, 1966)
Dhonnchadha, Máirín Ní and Dorgan, Theo (eds), *Revising the Rising: Essays* (Derry, 1991)
Donoghue, Denis, *Warrenpoint* (London, 1991)
Duff, Frank, *Miracles on Tap* (Dublin, 1961)
Duggan, John P., *Neutral Ireland and the Third Reich* (Dublin, 1985)
Dunne, Sean (ed.), *The Cork Anthology* (Cork, 1993);
    The Ireland Anthology (Dublin, 1997)

Eagleton, Terry, *Heathcliff and the Great Hunger* (London, 1995)
Eipper, Chris, *Hostage to Fortune: Bantry Bay and the Encounter with Gulf Oil* (St John's, Newfoundland, 1989)
Everett, Catherine, *Bricks and Flowers* (London, 1949)

Fanning, Ronan, *Independent Ireland* (London, 1930)
Farmer, Tony, *Ordinary Lives* (Dublin, 1992)
Farrell, M. J. (Molly Keane), *Taking Chances* (London, 1929);
    The Rising Tide (London, 1930);
    Mad Puppetstown (London, 1931)
Fingall, Daisy, Countess of, *Seventy Years Young* (London, 1937)
Fisk, Robert, *In Time of War* (London, 1983)
Fitzgerald, Garret, *All in Life* (Dublin, 1991);
    Towards a New Ireland (Dublin, 1996)
Fitzgerald, Kevin, *With O'Leary in the Grave* (Oxford, 1986)
Fitz-Simon, Christopher, *The Boys: A Biography of Mícheál Mac Liammóir and Hilton Edwards* (London, 1994)
Fleming, Lionel, *Head or Harp* (London, 1965)
Flower, Robin, *The Western Island or the Great Blasket* (Oxford, 1944)
Foster, Roy, *W. B. Yeats: A Life* (Oxford, 1997)

Gibbons, John, *Ireland: The New Ally* (London, 1938)
Gillespie, Elgy, *The Liberties of Dublin* (Dublin, 1974)
Gmelch, Sharon, *Tinkers and Travellers* (Dublin, 1975)
Gordon, Lady, *The Winds of Time* (London, 1934)

Gregory, Anne, *Me & Nu* (London, 1970)
Gregory, Lady, ed. Robinson, Lennox, *Journals* (London, 1979)
Grey, Tony, *Ireland This Century* (London, 1994)
Griffin, Victor, *Mark of Protest* (Dublin, 1993)
Gwynne, Stephen, *The Charm of Ireland* (London, 1927)

Healy, John, *Nineteen Acres* (Achill, 1978);
    No One Shouted Stop (Achill, 1988)
Hearn, Mona, *Below Stairs* (Dublin, 1993)
Hickey, D. H. and Doherty, J. F., *A Dictionary of Irish History: 1800–1980* (Dublin, 1987)
Hinkson, Pamela, *Irish Gold* (London, 1939)

Inglis, Brian, *Downstart* (London, 1990)

Johnston, Denis, *Orders and Desecrations* (Dublin, 1992)

Kavanagh, Patrick, *The Green Fool* (London, 1938);
    The Great Hunger (London, 1942);
    Tarry Flynn (London, 1948)
Keane, Molly, *Good Behaviour* (London, 1981)
Kearns, Kevin, *Stoneybatter: Dublin's Inner Urban Village* (Dublin, 1989);
    Dublin Tenement Life: An Oral History (Dublin, 1994)
Kelly, Bill, *Searching for a Place* (Portlaoise, 1992)
Kennedy, James, *The People who Drank from the River* (Dublin, 1991)
Kennelly, Patrick, *Sausages for Tuesday* (Dublin, 1969)
Keogh, Dermot, *Twentieth-Century Ireland: Nation and State* (Dublin, 1994)
Kiely, Jerome, *Seven Year Island* (London, 1969)
Killanin, Lord and Duignan, Michael, updated Harbison, Peter, *The Shell Guide to Ireland*
    (Dublin, 1989)

Lee, J. J., *Ireland 1912–1985: Politics and Society* (Cambridge, 1989)
Lee, Joseph and Ó Tuathaigh, Gearóid, *The Age of de Valera* (Dublin, 1960)
Lees-Milne, James, *Ancestral Voices* (London, 1975)
Leonard, Hugh, *Home Before Dark* (London, 1976)
Lindsay, Patrick, *With O'Leary in the Grave* (London, 1990)

Mac Amhlaigh, Dónall, trans. Iremonger, Valentine, *An Irish Navvy (Dialann Deoraí)*
    (London, 1964)
Mac Fhionnghaile, *Donegal, Ireland and the First World War* (Donegal, 1989)
McConville, Michael, *Ascendancy to Oblivion* (London, 1986)
McCourt, Frank, *Angela's Ashes: A Memoir of a Childhood* (London, 1996)
McDowell, R. B., *Land and Learning – Two Irish Clubs* (Dublin, 1994);
    Crisis and Decline: The Fate of the Southern Unionists (Dublin, 1997)
McGahern, John, *The Barracks* (London, 1960);
    High Ground (London, 1985)
MacLysaght, Edward, *Changing Times in Ireland Since 1888* (Gerrards Cross, 1978)
MacNamara, Brinsley, *The Valley of the Squinting Windows* (London, 1918)
MacRedmond, Louis, *To the Greater Glory* (Dublin, 1991)
Mac Thomáis, Eamonn, *The 'Labour' and the 'Royal'* (Dublin, 1979)
Manning, Maurice, *The Blueshirts* (Dublin, 1970)
Manning, Maurice and McDowell, Moore, *History of the ESB* (Dublin, 1984)
Mason, Thomas, *The Islands of Ireland* (London, 1936)

Miller, Kerby and Wagner, Paul, *Out of Ireland: The Story of Irish Emigration to America* (London, 1994)
Mitchell, David, *A 'Peculiar' Place: The Adelaide Hospital 1839–1989* (Dublin, 1990)
Mitchell, Geraldine, *Deeds Not Words: The Life and Work of Muriel Gahan* (Dublin, 1997)
Mitford, Nancy, *The Water Beetle* (London, 1960)
Moore, Brian, *The Emperor of Ice-Cream* (London, 1965)
Morton, H. V., *In Search of Ireland* (London, 1931)
Mullen, Pat, *Man of Aran* (London, 1934)
Mulloy, Bridie, *Itchy Feet and Thirsty Work* (Castlebar, 1990)
Mulloy, Martin, *The Book of Irish Courtesy* (Cork, 1968)
Mulvihill, Margaret, *Charlotte Despard* (London, 1989)
Murphy, Dervla, *Wheels Within Wheels* (London, 1979)
Murphy, John A., *Ireland in the Twentieth Century* (Dublin, 1975)

Neely, W. G., *Kilcooley Land and People in Tipperary* (Belfast, 1983)
Neeson, Eoin, *The Civil War* (Dublin, 1966)
Nesbitt, Ronald, *At Arnott's of Dublin 1843–1943* (Dublin, 1993)
Nicolson, Harold, *Diaries* (Collins, 1966, 1967, 1968)
Noone, Father Sean, *Bangor Erris: Where the Sun Sets* (Naas, 1991)

Ó hAodha, Mícheál, *The Importance of Being Mícheál* (Kerry, 1990)
O'Brien, Conor Cruise, *States of Ireland* (London, 1972)
O'Brien, Edna, *The Country Girls* (London, 1960);
    Mother Ireland (London, 1976)
O'Brien, Edward, *An Historical and Social Diary of Durrow, Co. Laois 1708–1992* (Kilkenny, 1992)
O'Brien, George, *The Village of Longing* (Dublin, 1987);
    Dancehall Days (Dublin, 1988)
Ó Broin, Leon, *Frank Duff* (Dublin, 1982);
    Just Like Yesterday: An Autobiography (Dublin, 1986)
O'Carroll, P. and Murphy, John A. (eds), *De Valera and His Times* (Cork, 1983)
O'Casey, Sean, *Autobiographies* (London, 1963)
O'Casey, Eileen, *Sean* (Dublin, 1971)
O'Connell, Peadar, *Islanders* (London, 1927)
O'Connor, Frank, *The Big Fellow* (London, 1937);
    An Only Child (London, 1961);
    My Father's Son (London, 1968)
O'Connor, Patrick, *All Ireland is In and Around Rathkeale* (Limerick, 1996)
O'Connor, Ulick, *Brendan Behan* (London, 1970);
    Celtic Dawn (London, 1984);
    The Troubles: Ireland 1912–1922 (London, 1989)
Ó Criomthain, Tomás, trans. Flower, Robin, *The Islandman (An tOileánach)* (London, 1934)
O'Donoghue, Florence, *No Other Law* (Dublin, 1954)
O'Dowd, Peadar, *Down by the Claddagh* (Dublin, 1990)
O'Faolain, Sean, *De Valera* (London, 1939);
    An Irish Journey (London, 1941);
    The Irish (London, 1947);
    Vive Moi (London, 1964);
    Midsummer Night Madness and other stories (London, 1980)
O'Flaherty, Liam, *Spring Sowing* (London, 1924);
    A Tourist's Guide to Ireland (London, 1929);
    The Informer (London, 1981)

O'Flaherty, Tom, *Aranmen* (Dublin, 1934)
Oliver Bell, Anne (ed.), *Diaries of Virginia Woolf* (London, 1984)
O'Malley, Ernie, *On Another Man's Wound* (London, 1936);
    The Singing Flame (Dublin, 1978)
O'Neill, Timothy, *Life and Tradition in Rural Ireland* (London, 1977)
O'Shea, Patrick, *Voices and the Sound of Drums* (Belfast, 1981)
Ó Súilleabháin, Diarmaid, *Where Mountainy Men Have Sown* (Tralee, 1965)
Ó Súilleabháin, Muiris, trans. Llewelyn Davies, Moya and Thomson, George, *Twenty Years A-Growing (Fiche Blian ag Fás)* (Oxford, 1933)
O'Sullivan, Patrick, *I Heard the Wild Birds Sing: A Kerry Childhood* (Dublin, 1991)

Pakenham, Frank, *Peace by Ordeal* (London, 1935)
Parkes, Susan, *Kildare Place: The History of the Church of Ireland Training College* (Dublin, 1984)
Peillon, Michel, *Contemporary Irish Society* (Dublin, 1982)
Pochin Mould, Daphne, *Valentia* (Dublin, 1978)
Pritchett, V. S., *Midnight Oil* (London, 1980)
Purcell, Mary, *Matt Talbot and His Times* (Dublin, 1976)

Robertson, Norah, *Crowned Harp* (Dublin, 1960)
Robin, Joseph, *Custom House People* (Dublin, 1994)
Robinson, Sir Henry, *Memories Wise and Otherwise* (London, 1923);
    Further Memories of Irish Life (London, 1924)
Robinson, Lennox, *Brian Cooper* (Dublin, 1931)
Robinson, Tim, *The Stones of Aran* (London, 1990)
Ryan, Desmond, *Sean Tracy and the 3rd Tipperary Brigade* (Dublin, 1946)
Ryan, Mary; Browne, Sean and Gilmour, Ken (eds), *No Shoes in Summer* (Dublin, 1995)

Sayers, Peig, trans. MacMahon, Bryan, *Peig* (Dublin, 1974)
Solomons, Bethel, *One Doctor in His Time* (London, 1956)
Somerville-Large, Peter, *Cappaghglass* (London, 1985)
Speakman, Harold, *Here's Ireland* (London, 1926)
Stephens, James, *The Insurrection in Dublin* (Dublin, 1916)
Stuart, Francis H., *Black List Section* (Illinois, 1971)
Sutherland, Halliday, *Irish Journey* (London, 1956)

Taylor, Alice, *To School Through the Fields* (Kerry, 1988)
Thomson, David, *Woodbrook* (London, 1974)
Toksvig, Signe, ed. Pihl, Lis, *Irish Diaries* (Dublin, 1994)
Tracy, Honor, *Mind You, I've Said Nothing* (London, 1953);
    The Straight and Narrow Path (London, 1956)
Treacy, Brendan (ed.), *Nenagh Yesterday* (Nenagh, 1993)
Twohig, Patrick J., *Green Tears for Hecuba: Ireland's Fight for Freedom* (Cork, 1994)

Ussher, Arland, *The Face and Mind of Ireland* (London, 1949)

Verschoyle, Moira, *So Long to Wait* (London, 1960)

Walsh, Maurice, *An Irish Country Childhood* (London, 1995)
Waugh, Evelyn, ed. Davies, Michael, *Diaries* (London, 1976)
White, George, *The Last Word* (Dublin, 1977)
White, Terence de Vere, *Kevin O'Higgins* (Dublin, 1948);

The Fretful Midge (London, 1959)
Wynne, Maud, *An Irishman and His Family* (London, 1937)

Newspapers, periodicals etc.

The Bell
The Blueshirt
The Capuchin Annual
The Catholic Bulletin
Country Living
The Dublin Magazine
Dublin Opinion
The Envoy
The Furrow
History Ireland
Ireland Over All
The Irish Bulletin
The Irish Ecclesiastical Record
The Irish Independent
The Irish Press
The Irish Tatler
The Irish Times
The Journal of the Medical Association of Éire
Kavanagh's Weekly
The Limerick Journal (Old Barrington edition)
The Modern Girl and Ladies' Home Journal
Poetry Ireland
Studies
The Tipperary Star

Index